P9-DHJ-237

# THE COMPLETE HANDBOOK OF POWER TOOLS

# THE COMPLETE HANDBOOK OF POWER TOOLS

**George R. Drake**

RESTON PUBLISHING COMPANY, INC.
Reston, Virginia
*A Prentice-Hall Company*

**Library of Congress Cataloging in Publication Data**

Drake, George R 1938–
The complete handbook of power tools

1. Power tools–Handbooks, manuals, etc. 2. Wood-working tools–Handbooks, manuals, etc. I. Title.
TT153.5.D7 684'.083 75-14286
ISBN 0-87909-150-9


*A Prentice-Hall Company*
Reston, Virginia 22090



10 9 8 7 6 5 4 3

Printed in the United States of America.

to

**MATTHEW MANDL**

a friend and fellow author

# CONTENTS

# PREFACE

Nearly everyone can become a craftsman if he has the proper power tools and knows how to use them. Notice I said *power tools*; I believe that it takes years of practice and a little inborn talent to be a craftsman if only hand tools are used. But, thanks to the technology of today, the power tool manufacturers have designed and developed power tools with numerous accessories so that anyone can use them to cut, drill, plane, shape, turn, and sand wood with precision. Through the use of the basic equipment, accessories, and inexpensive homemade jigs, the average person can create complex pieces of furniture, room accessories, decorations, personalized gifts, toys, and a multitude of intricate designs and patterns of yet-to-be-designed projects.

The objective of this book is to give *you* the know how in the use of power tools. The *you* I'm speaking of are the many men, women, and young adults who want to enjoy the pleasures, thrills, and personal rewards of having accomplished something with their own hands. You will take an idea, expand on it, and then turn a few pieces of rough lumber into a beautiful creation. You really won't save any money–not if you count your time and your investment in tools in addition to the cost of the material. Your creation will cost about as much as if you had gone to the store and bought it, but it will be completely designed, constructed, and *hand tailored* by you. You will have personalized it by adding your own ideas to something you saw or read about. One last thought: would you rather receive a set of store purchased candlestick holders or a set of lathe turned mahogany candlestick holders that your friend personally created for you? Your friends and loved ones have the same answer.

If you are one of the people who would like to turn a piece of rough wood into a finished product, then this handbook is for you. It's for the accountant, the craftsman, the do-it-yourselfer, the grandparent, the hobbyist, the housewife, the nurse, the retiree, the student in high school, vocational school, or adult education program, and the zoologist.

This handbook provides you with a complete description of the principal parts, operating controls, operating procedures, calibrations and adjustments, accessories, installation procedures, and hints and kinks for attaining professional results from each of the power tools discussed. All of the major power tools for home use are covered and are presented in alphabetical order for your convenience; the band saw, drill press, jigsaw (scroll saw), jointer, lathe, radial arm saw, sander (belt and disk), sander-grinder, shaper, table (arbor, bench, circular) saw, and thickness planer are presented. Chapter 1 sets you straight initially by discussing: your power tool needs; your workshop; floor plans; electrical and lighting considerations; motors, pulleys, belts, and speeds; power tool and workpiece support stands; storage; patterns; jigs, stop blocks and miter gauges; buying accessories; general power tool care; and safety precautions.

Appendixes A through G have been included to provide you with the mathematical processes and the conversion factors necessary for converting from the English system to the metric system (International System of Units) and from the metric system to the English system. Appendix H is a lumber conversion chart that converts standard sized lumber into board feet and Appendix I lists decimal equivalents of number and letter size drills. Appendix J illustrates many of the common joints used in woodworking. Appendixes K and L provide nail and screw reference charts, respectively.

Finally, a glossary defines all of the terms that you may be unfamiliar with, and a detailed cross reference index pinpoints the exact page for information that you need.

Happy woodworking!

*George R. Drake*
*Baltimore, Md.*

# ACKNOWLEDGMENTS


The author would like to acknowledge and thank the following companies and persons who generously donated the many photographs in this handbook:

| | *Figure No.* |
|---|---|
| *American Machine and Tool Company, Inc., of Pennsylvania,* Royersford, PA 19468–Mr. Henry M. Pollak, Vice President | 5-1, 6-1, 8-1, 10-1, 10-3, 11-1 |
| *ARCO Manufacturing Inc. of Racine*, Racine, WI 53403–Mr. Arthur W. Sateren, Sales | 8-1, 9-1, 9-4 |
| *The Black and Decker Manufacturing Co.*, Towson, MD 21204–Mr. Carl W. Starner, Public Relations Manager | 7-10, 7-12, 7-13, 7-16, 7-17, 7-19, 7-22, 7-23, 7-24, 7-26, 7-28, 7-30, 7-32, 7-33, 7-36, 7-37, 7-38, 7-42, 7-43 |
| *Mr. Howard E. Chaney*, Baltimore, MD | 1-10, 1-11 |
| *Dremel Manufacturing Company*, Racine, WI 53401–Mr. B. R. Springhorn, Advertising and Sales Promotion Manager | 4-1, 4-2, 4-15 |
| *Gilliom Manufacturing Co.*, St. Charles, MO–Mr. Lyle Gilliom | 2-1, 6-1, 8-1, 11-1 |
| *McGraw-Edison Company, Portable Electric Tools Division*, Geneva, IL 60134–Mr. Jack R. Terrazas, Assistant Advertising Manager | 3-1, 7-1 |
| *Nicholson File Company*, member of The Cooper | |

| | Figure No. |
|---|---|
| Group, Apex, NC 27502–Ms. Martha Wayda, Sales Promotion Manager | 4-13 |
| *Parks Woodworking Machine Company*, Cincinnati, OH 45223–Mr. D. P. Jenkins, Sales Manager | 12-1, 12-2 |
| *Rockwell International, Power Tool Division*, Pittsburgh, PA 15208–Mr. Daniel W. Irvin, Educational Director, Industrial Power Tool Division | 2-13, 3-3, 3-6, 4-1, 4-4, 4-5, 4-14, 4-16, 5-1, 6-3, 6-19, 6-20, 6-21, 7-7, 8-5, 8-7, 8-9, 9-1, 9-2, 9-3, 9-5, 9-7, 9-8, 9-9, 9-10, 10-4, 11-1, 11-5 |
| *Sears, Roebuck and Co.*, Chicago, IL 60684–Mr. C. D. Denno, Buyer, and Mr. J. R. Durham, Assistant Buyer | 2-1, 2-9, 2-10, 2-12, 3-12, 3-14, 3-17, 3-18, 3-19, 3-21, 3-22, 5-1, 5-6, 5-15, 6-1, 7-1, 7-2, 7-8, 7-9, 7-11, 7-14, 7-15, 7-20, 7-21, 7-27, 7-29, 7-31, 7-34, 7-35, 7-39, 7-40, 7-41, 8-1, 8-2, 8-3, 8-4, 9-1, 11-1, 11-4, 11-6, 11-7, 11-8, 11-9, 11-10, 11-11, 11-13, 11-14, 11-15, 11-16, 11-17, 11-19, 11-20, 11-22, 11-23, 11-24, 11-26 |
| *Shopsmith, Incorporated*, Tipp City, OH 45371–Mr. Larry A. Blank, Vice President, Sales | 3-8, 3-11, 3-13, 4-1, 4-9, 5-1, 5-17, 6-2 |
| *Sprunger Brothers, Inc.*, Ligonier, IN 46767–Mr. William E. Davis, Secretary Treasurer | 2-1, 3-1, 3-2, 5-1, 5-2, 5-3, 11-1, 11-2, 11-3 |
| *Toolkraft Corporation*, Chicopee, MA 01013–Mr. R. Hynes, Sales Manager | 2-1, 3-1, 5-1, 6-1, 6-8, 6-11, 8-1, 10-1, 10-2, 11-1 |
| *Wilton Corporation*, Des Plaines, IL 60018–Mr. Randall Bartow, Advertising Manager | 3-1 |

# chapter one

# YOU AND POWER TOOLS

If you are like most of us, you have built a project such as bookshelves, a table, a toy, or knickknack shelves using hand tools. You discovered it was no simple task to use hand tools. You sawed away from the marked guide line, tried to correct, and ended up with a mess. You made dadoes (grooves) with a sharp chisel that also gouged your work. Then you bored holes and set screws into place. Finally, you sanded–and sanded–until you thought your arms would drop off.

Hand tools seem simple enough in principle, but their use is tough. Perhaps you are wondering, "Am I able to use more complex power tools–or would I bungle the job with power tools too?"

Well, let me assure you–anyone–that you *can* use power tools and that you can use them accurately. *You* can become a craftsman with the aid of power tools. And, you will use little effort to produce quality results. All you need is the correct instruction from someone experienced in the use of power tools–and that is what this book is all about.

THE COMPLETE HANDBOOK OF POWER TOOLS has been written so that by reading about and then actually following the procedures:

*1* / You can readily determine your power tool needs.

*2* / You will have sufficient basic knowledge of the capabilities and limitations of a power tool before you buy it so that you can make a suitable power tool purchase.

*3* / You can learn the basic operation of a newly acquired power tool so that you can use it to make precision cuts immediately.

*4* / You will learn many techniques and shortcuts to enable you to get full utilization from your power tool and become a craftsman quickly.

Power tools perform many of the same functions as the hand tools that you probably now own and can use, but powered tools aid you in completing the task more efficiently, with less fatigue, and with more accuracy. Power tools increase your range of capabilities and save you time. With practice, you can easily learn the basic functions, the capabilities and the limitations of any powered tool that you may purchase. Once the fundamental operation of the basic tool is mastered, you can extend the range of capabilities of the tool by adding accessories.

With any tool the fundamental principles of operation—its use, the extent of the tool's capabilities, its limitations, safe operating procedures, and general care—are only learned through *practice*. When you first acquire a tool, you should plan to spend a few evenings with the tool practicing. Sit down in your easy chair and read the complete section of this handbook dealing with the power tool you've purchased; then read the manufacturer's instructions. Look at the tool; learn the names of its parts. With the tool electrically disconnected, place yourself in position next to the tool. Move its switches in the specified sequences. Move its adjustments. Note its safety features and note any unsafe conditions. Locate lubrication points. Familiarize yourself completely with the tool.

Clean up your shop and make room for your new power tool. Get hold of some scrap wood to use with your new tool, and check that all adjustments on the tool are secure. Plug your tool into the electrical power outlet and turn it on without touching the workpiece. Feel the power of the tool; respect it. Turn the power off. Place the scrap wood to the tool, apply power, and practice using the tool to perform its basic functions. Try more difficult operations. Extend your knowledge of the tool's capabilities and limitations by varying adjustments, changing angles and depths of cut, and by utilizing different cutters. Once these capabilities are mastered, add accessories to the basic tool. *Practice* with the accessories until you are thoroughly familiar with the complete operation of the tool. Now you've accomplished something. You are a master of the tool and you know its overall capabilities. You are ready to cut a workpiece on the powered tool. *THINK SAFETY*.

The keys to accurate and rapid completion of any wood cutting task involving the use of power tools are knowledge of the proper power tool and accessory for the job, knowledge of how to use the tool and accessory correctly, and knowledge of how to care for the tool and accessories. This book provides you with this knowledge. You'll be your own boss and you can build home improvements and construct projects of professional quality. You can do this because you'll have as much knowledge and you'll have more time than the professional. He has to hurry to make money. You can take your time and then have the personal satisfaction that *you* built it.

## 1-1 / WHAT ARE YOUR POWER TOOL NEEDS?

The logical order of purchasing power tools and the extent of the number you'll buy depends upon your tool needs—now and in the future. Perhaps at this stage, you're only interested in building occasional wooden toys for your children, building knickknack shelves, or cutting "blanks" for hand carving. Perhaps, then, the jig saw will suffice for your present demands. Or perhaps you're planning to build a recreation room complete with paneled walls, bookshelves, and built-ins. Then, you will want to buy a radial arm or table saw. If you want to build electronic chassis from blank metal boxes or drill metals, assemble furniture with dowels, or drill countersink holes for screw heads, then you'll need a drill press.

But, before you buy any power tool, read the introductory material to each chapter in this book in detail; learn what the tool does and what features it may have. Skim over the rest of the chapter so that you know how to operate the tool and what accessories are available.

Buy only quality made power tools from a reputable manufacturer. (Some are listed as contributors of photographs to this book—refer to the preface.) Buy the best tools you can afford—the tools will pay off your investment by giving you longer service, more accuracy, more availability of replacement parts, and greater resale value. Watch your newspaper and sales catalogs—there are often sales that will lower your tool costs; but beware of inexpensive tools that are often imported and are of low quality. Also be careful in buying multi-tools or tools with many accessories; this is usually the merchandiser's method of getting rid of those items that no one else wants. Many times, you'll never have practical uses for some of the accessories thrown in with the sale items.

Watch the newspaper classified columns ARTICLES FOR SALE and MACHINERY AND TOOLS. You can often make purchases of good, used power tools at large savings from someone who has lost interest in the hobby or needs cash quickly. When buying from advertisers in classified ads, call the advertiser and determine the type, size, age, and condition of the tool desired. Then check your tool catalogs and skim the applicable chapter of this book. Establish a price value in your mind. Then visit the advertiser and have him demonstrate the equipment. Look the accessories over carefully.

If possible, it is a good idea to buy tools from a manufacturer that has a repair facility or representative located in your city. Know before you buy that you can obtain replacement parts for the tool. Also be sure that the tool has a guarantee—and don't forget to mail it in. Finally, don't buy a tool unless a set of operating instructions, maintenance instructions, and a list of repair parts are included. These suggestions are particularly important if you are buying a used tool.

Low cost power tools can be purchased from several manufacturers. In some cases, the basic parts are provided in a "kit" with detailed plans that you can use to build the cabinet and stands. Generally, these low cost tools perform very well for their cost, but they are not precision tools. If your work is not to be too exacting, then perhaps the less expensive tools or the "kit" tools are for you. Remember the old axiom though—"you only get what you pay for." Figure 2-1 includes a band saw in which the complete cabinet is made in the home shop from wood. Figure 10-3 illustrates a shaper in which you build the housing. (In the photographs in Chap. 10 the author is using the shaper shown in Fig. 10-3, but has designed his own table top and added a stand.)

When purchasing power tools, be sure that you buy a size with sufficient horsepower and speed to accomplish your jobs. Don't consider only the job at hand, but consider future tasks. Tools with ball bearings outlast other tools. Motors with slip clutch gear trains allow the motor to operate even if the drive shaft becomes suddenly jammed. This prevents gear stripping and motor burnout. If a drive shaft stops rotating because of a jammed blade, etc., immediately remove electrical power.

You may sometimes wonder whether you should buy, borrow, or rent a specific power tool. The answer depends upon immediate need, anticipation of the frequency of use, cost of the tool, and your relationship with a friend or neighbor who owns the tool. In borrowing tools though, keep three principles in mind: use the tool only in its proper application, clean it after use, and return it as soon as you are finished. Adherence to these principles will keep you at peace with the neighbors.

To rent a power tool, refer to the yellow pages in your telephone directory under TOOLS–RENTING. Call the renter–you may decide it's cheaper in the long run to buy the needed tool in the first place. If you do decide to rent, know ahead of time how you'll need to use the tool and what accessories you'll need. Have your workpieces measured and marked for cutting before you rent.

## *1-2* / HOW TO USE THIS BOOK

The first page of each chapter in this book illustrates several manufacturer's models of the tool discussed in that chapter. Chapters are arranged alphabetically for your convenience and cover: band saw, drill press, jigsaw (scroll saw), jointer, lathe, radial arm saw, sander (belt and disk), sander-grinder, shaper, table (arbor, bench, circular) saw, and thickness planer.

Appendixes A through G at the end of this book provide tables for conversions from English to metric and metric to English. Appendix H is a lumber conversion chart that converts standard sized lumber into board feet so that costs can be estimated. Appendix I lists decimal equivalents of number and letter size drills, and Appendix J illustrates wood joints used in the construction of furniture and other projects. Appendixes K and L provide nail and screw reference charts, respectively.

A glossary enables you to learn the definitions of terms with which you are unfamiliar. A comprehensive index enables you to readily locate power tool descriptions, applications, accessories, adjustments, and procedures.

To begin your study of power tools read the completion of this chapter, which gives some general information about power tools and workshops. It discusses workshops–basement, attic, or garage; workshop floor plans; electrical power; lighting the work area;

motors, belts, pulleys, and speeds; power tool stands; accessory and hand tool storage; workpiece support stands; patterns; jigs, stop blocks, and miter gauges; tips on buying power tool accessories; power tool care and usage procedures; and general safety precautions.

## 1-3 / WORKSHOPS—BASEMENT, ATTIC, OR GARAGE?

The location of your workshop depends upon the size of your home, the availability of a spare room, basement, attic, or garage, and the space needed. The craftsman needs room for a large workbench, tool storage, lumber storage, and an assembly and paint area. In addition to location, other considerations should include adequate ventilation, temperature control, dampness control, and lighting.

The basement probably provides the most adequate area for a workshop. It is isolated from the rest of the home so that noise disturbances are held to a minimum. Dirt from sawdust and smell from glues and paints are also partially isolated from the rest of the home. As the basement is normally below grade, the surrounding earth tends to aid in keeping the basement warmer in the winter and cooler in the summer. Registers are easily placed in the heat and air conditioning ducts as required. Basements are often damp in the summer and can cause tools to rust, but dampness can be limited by use of a dehumidifier.

An attic is another area to consider for setting up a workshop. It may provide sufficient space and some isolation from the rest of the home. Dust, however, has a tendency to settle to the lower floor and to work its way into stored items. The attic is also usually too hot in the summer and too cool in the winter for comfortable working conditions, although additional heating/air conditioning ducts or portable units can be used.

Garages provide adequate room and isolation from the rest of the house, and dirt and noise are not problems. However, competition for space with the automobile(s), lawn and garden tools, and bicycles and toys often significantly limit shop space in garages. Heat, air conditioning, and dampness are also problems which are difficult to contend with in the garage.

## 1-4 / WORKSHOP FLOOR PLANS

Floor plans for your workshop should depend upon your needs, both present and future. How large an area do you need? What are your storage requirements? Can you place cabinets on the walls? Do you need a lumber or metal storage area? Which power tools do you own and which do you plan to purchase in the near future?

Figures 1-1 and 1-2 present some ideas for floor plans of different shops. Use the ideas to construct a plan for your workshop.

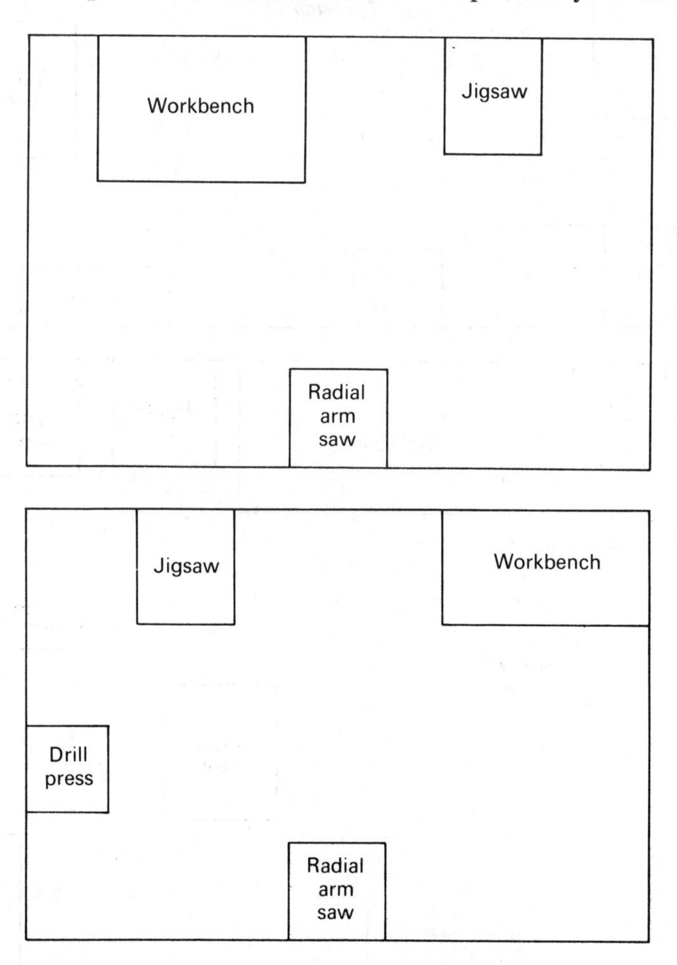


**FIGURE 1-1** / Suggested floor plans for beginning power tool workshops.

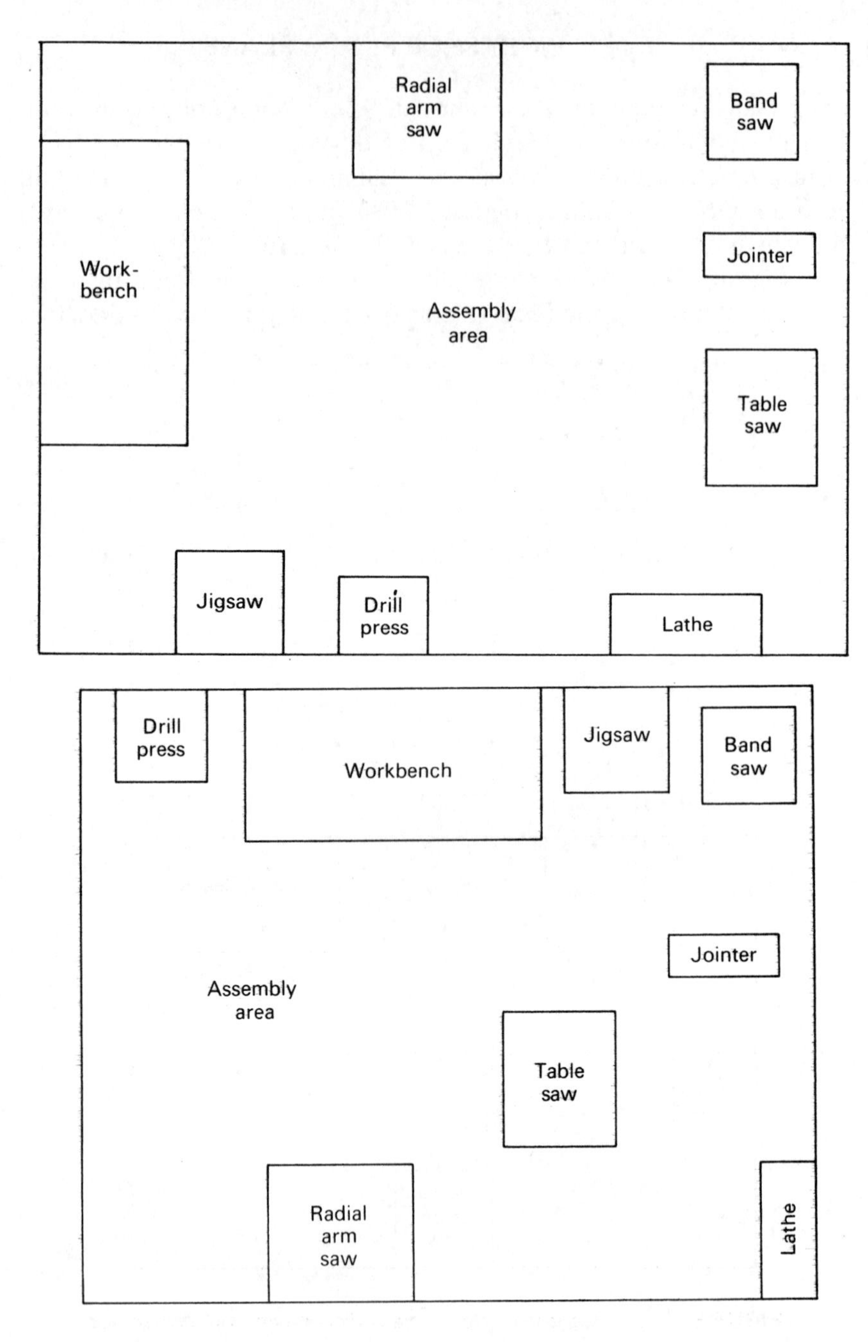


**FIGURE 1-2** / Suggested floor plans for more complete power tool workshops.

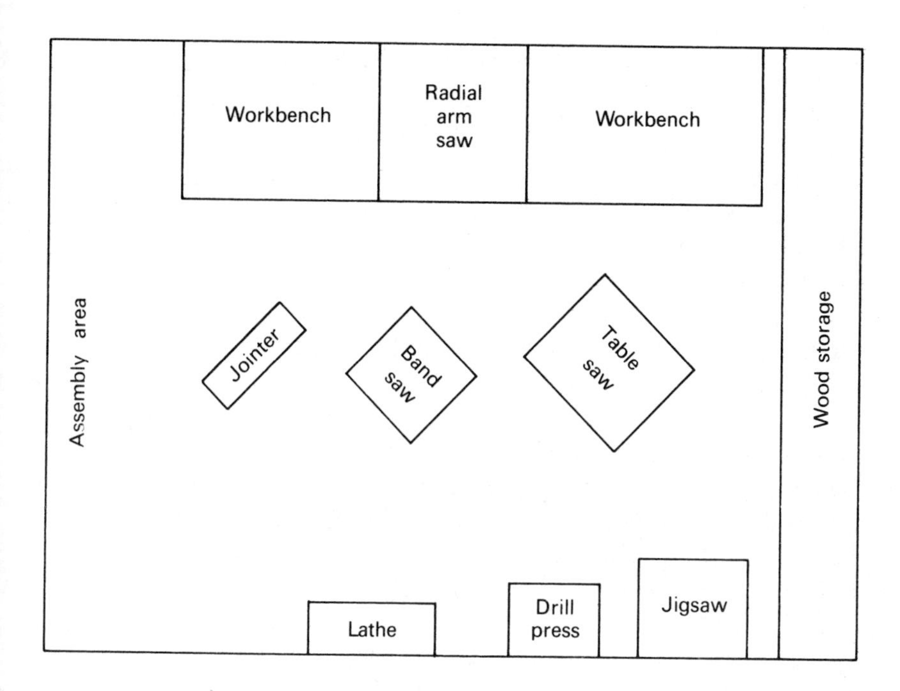


**FIGURE 1-2** / Continued.

You might want to make a scale model of your workshop. Use a piece of 1/4-inch grid line paper and let one square equal one square foot. Mark the overall space you have available. Use another piece of grid line paper and glue it to a piece of thin cardboard. Draw scaled outlines of your proposed workbench, power tools (and surrounding work area), storage cabinets, wood storage areas, and other items that you may have. Label the areas, power tools, and units on the outlines and then cut the outlines apart. Place the scaled outlines on the first drawing and arrange them until you have a satisfactory and convenient layout.

Next, consider electrical power (Sec. 1-5) and lighting (Sec. 1-6). Have wiring installed, being sure to consider present and future power tool installations.

The walls and ceiling should be painted a light color or white to reflect light around the workshop. Floors may be painted so that *lost* parts may be more rapidly found and dust and dirt may be more readily removed; be sure that the floor is not slippery.

## 1-5 / ELECTRICAL POWER

You should have two or perhaps three electrical power circuit lines in your shop. One power line should be for lighting and for an accessory outlet strip across your workbench. A second line from a separate fuse or circuit breaker should connect to power outlets for all of your power tools; convenience outlets should be located near your power tools. It is best if this second line comes from a circuit breaker that can be locked in the off position; this prevents children from being able to turn on any power tools.

The motors of some power tools such as radial arm saws are rated with higher horsepowers of 1-1/2- to 2-hp and may operate from either 115VAC, 230VAC, or perhaps from either power if the owner makes some simple wiring changes at the motor (this is detailed in the operating manual for the particular tool). Operation of larger motors is more efficient–hence less expensive–on 230VAC, but your home must be wired for 230VAC power. If you decide to put this third power line–230VAC power–into your shop, have an electrician install the service. Arrange for a locking type of circuit breaker.

## 1-6 / LIGHTING THE WORK AREA

Once you have established your workshop and have built or purchased a workbench, you are ready to locate the workbench. Consider placing it near a window which will aid in lighting the work area during daylight. You might like to have a curtain or shade that can be drawn to block direct sunlight.

Artificial light suggestions include incandescent lights, fluorescent lights, high intensity lights (also incandescent light), and flexible arm lamps. Incandescent lights of 100 to 150 watts can be placed in reflector sockets. The complete unit can be hung by a half knot in the line cord to a pulley. The pulley can be attached to a cable (such as AWG no. 8 or 10 aluminum TV antenna guy wire) so that it can be drawn across the work area. This enables you to place the light where you need it (Fig. 1-3). If you'd like to vary the intensity of the light, install a dimmer switch or light dimmer control box.

Fluorescent lights may be purchased in either wall or overhead mounting fixtures. From one to four tube models are available. A fluorescent fixture may also be hung with pulleys from cables as

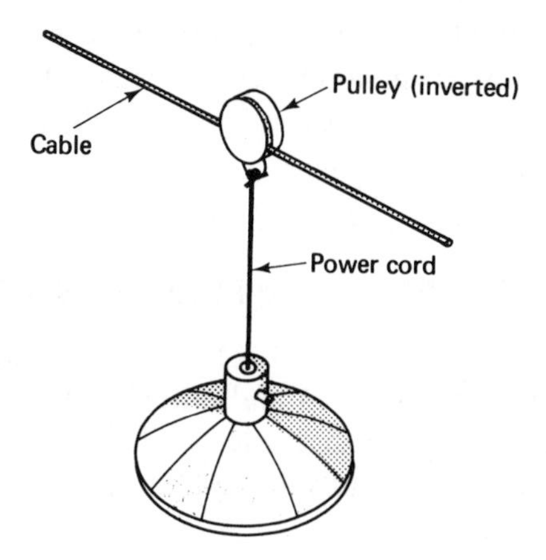


**FIGURE 1-3** / Incandescent lights installed in reflector sockets can be hung by a pulley on a length of cable.

shown in Fig. 1-4. The pulleys are attached to the fixture with eye bolts. Turn buckles attached to one end of each cable enable the cables to be drawn tight. This method of suspending the fixture allows the light to be moved to a convenient location over any work area along the length of the cables. Fluorescent light fixtures that have light diffusers installed provide nearly shadow free light.

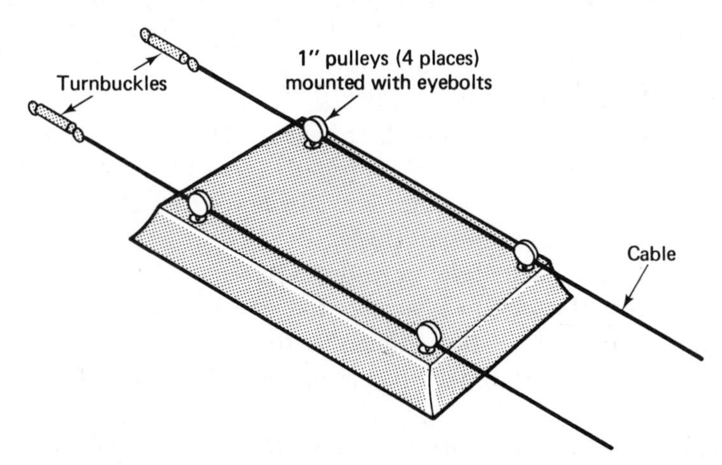


**FIGURE 1-4** / Fluorescent fixtures can be hung on pulleys and cables, allowing the fixture to be easily moved over your work area.

High intensity lamps can be mounted on the work surface or mounted to a wall behind the workbench or power tool. These lamps are recommended where high intensity light is needed over a small work area. Flexible arm lamps are fluorescent lights that may be bench or wall mounted. These lamps provide more overall surface light than the high intensity light.

## 1-7 / MOTORS, BELTS, PULLEYS, AND SPEEDS

This section provides you with some valuable information. Refer to it often during tool installation and initial set up. Information about motor wiring, motor mounting, belts, pulleys, calculating tool speeds in revolutions per minute and surface feet per minute, and motorized power tools are included.

### *Motor Wiring*

If your power tool motor is powered by 105-120 VAC and is equipped with a three-conductor cord and a three-prong grounding type plug, connect it to a properly grounded three-prong receptacle [Fig. 1-5(A)]. The green (or green and yellow) conductor is the ground conductor; this conductor is *never* connected to a live terminal. If your shop does not have properly grounded three-pole receptacles available, use an adapter and connect it as shown in Fig. 1-5(B). The green (or green and yellow) grounding wire extending from the adapter must be connected to a permanent ground such as a properly grounded outlet box screw.

If your motor operates on a voltage of 210-250 VAC, connect the grounded power plug to a properly grounded outlet box as shown in Fig. 1-5(C). No adapter is available for 210-250 VAC plugs.

If you must use extension cords, use only heavy duty three-wire extension cords which have three-prong grounding type plugs and three-pole receptacles that accept the power tool's plug. Long extension cords reduce the voltage at the motor and could cause damage. Replace or repair damaged or worn extension cords immediately.

The direction of rotation of a motor can be easily changed. Procedures for reversing the rotation direction are printed on the plate of the motor that covers the wiring. With the motor power disconnected from the electrical outlet, remove the screws which hold the plate. Remove the plate and read the directions. The

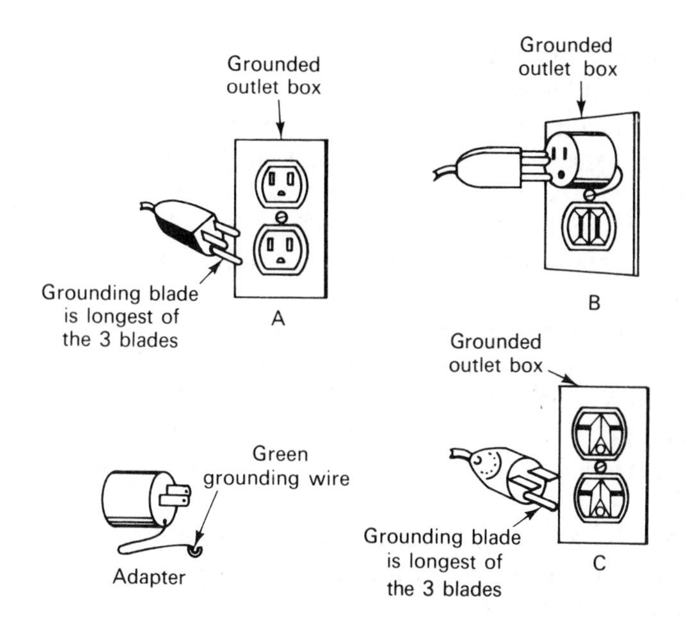


**FIGURE 1-5** / Power connections.

procedure consists of simply reversing two wires within the housing. After reversing the wires, reinstall the plate taking care not to catch the wires between the plate and the motor housing.

Motor *reversing switches* are available commercially and are desirable additions for the lathe and shaper motors as it is often desirable to change the direction of rotation of the tool spindles. Specific wiring instructions come packaged with each switch. Position the switch at a convenient location on the power tool stand.

If your motor has a red reset *relay* button on it, the button is an overload relay to protect against overloading the motor or against low voltage. If the motor shuts off by itself, let it cool three to five minutes before pressing the reset button. If the trouble is repeated, determine the cause. Many times the trouble stems from the use of an extension cord which is too long in size, or the wire within the cord is too small to carry the current required.

### *Motor Mounting*

Motors are most conveniently located behind the tool on the power tool stand or bench; they are also often mounted on the stand below the tool, but this sometimes necessitates cutting a hole in the power tool stand to allow for passage of the drive belt. Motors are also sometimes mounted above the tool or behind the tool on a wall.

When the motor is mounted behind the tool, bore holes in the stand top to the rear of the motor base mounting slots. This allows the motor to be shifted back slightly allowing for greater center distance when a smaller motor pulley is used; this location of holes also allows for setting correct belt tension.

A similar arrangement for mounting the motor below the tool is possible, except shim blocks should be used under the motor when it is used with a larger pulley. Remove the shims for a smaller pulley. Locate the motor with the pulleys (motor and saw) in line, drive shafts parallel, and with the belt just tight enough to prevent slipping.

Motors are often mounted below the tool on a hinge arrangement so that the weight of the motor provides tension on the belt to the tool. Bolt one side of the motor to one end of the hinge. Bolt or screw the side of the hinge to the tool stand so that the motor is raised about 1/2-inch from the motor table when the belt is taut from the tension produced by the weight of the motor. Now place a 6 inch bolt through the motor table (fasten to the table with a nut) and through the end of the motor that is raised in the air (Fig. 1-6). Place a nut at the top of the bolt to prevent the motor from jumping off of the bolt when electrical power is first applied to the motor.

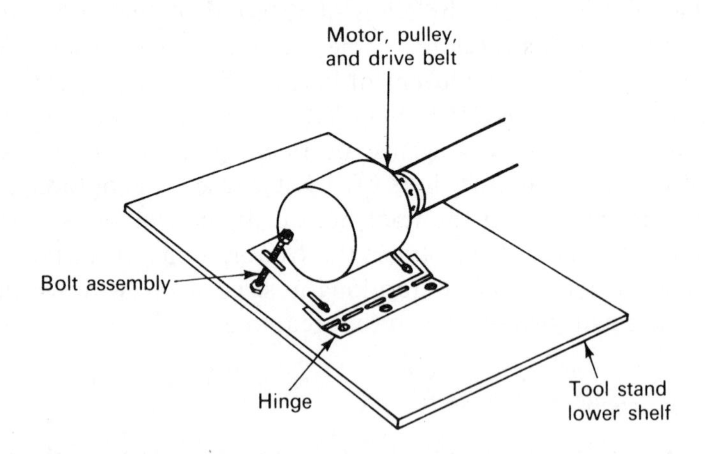


**FIGURE 1-6** / Motors are often mounted on hinge assemblies so that proper tension is placed on the drive belt.

*Belts and Pulleys*

The power to run tools is transmitted from an electric motor to the tool by means of a belt running on pulleys. Belts transmit power because of friction between the belt and pulleys. Belts are made of canvas, rubber, or leather, often neoprene impregnated. Flat belts are used with flat pulleys and V-belts are used with grooved pulleys. Some belts are said to be "A" belts because their cross sectional views look like the letter A.

It is often necessary to measure a belt for one of your tools; there is only one correct method of measuring the width and length of the belt needed. (Refer to Fig. 1-7.) To measure the width of the belt, measure across the wider surface of the belt, as shown. Measure the length with a steel tape and measure around the *outside* edge of both pulleys. Do not measure the grooves. Belt lengths of 17 to 50 inches are available in 1 inch incremented lengths; lengths between 50 and 72 inches are available in increments of 2 inches.

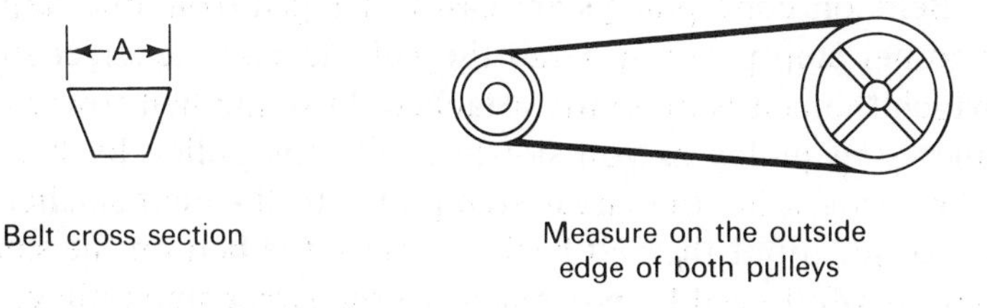


**FIGURE 1-7** / Belt measurements must be made correctly.

Pulleys are used in pairs to increase, decrease, or keep the speed of the tool the same as the speed of the motor. Pulleys, properly belted, are also used to change direction of rotation.

Pulley diameters are specified for the *outer* edge of the pulley. Different configurations include pulleys with hubs, pulleys without hubs for side by side mounting of drives, and *cone* pulleys with three to eight different diameter pulleys (steps) in one stacked cone-shaped arrangement. Pulleys are available with 1/2-, 5/8-, and 3/4-inch bores. Some pulley hubs have *keyways* (grooves) inside them for insertion of a rectangular shaped *key* to aid in keeping the pulley from moving on the shaft. Pulleys slide over the shafts of motors and are secured in place with a setscrew against the "flat" (a flat machined surface on the shaft).

The *drive* pulley (on the motor) and the *driven* pulley (on the tool) must be aligned at installation. Move the motor until the planes of the two pulleys are parallel. Then secure the motor.

When step cone pulleys are used on tools and motors so that the speeds of the tool can be varied, the drive and driven pulleys must have the exact same diameter. The largest cone pulley of one pulley is mounted parallel to the smallest cone of the other pulley. Thus, the circumference (and hence, the belt length) is always the same regardless of which step of the pulleys is being used. The belt always remains parallel to the cones—you cannot, for example, place a belt between the large cones of the two pulleys.

With the motor properly mounted and the belt installed, the belt should not deflect more than one inch when you press against one side with a moderate force. The main factor here is that the belt does not slip on the pulleys—but the belt should not be so tight that it causes wear to the belt or shaft and spindle bearings. (Refer to Sec. 1-14 and Fig. 1-22.)

Belts on cone pulleys are easily changed from one step position to another step position. Grab the belt nearest the larger step pulley to which the belt is presently attached. Push the belt toward the next smaller step pulley as you slowly rotate the pulley by hand so that the belt works off the larger step pulley to the next smaller step. Do the reverse to put the belt back on; place the belt on the smaller step pulley first followed by movement to the larger step pulley.

Sometimes several similar tools can be installed on a *line shaft* where only one motor is required to drive more than one tool. For example, you could run a grinder and separate polishing wheels from a drive shaft common to both tools. The motor drives the shaft which is suspended in blocks and has several pulleys along its length. Belt drives from the pulleys drive the various tools.

### *Calculating Tool Speeds*

Since most electric motors run at about 1725 and 3450 rev/min, there is often a need to either decrease or increase these speeds at the tool spindle. These changes in speed can be made by using the correct size pulleys at the motor and at the tool. The pulley at the motor is known as the *drive* pulley; the one at the tool is the *driven* pulley. Speeds can be determined by the equation:

$$DN = dn$$

*where:*

D = diameter of the *drive* pulley

N = number of revolutions per minute of the *drive* pulley

d = diameter of the *driven* pulley

n = number of revolutions per minute of the *driven* pulley

For example, if the tool is to be operated at approximately 800 rev/min, what size *drive* pulley is required if the tool driven pulley is 4 inches and the motor speed is 1725 rev/min?

$$DN = dn$$

$$D = \frac{dn}{N}$$

$$= \frac{(4)(800)}{1725}$$

$$= 1.85 \text{ or approximately 2 inches}$$

The speed of some tools such as the band saw is often stated by the blade speed in *surface feet per minute* (SFM). This speed is the rate at which the blade is traveling. Likewise, it is often desirable to know the surface speed of the drive belt between the motor and the tool. Surface speed S in feet per minute is calculated by the equation:

$$S = 0.2618\ DN$$

*where:* D = diameter of the pulley or wheel in inches

N = number of revolutions per minute of the pulley or wheel

For example, if a band saw has 10-inch wheels driven at 862 rev/min, what is the surface speed of the band saw blade?

$$S = 0.2618\,DN$$
$$= 0.2618(10)(862)$$
$$= 2257 \text{ surface feet per minute}$$

*Motorized Power Tools*

*Motorized* power tools have the motors built *into* the tool. A *timing* belt located between the motor shaft and the tool arbor pulley drives the arbor. The timing belts should be checked periodically for proper tension and replaced when badly frayed or broken. Remove the nuts or screws holding the belt guard in place; remove the guard. Loosen the motor mounting nuts. To adjust the timing belt tension, use a screwdriver to push the motor away until the belt can be deflected about 1/8- to 1/4-inch by using a moderate pressure between your thumb and forefinger. Once set to the proper tension, tighten the motor mounting nuts and replace the belt guard. To replace a belt, slide the motor mount toward the arbor pulley, place the belt on and slide the motor away. Then proceed as discussed for tightening the belt.

## *1-8* / POWER TOOL STANDS

Power tool stands are of several varieties: fixed, attached, sold with a power tool; metal stands that are adjustable for many manufacturer's tool bases; home-built wood stands; and workbenches. Fixed, attached stands are most likely sold with radial arm and table saws and are the most convenient and probably the most expensive stands.

Adjustable steel stands (Fig. 1-8) that are sold by several manufacturers are quickly and easily assembled with bolts and nuts. The slotted construction of the legs and support brackets allows adjustment in the width, depth, and height of the table to accommodate your tool and to place the tool at a convenient working height. The legs can be bolted into the floor, or accessory rubber feet or casters can be bolted into the legs. If casters are installed, two of the four rubber-wheeled casters should have *brakes* included so that the stand can be locked into place. You can also build and bolt wood work surfaces to the table tops and can add drawers, shelves, compartments, and dust shoots to the tables as your requirements demand.

**FIGURE 1-8** / The steel adjustable power tool stand is easily assembled and fits a variety of power tools.

You can build your own power tool stands (Fig. 1-9) from 2 by 4 inch, and 1 by 4 inch fir lumber and 1/2-inch A-D grade (one side smooth, one rough) plywood. Design the top to accommodate your power tool and motor; leave some excess room to hold operating tools, accessories, or small workpieces. You may also locate the motor below the power tool on a shelf. This requires cutting a hole into the stand top to allow the motor drive belt to drive the tool pulley.

Cut the stand top first. Determine the height of your stand top—the cutting area of the tool is usually most convenient at about waist height or slightly higher. However, this depends upon the particular tool and your desires. Cut the stand legs to the proper length for the determined height. Cut the two ends of each leg at an angle of 10° so that the stand top is level and the leg sits flat on the floor but the leg is angled out 10° for strength and stability. Cut dadoes (grooves—Sec. 7-7) into each leg to accept braces between the legs; if you don't have the tools for dadoing, place the braces on the inside of the legs. Screw and glue the legs to the braces and then the top of the legs. Measure and cut the bottom shelf (which also adds strength to the stand). Screw it into place. Countersink the screw heads and fill the holes with wood filler. You can complete the job

**FIGURE 1-9** / You can build your own tool stands to your specifications from 2 by 4 and 1 by 4 inch fir and 1/2 inch plywood.

by adding two coats of gray enamel to the stand.

You can conveniently build drawers, trays, or compartments for power tool accessories into the stand. You can also build a dust shoot or a dust box to shoot dirt out of the tool into a waiting box or into a fixed box that can later be removed and dumped. Make the shoot or dust box from 1/4-inch plywood or masonite. Varnish and wax the finished shoot or box to prevent sawdust from clinging to the sides.

Home built stands are less expensive and meet your requirements because you've custom built them. However, you might consider buying standard commercial adaptable stands that you can modify.

If you only have one power tool such as a jigsaw, sander, sander-grinder, or drill press, you can locate the tool on one end of your workbench. Bolt the tool and motor to the workbench. However, this may make the tool too high for safe, easy use.

If your power tool does not have a self-contained power on-off switch, locate a power switch at a convenient operating position where the switch cannot be accidentally turned on and where it can be easily reached in an emergency. Tie the power cord out of the operator's way at locations along the stand.

## 1-9 / ACCESSORY AND HAND TOOL STORAGE

Accessories and hand tools for use with power tools can be stored in power tool stand drawers, trays, or compartments, in workbench drawers, in closets, or they can be hung from pegboard. Each type of storage has its advantages and disadvantages; the choice is up to you, but the storage area should allow for the arrangement, convenient selection, and protection of each accessory and tool. Common types of accessories and tools should be grouped together. Place the accessories and tools that you use most often in a convenient location to the associated power tool. Those that are seldom used can be placed in the back of drawers, in the lower drawers, or in storage cabinets away from the normal working area. Some tools require special holders or may require a preservative or a rust inhibitor. Locate these tools near each other but keep them from touching one another.

Workbenches and storage areas are the places where you'll do your work and store your hand tools, some power tool accessories and tools, supplies, parts, and partially completed projects. The size, shape, and quantity of workbenches and storage areas depend upon your needs.

Figures 1-10 through 1-12 suggest some ideas for workbenches and storage areas. For workbenches, you can consider buying the complete bench or make one to your own design specifications. A workbench is a good construction project to begin with because no finishing is required. If you don't like the idea of building drawers, consider buying two unfinished chests of drawers. Then screw two or three 2 by 12 inch boards across the top. You may also consider placing an old door on top of the chests (Fig. 1-12). If you want to put a fairly durable and tough top on the bench, nail or glue a piece of tempered masonite to the top. Paint the chests with a good enamel paint, but don't paint the workbench top.

Unfinished kitchen cabinets make excellent storage cabinets, or perhaps you know someone who is remodeling their kitchen and discarding old cabinets. Also consider buying secondhand cabinets and give the cabinets a new coat of paint.

Pegboard and assorted hooks make excellent hangers for many hand tools and power tool accessories. Place a piece behind your bench and power tools for easy access to the tools and accessories that you use most often. Place other pieces next to the bench or

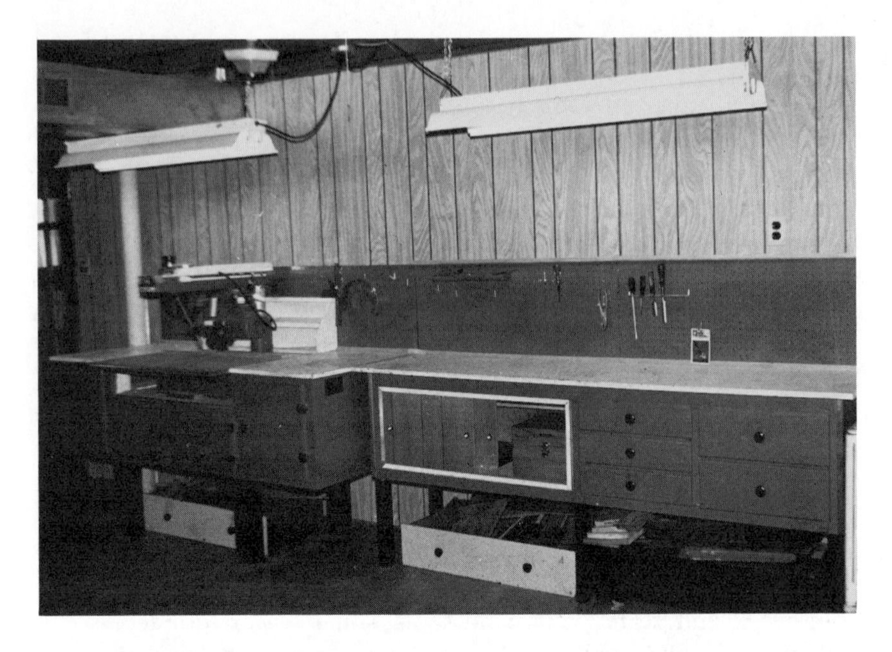

**FIGURE 1-10** / This workbench provides a large work area and lots of storage space. Note that lumber is stored underneath.

**FIGURE 1-11** / Different sized cabinets and drawers have been built for storage. Old kitchen cabinets make ideal storage areas.

FIGURE 1-12 / A sturdy workbench can be constructed from two unfinished chests of drawers and a door.

around the workshop at convenient places. Paint the pegboard with a glossy white paint to protect it and to reflect light. Magnetic bars may be used to hang iron alloy tools. Other suitable items for hanging tools include nails, spring clips, strips of leather or inner tube, wooden pegs, and holes or notches in a piece of wood.

Wood (or metal) storage areas can be made by dropping U-shaped frames from the rafters or by placing 2 by 3 inch supports from the rafters to the floor. Place cross braces as required (Fig. 1-13). Store your wood by type and size in the spaces created by the dividers.

Make a habit of always returning power tool accessories, hand tools, and scrap wood back to its own storage space—in essence, *a home for each tool*. By doing this, you will usually know exactly where your accessories, tools, and wood are when you need them. (This is often a difficult task if there are some young craftsmen in your family!)

## 1-10 / WORKPIECE SUPPORT STANDS

A workpiece support stand (Fig. 1-14) is a very useful device for the support of a long workpiece that is being sawed or planed. The

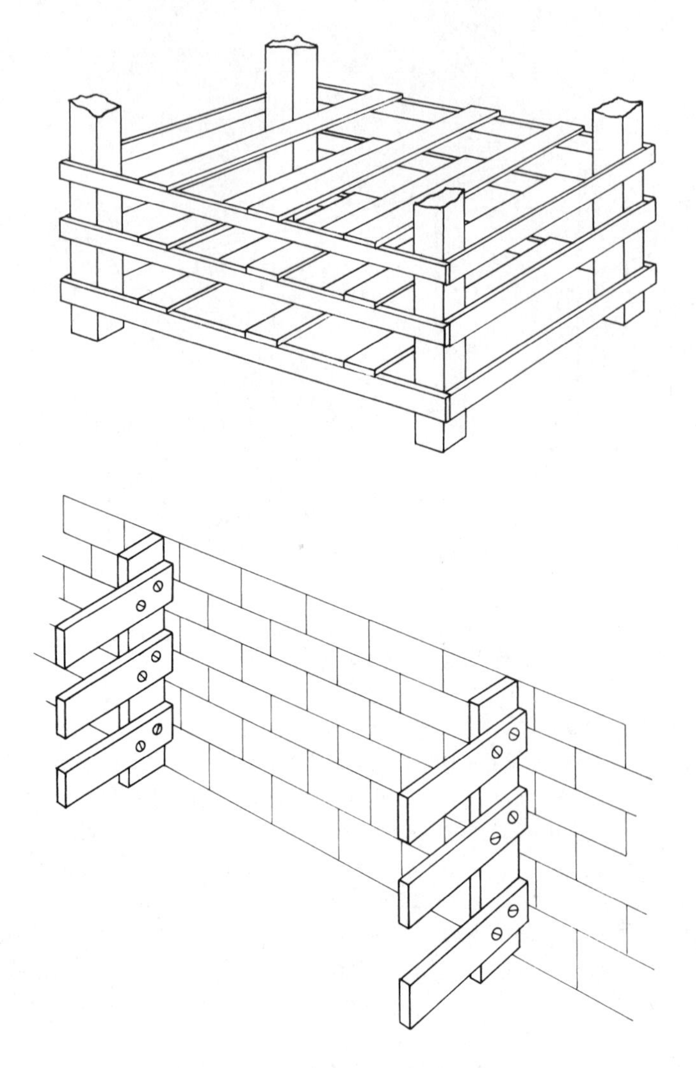

**FIGURE 1-13** / Wood storage areas.

support stand prevents the workpiece from bending, a condition that causes binding of the blade, inaccurate cuts and is a hazard to the operator. The stand is adjustable and is set to the height of the saw, plane, or other table. As the workpiece is pushed through the tool, the cut portion is pushed onto the stand; the top of the stand rotates to accommodate the easy movement of the workpiece across the stand. You can build your own stand easily or you can purchase a commercial one.

You can build a workpiece support stand (Fig. 1-15) from scrap

**FIGURE 1-14** / A workpiece support stand is used when long pieces of wood are cut or planed.

1 by 4 inch soft wood. Rip the 1 by 4 inches to 1 by 2 inches for the narrower pieces and to 1 by 1 inch for the four slide guides. The fixed stand height should be at least three inches shorter than your lowest power saw or plane table top—about 30 inches maximum. The base should be 15 inches in both width and depth. The entire stand is simply nailed and glued together.

When the fixed assembly is completed, build the movable assembly to fit into the slides. The roller is made of 1-1/4-inch wood closet rod; a nail on each end acts as an axle. The movable assembly is bolted to the fixed assembly with a single 2-1/2-inch carriage bolt, flat washer, and a wing nut. The carriage bolt is placed through the fixed assembly near the top. Rub some soap onto the slides to make the assemblies operate easily.

As an alternative to the roller top, you can place a piece of rectangular shaped wood in place of the roller. Screw this piece into place and then add ball casters to the top of the piece of flat wood. The ball casters have the advantage that they roll in any direction.

## *1-11* / PATTERNS

You can buy or make your own patterns for workpieces. *Scaling* is easily done as shown in Fig. 1-16 which is a scaled drawing of a push

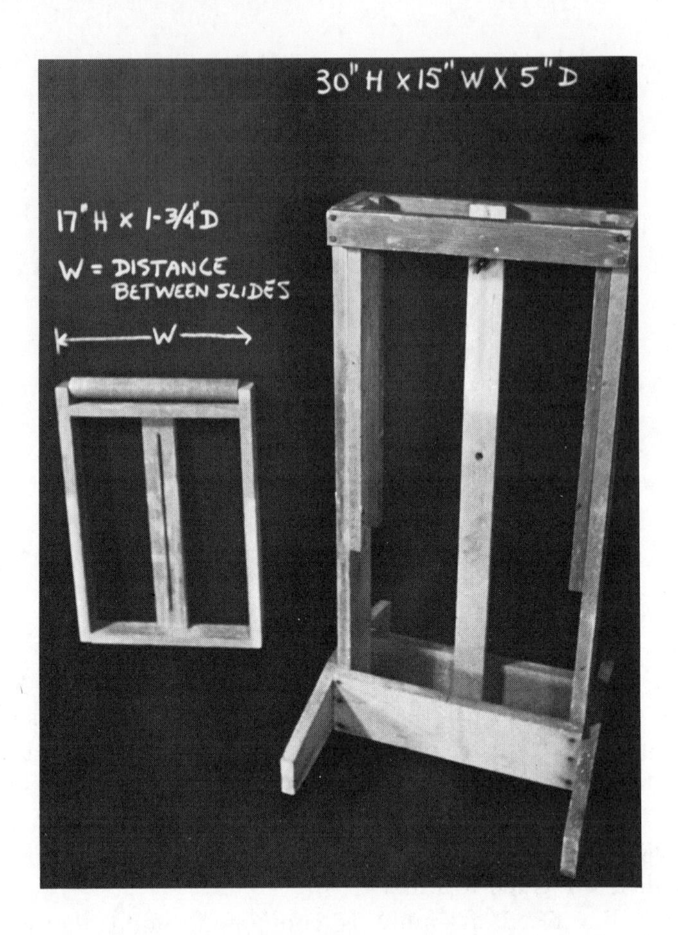


**FIGURE 1-15** / The workpiece support stand is made of scrap wood and has both a movable and a fixed assembly.

stick that should be a part of every workshop. The push stick is used to push narrow workpieces through a cutter when rip sawing on the radial arm or table saw, planing on the jointer, or shaping on the shaper.

Note the *scale* in the illustration: one block equals 1 square inch. This means that the distance between any two parallel lines (called grids) equals 1 inch on the actual workpiece. Therefore, to draw the workpiece pattern to the actual scale, you need to have a piece of *grid lined paper* with one inch squares on it. This paper is readily purchased in a stationary store; in fact, you can get paper with grids of 1/16-, 1/10-, 1/8-, 1/4-, 1/2-, 1 inch and in centimeter

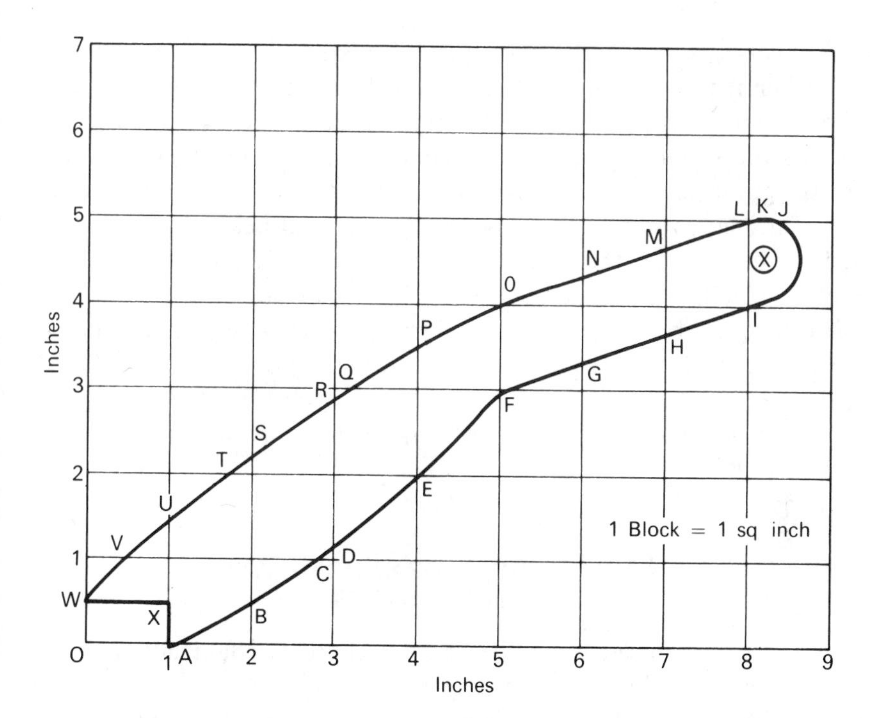


**FIGURE 1-16** / Pattern for a push stick.

and decimeters (metric for 1/100 and 1/10 of a meter, respectively). Or, you can draw your own grid lines on a piece of paper. Scales may also be: 1 block equals 1/2-square inch, 1/4-, 1/8-, 1/10-inch, 6 inches, 1 foot, etc.; this simply means that the distance between adjacent parallel lines on the pattern represents 1/2-inch, 1/4-inch, etc.

With your pattern and grid lined pattern on hand, number both sets of grid lines (Fig. 1-16) identically. On your grid lined paper, mark and identify points crossing grid lines on the pattern—you may assign letter designations as shown on the illustration to get started. For example, on your grid line paper, locate point A on the 0 inch vertical line and 1 inch horizontal line; B half way between the 0 and 1 inch vertical line on the 2 inch horizontal line and so on for the remaining points C to X. Now connect the points with lines using a straight edge and perhaps a French curve (a drawing template) as guides. You now have a full size pattern that can be cut out and attached to the workpiece or traced over with carbon paper underneath to transfer the full size pattern to the workpiece.

You can apply the principles discussed to make any pattern, whether it is designed from scratch or from an idea from a picture. For example, suppose you see a picture of a Canadian goose flying across the sky in a magazine and you would like to make a silhouette of the goose for your recreation room wall. Decide how big you want the finished product–let's say 15 inches from beak to tail. Make a grid system across the picture so that there are 15 equal blocks from beak to tail. Make your full size paper with at least 16 one inch blocks across by the necessary height (as shown on your grid on the magazine picture). Transfer and connect the points and you have a full size pattern.

These basic principles can be applied to any workpiece of any size. Try it!

## *1-12* / JIGS, STOP BLOCKS, AND MITER GAUGES

A jig is a device used as a guide or template to mechanically maintain the correct positional relationship between a workpiece and the tool or between parts of a workpiece during assembly. You will find jigs very handy–sometimes the jig can be used with more than one tool in your workshop. As your shop grows and as your knowledge expands, you'll be designing jigs for your own tools. To give you some ideas for jigs, I've incorporated two in this section and others are scattered throughout this book. The jigs included here are a "rip fence" and a "right angle" that can be used with tools such as the jigsaw and band saw which are usually considered freehand tools and therefore usually do not have these attachments. The "rip fence" and "right angle" permit straight line cuts to be made.

For rip cuts, construct a perfectly square T of two pieces of hardwood screwed together. Then clamp the T at the width dimension of the workpiece from the blade (Fig. 1-17). Slide the workpiece along the "rip fence" to make accurate rip cuts. (If you don't want to make a T that will save time in setups, simply clamp a piece of wood parallel to the table edge.)

By using the constructed rip fence and a right angle jig as shown in Fig. 1-18, you can make crosscuts. If you have a number of repeated miter cuts to make at the same angle, cut a jig similar to the right angle jig, but at the desired angle.

*Stop blocks* (Figs. 1-19 through 1-21) are used when you have a

**FIGURE 1-17** / Make a "rip fence" for your jigsaw or band saw.

**FIGURE 1-18** / Use the "rip fence" and a right angle jig for cross-cutting.

number of workpieces to be cut to the same length or holes drilled in the same location in several workpieces. Clamp a piece of scrap wood with a square edge in position. Then, using a miter gauge or rip fence, hold the workpiece firm and against the stop block. Make the cut and repeat for additional workpieces. A *step* stop block can also be used for several different sizes.

**FIGURE 1-19** / Clamp the stop block securely.

A *miter gauge* is a T-shaped square used on the table saw, disk sander, shaper, bandsaw, and to a lesser extent on the jigsaw to guide workpieces to a cutter at an angle of 90° or at some other angle between 90 and 45 or 30° left and right. The miter gauge consists of a slotted T-shaped head, a rectangular guide bar of metal approximately 3/8-inch thick by 3/4-inch wide by 12 inches long, a pointer, and a lock knob. The guide bar fits the groove of a table; it is attached to the head with a threaded stud and lock knob. The head is graduated in degrees from 90 to 45 or 30° left and right.

In use, the miter gauge is placed in the table groove and the head is set to the miter angle desired. The workpiece is then held firmly against the head of the gauge and is advanced to the cutter.

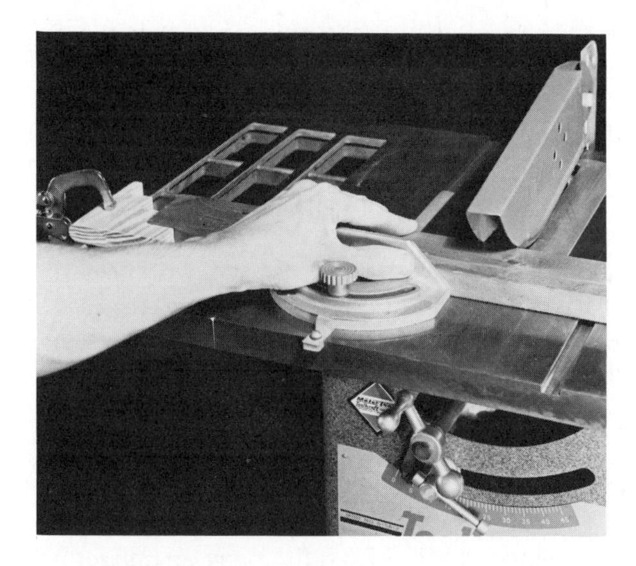

**FIGURE 1-20** / A step stop block is used for varied sizes of workpieces. Hold the workpiece firmly against the miter.

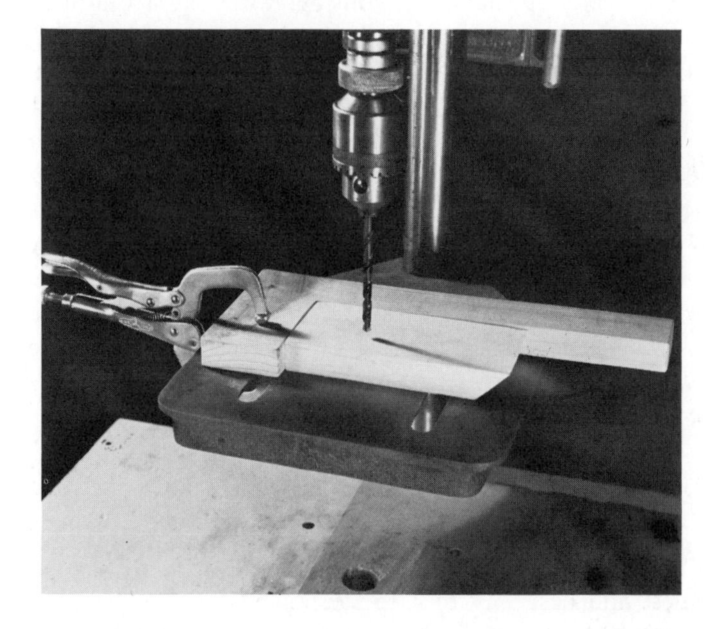

**FIGURE 1-21** / The stop block can be used for locating holes in workpieces of the same size.

The miter gauge is easily calibrated by inverting the gauge in the table groove, with the head against the table edge. Loosen the locking nut, push the assembly forward until the head is flat against the table edge, and then lock the assembly by tightening the knob. Turn the gauge over and reset the pointer exactly to 90°.

Some miter gauges may incorporate additional desirable features such as positive *stops* at 90 and 45°, stop rods for use in cutting a number of the same size workpieces, and workpiece hold down clamps. Unfortunately, few miter gauges are for use in tables manufactured by different companies; each company seems to have different sized table grooves.

## *1-13* / TIPS ON BUYING POWER TOOL ACCESSORIES

Accessories for power tools often fit many manufacturers' tools. Therefore, you may buy a manufacturer's product because his accessory may have some advantage over another's and perhaps one is on sale. Before buying, however, consider what the accessory is and know the dimension specifications, if required. For example, you can buy a table saw blade from numerous manufacturers, but you must know the maximum diameter blade that can be used on your saw, the size of the saw arbor (blade shaft hole), and the type of workpiece that you want to cut.

When you are selecting cutting blades, keep in mind that tungsten carbide blades and tungsten carbide tipped blades cost a good deal more than standard blades, but they outlast the standard blades ten to one. Tungsten carbide blades have no teeth; instead, particles of tungsten carbide are fused to the blade. Tungsten carbide blades cut wood, ceramic, countertop material, slate, cement, brick, asbestos, pipe, and stainless steel.

## *1-14* / POWER TOOL CARE (CLEANING, LUBRICATING, SHARPENING)

The simplest and best way to care for power tools and accessories is to *use them in the proper way and only for their intended purposes.*

The specific care of each power tool is covered separately in each tool chapter, but here are some general tips on care applicable to all power tools and accessories:

*a* / Keep tools clean at all times.

*1* / When new power tools are unpacked, you will discover that a protective coating was placed on unpainted surfaces to prevent rusting. Remove the coating by rubbing the surface with a rag dampened with kerosene or varsol.

*2* / Brush dust away from the tool after each use. Occasionally use a vacuum cleaner to clean dust from around the motor. (Hold the vacuum nozzle close to the cooling fins of the motor and draw the dust out.)

*3* / Remove gum, pitch, and dirt from accessories with a rag dampened in turpentine. Scrub with an old toothbrush saturated with turpentine if necessary or use steel wool or a wire brush.

*4* / Paste wax for metal surfaces (automobile paste wax) should be applied at regular intervals to the exposed metal table tops and other ferrous metals of your tools. The wax not only protects the metal against rust, but it also provides a smoother surface making it easier to feed your workpiece to the cutter.

Apply the wax and let it dry. Rub it to a shine. It's also a good idea to wax the painted parts of the tool occasionally. The wax will protect the tool against sprays and helps prevent dust from clinging to it.

*b* / Remove burrs by rubbing them with an oilstone. Dull blades should be sharpened in accordance with specific procedures in each chapter. Usually, it is best for the homeowner to take the blades to a professional for sharpening. Resharpening is inexpensive.

*c* / Most new electric motors do not require lubrication. Others require the addition of a light machine oil periodically. For specific instructions, refer to the manufacturer's instructions. Generally, however, plan to apply a light oil semiannually into the motor at oil caps provided.

Apply a few drops and wait for it to soak in–continue to apply a few drops at a time until the oil reservoir is full. Then operate the motor for one minute and recheck. Replace old grease as recommended by the manufacturer.

*d* / For proper operation of any power tool, it is important that the drive belt is at proper tension. Improper tension can reduce the life of the belt, pulleys, and bearings. To check for proper tension (Fig. 1-22) place a ruler perpendicular to the belt and depress the top belt section moderately with your finger; with proper tension, the belt should depress 1/2-to 1 inch. If the tension is not correct, loosen the motor bolts and slide the motor until the tension is correct. Retighten the bolts.

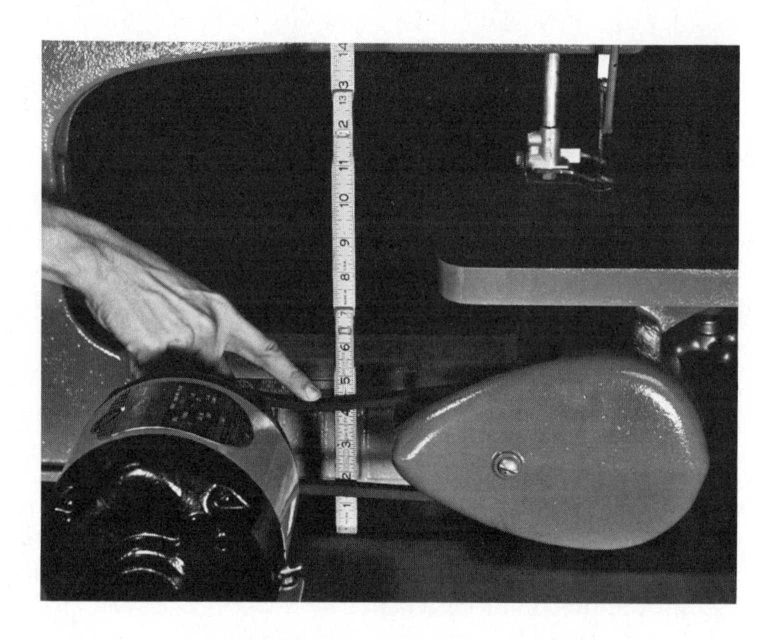

**FIGURE 1-22** / Checking belt tension.

*e* / Refer to Sec. 1-7 for checking belt tension on motorized power tools.

*f* / Check power cords for frays, cracks, or cuts. Replace the cords in accordance with the manufacturer's instructions if any frays, cracks, or cuts are located.

*g* / In small power tools, inspect the motor brushes regularly for wear. Excessive sparking indicates worn brushes or springs. Remove and replace the brushes and springs in accordance with the tool manufacturer's recommendations. When new brushes are installed, contour the end of the brushes to fit against the commutator. Do this by placing a fine abrasive paper against the commutator and lightly rubbing the brush against the abrasive paper. Check the commutator too. If it is dirty, rub it with a fine abrasive paper; then wipe it with a rag slightly dampened with lacquer thinner. Finally, brush and vacuum out all dirt.

*h* / Tools and accessories should be stored properly either by hanging or by placing them in drawers. If tools with cutting edges such as lathe chisels and gouges are kept in drawers or in a tool box, they should be protected from touching each other. Keep metallic tools and metal tool work surfaces lightly coated with a light oil. If tools are to be stored over a long period of time (over a month), apply a rust preventative, such as a light grease, to all metal parts.

## 1-15 / POWER TOOL USAGE PROCEDURES

The application of each of the power tools is separately described under each tool, but here are some general tips applicable to each tool:

*a* / Always be safe. Support and clamp the workpiece firmly. Take a safe operating position where you can reach the workpiece completely in a balanced position. Do not stand in the line of the cutter. Power cords should be out of the way. The shop should not be cluttered and you should have ample workspace. Be aware of what to do should an accident occur.

*b* / It is always a good idea to try operations on a scrap workpiece first. This will give you a checkout of your procedures, enable you to adjust the tool (such as angle, depth of cut, speed, and feed rate), and may prevent you from making an error and ruining your workpiece.

*c* / When cutting materials, slower speeds are used for harder materials; higher speeds for softer materials.

## *1-16* / GENERAL SAFETY PRECAUTIONS

Always concern yourself and others with safety. Power tools can be dangerous and can maim you or your loved ones permanently. Read the following DO's and DON'T's and reread them frequently; they are applicable to every chapter in this book. Use the workshop safety check list in Table 1-1 now and recheck it on occasion—in fact, schedule periodic safety checks for your work area. A YES in every column indicates a safe workshop.

**DO** use goggles, a face shield, or safety glasses for all cutting operations.

**DO** take your time in working with all tools.

**DO** stand aside when turning power on.

**DO** plan ahead.

**DO** keep guards in place and in working order.

**DO** wear nonslip rubber soled shoes.

**DO** support long workpieces.

**DO** inspect and remove all nails or other fasteners from workpieces prior to any cutting operations.

**DO** take work breaks to reduce fatigue.

**DO** secure workpieces with clamps.

**DO** follow manufacturer's recommendations.

**DO** check that adjusting keys and wrenches are removed from the tool before power is applied.

**DO** store your tools and accessories properly.

**DO** use tools in good light.

**DO** keep your tools sharp. Sharp tools are the easiest to use and the safest.

**DO** make all adjustments with the electrical power turned off.

**DO** keep hands at a safe distance from cutters.

**DON'T** wear neckties, long sleeved shirts, shorts, or jewelry while working in the shop.

**DON'T** work when you're tired.

**DON'T** force the tool. The tool will do a safer job if you let it cut at its own rate.

**DON'T** allow your children to use sharp tools or power tools unless you are closely supervising them.

**DON'T** overreach.

**DON'T** leave a tool running when unattended.

**DON'T** store any rags that are dampened with oil or kerosene. Throw them out.

**Table 1-1**
**WORKSHOP SAFETY CHECK LIST**

| | *Yes* | *No* |
|---|---|---|
| Tools and accessories are properly stored. | | |
| Tools are sharp. | | |
| Wood and metal are properly stored. Nails are removed from used lumber. | | |
| Power tools, cords, and plugs are in good condition. | | |
| Power to power tools can be removed by central circuit breaker. | | |
| Safety glasses, goggles or face shield are available. | | |
| Shop work areas and floor are clean. | | |
| Tool tables are uncluttered and clean. | | |

# chapter two

# BAND SAW

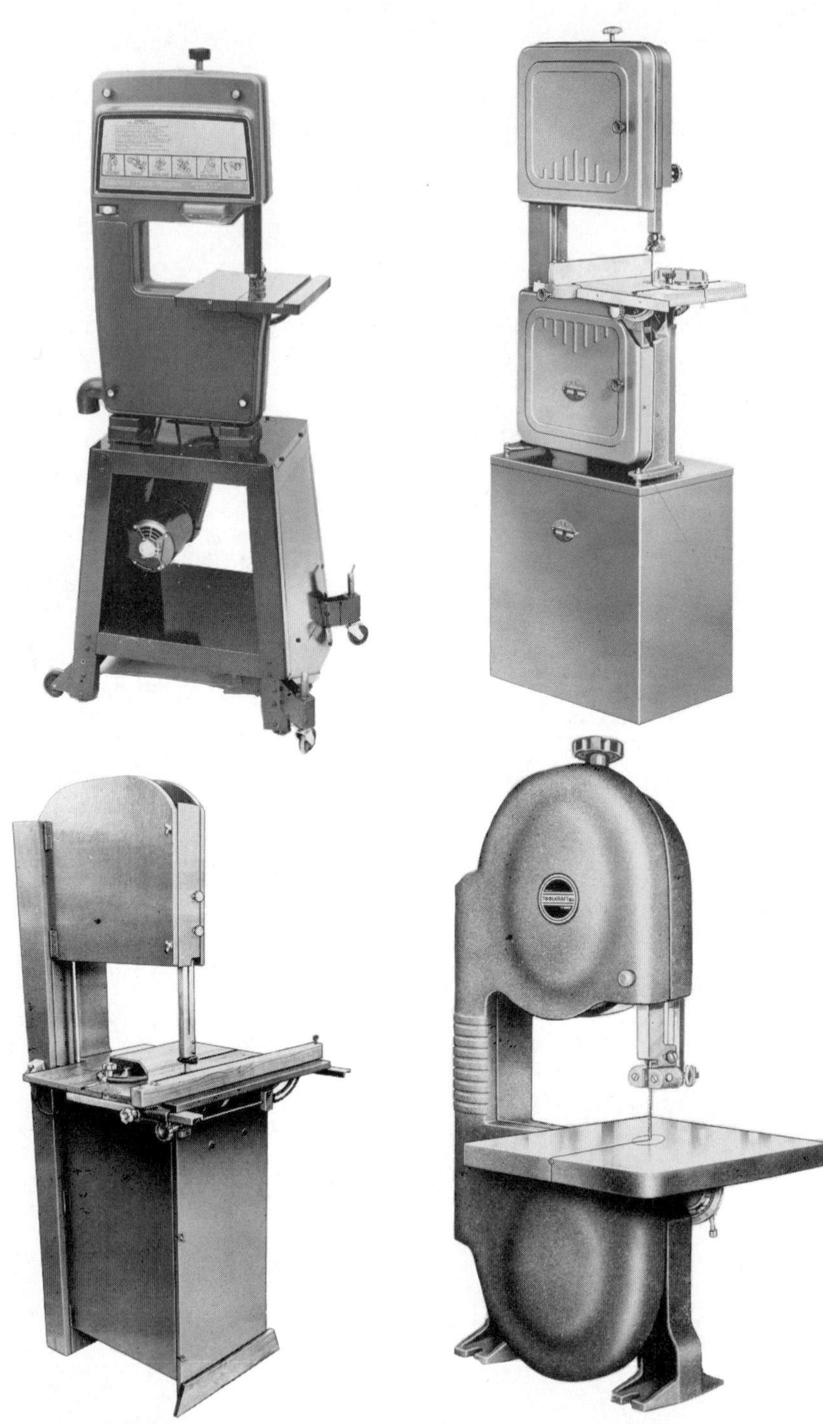

**FIGURE 2-1** / Band saws cut intricate shapes, scrolls, curlicues, and straight lines in wood workpieces up to about 6 inches thick.

The band saw is used in the home workshop to cut intricate shapes, scrolls, curlicues, inside contours and straight lines in thick wood workpieces or thin metals. It is also used to resaw thick boards into thin boards. The band saw cuts much heavier stock than the jig or other saws and does it faster and smoother. The band saw's flexible steel blade is a circular, continuous ribbon that cuts up to 6-1/4-inch thick wood; a piece can be added to the frame of some band saws to increase the thickness of cut capacity to 12 inches.

The band saw is useful for rough cutting wood that is to be carved, for cutting tapered and curved legs for furniture, and for precutting wood to be turned on a lathe. It makes intricate cuts like the jigsaw but does not have the capability (as the jigsaw has) for making internal cuts in a workpiece.

## *2-1* / DESCRIPTION AND MAJOR PARTS

Figure 2-2 illustrates the major parts of the band saw: frame, cover, wheels, tilting table, blade, blade guide assemblies, and the motor and drive system. The frame houses the major parts of the band saw with the exception of the motor, belt, and motor pulley that can be mounted below (usually) or behind the band saw. With the cover closed to protect the operator from the traveling blade, the band saw, excluding the motor and power tool stand, measures from approximately 12 by 19 by 32 inches for a 10 inch band saw to 17 by 27 by 43 inches for a 14 inch band saw.

The *size* of a band saw is determined by the number of inches from the blade to the frame—for home workshop use it is usually from 9 to 14 inches. This dimension is known as the *throat* dimension and is the widest dimension of a workpiece that can be

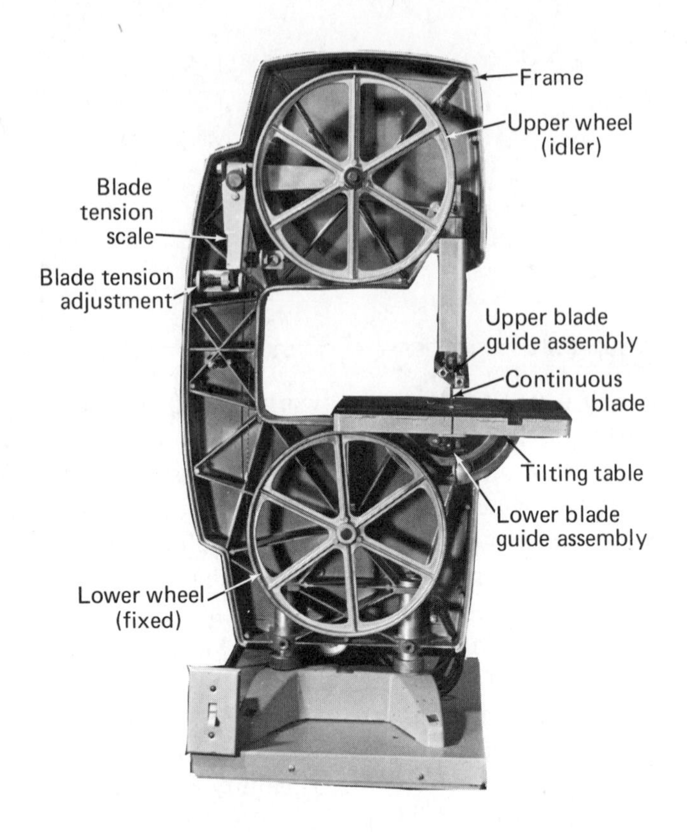


**FIGURE 2-2** / Major parts of the band saw.

cut on that particular model. Advertisers often state that a saw cuts to the center of a 20 inch diameter circle; this means that the saw has a throat of 10 inches.

The cast and machined wheels transmit power to the blade and maintain the blade in its travel path. Power is fed from the electric motor, belt, pulley, and drive shaft to the lower wheel. Because of the saw blade around the two wheels, the upper *idler/tension* wheel also rotates, providing a continuous cutting edge past the table for sawing. The upper wheel is not on a fixed shaft as is the lower wheel; the upper wheel can be raised or lowered in a slotted guide to increase or decrease tension on the blade, and can also be tilted so that the upper wheel is exactly parallel (in alignment) to the lower wheel. When the blade travels over the center of the upper wheel as well as the center of the lower wheel, the blade is known to be *tracking* correctly. The tilting adjustment is known as the blade tracking adjustment. Some band saws incorporate a blade tension scale that indicates the correct tension for different width blades. The scale reads from the inside or the outside and is an asset in setting correct blade tension.

The perimeter of the wheels are covered with rubber in one of two manners. The wheel can have a groove in the center to accept a rubber band having a center projection that fits into the groove or, if the wheel is not grooved, a flat rubber band is glued to the wheel. This rubber band encircling the wheel helps to hold the blade onto the wheel, and it also provides a cushion to the blade teeth having a *set* in the direction of the wheel. Without this cushion, the blade teeth would become damaged and dulled.

The tilting table varies in size from about 10 by 10 inches to 14 by 14 inches, increasing in size as the machine throat size increases. The table is mounted on a single or a double trunnion and tilts 45° to the right and 5 to 10° to the left. A table tilt adjustment locks the table at any angle (between 10° left and 45° right) indicated by a table tilt pointer on a table tilt angle scale. The table top has a hole in the center of about 2 inch diameter for the blade to pass through. A removable slotted aluminum table insert fits into the hole to support small workpieces. A slot from the center hole to the forward edge of the table is an access slot for removal and installation of the blade. A setscrew is usually placed into the end of this slot. The table is often drilled in the edge for a rip fence and grooved across the top for a miter gauge.

For home workshop use, band saw blades vary in width from 1/8- to 1/2-inch and in length from approximately 54 to 94 inches; the length is dependent upon the wheel circumferences and the distance between the wheels. Blades are discussed in detail in Sec 2-2.

A lower and an upper blade guide assembly prevent the blade from being pushed to the rear or to the sides and from twisting when workpieces are cut. This prevents the blade from coming off of the wheels and from breaking. The lower blade guide assembly is located in a fixed position just beneath the table. The upper blade guide is adjustable in height and is set just above the top of the workpiece. An adjustable finger guard to aid in preventing accidents with the blade is part of the upper blade guide.

Each blade guide consists of a roller located behind the blade and two hardened steel blade guide rods or rollers for the left and right sides of the blade; although roller guides are best, the rods are used in the less expensive home workshop models. The roller runs on a bearing and is adjustable from 1/8- to 1/2-inch for rear support of the blade. The rods are adjustable also.

The band saw blade should travel at 1400 to 2500 surface feet per minute for general wood cutting. This is usually accomplished by using a 4 inch driven pulley on the band saw and a 1725 rev/min 1/4-, 1/3- or 1/2-hp motor with a 2 inch drive pulley. The blade wheels are driven between 450 and 900 rev/min. (Refer to Sec. 1-7 for more discussion on pulley speeds and belt speeds.)

Band saws may also incorporate a built-in work light and a built-in sawdust ejection system that connects to a shop vacuum.

## 2-2 / BLADES

Blades for the home workshop band saw are available in lengths of 54 to 94 inches and widths of 1/8- to 1/2-inch. Select the length according to your manufacturer's instructions or by the equation:

$$L = 3.14D + 2\ell$$

*where* $L$ = band saw blade length.

$D$ = outside diameter of blade wheel (this equation assumes that the two wheels are of equal diameter).

$\ell$ = the distance between the centers of the two wheels when the tension adjustment has positioned the upper wheel to the bottom of the guide.

After L is calculated, select the next larger band saw blade available. Blade widths of 1/8- to 3/8-inch widths are used on band saws up to 10 inches; 1/8- to 1/2-inch on saws up to 14 inches. The number of teeth per inch vary also from 5 to 25.

The widest blade possible should always be used for straight cuts. Narrower blades should be used for intricate curved cuts; the radii of the cuts possible by each blade are dependent upon the blade width. Figure 2-3 illustrates the minimum radii that can be cut for each blade width. For example, a 1/4-inch width blade cannot cut around a radius of less than 3/4-inch.

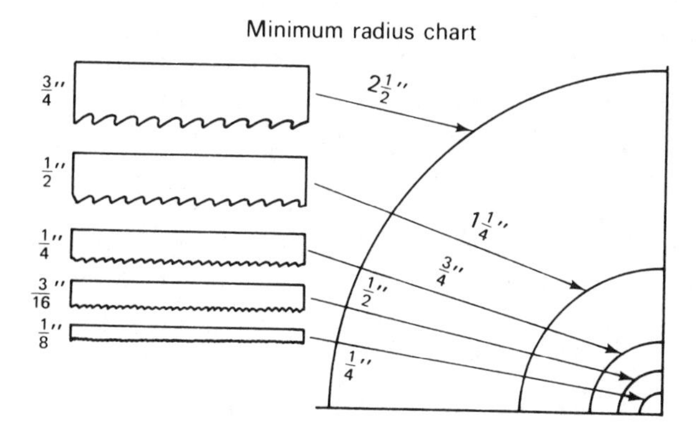


**FIGURE 2-3** / Smaller width blades are used for small radii cuts.

Finer tooth blades—more teeth per inch—are used for thin cross sections such as sheet metal, light tubing, and for extra hard materials. Fine tooth blades are for minimum splintering and smooth finishes. Coarser tooth blades are used for thick cross sections, soft and stringy materials, or for thin stock at extremely high speeds. For general use, 5 to 6 teeth per inch in the narrow width blades give very smooth and satisfactory cuts with minimum splintering. Use as coarse a tooth saw as can be used for the workpiece. The coarser teeth cut faster. The larger tooth gullets have more sawdust capacity that cleans the cut faster and easier. Table 2-1 can be used as a guide for selecting blades. When specifying blades, it should be noted that there is always one more *point* to the inch that *teeth* to the inch.

Blades have one of two types of *teeth*—skip or saber tooth—and one of three types of *set*—alternate, raker, or wavy (Fig. 2-4). The skip tooth blade is for cutting wood, plastic, hard rubber, building materials, bakelite, nonferrous soft metals such as aluminum and copper, and similar stock. The skip tooth leaves a narrow kerf and helps to keep the kerf free of chips. The wide tooth spacing—every other tooth is in effect skipped—provides for effective chip clearance and a high cutting speed.

The saber tooth blade, also called a hook tooth blade, is similar to the skip tooth but the cutting edge of the tooth has a hook of 8 to 15°. This hook makes the blade feed easier and cut faster as the hook quickly removes the chips. The saber tooth blade is recommended for use on wood, plastics, paper, and nonferrous metals. Plastics and woods generally respond best to the saber tooth blade.

Table 2-1
BAND SAW BLADE SELECTION CHART

| *For sawing* | *Width (in.)* | *Teeth per in.* |
|---|---|---|
| Wood (fine scroll cutting) | 1/8 | 15 |
| Wood (hardboard, plywood, chipboard) | 3/16 | 15 |
| Wood | 1/4 | 6 to 7 |
| Wood | 3/8 | 6-1/2 to 7 |
| Wood | 1/2 | 7 |
| Plywood | 1/8 | 15 |
| Plywood | 1/4 | 15 |
| Brass, non-ferrous metals | 1/4 | 10 |
| Steel | 3/16 | 24 |
| Steel | 1/4 | 10 |

The alternate tooth set is principally used on wood saw blades. The teeth are arranged so that one is to the right, the next alternates to the left, back to the right and so on. The raker tooth set has a straight unbent chip-clearing tooth located between the alternate left and right bent cutting teeth. The raker set is used primarily in the coarse-tooth metal cutting blades. The wavy tooth set has two or more teeth bending alternately to the right and to the left in graduated degrees. The wavy tooth set is most commonly found in the finer tooth saw blades used in cutting thin metal and hard steel stock.

A good rule to follow is that if the proper blade is chosen, two teeth should always rest simultaneously on the workpiece. If two

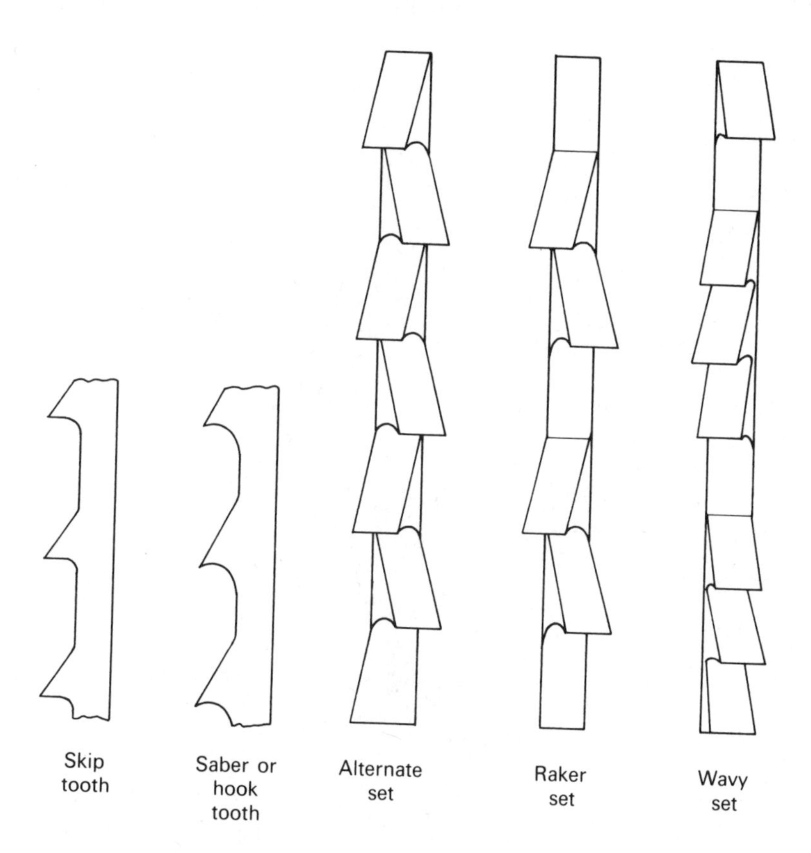


**FIGURE 2-4** / Blades have one of two types of teeth and one of three types of sets.

teeth can not simultaneously rest on the workpiece, sandwich the workpiece with a piece of scrap wood to increase the overall thickness.

Dull blades should be replaced—they are inexpensive; cracks in blades can be stopped by drilling a tiny hole (no. 60) through the blade at the end of the crack.

## 2-3 / OPERATING CONTROLS AND ADJUSTMENTS

There are only two primary adjustments to be made on the band saw prior to each operation: setting of the table tilt angle and placing the upper blade guide assembly. If a rip fence and a miter gauge are available, these adjustments must also be made. Set the operating controls and adjustments as follows (Fig. 2-5).

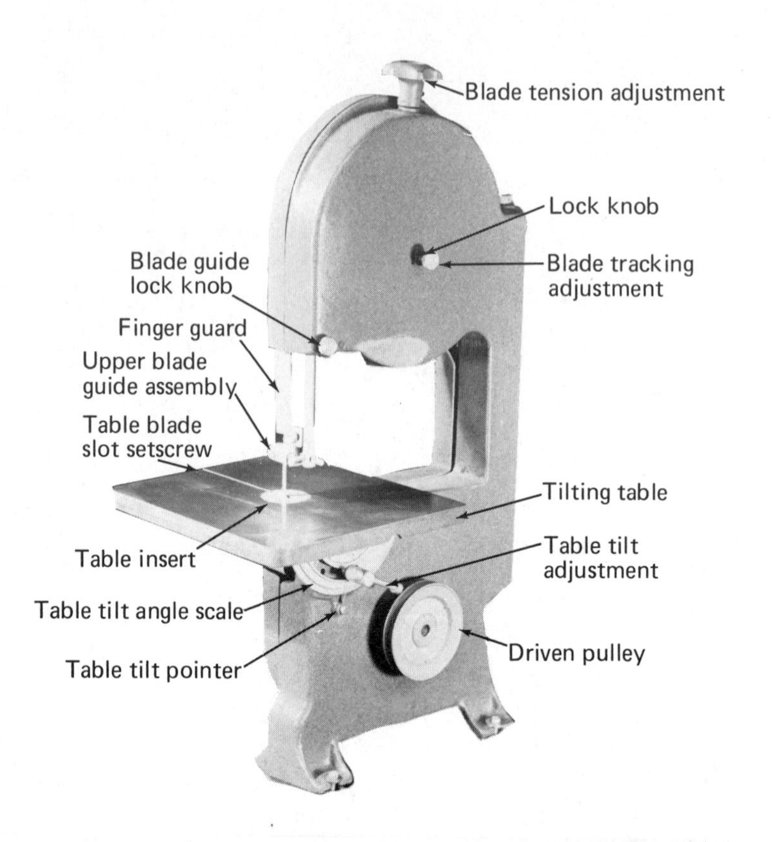


**FIGURE 2-5** / Band saw operating controls and adjustments.

1 / *table tilt*—Loosen the table tilt adjustment. Rotate the table in the trunnion to the desired angle of cut as indicated on the table tilt angle scale. Tighten the table tilt adjustment.

2 / *upper blade guide assembly*—With the power off, locate the workpiece next to the blade. Loosen the blade guide lock knob and set the upper blade guide assembly within 1/4-inch of the workpiece for maximum blade support and operator protection. Tighten the blade guide lock.

## 2-4 / OPERATION

The basic operation of the band saw is quite simple. Perform the following procedures:

1 / Select and insert the correct size blade: number of teeth depending upon the material to be cut and width depending upon the minimum radius to be cut around. Always use the widest blade possible, but remember that if the blade is too wide for the curve attempted, the blade may cramp in the saw kerf and break. Refer to Table 2-1 for band saw blade selection and to Sec. 2-8 for blade insertion procedures.

2 / Arrange the pulleys for a slow saw speed for cutting metals and hardwood or to a fast speed for cutting soft woods (refer to Sec. 1-7).

3 / Set the tilting table to the desired angle.

4 / Adjust the rip fence or miter gauge, if applicable.

5 / Place the workpiece on the tilting table adjacent to the blade. Lower the upper blade guide assembly until it is within 1/4-inch of the workpiece.

### *CAUTION*

***Never use a dull blade on the band saw, and never apply electrical power until the wheel cover (or door) is secured, the upper blade guide assembly is lowered, and the finger guard is in place. Review the safety precautions in Sec. 1-16.***

6 / Apply electrical power to the motor. Allow the saw to reach full speed. Perform the sawing procedures in Sec. 2-5.

Some common problems that arise in band saw operation are blade weaving, flutter, overheating, and excessive breakage. Weaving can be caused by the upper blade guide being too high, a dull blade, or the blade guides being too far apart or too far behind the blade. Flutter can be caused by insufficient tension, pitch and dust or lumps on the wheels, or by improper blade guide adjustment. Overheating can be caused by too little blade clearance from the blade guides, pitch and dust on the blade, too heavy a feed or crowding in the blade turns, or a dull blade. Excessive breakage can be caused by too much blade tension, blade guides out of adjustment, wheels misaligned, or crowding in the blade turns.

## 2-5 / SAWING PROCEDURES

Most sawing operations on the band saw are freehand. Occasionally you may have a need to cut thick workpieces square and thus a miter gauge or/and a rip fence may be used. A rip fence (or a board clamped to the table) is used in resawing boards into thinner boards.

Before sawing, mentally visualize the path of the cuts to be made so that the simplest method of cutting is achieved. Many cuts on larger workpieces will be limited by the frame of the band saw; by correct planning, you can work around many such situations. Where there is a choice of starting points, make the shortest cuts first—backing out of a short cut (with power off) is easier than backing out of a long cut. Where there are combination cuts, make a number of smaller cuts.

### *CAUTION*

***Never apply forward pressure with either hand directly in line with the blade. Use a push block for pushing small workpieces through the blade.***

Use one hand to feed the workpiece into the blade and the other hand to guide the workpiece (Fig. 2-6). Generally, feed slowly with moderate pressure letting the saw do the work. Use a light feed on thin cross sections, for radius cutting, and for blades 1/4-inch or less wide. Heavier feeds are used on hard materials. Guide the workpiece into the blade so that the cut is just to the outside of the pattern line. Finishing of the workpiece by sanding will trim the workpiece to the pattern line.

You simply can't make too sharp of turn cuts with the band saw. Refer to Sec. 2-2 and Fig. 2-3. Don't try to cut smaller radii than the minimum radius recommended. Use a narrow blade for curve cutting, but use the widest blade that you can for minimum radii cuts. If it is necessary to make a wide blade go around a short curve, break the cut into a number of short tangent cuts or eliminate the strain on the blade by using radial cuts to the curved line so that scrap pieces are cut away in small pieces and hence do not bind the blade. You can use the blade to *chip* away material in a narrow slot. You can also avoid backtracking the blade by boring holes in the workpiece to allow shifting of the workpiece in position.

**FIGURE 2-6** / One hand is used to feed the workpiece and the other is used to guide the workpiece.

*CAUTION*

***In the following procedure on compound cuts, do not insert brads into the area where the band saw blade will cut them.***

On compound curved cuts (cuts on more than one side of the workpiece so that the cuts intersect one another), cut on one side first. Then tack the pieces back together with brads, preferably in the scrap wood area, and then rotate the workpiece 90° and cut the other side (Fig. 2-7). The pieces are tacked back in place to provide a flat workpiece to the band saw table. This technique of compound cutting is good for precutting model pieces or pieces to be turned on the lathe.

To rip a board, place a wide blade (3/8- or 1/2-inch) on the saw: fine teeth for smooth cuts and wide coarse teeth for fast straight cutting. A narrow blade will tend to wander in the softer boards. Attach the rip fence or clamp a straight board to the table to use as a rip guide. If you are resawing thick boards, it may be necessary to

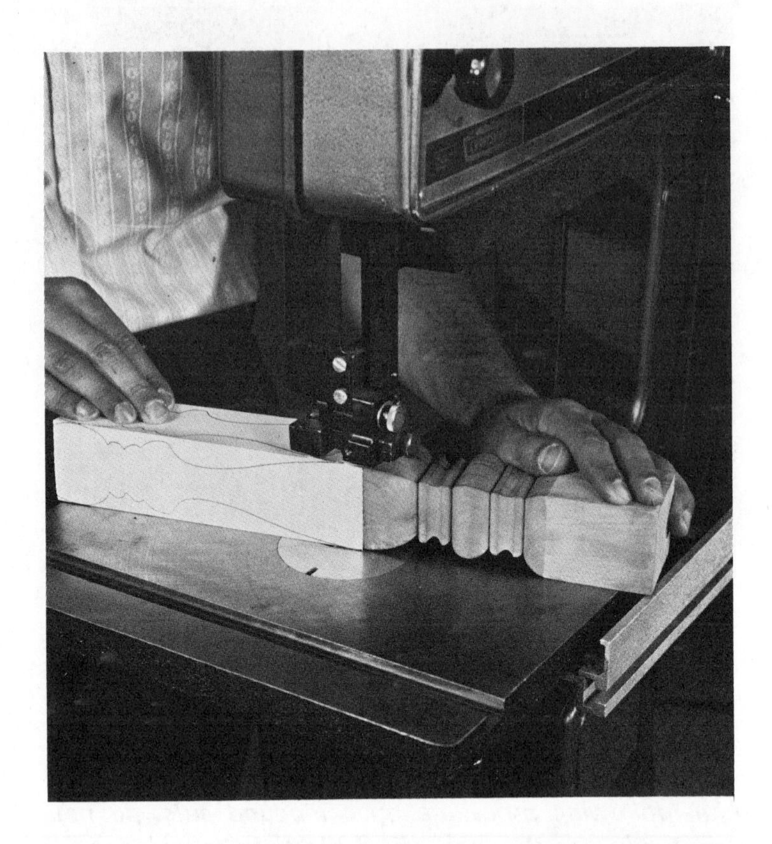

**FIGURE 2-7** / Compound cuts are easily made on the band saw.

screw a wide board vertically onto the rip fence to keep the workpiece vertical during cutting. Push the workpiece through the saw with a push stick. Use the other hand to guide the workpiece along (against) the rip fence.

You can rip or resaw a workpiece without a fence fairly accurately with a pivot guide (Fig. 2-8). Clamp the pivot guide directly opposite the blade. Mark the cut line on the workpiece. With one hand, push the workpiece against the pivot block. This method of ripping has the advantage of permitting the workpiece to be pivoted if leading of the blade occurs (the blade cuts to one side more than the other because one side is sharper). If a fence is available, you may need to screw an extra board to the fence to support wide workpieces for resawing. Note the positions of the hands when resawing, as shown in Fig. 2-9.

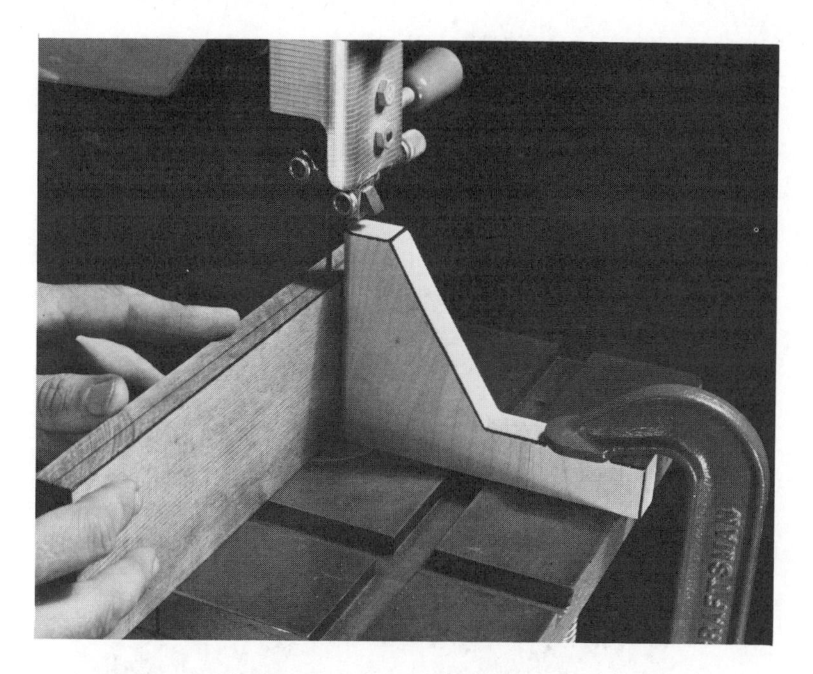


**FIGURE 2-8** / A pivot guide can be used for ripping or resawing if a fence is not available. You can also clamp a straight board to the table.

Miter cuts are made in the same manner as described in Sec. 1-12. Miter and rip fence aids can be constructed as described in Sec. 1-12.

Circular workpieces can be cut on the band saw either freehand or with a jig. Draw the pattern with a compass. For freehand cutting, keep the cut just to the outside of the pattern line, then sand the workpiece to the pattern line. A jig can also be used (refer to Sec. 4-5).

A series of equal size arcs can be ripped on the band saw. Move the rip fence over to the blade and scribe a line on the fence where the blade teeth meet the blade. Position the fence a distance from the blade that is equal to the width of the arc to be cut. Cut the first outside arc freehand and smooth it to the pattern line. Then feed the workpiece into the blade by keeping the workpiece in contact with the fence at exactly the point at which the line is drawn on the rip fence. If you don't have a rip fence, clamp a straight board to the table in place of it.

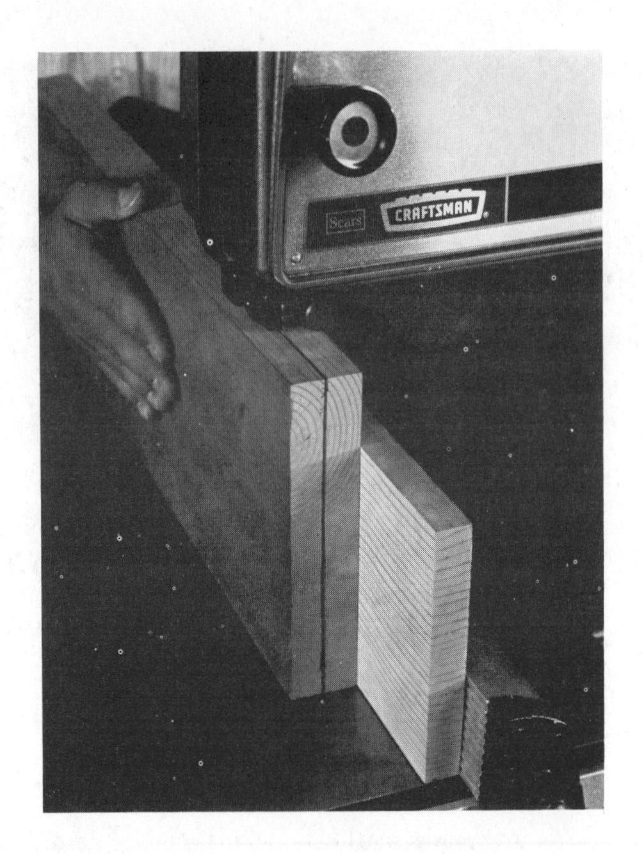


**FIGURE 2-9** / Resawing a workpiece when a fence is available.

Beveled cuts are made by tilting and locking the table to the desired angle (Fig. 2-10). Lower the upper blade guide as far as possible to support the blade and to protect your hands from the blade. Take extra care not to put additional pressure on the side of the blade (because the upper blade guide assembly is higher than normal). Follow the pattern line as if a straight line were being cut.

A number of duplicate tapered cuts (Fig. 2-11) can easily be made once the original taper is cut into a tapered pattern block. Simply place the workpiece into the taper pattern block, set the rip fence or a clamped board at the required distance from the blade, and pass the workpiece through the saw blade. Hold the workpiece firmly against the tapered pattern block and against the rip fence. This same technique can also be used on the table saw.

You can cut a number of similar workpieces all at once on the

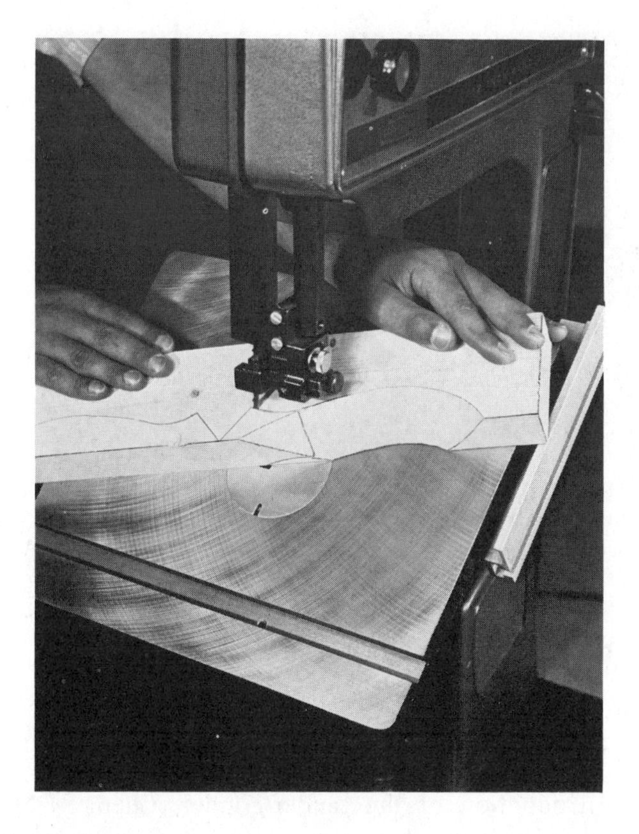

**FIGURE 2-10** / Beveled cuts are made by tilting and locking the table at the desired bevel angle.

band saw. Stack the workpiece materials together, and place small brads into the *sandwiched* stack at places that will be scrap material; it may be necessary to put one or two brads into the finished workpiece area. Draw the pattern on the top piece. Cut the sandwich and you'll simultaneously cut a number of workpieces. Back thin sheets of metal with wood. Thicker sheets will cut smoothly without a backing.

Plastics can generally be cut easily. Some are softened at a low temperature and the friction of the saw blade may cause the cut to be stringy or to have a heavy burr. These can be removed from the workpiece with an abrasive paper. Other plastics are brittle and chip easily. A strip of adhesive tape applied to the bottom side of the workpiece under the pattern lines will prevent or reduce this

**FIGURE 2-11** / Cutting a number of duplicate tapered workpieces.

chipping. Cut plastics at a slow speed and with a slow feed. Use a skip tooth blade with alternate set teeth.

## 2-6 / SANDING

Since the introduction of the sander-grinder (Chap. 9) by several power tool manufacturers, band saw manufacturers have adapted the band saw to a sander-grinder arrangement. A sanding attachment consisting of a flat or curved platen with guides and mounting brackets are attached to the upper blade guide assembly. The 1/2-inch sanding belt is then placed onto the wheels in place of the saw blade. Lower the upper blade guide assembly with the sanding attachment into position.

The sanding attachment eliminates tedious hand sanding of irregular shaped stock. Hold the workpiece against the tilting table for support, and press the workpiece gently against the sanding belt against the platen (Fig. 2-12).

## 2-7 / ACCESSORIES

The two most useful accessories for the band saw are the miter gauge and the rip fence. However, your band saw must have machined slots

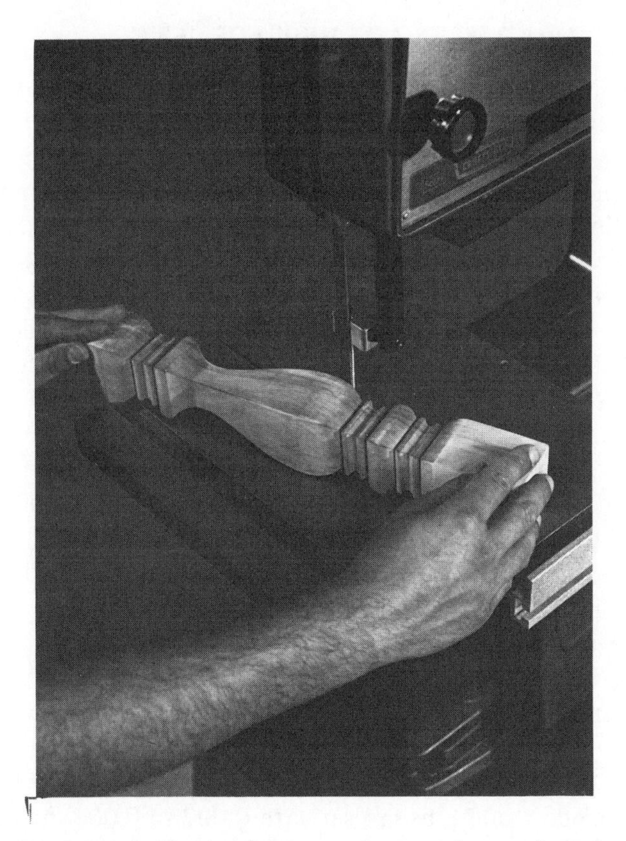

**FIGURE 2-12** / The band saw can be used for sanding after the addition of an adapter kit.

in the table for the miter gauge and holes drilled in the table for the rip fence attachment. The miter gauge holds workpieces at angles from 0 to 45° right or left for angled cuts. The rip fence locks to the front of the table and is used as a guide in ripping planks and boards. The rip fence tilts to an angle of 45° left. Use a 1/2-inch saw blade during ripping operations with the rip fence.

A sanding attachment with abrasive belts is available for some machines (Sec. 2-6). Lamp attachments, a mechanical link switch rod to the motor (if it is mounted below), and retractable casters for table mounted band saws are also available. Some manufacturers also have a *riser* available that can be installed into the frame. The riser increases the cutting thickness capacity by about two times the original capacity; longer blades are required.

## *2-8/* BLADE REPLACEMENT

Several adjustments that must be made when a band saw blade is replaced are *tracking, tension,* upper and lower *blade guide pins,* and *blade thrust support wheel.* The blade tracking adjustment is located on the rear of the frame and adjusts (tilts) the upper wheel anguarly in a vertical plane. It is adjusted so that the blade *tracks* in the center of the upper and lower wheels. A lock nut secures the adjustment once the wheel angle is correctly set. Some band saws do not have a variable angle upper wheel; thus, the blade tracking adjustment is not required. Instead, another blade roller guide is located inside the frame on the left side to cause the blade to track correctly.

The tension adjustment is usually located on the top outside of the frame, but it is also sometimes within the frame. The tension adjustment causes the upper idler wheel to raise or lower to increase or decrease the distance: hence the tension of the blade between the upper idler wheel and the lower fixed wheel.

Two sets of two blade guide pins and a blade thrust support wheel are located (Fig. 2-13) in both the lower and the upper blade guide assemblies. The blade guide pins are usually round or square steel rod, but may be ball bearing rollers on expensive band saws. The blade thrust support wheels are ball bearing rollers.

The blade guide pins are set with 0.002 to 0.003 inch clearance between each guide pin and the blade. The setting of this clearance is performed easily by inserting slips of paper between the guide pins and the blade; squeeze the guide pins, paper, and blade together and tighten the setscrews to hold the guide pins at the proper adjustment. Set the blade guide pin lateral adjustment so that the pins are just behind the blade gullets; only the teeth of the blade should project from the guide pins. Finally, set the blade thrust support wheel 1/64-inch behind the blade. When a workpiece is placed against the blade, the blade will run against the thrust support wheel.

Blade replacement jobs range from hard to easy on band saws. If your saw does not have a tilting upper wheel, the job is easy; follow the procedures described later in this section. If your saw has a tilting upper wheel, blade replacement is harder; follow these procedural steps:

*1* / Remove or open the wheel cover or door.

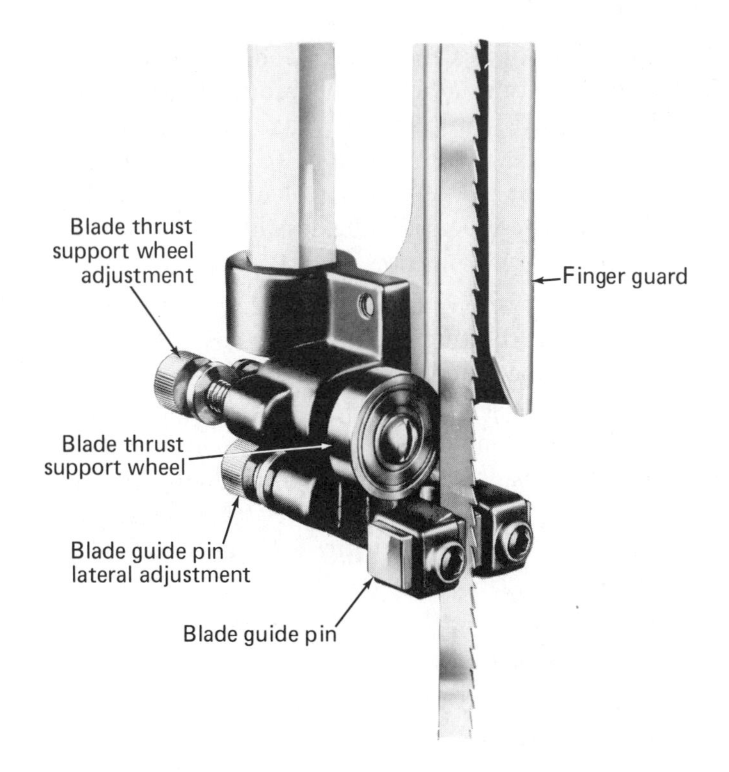


**FIGURE 2-13** / The upper blade guide assembly must be set correctly for the blade.

*2* / Loosen the upper wheel tension by rotating the blade tension adjustment.

*3* / Remove the table blade slot setscrew or latch and the table insert. Retract the blade guide assemblies as far as possible.

*4* / Remove the blade. Wipe any oil from the new blade and install it lightly on the center of the wheels.

*5* / Take up the blade tension slightly by rotating the blade tension adjustment.

*6* / Position the blade in the upper and lower blade guide assemblies.

*7* / Increase the tension on the blade. The tension should be sufficient for narrow blades to prevent blade weaving and excessive vibrating. The wider the blade, the higher the permissible tension. Too much tension will break the blade at the weld joint. If you are fortunate enough to have a blade tension scale on your band saw, increase the tension until the scale indicates the proper tension for the blade installed. If you have no blade tension scale, raise the upper blade guide assembly to its uppermost location. Press against the side of the blade with your finger; if the tension is correct, the blade should flex about 1/8-inch from its normal position.

*8* / Check that the blade tracks correctly in the center of the wheels by rotating the lower wheel about 20 turns by hand. If the blade starts to move from the center of the wheels, adjust the blade tracking adjustment until the blade tracks in the center. It is the best practice to back out the blade guide pins to facilitate tracking. When tracking is correct, check the blade tension again and adjust as necessary. Figure 2-14 illustrates the use of a board to align the wheels.

*9* / Set the lower and upper blade guide pins and blade thrust support wheel as previously described.

*10* / Again rotate the wheels about 20 turns by hand to check all adjustments.

*11* / Reinstall the wheel cover or close the door.

*12* / Apply power to the saw and let it run for a few minutes without a workpiece to seat the blade and to check for weld defects and improper adjustment.

If your saw does not have a tilting upper wheel, perform steps 1 through 7. It is best to back the blade guide all the way out prior to inserting the blade. Perform steps 9 through 12. It is not necessary to adjust the blade thrust support wheels in the upper and lower blade guide assemblies with this type of saw because they are fixed. The blade will track correctly. During operation with no workpiece in the saw, the blade does *not* touch the upper blade guide assembly blade thrust support wheel; this is normal operation and contact is made when a workpiece is pushed into the blade.

## 2-9 / CALIBRATION AND MAINTENANCE

The table should be checked periodically to verify that it is perpendicular to the blade when the table tilt pointer indicates 0°

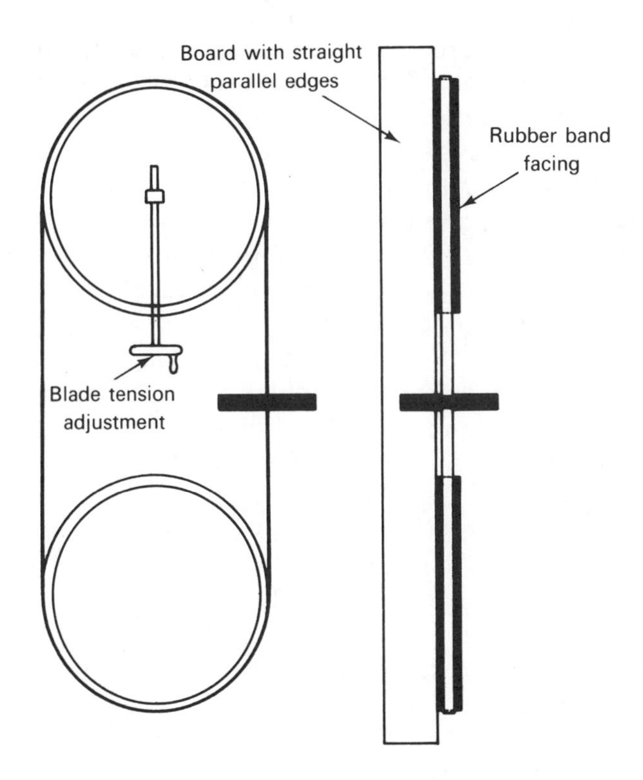


**FIGURE 2-14** / Aligning the band saw wheels.

(90° on some models). To do this, place a square or triangle against the side of the blade and table. If the table is not perpendicular to the blade, release the table tilt adjustment and level the table until the square indicates a perpendicular condition. Lock the table tilt adjustment. If the table tilt pointer does not indicate exactly zero, loosen the pointer or scale screws and set to indicate zero; retighten the screws and make a final check for perpendicularity.

If your band saw table does not tilt to the left, then it probably has a 0° (or 90°) *stop bolt* inserted underneath the table. With the table set perpendicular to the blade and the table tilt pointer to 0° (or 90°), the bolt head should set flat against the band saw frame. If it does not, adjust the bolt flat against the frame when the pointer indicates 0°. Tilt and return the table to 0° several times to verify the correct adjustment. Miter gauges and perpendicularity of rip fences should be checked and calibrated in accordance with the procedures in Sec. 1-7.

Tension should be removed from band saw blades during

periods of nonuse. During long periods of nonuse, remove and store the blades. This prevents the blade from taking a set or bend due to the wheel pressure and curvature. Wipe blades to be stored with an oily rag. A coat of beeswax makes a good lubricant; it also helps the blade pass through a cut more easily.

Blades that are caked with sawdust and pitch act as dull blades tearing rather than cutting the wood fibers. This puts stress on the blade causing eventual breakage. To remove caked sawdust, soak the blade in kerosene and then wipe, scrape, or use a toothbrush to remove the sawdust. Often a kerosene soaked rag does the job. Steel wool or a wire brush will remove stubborn dirt and pitch.

The rubber covering the wheels should remain soft to allow the set of the blade teeth to sink into it. If the rubber is hard, unnecessary strain is placed on the gullets of the blade teeth, often causing cracked and broken blades. Hard and cracked rubber should be replaced. On models having grooved wheels, simply remove the rubber band and replace it; on models on which the rubber is glued on, remove the rubber and old glue completely, using a knife and steel wool. Apply new rubber adhesive and the new rubber band.

Clean the inside of the band saw occasionally with a vacuum cleaner. Use a soft brush to remove dust from bearings, tension scale, blade guides, and other parts of the band saw. Use a stiff bristle brush to clean metal chips from the rubber tires. Also remove the table insert and clean away any dirt that may have accumulated under it.

Place a drop or two of light machine oil on the shafts of the blade thrust support wheels. Place a small amount of graphite on the upper blade guard assembly support shaft, on the trunnions, and on the threads of control knobs.

Inspect the blade guide pins occasionally for wear. At the first sign of scuffing or scoring, resurface them. Grip a pin securely in a locking plier wrench, and hold the end to be resurfaced against a sander grinder, disk or belt sander, or a grinding wheel. Be sure to maintain the same angle as on the guide pin. Use light pressure and do not let the pins get hot.

## 2-10 / HINTS AND KINKS

Where storage room permits, hang band saw blades in a single loop. If storage room does not permit this, fold the blade into three loops for storage. Hold the blade in front of you with the teeth pointing away. Hold the blade in the centers with your right hand up and the left hand down. Note the original position of the hands and the thumbs, as this is the secret to folding. Grasp the blade tightly with the thumbs and while *maintaining* the grasp, rotate the right hand *away* from your body and the left hand *toward* your body. Maintain the grip and the blade will automatically fold into three loops. Be careful not to kink the blade. Tie the loops with soft covered wire or cord.

Wipe the blade with an oily rag prior to storing. Hang the blade on a peg, a notched board, or even under and inside of the band saw tool stand.

## 2-11 / INSTALLATION

Clearance is required in front of and behind the blade for long workpieces. The left side of the band saw can be mounted near or against a wall.

The band saw should be mounted on a power tool stand with a top of about 18 by 24 inches. The band saw tilting table should be about 42 inches off of the floor. The motor can be mounted on the table or under the table. Position the band saw on the power tool stand so that workpieces will be off the side of the table when the tilting table is set to 45°. Perform the calibration and maintenance procedures of Sec. 2-9.

chapter three

# DRILL PRESS

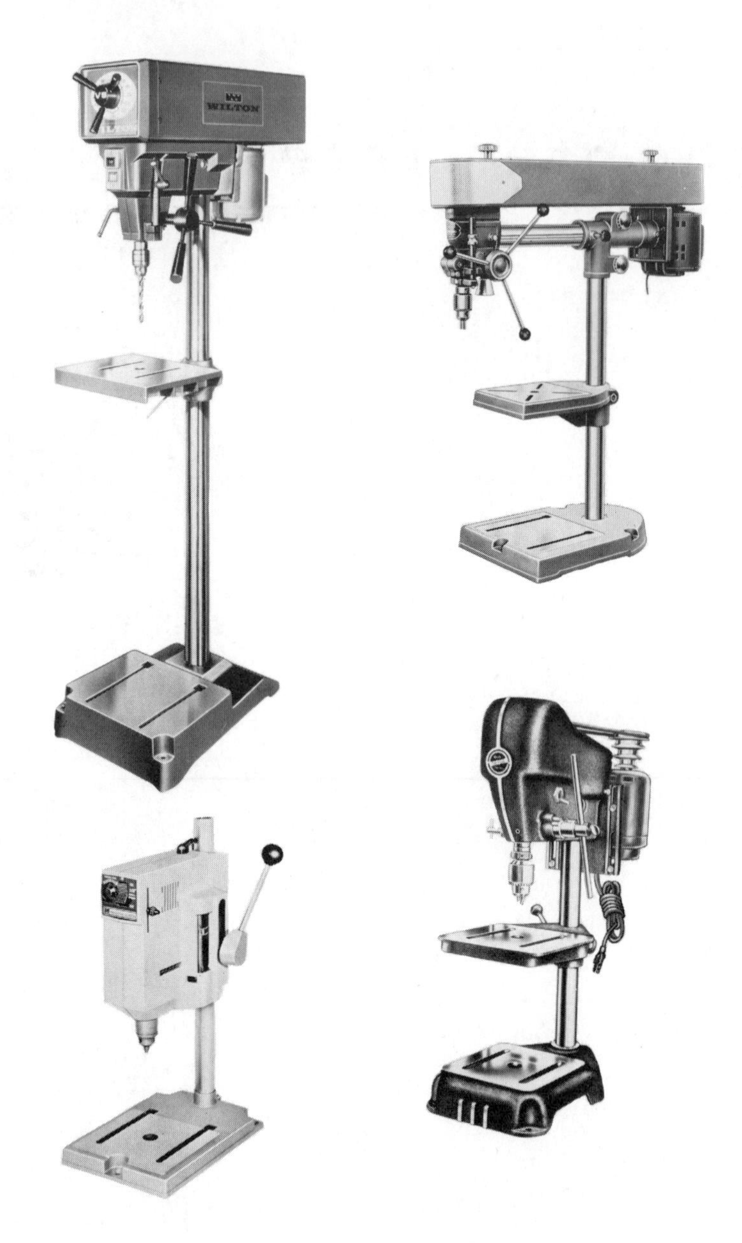


**FIGURE 3-1** / Drill presses are multipurpose tools that, with accessories, perform many functions in addition to drilling holes.

Probably the first hand powered tool you owned was the hand held electric drill. You purchased it because of its multipurpose uses when various attachments were placed into the chuck or onto the threaded arbor when the chuck was removed. Through use, however, you found that the hand electric drill was limited in accuracy and application without a stand or guide.

The drill press is also a multipurpose tool, but it is probably the second bench tool you'll buy for your workshop; the radial arm saw is the recommended first tool. The main function of the drill press is to securely fasten and turn drills and bits for cutting holes in workpieces of many types of material. The drill press is sturdily built to provide accurate drilling at the proper speed to suit the cutting tool and the material.

Secondary functions of the drill press are sanding, routing, shaping, mortising, and making dovetails. Sanding is performed by the addition of a clamped-on auxiliary table made in the shop from wood and a sanding drum and adapter placed on the spindle in place of the chuck; some drum sanding can be performed by placing a drum with a 1/4-inch shaft into the chuck. In the routing of designs into workpieces or the cutting of molding, trim, inlays, joints, and trim work, a routing bit is placed in a collet chuck or adapter, and the workpiece is carefully moved under the bit.

The shaping of decorative molding, rabbeting, beading, fluting, the cutting of door lips, and the cutting of picture frame molding can be done by using shaping attachments that include cutters, a fence, and a larger auxiliary table (made in the workshop).

The cutting of mortises–rectangular cuts of considerable depth in a piece of wood for receiving a corresponding projection (tenon) on another piece of wood to form a joint–is accomplished by the addition of mortising attachments including a mortising chisel housing, fence and hold down assembly, mortising bit, and a hollow chisel. Dovetails–joints to join drawer sides and fronts together–are made with the use of a dovetail bit, and plates, a comb, stop, clamps, and other hardware.

Drill presses are not meant to take the place of routers, shapers, and sanding tools. Instead, they are used with the necessary attachments if you do not have sufficient need or sufficient funds to purchase separate tools. Drill presses do not run with as high speeds as the router or shaper, but the speed is adequate for light duty routing and shaping.

The size of a drill press is determined by the distance between the chuck center and the vertical support column. This is the *throat* size and is the largest radius of a circle that could be drilled. For example, a 6 inch drill press can cut a hole in the center of a circular workpiece having a radius of 6 inches; this is a diameter of 12 inches. Home workshop drill press throats are from 5 to 6 inches–they drill to the center of 10 to 12 inch diameter circles.

## 3-1 / DESCRIPTION AND MAJOR PARTS

The major parts of the bench drill press (Fig. 3-2) are the head, base, column, and table. The head houses all of the working parts of the drill press including the *motor, spindle drive system, spindle, quill, chuck,* the *speed* and *feed adjustments* and the *depth gauge* and *stop* or *lock.*

The motors most often recommended for the drill press are 1/3- or 1/2-hp turning at 1725 rev/min. This results in spindle speeds of approximately 370 to 5500 or more rev/min depending upon the belt/pulley or gear systems. Motors are mounted at the rear of the head with the motor shaft on top spinning clockwise (looking down on top of the shaft).

The motor drives the spindle drive system. This system consists of fixed pulleys and a belt, or variable speed pulleys and belt(s), or a geared drive system. The geared drive system has no pulleys or belts, is expensive, and is generally for industrial use rather than home workshop use. Meshing gears are made in pairs–one fiber and one steel–for quiet operation.

The fixed pulleys and belt system is the least expensive drive

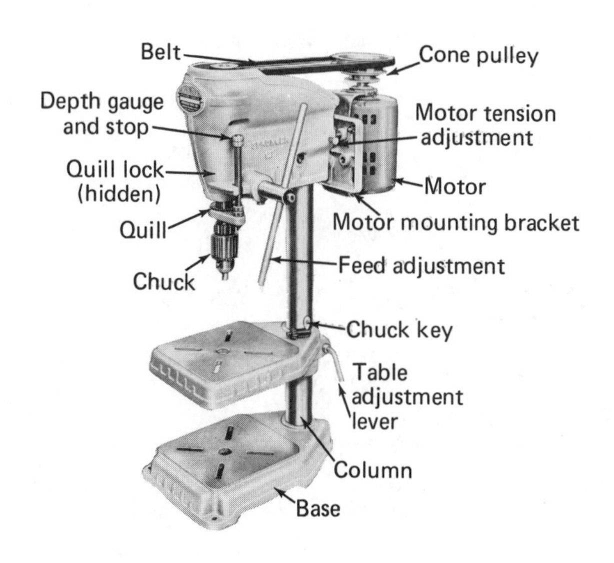


**FIGURE 3-2** / Major parts of the drill press.

system. Two four-to-eight *step* cone pulleys of equal size are used; one on the motor shaft and one placed in an inverted position on the sleeve of the spindle assembly. With four step pulleys and a 1725 rev/min motor, four speeds are available at the chuck–approximately 860, 1210, 2225 and 3450 rev/min. A six step cone pulley system with a 1725 rev/min motor has speeds of approximately 370, 625, 1125, 1950, 3480, and 5500 rev/min. Eight step cone pulleys with a 1725 rev/min motor have speeds of approximately 380, 480, 720, 1325, 2300, 4250, 6400, and 8550 rev/min. Belts are changed easily by hand between the various cone pulley diameters. Four speeds meet the normal demands of the home workshop. The extended lower speeds are useful in metal drilling, and the extended higher speeds permit higher quality routing and shaping.

The variable speed pulley system may consist of one or two variable speed pulleys and one or two belts (Fig. 3-3). The variable speed pulleys are designed so that the groove width of the pulley can be changed. This in turn changes the diameter of the pulley and thus the speed of the spindle assembly.

The *spindle* is turned by the driven pulley and provides the turning of the chuck or other attachment. The upper end of the spindle is splined and mates with a splined bearing mounted sleeve. This splining ensures a positive drive of the spindle even though the

**FIGURE 3-3** / This drill press has variable speed pulleys.

spindle moves up and down to set the depth of cut. The lower end of the spindle is tapered or threaded to fit a chuck or accessory attachment adapter. On some drill presses, the spindle is interchangeable.

The spindle and its bearings are enclosed by a steel sleeve called a *quill.* The quill does not rotate but it does support the spindle; it has gear teeth down the back side that mesh with a pinion gear which is driven by the feed adjustment handle to lower the quill/spindle/chuck assembly. A spring returns the quill when the feed adjustment is released. The quill can be locked at any position by the *quill lock.* Quill travel—and hence the depth of cut—is about 3-1/2-inches on home use drill presses.

A *chuck* is a three-jaw assembly used to grip an infinite range of round accessory shafts to the maximum capacity of the drill chuck. The three-jaw configuration has the ability to always hold the shaft within the center line of the drill. The chuck size determines the largest drill size that can be used in the drill press. For home use, this is from 0 to 1/2-inch diameter. The chuck fits onto the spindle by either a tapered or a threaded fit.

*Speed adjustments* are made by changing the position of the belt on a fixed pulley system. On variable speed systems, a dial or rotating handle is used to change the speed.

*Feed adjustments* are made by rotating the feed adjustment handle toward (counterclockwise) the operator. The rate of feed and the feed pressure are determined by the operator.

The *depth gauge* indicates the depth of extension of the quill, and hence, the penetration of the drill into the workpiece. Markings are graduated in 1/16-inch. Two stop nuts can be spun down the gauge to limit the travel of the quill (one nut locks the other) for repetitive depth drilling. Another type of depth gauge is a collar with a setscrew on the feed adjustment shaft. The collar can be rotated and locked in position to a given depth. When the feed adjustment is rotated, the collar rotates with the adjustment shaft; when a protrusion on the collar strikes a stop on the head casting, the feed adjustment travel is ended at the preset depth.

The *base* of the drill press provides the support for the column that holds the head and table. The base has a center hole and slots in its casting; the hole is for the drill to pass through, thus preventing damage of the base by the drill tip. The slots are for bolting on jigs or vises to hold workpieces securely in place while operations are performed. The base of approximately 10 by 12 inches is bolted to a bench or power tool stand or to the floor, as in the case of floor model drill presses. Incidentally, the bases of floor model drill presses are larger and weigh considerably more than the bases of bench type drill presses.

The *column* of the drill press mounts in the base and provides a "track" to which the table and head are mounted and fastened by means of column locking sleeves and nuts. Table and head adjustment handles loosen and tighten the locking device, thus allowing the table and head to be located at any height and at any location 360° around the column. Normally, the head is locked at the top of the column, and the table is locked below the drill in the chuck.

The *table,* about 9 by 10 inches, supports the workpiece. A hole in the center of the cast table allows the drill point that has passed through the workpiece to pass through the table rather than to drill into the table. Slots in the table permit a vise or auxiliary table to be bolted to the table to facilitate clamping of the workpiece. As previously mentioned, by loosening the table adjustment via the level, the table can be raised or lowered or rotated 360° around the column. Some tables also tilt and lock into any angular position from a horizontal to a vertical position; this is a handy feature when it is necessary to drill a hole into a workpiece at an angle.

The drill press discussed thus far has been of conventional design. Three additional drill press designs–radial, drill-router, and a small motorized press–are now discussed. The overall dimensions of the conventional bench mounted drill press are approximately 12 inches wide, 19 inches front to rear, and 34 inches high. Floor models are about 70 inches high.

A *radial* drill press (Fig. 3-1) is similar to the design of the drill press in Fig. 3-2; however, in addition to the vertical column, there is also a tubular horizontal shaft that allows the complete head assembly to move forward and backward, around in a circular path of 360°, and to tilt 90° left and right. The tilt angle is indicated on a scale. This tilting feature lets the cutting tool operate at many angles. An index pin locks into a groove to align the head with the vertical column. The throat capacity–the distance from the cutting tool tip to the vertical column–is about double that of the conventional drill press. Throat distances on radial drill presses vary because of the movable shaft from approximately 5 to 16 inches, and tables are longer too–about 16 by 24 inches. The overall size of the radial drill press is approximately 20 inches wide, 35 inches deep, and 37 inches high.

There are three advantages of the radial drill press over the standard drill press: the head tilts up to 90° left or right for easy angle drilling, the head moves in and out to increase or decrease the throat distance as necessary, and the head rotates in a 360° horizontal plane.

The *drill-router* is a relatively new tool. It has two spindles–one *drill spindle* protruding from the head, as in ordinary drills, plus the addition of a *router spindle* protruding from the top of the head. The drill spindle rotates between 500 and 2500 rev/min; the router spindle rotates at 4000 to 21,000 rev/min. A solid state gear-driven speed change system without belts and pulleys provides an infinite number of speeds. A spindle guard is moved from one spindle to the other, and the entire head is rotated in a 360° circle to place the desired spindle in operating position. Two available models have 8-1/2- and 10-inch throats, 12 by 14 inch tables, and are powered by a 5/8-hp motor built within the head. Chuck capacities are 0 to 1/2-inch with a quill travel of 6 inches.

Small motorized drill presses similar to the one illustrated in Fig. 3-1 are 18 inches high and have chuck capacities of 3/8-inch. They have 1/4-hp motors rotating at variable speeds from approximately 700 to 2000 rev/min. These small drill presses can drill holes to 3/4-inch in wood and 3/8-inch in steel.

## 3-2 / DRILLS AND OTHER BORING TOOLS

Drills and other boring tools and circle sawing tools (Fig. 3-4) are used to bore or saw a round hole into a piece of wood, metal, plastic, masonry, or other material. The hole may be used for a fastener such

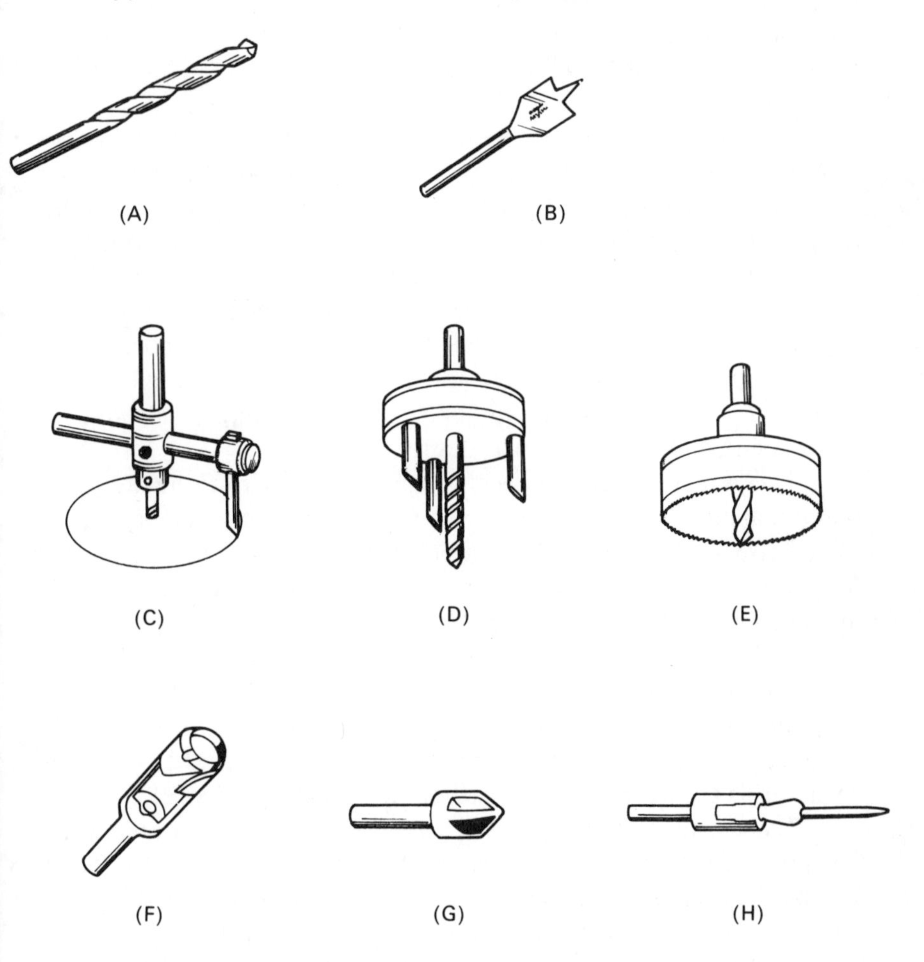


**FIGURE 3-4** / Drills and other boring tools and circle sawing tools: (A) twist drill; (B) power wood boring bit; (C) fly cutter; (D) three point cutter; (E) saw blade cutter; (F) plug cutter; (G) countersink; (H) screw pilot bit.

as a screw, bolt, rivet, pin, or dowel. The hole may also be used for another assembly such as a lock or as an opening to pass an object through.

The terms *drill* and *bit* are used rather interchangeably to denote a tool or instrument with an edged or pointed end for making holes in workpieces by revolving. In home workshop use, the *twist drill* is usually the tool used to make holes in metal, wood, and other materials; twist drills are available in sizes from 1/32-inch to 1/4-inch in diameter. Larger holes in wood workpieces are usually made in the home workshop with *power wood boring bits.* These bits extend the range of hole drilling in wood workpieces from 1/4-inch to 1-1/2-inches. *Circle cutters* then extend this range even further to about 7 inches. *Plug cutters* cut slightly beveled plugs from wood for insertion into screw holes in a workpiece to hide the screwhead. *Countersinks* are used to cut a tapered hole below the surface so that a screwhead can be driven flat with the surface. A *counterbore* enlarges the top part of a hole so that a screwhead can be sunk below the surface, and the remaining area above the screwhead is filled with a plug or a wood filler. A combined countersink/counterbore known as a *screw pilot bit* is used to simultaneously drill all of the "opening" for the screw pilot (threads), shank, head, and to countersink and counterbore as desired.

The remainder of this section provides descriptions, uses, and maintenance of twist drills, power wood boring bits, circle cutters, plug cutters, countersinks, counterbores, and screw pilot bits. The *how-to-use* instructions of these drills/bits including speeds, feeds, and cutting fluids is described in Sec. 3-5.

Twist drills are among the most popular bits because they can be used for boring holes in either wood or metal. The point is the only cutting area; the flutes (two spiral grooves) remove cut material from the boring and allow lubricant to flow to the cutting point. Twist drills are made of either carbon or of high speed steel.

Twist drills vary in diameter; their length is proportional to the diameter. Twist drills are sold singularly or in sets of 13, 15, 21, or 29 sizes. The bits in these sets are incremented in size by 1/64-inch and provide a convenient storage medium. Twist drills normally have shanks the same diameter as the tip and flute area up to the 1/4-inch diameter shank size. Shank size may then remain at 1/4-inch while the tip and flute diameter increase. Likewise, 1/2-inch is another standard shank size. *High speed steel* (HSS) twist drills are recommended over carbon steel drills because the HSS drills can be run at higher speeds, cut harder metals, and last longer.

Twist drills may be sharpened on the grinding wheel using a drill point gauge and holders that are available commercially. The correct angle at the cutting edge of the drill point lip is 59°. After the cutting edge is ground, the lip heel is ground at 12°. Unless you use drills extremely often and wear them out often, it is more practical to purchase replacement twist drills than to regrind the points.

Because many electric hand drills accept only up to 1/4-inch shank drills, wood drills with 1/4-inch shanks (for 1/4-inch or larger chucks) but with the capability of drilling from 1/4- to 1-1/2-inch holes are available; these are known as power wood boring bits. Various sizes are often available in sets of four, six or eight. Hollow ground points start the hole and guide the drill. Machine sharpened cutters bore the large diameter holes.

To sharpen a boring bit by hand, clamp the bit in a vise and stroke it with a flat 8 inch mill file at an angle of 15°. Power sharpen on a fine grain round corner wheel and use an oilstone to remove burrs.

A circle cutter (C, D, E, Fig. 3-4) may be one of three types: a *fly cutter,* a *three point* cutter, or a *saw blade* type cutter. The fly cutter has an adjustable arm with a single cutter that extends from a center drill; graduations are in 1/16-inch and a setscrew locks the extended bar at the desired circle radius. Holes up to 7 inches in diameter can be cut in wood, steel, brass, aluminum, and plastic. The center pilot drill keeps the cutter in alignment.

The three point cutter has an adjustable diameter setting from 1-1/8- to 2-1/2-inches, readable on a dial indicator. It cuts wood and plastic. To set the diameter, turn the hex nut one-quarter turn, set the diameter, and retighten the nut.

The saw blade type hole cutter cuts wood, plastic, and wallboard. First purchase a mandrel, and then add the hole saw diameter attachment of your choice. Sizes of attachments are from 3/4- to 2-1/2-inches; maximum depth of cut is 3/4-inch.

Plug cutters cut thin plugs or dowels for insertion in holes drilled for countersunk screw holes (plugs) or for joining two pieces together (dowels). Dowels up to about 2 inches in length can be cut. The advantage of cutting your own plugs is that the plug material will match the workpiece in color and grain because the plugs are cut from scrap workpiece material. The plugs should be cut with a slight bevel to ensure an easy insertion and perfect fit. Plug diameters available are 3/8-, 1/2-, 5/8-, and 3/4-inch.

Countersinks with 1/4-inch shanks and five fluted heads with 82° angles are available for enlarging the upper part of a hole by chamfering to receive the cone-shaped head of a screw or bolt. Combination countersinks/counterbores are sold in combination size sets for use with screws; they are known as wood screw pilot bits. (Countersinking is boring a conical shaped hole in order that the conical head of a flat head screw will recess flat with the surface. Counterboring is boring below the surface of the wood in order that a screw will go below the surface—the hole may then be plugged with dowel or dowel buttons or filled. Refer to Fig. 3-5.) The combination countersink/counterbore wood screw pilot bit drills the proper screw thread and shank size, countersinks and counterbores for a plug or wood filler filling in one operation. The shanks of the wood screw pilot bits are 1/4-inch in diameter. The depth of countersinking/counterboring is adjustable.

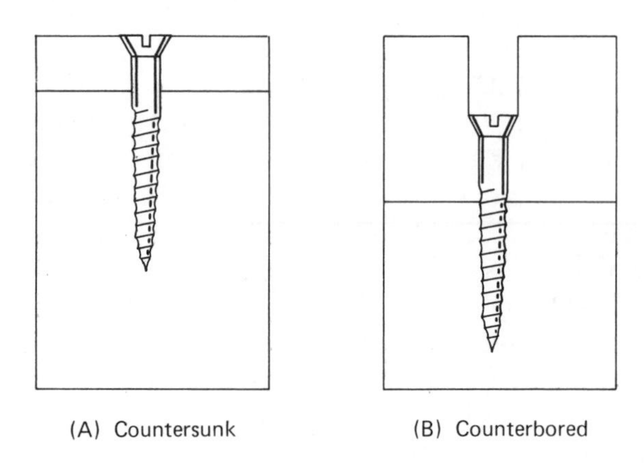


**FIGURE 3-5** / Illustration of a screw inserted in (A) a countersunk hole and (B) a counterbored hole.

## 3-3 / OPERATING CONTROLS AND ADJUSTMENTS

Operating controls and adjustments for the drill press (Fig. 3-2) include placing a bit or other shaft into the chuck, chuck tightening, table locating, locking the quill, setting depth of cut, feed adjustment, and variable speed adjustment. With the exception of the feed and variable speed adjustments, all other controls and adjustments are performed prior to applying power to the motor. Belt changes between various sections of cone pulleys are discussed in Sec. 1-7.

1 / *chuck tightening*—Prior to installing a drill or accessory shaft into the chuck, inspect the drill or shaft for burrs or marred shanks. Such drills or shafts will not run properly in the drill chuck. Remove the burrs or other surface mars with a grinding stone. Then insert a drill or accessory shaft into the chuck (insert about three-fourths of the shaft). As you hand tighten the chuck, rotate the shaft to ensure that the shaft seats properly in the chuck. Then use the chuck key to tighten the chuck. *Remember to remove the chuck key from the chuck.* Momentarily turn the motor on and off, and check that the drill or accessory is "spinning true" in the centerline of the chuck, i.e., the drill or accessory has been properly seated in the chuck. This procedure is important when you are using small diameter drills.

***NOTE***

***Do not insert any shaft with a burr into the chuck. Remove the burr with a grinding stone.***

2 / *table location*—After the drill has been properly inserted into the chuck, place the workpiece on the table, loosen the table adjustment lever, and raise the table until the workpiece is just below the drill point. Remove the workpiece and ensure that the table center hole is located directly under the drill. Tighten the table adjustment level. With the motor power still off, rotate the feed adjustment toward you, lowering the drill to the table center hole to ensure the table is correctly located. Some tables also tilt. Loosen the adjustment level and rotate to the angle desired.

3 / *locking the quill*—When a sanding drum, buffing wheel, router bit, or a similar attachment is being used, it is often

desirable to lower the quill and lock it in a fixed position. To do this, lower the quill to the desired position by rotating the feed adjustment; then hand tighten the quill lock by rotating it clockwise. To unlock the quill, rotate the quill lock counterclockwise; the spring in the quill assembly will return the quill to its uppermost position. Normally the quill lock is *lightly snugged* against the quill; this allows normal movement of the quill but prevents the quill and pinion gear from coming apart if the quill is lowered beyond the recommended travel.

4 / *depth of cut*—It is often desirable to drill a hole or a series of holes to a limited depth. This is performed by locating the workpiece and then lowering the drill tip to the workpiece. The gauge stop nuts are then set to the desired depth (Fig. 3-6). When the feed adjustment is rotated lowering the quill and drill, the motion is stopped when the depth gauge stop nuts meet the frame. An arrangement that is different from the depth gauge shown in Fig. 3-2 consists of a cam and a collar calibrated in 1/16-inch increments on the feed adjustment shaft. On this arrange-

**FIGURE 3-6** / Setting the depth stop for a hole of predetermined depth.

ment, the cam is locked to the desired depth with a setscrew. At the end of the set depth travel, the cam stops against the frame halting the travel of the quill.

5 / *feed adjustment*—The feed adjustment is rotated in a counterclockwise direction to lower the drill to the workpiece. When the drill enters the workpiece, the adjustment pressure must increase somewhat to cause the drill to cut. The amount of feed pressure and the rate of feed are dependent on the drill type and size and on the workpiece material. Let the drill do the cutting. (Refer to Sec. 3-4 for further discussion on feeds.)

6 / *variable speed adjustment*—Drills having a variable speed adjustment have a knob or a spoke and hub assembly located on the front of the head for adjusting the speed. This *variable speed adjustment is always made with the motor power turned on.* Set the speed to the approximate values given in Sec. 3-4.

## *3-4* / OPERATION

Observe the following cautions prior to operation of the drill press:

### *CAUTIONS*

1 / *Make all adjustments other than variable speed settings and feed adjustments with electrical power turned off.*

2 / *Ensure that the chuck key is removed from the chuck.*

3 / *Ensure that the drill point or other tool is not touching the workpiece when power is applied to the motor.*

4 / *Clamp the workpiece to the table.*

5 / *Observe the general safety precautions of Sec. 1-16.*

Perform the following procedures to operate the drill press. Do not apply motor power until directed.

*1* / If the drive system is composed of belt(s) and pulleys, set the belt on the proper pulley combination for the desired speed. Refer to Table 3-1 and Sec. 1-7.

*2* / Install the drill or other attachment into the chuck or onto the spindle or adapter, as applicable. Ensure that the chuck key is removed.

*3* / Raise the table, backup scrap wood, and workpiece as close to the drill bit or accessory as possible. Tilt the table, as required. Ensure that the table center hole is centered under the drill.

*4* / Clamp the workpiece and any scrap backup material in position.

*5* / If operations such as routing, sanding, or buffing are to be performed, lock the quill at the desired height.

*6* / If a hole is to be drilled, countersunk or counterbored to a certain depth, set the depth gauge and scale accordingly.

*7* / Turn the motor on and let it reach full speed.

*8* / If you are using a variable speed drill, set the desired speed (refer to Table 3-1).

*9* / Perform the applicable procedures for drilling (Sec. 3-5); sanding, buffing, grinding, and filing (Sec. 3-6); routing (Sec. 3-7); shaping (Sec. 3-8); dovetailing (Sec. 3-9); or mortising (Sec. 3-10).

## 3-5 / DRILLING PROCEDURES

This section begins by detailing four areas that are used in every drilling procedure: holding the workpiece securely, selecting the proper drilling speed, feeding the drill into the workpiece, and cutting fluids. Accurate holes are bored and the boring tools remain sharper longer when the workpiece is held securely, the correct fluid is used, and the proper speeds and feeds are selected and used.

The next areas covered in this section are the specific procedures for drilling and cutting holes in wood, metals, and other materials. Procedures for using twist drills, power wood boring bits, circle cutters, plug cutters, countersinks, counterbores, and screw pilot bits are included.

*Holding the Workpiece Securely*

Workpieces must always be held tightly in some fashion on the drill press table to prevent the drill from "snagging" into the workpiece causing the workpiece to spin dangerously. Remember that one of your hands has to be on the feed adjustment. This leaves one hand for holding the workpiece–a sometimes dangerous condition. *It is recommended that all workpieces be clamped in some manner.* All workpieces requiring accuracy in the drilling of holes should also be clamped; all metal workpieces should always be clamped.

The simplest method of holding a large wooden workpiece on the drill press table is to brace one end of the workpiece against the left side of the column; hold the workpiece with your left hand about 3 inches from the drill. This bracing method will prevent the workpiece from rotating if the clockwise turning drill snags in the workpiece.

Another easy method for bracing workpieces is to simply clamp the workpiece to the table with one or two C-clamps (Fig. 3-7). Pieces of scrap wood are placed between the workpiece and the clamp to prevent marring of the workpiece. A fence (Fig. 3-8) or a

**FIGURE 3-7** / Workpieces are easily clamped to the drill press table. This prevents the workpiece from moving, thus ensuring accurately drilled holes and a higher degree of safety.

straight board may also be used to prevent rotation of the workpiece. Place the fence or clamp—or bolt the board—at the required distance from the hole center mark. This procedure is particularly useful when a number of holes along a line are to be drilled, or when a number of similar workpieces are to have holes drilled the same distance from the drill center.

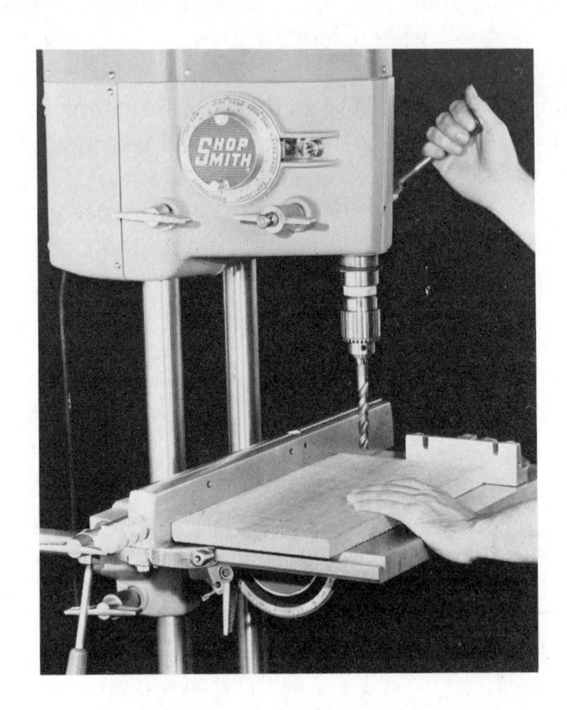


**FIGURE 3-8** / A fence or board clamped to the drill press table prevents the workpiece from turning. It also allows you to drill a number of holes of equal distance from the drill point.

The workpiece itself can be bolted to the table by passing bolts through the slots in the table top. Or, bolts can simply be fastened through the slots and the workpiece braced against the bolts in the same manner as against a fence or the drill press column.

A drill press vise (Fig. 3-9) is particularly effective in clamping small workpieces. The center of the vise between the jaws is open to allow clearance for the drill after it passes through the workpiece. The jaw faces are flat, but two additional accessory pieces for holding irregular and round shaped workpieces are included with the vise. The jaws may be opened about 3 inches. Mounting lugs are provided on the base for mounting the vise to the drill press table. The vise can be placed on its base or sides for making quick setups. Some drill press vises are mounted to a tilting-type base or a combination swivel/tilting base; this arrangement gives even more versatility because the jaws can be set at an angle of from 0 to 90° in a 360° circle.

**FIGURE 3-9** / A drill press vise is used to hold small workpieces securely.

If you need to clamp a round workpiece but you don't have a drill press vise, construct a jig by bolting two round pieces of pipe or dowel together (Fig. 3-10). Clamp the jig to the table and then place the round workpiece in the curved opening created by the joined pipes or dowels.

Round or other irregular shaped workpieces can also be held between a tilting table and fence (Fig. 3-11) or you can buy V-blocks. Finally, a hold down guide (Fig. 3-12), available as an accessory for drill presses, combines both a fence and a clamp into one unit. The two-pronged clamp holds the workpiece on either side of the drill.

### *Drilling Speeds*

The proper rotation speed of a drill or other cutting tool is important

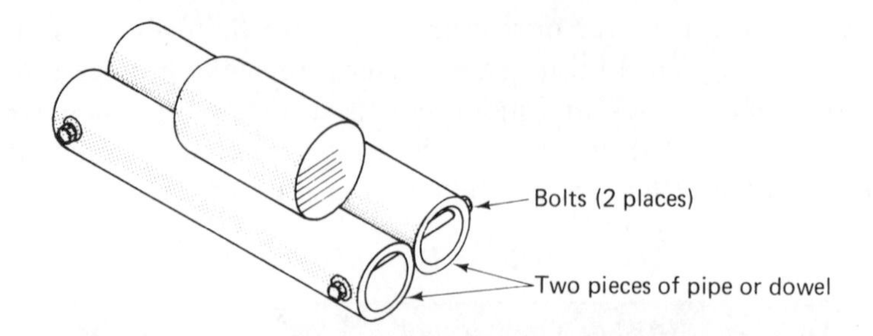


**FIGURE 3-10** / A jig for holding round workpieces can easily be made from two pieces of pipe or dowel.

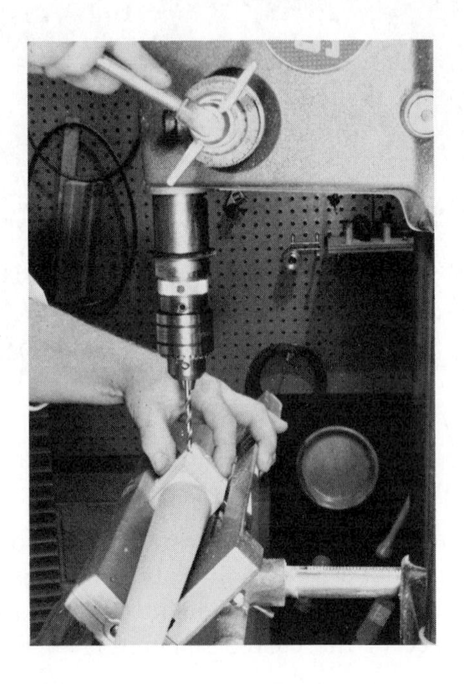

**FIGURE 3-11** / Round workpieces can also be held between a fence and tilting table.

for the extension of drill life. In general, low speeds are used when drilling hard materials and large holes (1/2-inch or larger). Small drills are run at high speed but with a light slow feed. If you notice that the workpiece is starting to smoke, reduce the drill speed immediately. Use table 3-1 as a guide to proper drill press speeds—use the speed of your drill press that is nearest to the speed indicated in the table. An asterisk in the speed column of the table indicates that the highest speed within the acceptable range is preferred; where only a range of speeds is given, use your closest speed to the center of the range. Any manufacturer's instructions on speed should be used, however, in preference to the table. (Speeds of your drill press for various pulley step sizes should be calculated and the results affixed to your drill press for easy access. Refer to Sec. 1-7 for calculations.)

**Table 3-1**
**DRILL PRESS SPEEDS**

| *Operation* | *Material* | *Speed in RPM* |
|---|---|---|
| Buffing (with a disk cloth wheel with a drum buffer) | | 2400<br>up to 4000 |
| Carving (with small router bits) | Wood | 5000 or higher |
| Countersinking/counterboring—see drilling, wood screw pilot bits | | |
| Dovetailing | | 5000 to 9000* |
| Dowel cutting (also see plug cutting) | Wood | 1300 |
| Drilling | | |
| Expansive bit | Wood | 700 or less |
| Fly cutter (circle cutter) | Wood<br>Metal | 500 or less<br>500 or less |
| Hole saw (circle cutter, saw blade cutter) | | 500 or less |
| Wood screw pilot bits | Wood | 600 to 1300 |

**Table 3-1 (continued)**
**DRILL PRESS SPEEDS**

| Operation | Material | Speed in RPM |
| --- | --- | --- |
| Twist drills | Aluminum—drills up to 1/4-in. | 5600 |
| | drills 1/4- to 1/2 in. | 1950 |
| | Brass, Bronze—drills up to 1/4-in. | 4500 |
| | drills up to 1/2-in. | 2200 |
| | Cast iron—drills up to 1/4-in. | 1200 |
| | drills 1/4- to 1/2 in. | 620 |
| | Glass—drill with a brass tube | 600 |
| | Plastics | 500 or less |
| | Steel, mild—drills up to 1/4-in. | 1200 |
| | drills 1/4- to 1/2 in. | 620 |
| | Steel, hard—drills up to 1/4-in. | 700 |
| | drills 1/4- to 1/2-in. | 350 |
| | Wood—drills up to 1/4-in. | 5600 |
| | drills 1/4- to 1/2-in. | 3500 |
| | drills 1/2- to 1 in. | 1950 |
| | drills over 1 in. | 700 |
| Wood boring bits | | 1000 to 1500 |
| Filing (cutter known as a rasp or rotary cutter) | Wood | 4000 |
| Grinding | | 2400 |
| Mortising | Wood—with 1/4-in. chisel | 3600 |
| | with 3/8-in. chisel | 2800 or less |

**Table 3-1 (continued)**
**DRILL PRESS SPEEDS**

| *Operation* | *Material* | *Speed in RPM* |
|---|---|---|
| | with 1/2-in. chisel | 2800 or less |
| Planing | Wood | 5000 to 9000* |
| Plug cutting | Wood | 2400 |
| Polishing | | 1500 to 2400 |
| Reaming | | 2/3 of drill speed |
| Routing | Wood | 4000 to 21,000* |
| Sanding (drums) | Wood | 1300 to 2400 |
| Shaping | Wood | 4000 to 10,000* |
| Wire brushing | Metal | 1300 to 2400 |
| | Wood | 2000 |

*The higher speeds are preferred where an asterisk is given. Where a range is given, select a mid-range.

*Feeding the Drill*

The feed of a drill press and cutting tool is the cutting rate and pressure required to bore the desired hole. The feed rate is determined by operator "feel" and experience which you must acquire. A few general guidelines will help you to initially gain the "feel":

*1* / The feed pressure and rate required in wood is determined by the type of wood and the grain structure. Don't force the drill, but let the drill do the cutting. Use a steady, moderate pressure and back the drill out occasionally to remove chips; this prevents binding, jamming, and the build up of excessive heat.

2 / Use a light feed pressure on thin drills to prevent them from bending and/or breaking.

3 / The feed pressure on metals and other materials depends on their hardness. Less pressure is used with harder materials; a very light feed pressure and rate is used with plastics.

4 / Feed carefully with light pressure when approaching the breakthrough point at the back of any material. This will prevent jagged cut edges and drill breakage.

5 / When using a fly cutter or an expansive bit, use a light feed pressure to prevent gouging of the workpiece and breaking of the tool.

### *Cutting Fluids*

Cutting fluids are used when drilling metals to aid in cooling, lubricating, and finishing the workpiece. As a coolant, the cutting fluid cools both the workpiece and the drill by carrying the heat away. The fluid lubricates the surface between the drill and the workpiece thus decreasing friction, heat, and tool wear. The lubricating effect also prevents chips from sticking. Finally, the cutting fluid acts as an agent to produce a desired finish on the machined surface of a workpiece. Table 3-2 lists recommended cutting fluids for various metals.

A soluble oil is an oil that is thinned with water prior to use. Mineral oils are obtained from the distillation of petroleum–paraffin, kerosene, and mineral seal oil. Sulphurated oils have excellent coolant and cutting qualities in hard metal applications. Lard oil is the best type of lubricating oil. Soda water is made by dissolving sal soda in water.

### *Boring into Wood*

To bore a hole into wood, first carefully measure and mark the center point of the hole to be drilled. Determine the size of the hole,

Table 3-2
CUTTING FLUIDS

| Workpiece material | Cutting fluid |
|---|---|
| Aluminum | Kerosene, turpentine |
| Bakelite | None |
| Brass | None |
| Bronze | Soluble oil, lard oil, dry |
| Copper | Soluble oil |
| Iron, cast | None |
| Iron, malleable | None |
| Iron, wrought | Soluble oil, soda water |
| Lucite | None |
| Magnesium | Low viscosity neutral oil |
| Monel metal | Lard oil, soluble oil |
| Plastic | None |
| Steel, manganese and soft | Soluble oil, sulphurized oil, mineral lard oil |
| Steel, stainless | Sulphurized mineral oil |
| Steel, tool | Soluble oil, mineral lard oil, sulphurized oil |
| Wood, hard | Light oil, wax, soap (refer to text) |

select your boring tool, and insert the tool into the drill press chuck. Use an awl to make a small prick point in the wood; the point should be of sufficient diameter and depth to accept the point of the boring tool. Place the workpiece on the table and raise the table until the workpiece is near the boring tool. Secure the table, making sure the table center hole is under the drill. Clamp the workpiece to the table or hold it in some manner so that it cannot rotate because of the torque of the boring tool. Turn the motor on and rotate the feed adjustment slowly to insert the tool point into the prick point made by the awl. Increase the feed slowly until the boring tool is through the *surface* of the wood. Increase the feed and continue boring. Reduce the feed pressure when you think the boring tool is nearly through the wood. When the boring tool point comes through the other side of the material, release the feed adjustment to remove the boring tool from the workpiece. Turn the workpiece to the opposite side of the wood where the point came through, and follow the above process gently on the back side until the hole is complete. This process will prevent the boring tool from splitting the wood when the tool comes through the workpiece.

Instead of turning the workpiece over to finish boring the hole, a simpler method is to place a piece of scrap wood under the workpiece. Bore completely through the workpiece—and into the scrap wood; the scrap will prevent the back of the workpiece from splintering.

If a hole is to be drilled deeper than the drill press quill can extend, drill to about three-fourths of the quill travel. Turn the drill press motor off and raise the table around the drill. Hold the workpiece firmly (clamp it!) and apply electrical power. Continue to drill to the required depth. An alternate to this approach is to drill from both sides of the workpiece and use stop blocks to align the workpiece.

When drilling hardwoods, pull the drill partially out occasionally to remove the dust. A light oil, wax, or soap can be used as a lubricant to aid in drilling. However, these lubricants may prevent you from using a desired wood finish (such as penetrating oil stain) later on, so use lubricants on wood with discretion.

It may be necessary to drill a hole at an angle within the workpiece. This is easily accomplshed if you have one of the following: a radial drill press with a rotating head, a tilting table, or a vise with a tilting base. If you have none of these, then you must make a wooden jig with some wedges to set the workpiece to the desired angle. Whichever of the four methods is used, however, the single most important procedure that must be performed to ensure an accurately drilled hole is to clamp the workpiece securely (Fig. 3-12). A clamped workpiece will prevent the workpiece from "creeping" as the pressure of the tip of the drill attempts to make the initial entry into the workpiece. An awl or centerpunch should also be used to make a small hole into which the drill tip is placed prior to power application to the drill motor. Figure 3-13 illustrates the use of a fence and tilting table to aid in angle drilling.

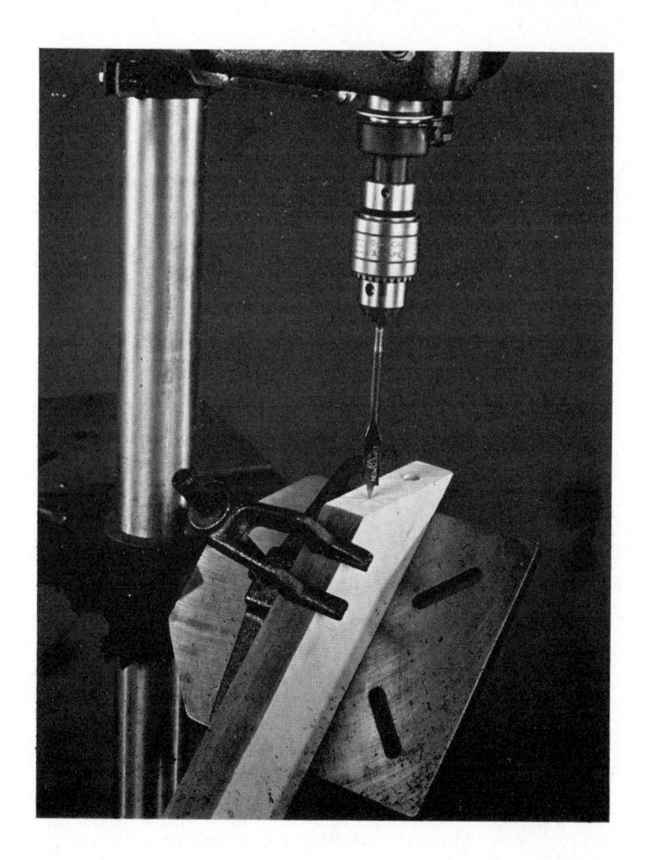

**FIGURE 3-12** / Workpieces should be firmly clamped for angle drilling.

To drill a clamped workpiece at an angle with the radial drill press, simply rotate and lock the head at the desired angle indicated on the tilt scale. In the case of the tilting table, loosen the locking device and tilt the table; lock the table in position. If no tilt angle scale is provided, measure the angle with a protractor or bevel. If you use a vise with a tilting base, set the vise to the angle indicated on the base scale. Be sure to clamp the vise to the drill table.

To use power wood boring bits, insert the shank into the chuck. Align the bit shank flats against the chuck flats and hand tighten the chuck. Check proper seating of the bit by trying to rotate it in the chuck as you continue to snug the chuck flats against the shank flats. When properly aligned, tighten the drill chuck with the chuck key. Clamp the workpiece with a backup scrap board to the table. With the drill at 1000 to 1500 rev/min, feed the bit slowly into the

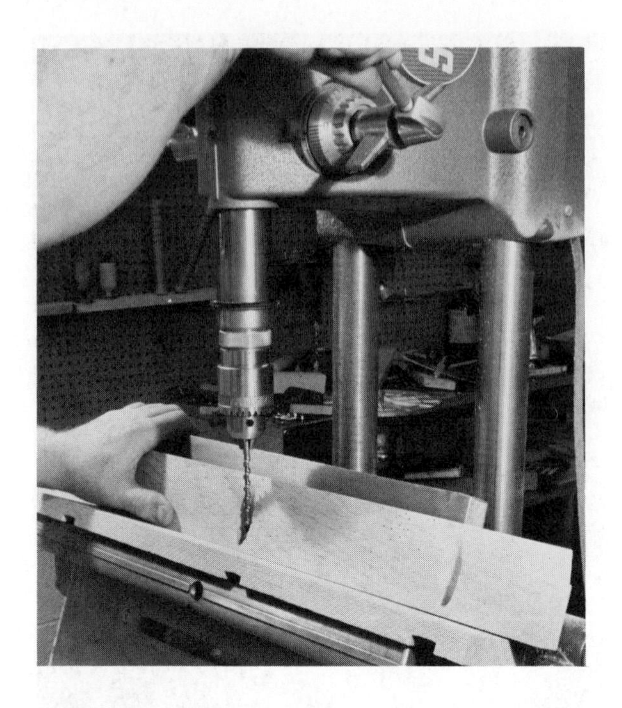

**FIGURE 3-13** / Another method of holding the workpiece for angle drilling is with the fence and a tilting table.

workpiece. After the flanges of the bit have cut through the wood surface, the feed rate can be somewhat increased. In deep holes over 3/4-inch, occasionally raise the bit slightly to remove dust and shavings and to cool the bit. Reduce feed pressure on the drill when the bit is nearly through the wood. Do not let the bit become excessively hot while drilling—excessive heat can damage the hardened edge.

When drilling with a bit that has a cutter on *one* side only—as an expansive bit or a fly cutter—be sure to clamp the workpiece securely and operate the drill press at a speed of 700 rev/min or less. Start the bit into the work very carefully and feed with a light pressure to prevent gouging the workpiece or breaking the bit. Hole saws (saw blade cutters) are run at speeds of less than 500 rev/min. The selected size blade is placed onto a mandrel. Clamp the workpiece to the table with a piece of scrap wood under it (Fig. 3-14).

To use a plug cutter, install the 1/2-inch cutter shank into the drill chuck. To cut a plug for capping a countersunk screw hole, cut

**FIGURE 3-14** / Cutting large holes—notice the backup scrap wood and the clamp on the workpiece.

with the grain running across the diameter of the plug at about 2400 rev/min as shown in A of Fig. 3-15. Dowels are cut running with the grain at about 1300 rev/min as shown in B of Fig. 3-15.

Countersinks are used in wood or soft metal when it is desired to place the head of a fastener such as a flathead screw or a bolt flush with the surface. The fastener hole is drilled first. The countersink tip is then placed into the fastener hole and is drilled. Periodically remove the countersink and hold the fastener head to the hole to gauge proper depth.

In using the wood screw pilot pit (countersink/counterbore), no predrilling of a pilot hole is required, but a pilot hole is recommended for accurate drilling in hardwoods. Use an awl to start a point for the countersink/counterbore. Run the drill at 600 to

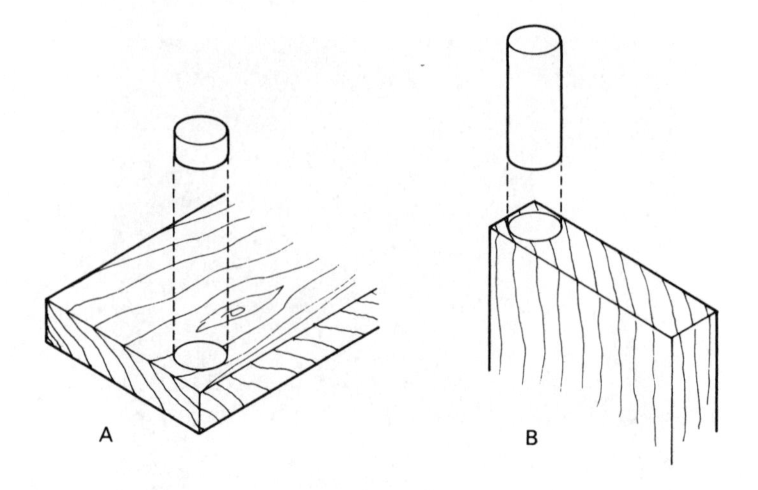


**FIGURE 3-15** / Screw caps are cut with the grain running across the diameter of the plug; dowels are cut running with the grain.

1300 rev/min and do not let the point become excessively hot during use.

*Boring into Metal*

Twist drills are used to bore holes into metal. After the proposed hole center point has been carefully located, use a center punch to make an indenture in the metal. Place the center punch point against the marked point—hold the punch perpendicular to the workpiece. Strike the anvil end of the punch with a hammer to make the indenture. The angle of the conical indenture made by the point matches the angle of the tip of a twist drill.

If a small diameter hole is to be drilled, place the tip of the twist drill into the indenture and begin drilling at a slow feed and pressure. The drill speed should also be slow. Increase pressure and feed as the drill enters the metal. For deep holes, lubricate the drill point. (Refer to Table 3-2.) Occasionally raise the drill point; this causes the metal chips (or ribbons) to break off. As the drill point is about to break through the metal, decrease the feed and pressure. This will help prevent burring of the metal. Don't let the drill get too hot. If a larger diameter hole is to be drilled in metal, first center punch the hole location and then drill a small pilot hole through the workpiece. Follow this by the larger drill.

Twist drills do not drill perfectly round holes. To correct this, machine shops use *reamers* to finish a slightly undersized diameter hole to a round hole of proper diameter; these reamers are normally not found in the home workshop because twist drills do drill holes to the desired accuracy for the home workshop. A reamer is slightly tapered on the end to fit the drilled undersized hole. After the undersized hole is drilled, the correct reamer is placed into the drill chuck, and the speed is set to about two-thirds the drilling speed. The quill is lowered and the hole is reamed to the proper size.

Sometimes the drill will slip from the starting hole and begin to drill a hole elsewhere. To correct this, first determine the cause—it is usually a dull drill or an inadequately clamped workpiece. Then use a cape chisel to cut some of the metal on the side where the drill should return. Enter the drill into the workpiece again, and the drill will move to the chiseled side of the hole.

### Boring into Other Materials

Two other materials which are frequently bored are masonry and plastics. Masonry (including brick, slate, concrete, etc.) is bored at a medium speed with a special carbide tipped drill that has a wide spiral fluted shank to provide fast, easy drilling and quick dust removal. Drill sizes range from 3/16- to 1-inch, with shank chuck sizes of 1/4-inch for the smaller drills and 1/2-inch for the larger drills.

Plastics made of acetate or acrylic are drilled best by a *scraping* action. You can use the same twist drills used for cutting wood and metal, but an old twist drill of proper diameter with a tip reground to 140° (Fig. 3-16) will drill easier and produce a better hole. Drill at

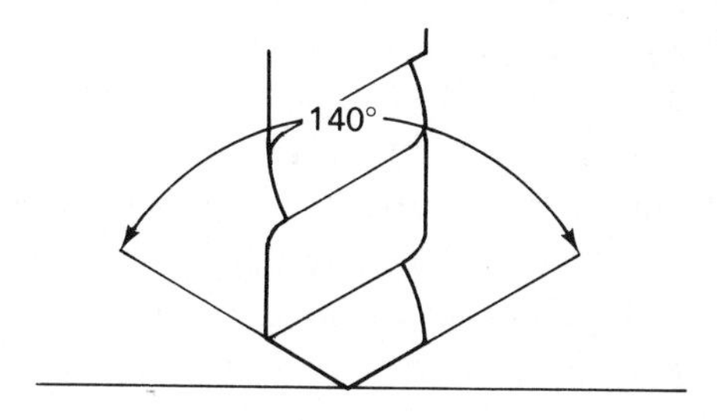


**FIGURE 3-16** / Twist drills are reground to 140° to drill acetate and acrylic plastics.

a very light feed and speed of about 500 rev/min. Lift the drill frequently to prevent burning and back the boring area with a piece of wood.

*Miscellaneous*

A number of holes can be drilled around a circle at a given radius on a circular workpiece by using the jig described in Sec. 4-5. Clamp the jig to the drill press work table so that the pivot pin is the given radius from the drill point. Rotate the workpiece on the pivot to position the workpiece for hole drilling.

Holes along a straight line of a workpiece are easily drilled if a fence or a scrap board is clamped to the drill press table as a guide. The workpiece is slid along the guide. Repetitive holes can be drilled at identical locations on a number of workpieces by using a clamped scrap board and workpiece stops (refer also to Sec. 1-12).

## 3-6 / SANDING, BUFFING, GRINDING, AND FILING PROCEDURES

Sanding, buffing, grinding, and filing operations are easily performed on the drill press with the addition of accessories. The various accessory wheels or drums are sometimes mounted by a shaft into the drill press chuck; others are mounted on collared and threaded spindles or other special adapters where the chuck is removed and the adapter is attached.

In using the sanding, buffing, grinding, and filing accessories, avoid long quill extensions. Instead, raise the table. Feed the workpieces into the direction of rotation of the accessory.

Sanding drums are used to sand irregular sizes and shapes. A piece of 3/4-inch plywood is clamped or bolted to the table as an auxiliary sanding table (Fig. 3-17). A hole 1/4-inch in diameter larger than the sanding drum is cut so that the sanding drum can be positioned below the surface in order to finish the entire edge of the workpiece. Place the drum in the hole of the secured auxiliary table and lock the quill. Operate the drill press at 1300-2400 rev/min. Drums are expandable for receiving and holding various grit sleeves.

Buffing and polishing wheels are used with polishing compounds to shine metal workpieces (Fig. 3-18). Fiber and steel wire brushes—in cup and disk shapes—are used to scrub, wax, remove

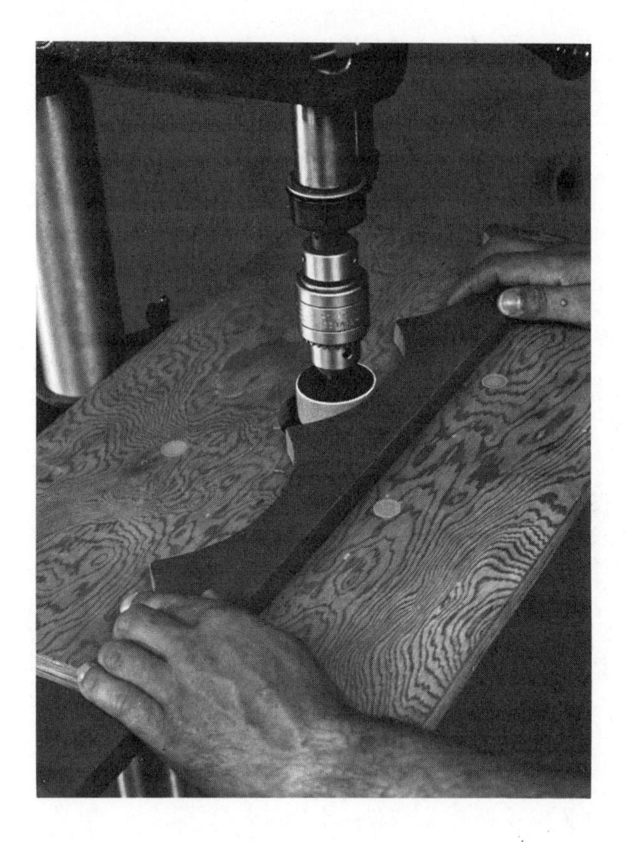

**FIGURE 3-17** / The sanding drum sands irregular sizes and shapes.

finishes, and polish metal to a dull surface finish. The wheels mount to the drill press chuck with either a shaft or a 1/2-inch arbor hole for mounting to an adapter. Disk type buffing wheels are run at about 2400 rev/min–drum types at speeds up to 4000 rev/min. Fiber and steel brushes are used on metal at speeds of 1300 to 2400 rev/min and on wood at 2000 rev/min. The appropriate buffing compound should be used with the metal being polished; refer to Sec. 9-10.

Surface grinding can be accomplished by using a 4 inch grinding cup or an abrasive wheel with a recessed mounting hole for a 1/2-inch spindle. Many grit sizes are available. To grind a workpiece, first ensure that the workpiece is secured in a vise. Lower the quill and lock it in position for grinding off a *very* small amount on each pass. Clamp a fence or a straight piece of scrap wood to the table to

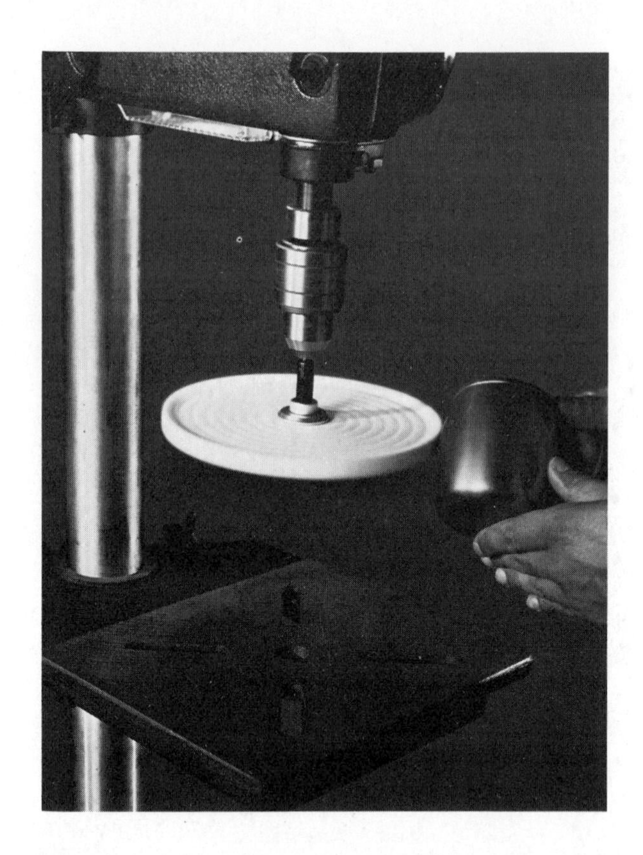

**FIGURE 3-18** / The drill press can accept many accessories. A buffing wheel is shown here.

act as a fence. Be sure to wear safety goggles or a face shield. Operate the drill press at about 2400 rev/min, and with the vise against the fence, pass the workpiece slowly and carefully under the wheel; grind the entire surface before changing the depth again. Another procedure for surface grinding is to place a column clamp under the table clamp. Loosen the table clamp; bolt the vise to the table. Rotate the table and workpiece slowly and carefully under the grinding wheel and make a complete pass before changing the depth.

Filing is accomplished by placing a cutter known as a *file, rasp,* or *rotary cutter* into the drill press chuck and then passing the workpiece by the cutter. Filing is for fast removal of material and is not intended for very smooth finishing. Insert the cutter into the chuck and use an auxiliary table with a hole in it as previously discussed for the sanding drum. Lower the quill and lock it to the desired position—or raise the table. Operate the drill press at about 4000 rev/min.

## 3-7 / ROUTING PROCEDURES

The router accessory for the drill press is used to produce intricate contours in wood, multicurved moldings and edges, relief panels, trim work, sign engraving, and delicate grooves for intricate inlays. Router bits can also make rabbet joints, dadoes, grooves, and bead moldings The drill press with a router attachment does not do the smooth precise work of the actual router tool itself, but it does do a sufficient job for most applications. The lack of smoothness is due to the lower speed of the drill press router—about 4000 to 5000 rev/min maximum, whereas a router turns at 18,000 to 22,000 rev/min. There is at least one exception to the low speed drill press, however. One manufacturer has a *drill-router;* the head has two spindles—one that rotates at a variable speed from 4000 to 21,000 rev/min for routing and shaping operations. Router bits with 1/4-inch shanks are placed into the spindle adapter.

To rout with the drill press, attach the desired router bit to the drill press in accordance with the manufacturer's instructions. In most cases, the drill chuck is removed and replaced with a collet chuck or adapter. Install the router bit. If necessary for a larger workpiece, install an auxiliary plywood table clamped or bolted to the drill press table. (You can use the same auxiliary table as for the sanding drum, Sec. 3-6.)

Set the drill press speed to the highest speed available (not less than 4000 rev/min for grooving or carving hardwoods, nor less than 5000 rev/min for soft woods). Lower the quill to the desired depth of cut and lock the quill in position; you should not cut more than 1/4-inch in hardwood nor more than 1/2-inch in soft wood per pass. Use a fence or a piece of scrap wood clamped to the table whenever possible to eliminate the tendency of the workpiece to rotate clockwise because of the rotating router bit. A fence or straight scrap piece is required for making accurate straight routing cuts. Hold the workpiece firmly with both hands and feed the workpiece slowly to prevent bending or burning the bit as you guide the workpiece along the guide or free hand along the pattern line (Fig. 3-19).

**FIGURE 3-19** / The router bit can be used freehand, but be sure to hold the workpiece firmly.

Router bits (Fig. 3-20) cut on the side of the bit, not on the tip as a drill cuts. Therefore, do not try to drill with the bits. To start a groove *inside* of a workpiece surface, drill a hole first. Then insert the router into the hole and start the router. Be careful–don't drill quite as deep as the bit will rout.

The rounding off–"edge carving"–of the top edge of a straight or curved workpiece is done with a router bit with a *pilot* on the bit. With the pilot, you don't need a guide; the pilot follows the sawed cut (edge) and also regulates the depth of cut. Feed the workpiece against the clockwise rotation of the cutter.

The carving of flutes and freehand designs with router bits is done without the use of pilots. Guides can be clamped to the table. Lock the quill to the desired location for fixed depths or raise and lower the quill for carving. Use a light feed pressure.

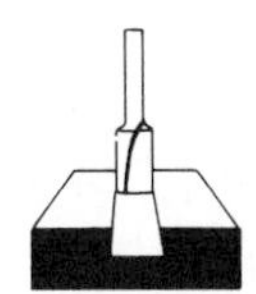

Straight—for general stock removal, slotting, grooving, rabbeting

Veining—for decorative free-hand routing such as carving, inlay work

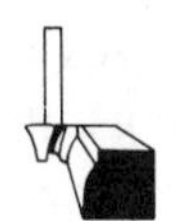

Sash bead—for beading inner side of window frames

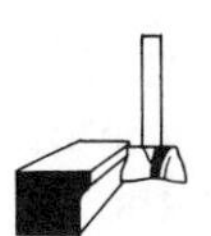

Sash cope—for coping window rails to match bead cut

Core box—for fluting and general ornamentation

Dovetail—for dovetailing joints. Use with dovetail templet

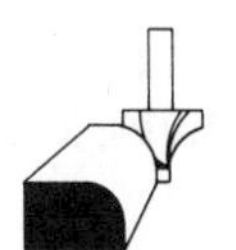

Corner round—for edge rounding

Bead—for decorative edging

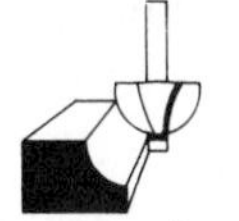

Cove—for cutting coves

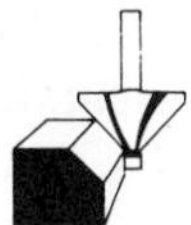

45° bevel chamfer—for bevel cutting

Mortise—for stock removal, dados, rabbets, hinge butt mortising

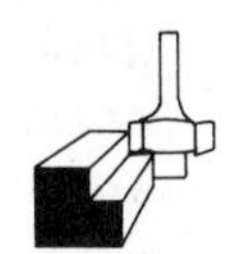

Rabbeting—for rabbeting or step-cutting edges

Roman ogee—for decorative edging

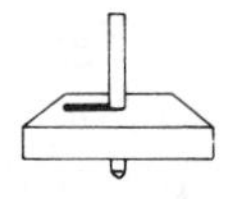

Panel pilot—for cutting openings and for through-cutting

Pilot spiral (down)—for operations where plunge cutting is required in conjunction with templet routing, using the pilot guide

Straight spiral (down)—for through cutting plastics and non-ferrous metals; also for deep slotting operations in wood

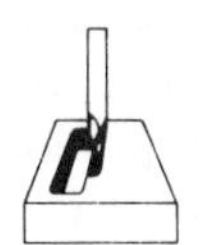

Straight spiral (up)—for slotting and mortising operations particularly in non-ferrous metals such as aluminum door jambs

V-groove—for simulating plank construction

Spiral—for outside and inside curve cutting

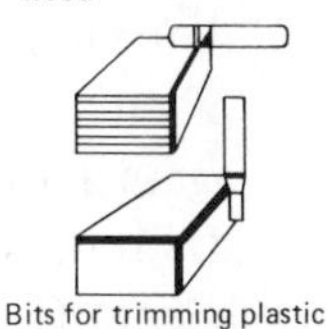

Bits for trimming plastic laminates. Solid carbide or carbide-tipped bits for flush and bevel trimming operations Solid carbide self-pivoting flush and bevel trimming bits

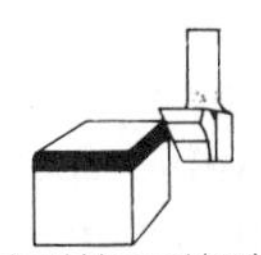

Solid-carbide combination flush/bevel trimming bit

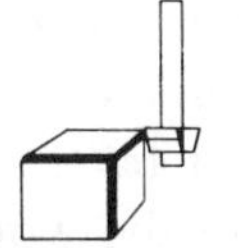

Carbide-tipped bevel trimmer bit

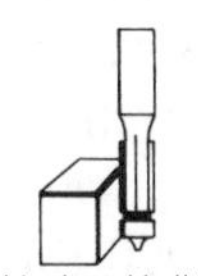

Carbide-tipped ball bearing flush trimming bit

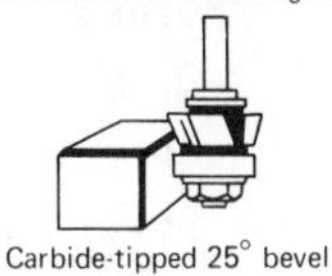

Carbide-tipped 25° bevel trimmer kits

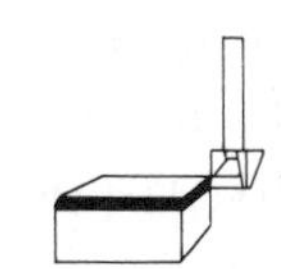

Carbide-tipped combination flush/bevel trimming bit

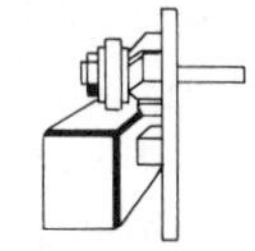

Carbide-tipped 15° backsplash trimmer—with $\frac{5}{16}$" diameter hole

**FIGURE 3-20** / Router bits.

Circular grooves can be cut in a workpiece at any radius from the center by using a jig with a center pin (refer to Fig. 4-11). Fasten the jig to the drill press table with clamps or a bolt.

## 3-8 / SHAPING PROCEDURES

Shaping attachments can be added to the drill press to convert it to a tool to cut moldings, tongue and groove joints, flutes, and beads on straight or irregular workpieces. Necessary accessories include cutters with 1/2-inch bores (these are the same cutters used on the bench model shaper—refer to Fig. 10-4), a shaper fence, and a larger auxiliary table that can be made from 3/4-inch plywood and bolted or clamped to the drill press table (this auxiliary table can be the same as used for the sanding drum, Sec. 3-6). The desired shaping cutter is mounted to the drill press spindle on a special adapter that replaces the drill press chuck. The shaper fence (Fig. 3-21) is attached to the auxiliary table. The fence has two sections with a gap between them to allow the rotation of the cutter. The right section (outfeed) of the fence moves in and out to provide support for the workpiece when the edge has been cut off by the shaper cutter; the movable section of the fence is comparable to the jointer tables turned 90°. The fence guides the workpiece by positioning it. The fence also helps determine the depth of cut. Spring steel hold down attachments often accompany the fence to hold the workpiece *down* and *in* against the cutter. The drill press head can be completely inverted, if desired, to position the shaper exactly the same as a separate bench shaper (Chap. 10).

Always try to position the workpiece to cut with the grain. If necessary to cut against the grain, feed the workpiece very slowly. If you are shaping a square workpiece, shape the across-the-grain edges first, followed by the with-the-grain edges; this will help prevent chipping. Set the drill press speed to the highest possible speed—never less than 4000 rev/min. Hold the workpiece firmly against the table and the infeed section of the fence and toward the direction of rotation of the cutter. Use the hold down attachments. Keep the quill extension short and locked tightly in position—raise the table, if necessary, to keep the extension short because there is a lot of side thrust otherwise on the quill.

With the fence and quill adjusted for a shallow cut, carefully feed the workpiece from the infeed table, through the cutter, to the

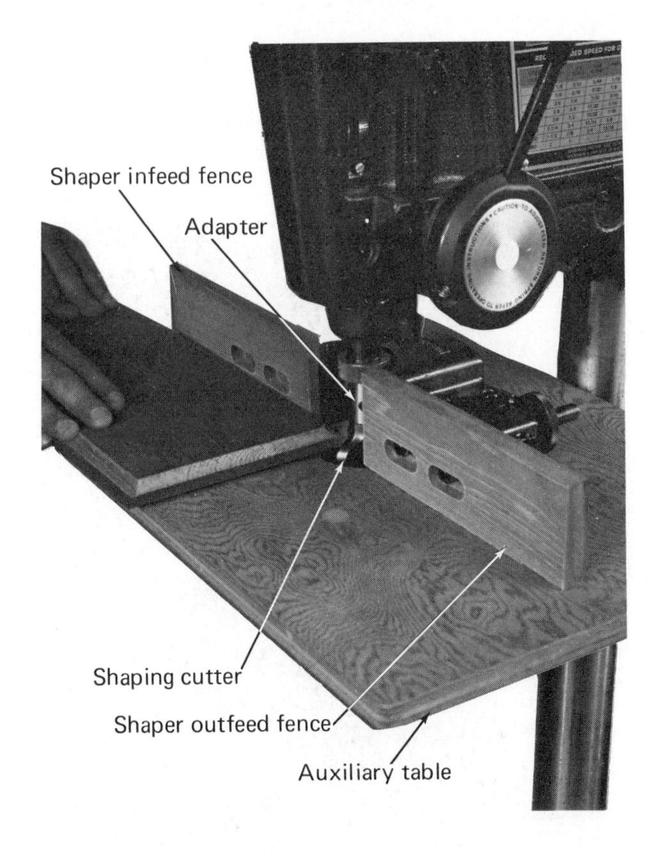


**FIGURE 3-21** / The drill press can be converted to a shaper.

outfeed table. With motor power off, adjust the outfeed fence to meet the cut edge of the workpiece. Thus, the fence is against the uncut portion of the workpiece as well as against the cut portion of the workpiece. Continue to make repeated passes, adjusting the quill and fence as required, until the workpiece is completed.

## 3-9 / DOVETAILING PROCEDURES

Dovetail joints are used to join drawer fronts to side pieces and to join bookcases. These strong joints are made accurately on the drill press (Fig. 3-22) by the use of dovetail attachments that include a 1/2-inch dovetail bit, end plates, a comb, stop, clamps, screw fittings, and wood parts. The attachments clamp the workpieces at right angles allowing both one side of the drawer front and a side piece to be cut simultaneously by the dovetail bit. The comb and stop act as a template to control the spacing and depth of cut. The other hardware ensures accurate alignment of the workpieces for accurate cuts.

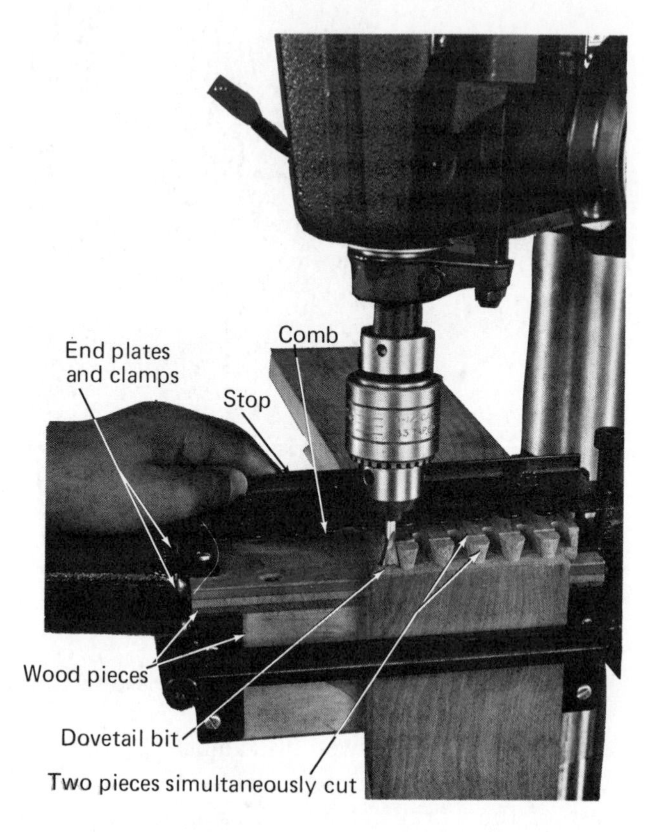


**FIGURE 3-22** / Dovetail joints are used to join drawer fronts together.

Although any manufacturer's dovetail cutting fixture can be used with any drill press, you should specifically follow the manufacturer's instructions in the use of the fixture you purchase. For reference, the essentials of cutting dovetails are included in the event you want to know what you're getting into beforehand, or if you've lost your instructions.

Two pieces of scrap wood (Fig. 3-22) are attached to the dovetail fixture end plates. The workpieces to be joined are cut to exact size and the ends are smoothed. The two workpieces are then butted together at the left side of the plates with the edges trued. The drawer front is horizontal with the outside face down on the table; the drawer side is vertical with the outside face turned in against the scrap wood. All clamp knobs are secured to firmly hold the workpieces.

The comb and stop are set in place next as follows. Measure from the edge of the *drawer front* (the horizontal workpiece) back the *thickness* of the *drawer side* (the vertical workpiece), subtract 1/8-inch, and mark this point on the drawer front. Draw a straight line through this point across the *width* of the drawer front. Place the comb on top of the drawer front, and line up the outer rounded edges of the comb teeth exactly flush with the edge of the drawer side. Look to see if the drawn line is visible through the comb; if it is, place the stop exactly parallel to the line and clamp it tight. If the line is not visible, slide the comb back until the line is just barely visible and clamp the comb; do not use the stop.

Lower the quill with the dovetail bit until the bit is set to cut exactly 3/8-inch below the surface of the drawer front. Lock the quill. Check that the horizontal workpiece is absolutely flat on the wood of the dovetail fixture and that the fixture is flat on the table; the vertical workpiece should be hanging over the side of the table. Set the drill press for a speed of 5000 to 9000 rev/min–the faster the better.

Apply power to the drill press motor and, starting at either side of the dovetail fixture, move the workpieces into the dovetail bit. Move the workpieces so that the bit runs into the comb as far as it can go, keeping the shank of the bit in constant contact with the comb. Continue to the other side of the comb. You may find that you'll need to rotate the table–if you do, place a *column clamp* (available as another accessory) under the table.

## 3-10 / MORTISING PROCEDURES

Mortises–rectangular holes–that mate with tenons–nearly rectangular projections–are used in combination to form sturdy joints for chairs, tables, cabinets, windows, screens, doors, etc. Mortises are made in workpieces on a drill press to which mortising attachments are added (Fig. 3-23). These attachments include a mortising chisel housing, fence and hold down assembly, hollow chisel, and a mortising bit. The mortising chisel housing mounts onto the quill and accepts the mortising chisel. The chisel is square and hollow and has four sharpened edges. The mortising bit (available in 1/4-, 3/8-, and 1/2-inch sizes) passes through the hollow chisel and is inserted into the drill press chuck. The fence and hold down assembly is bolted to the drill press table and is used to position and hold the workpiece during mortising operations.

The rectangular holes are made in the workpiece by the

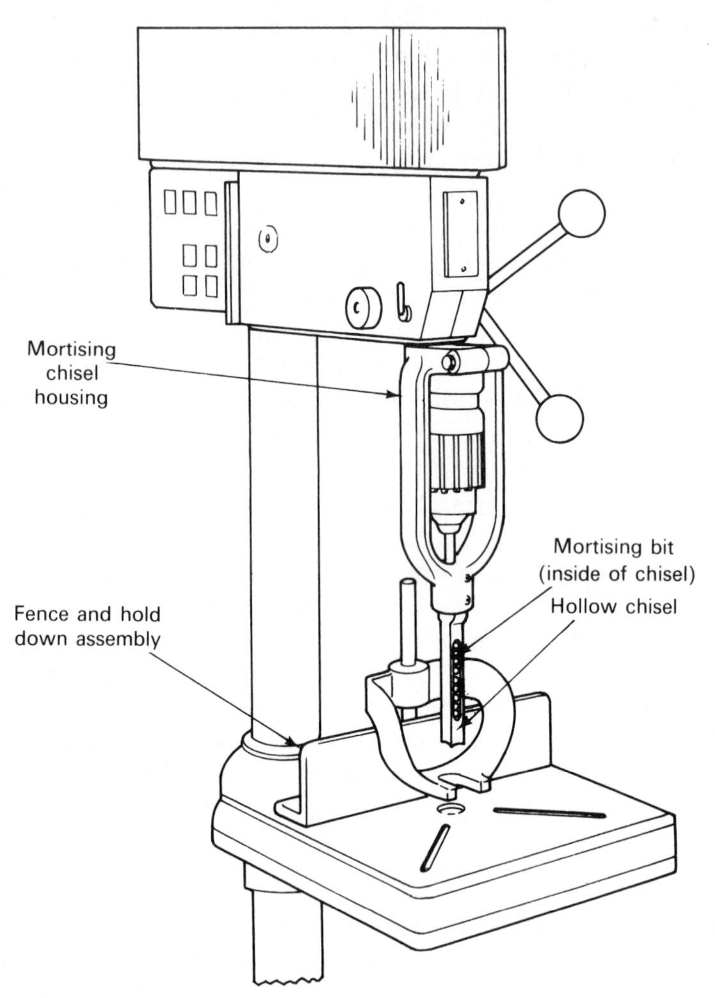


**FIGURE 3-23** / The mortising attachment is used to make square (rectangular) holes—mortises—for tenons.

combined action of the drill removing the majority of the wood and the four-sided hollow chisel that shaves and cuts the remaining wood around the circumference of the hole made by the mortising bit. The chisel and bit are purchased in sets for 1/4-, 3/8-, or 1/2-inch square holes. Longer and/or wider rectangular holes are made by taking additional cuts that overlap each other by one-third of the chisel width.

Mortises may also be made with a router bit. The procedures are described subsequently; also refer to Sec. 3-7.

As with other accessories, attach the mortising accessories in accordance with the manufacturer's directions. The mortising chisel housing is installed by removing the chuck (Sec. 3-12), sliding the housing onto the quill and tightening the bracket, and replacing the chuck. Select the desired mortise width (1/4-, 3/8-, or 1/2-inch) and install the hollow chisel. Install the corresponding mortising bit into the chuck so that there is a 1/64-inch clearance between the bit and the chisel bottom. Tighten the chuck and then rotate the chuck by hand to check bit/chisel clearance. Adjustment of the bit/chisel clearance is critical—follow the manufacturer's recommendations. Bolt the fence and hold down assembly in position to the drill press table. Place the workpiece against the fence and secure the workpiece with the hold down.

Operate the drill press at 3600 or less rev/min for the 1/4-chisel, and 2800 or less rev/min for the 3/8- and 1/2-inch chisels. Start at one end of the proposed mortise, rotate the feed adjustment using short successive cutting strokes. Raise the chisel slightly after each stroke to get rid of chips inside the hollow chisel. Move the workpiece along the fence and clamp it with the hold down prior to each new cut. Take additional cuts that overlap each other by one-third until the mortise is completed.

Mortises may also be made with a router bit or just a drill bit and a hand chisel (Sec. 3-13). Since a router bit cuts on the sides only, rather than on the tip, a hole must be drilled first. Then with the motor off, place the router bit in the hole. Clamp a pair of scrap boards to the drill press table. Let the workpiece slide between the two clamped boards. Put soap on the scrap boards to make the workpiece slide easier. Now apply power and slide the workpiece through the router bit as many passes as necessary to get the required depth and width.

## 3-11 / ACCESSORIES

The more elaborate accessories that convert the drill press for sanding, buffing, grinding, filing, routing, shaping, dovetailing and mortising have already been discussed. Other accessories are the rotary planer, tilting table column collar, hold down clamp, vise, universal compound vise, and a rotary indexing table.

The rotary planer converts the drill press to a 2-1/2-inch planer to true, remove paint and varnish, plane, rabbet, and finish wood surfaces. The high speed steel rotary cutter uses a special adapter in place of the drill press chuck. It is operated between 5000 and 9000 rev/min. Use an auxiliary wood table with a back to act as a fence for large pieces; for smaller workpieces, clamp a piece of straight scrap wood to the table to act as a fence. Make a number of shallow passes resetting and locking the quill for each pass. Feed the workpiece to the cutter from the left to the right.

A tilting table is a desirable accessory because it permits drilling holes easily at an angle (a tilting table is not required if you own a radial drill press). The table moves up and down, around, and tilts from horizontal to vertical. Index pins permit instant alignment at 45 and 90°. It's best to buy the tilting table from your drill press manufacturer to ensure that the drill press column clamp fits the drill press column.

Another valuable but inexpensive accessory is a *column collar.* The collar fits around the column and is secured below the drill press table. The table column clamp can then be loosened allowing it to rotate freely without sliding down the column.

Drill press manufacturers also sell hold down clamps as accessories. The clamp shown in Fig. 3-12 has two prongs that hold the workpiece on each side of the drill. The clamp also incorporates a fence and bolts to the slots in the table. Buy the clamp from your drill press manufacturer, or be sure that the bolt arrangement will properly fit the slots in your drill press table.

A drill press vise is necessary for holding small and irregularly shaped parts for drilling. These special vises are made by a number of manufacturers; any are suitable as long as they incorporate the features you want. The vise jaws open 3 inches and have two additional pieces to hold irregularly shaped workpieces. Some vises incorporate a tilting base that allows the vise to tilt from 0 to 90°. The vise is either hand held or is bolted through mounting lugs to the table. The vise is flat on its sides and bottom to permit placing the vise on any of these surfaces.

A universal compound vise bolts to the drill press table. One jaw swivels—the other has a movable face. The jaws open to 4-1/2-inches. This vise is used for precision drilling and is not usually found in the home workshop. It also adapts to lathes, milling machines, and grinders.

The rotary indexing table, likewise, is for precision operations including drilling, milling, routing, and shaping. Its dial is calibrated in 3 minute intervals with a 0.001 inch tolerance. The 8 inch table rotates 360°. It is a very expensive vise/table and is not often found in the home workshop.

## 3-12 / CALIBRATION AND MAINTENANCE

Calibration and maintenance of the drill press includes setting a tilting table perpendicular to the chuck, adjusting the quill return speed, oiling various parts, and cleaning the chuck jaws. Procedures for removing and replacing a drill press chuck and a spindle are also included.

A tilting drill press work table can be set perpendicular to the chuck as follows. Insert a pencil into a home-built wire jig that is placed in the chuck and holds a pencil at about a 3 inch radius from the chuck center. Place a piece of cardboard on the table and rotate the chuck so that the pencil draws a circle on the cardboard. Failure to draw a part of the circle at any point indicates that the table is not perpendicular to the chuck.

The speed (and force) of the quill return can be adjusted by relocating the *tail* of the return spring. Relocate the tail of the spring a half or full turn in one direction or the other to increase or decrease spring tension.

Oil the bearings in the drill press spindle by placing several drops of SAE 20 oil on the upper part of the spindle and allowing the oil to run down to the bearings.

*NOTE*

*Do not lower the quill too far (usually no more than 3 inches) in the following procedure or it will disengage from the pinion gear. Lowering the quill too far can be prevented by loosening the quill lock just enough to let the quill move.*

Also lightly oil the outer surface of the quill and the thrust ball bearings (sealed ball bearings do not require lubrication—refer to the manufacturer's recommendations). A light coat of grease should always be deposited on the quill gear teeth. Mechanical variable speed changers should have a drop of oil occasionally as recommended by the manufacturer.

Keep the chuck jaws clean at all times; caked dust is easily removed with a child's toothbrush that reaches easily inside the jaws. Whenever the chuck is removed, clean the Morse taper and apply a light coat of oil before reinstalling. Wax the table top, the column, and any other exposed iron or steel parts to prevent corrosion.

The drill press chuck is occasionally removed to permit attachment of an accessory adapter, to perform maintenance, or to attach a mortising chisel housing. Follow the manufacturer's specific instructions for removing the chuck. Be sure to have some method of catching the chuck when it drops from the spindle; this will prevent damage to the chuck. Chucks may be removed from tapered spindles by placing a rod (about 3/16-inch diameter) or a center punch into a hole provided in the spindle adapter retainer nut that is located immediately above the chuck and lightly tapping the nut to the left, forcing the chuck off the taper. As an alternate, wedges (specifically made for the purpose) can be placed between the nut and chuck and tapped lightly until the chuck drops off.

Some drill presses have replaceable spindles for use with attachments such as buffing wheels, etc. Replacement necessitates the removal of the quill and spindle assembly. Follow the manufacturer's instructions specifically. Basically, the instructions first call for the release of the quill return spring. While the chuck (and hence the quill and spindle) is held, the quill lock is loosened. The chuck and assembly is then pulled down.

To reassemble, push the spindle and quill assembly up in the bore until the quill engages with the pinion gear. Push the quill as far up as possible and hold it in place with the quill lock; it is necessary to "wiggle" the spindle and chuck to get it to set in the pinion gear and mating collar. Replace the spring and "load" the spring force.

Boring tools have cutting or screw lead points, cutting edges, and in some cases, cutting flutes. To prevent damage to these tools, store them so that they cannot bang into each other or into other tools. Use a soft wire brush to remove clogged wood, metal, or other particles from boring tool flutes after each use. Wipe them occasionally with a rag dampened with light oil; this will prevent rusting. Remove burrs from the shanks of drills with a metal file or a stone.

## *3-13* / HINTS AND KINKS

Because there are so many accessories for the drill press, there are likewise many hints and kinks that can be used to bypass using the additional accessories needed on the drill press. In many cases, the additional functions of the drill press beyond the basic function of drilling holes are duplicated on other tools: shaping on the shaper–planing on the jointer–mortising with a drill and a hand chisel–dovetailing with a router–to name a few. Several hints and kinks are included here, but there are many others and with your ingenuity, you can design numerous jigs and find many ways of accomplishing work on the drill press.

Several ways have already been mentioned to keep a workpiece from moving–mostly spinning–if a drill grabs into the workpiece. Another easy, cheap method is to simply place bolts through the drill press table at the desired location and tighten the bolts with a lockwasher and nut (located on top of the table). A more sophisticated method would be to bolt a scrap board to the table and use wing nuts on the bolts; this arrangement would allow limited use of the board as a fence.

If you have some countersinking or counterboring to perform, and you don't own a set of wood screw pilot bits (Sec. 3-2), proceed as follows. First, drill a hole slightly smaller in diameter than the threaded portion of the screw; drill through one workpiece and into the second workpiece, but to a depth slightly less than the screw length. (If you are also counterboring, the counterbore depth has to be added to the screw length.) Now drill a slightly larger hole the diameter of the screw shank for a distance equal to the length of the screw shank. Finally, using a drill equal to or slightly larger than the screwhead size, drill to the depth desired for the countersunk or counterbored head. Use the depth gauge and stop when a number of repetitive holes are to be drilled. The counterbored hole can be filled with a wood filler or a plug.

Bolt a large piece of 3/4-inch plywood to the base of a bench mounted drill press. The plywood serves as a table for large workpieces (the drill press table is rotated out of the way and the head is lowered on the column, as required) and as a surface for holding workpieces and tools when the drill press operations are being performed on the drill press table.

Mortise joints can be made with elaborate accessories (Sec. 3-10) if you have the money and a need to make a large number of mortise and tenon joints. If you only make an occasional mortise or two, make them inexpensively using a drill bit to remove the majority of the material and a sharp, hand wood chisel to clean out the additional material. Use a fence to guide the workpiece when drilling, and set the depth stop to the proper depth.

A hole drilled at an angle in a workpiece where the greatest accuracy is not required is easy to accomplish. Draw a straight line on the edge of the workpiece parallel to the center line of the proposed hole through the workpiece. Place an X at the point where the drill is to enter the workpiece. Use an awl or a center punch to make an indentation to guide the drill tip at the center of the X. Place the workpiece on the tilting table, or place a wedge under the workpiece until the drawn line on the edge of the workpiece is vertical and the drill tip is at the center of the X. Clamp the workpiece, wedges, vise, or other devices used.

## 3-14 / INSTALLATION

Mount and bolt a bench model drill press on the front of a workbench or in the center of a tool stand. Adjust the tool stand legs so that the drill press table is level and the chuck (with the head at the top of the column) is 46 to 48 inches from the floor. The tool stand or floor model drill press can be located with the back of the drill press near a wall. Leave room on either side of the table for long workpieces extending beyond the table.

The drill press motor is mounted on the rear of the drill press head on a motor mounting bracket (Fig. 3-2). First, mount the motor pulley to the motor shaft and fasten it securely; if a cone pulley is used, the position on the motor must be inverted from the position of the driven pulley at the spindle, i.e., the largest pulley of the cone on the motor will be opposite the smallest pulley of the cone on the spindle.

Second, mount the motor with the pulley on top onto the motor mounting bracket (Fig. 3-2) at the rear of the drill press head. The motor must rotate in a clockwise direction when looking down on the pulley. Mount the motor so that the driven and drive pulleys are opposite each other (one inverted).

Place the belt correctly around a set of steps of the cone pulleys. Loosen the two motor tension adjustment screws (one on each side of the head near the motor mounting bracket). Move the motor mounting bracket in or out until the pulley belt deflects about 3/4-inch when pressed in the center with a moderate force. Tighten the motor tension adjustment bolts. Perform the calibration and maintenance procedures of Sec. 3-12.

chapter four

# JIGSAW (SCROLL SAW)

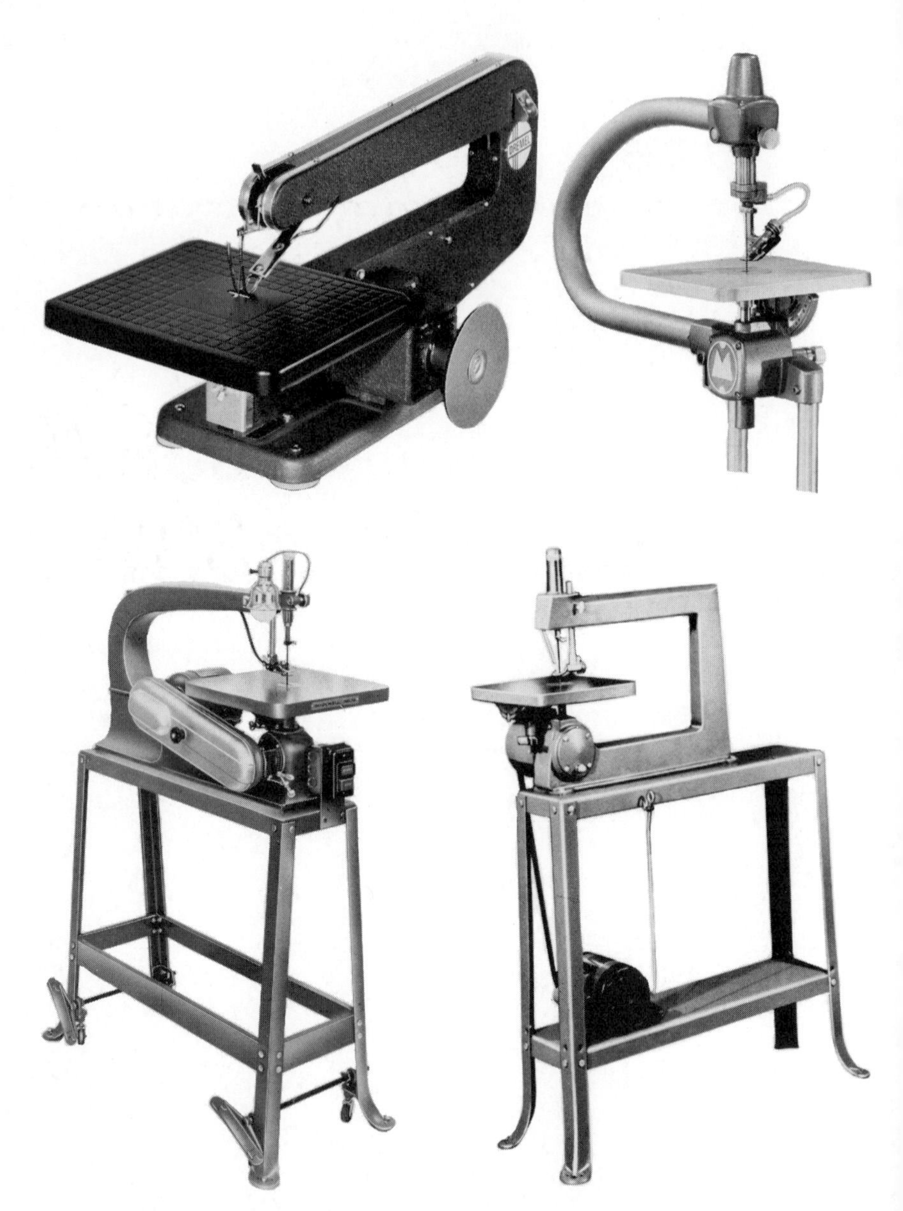


**FIGURE 4-1** / Jigsaws (scroll saws) are used to cut intricate designs in wood, plastic, thin and soft metals, paper, cloth, leather, and similar materials.

The jigsaw, also called a scroll saw, is known for its ability to cut curves and sharp corners of designs and patterns in model making, furniture, and toys, and to rough saw large pieces for carving. Used correctly, it is a precision tool for intricate work including fine frets, inlays, puzzles, marquetry work, and other ornamental objects of great variety. Although primarily a freehand saw, the jigsaw can be adapted with simple shop-built accessories for making straight line and circular cuts. The blade can be rotated 90° left or right on some models for ripping.

The jigsaw is the only bench power tool that can make cuts *inside* a workpiece without leaving a saw kerf. It cuts patterns in wood, plastic, thin and soft metals, and in paper, leather, and cloth when special methods are used (discussed later). The jigsaw is considered the simplest and safest of the bench power tools and is therefore ideally suited as the first power tool for youth (Fig. 4-2). The jigsaw is relatively low in cost and uses inexpensive replaceable blades.

## *4-1* / DESCRIPTION AND MAJOR PARTS

The major parts of the jigsaw (Fig. 4-3) are the cutting tool frame, tilting table, hold down assembly, lower and upper plunger assemblies, and the motor (although the motor is usually a separately priced item when purchased). The cutting tool can be a blade, file, or sanding attachment (Secs. 4-2, 4-6, and 4-7). Overall jigsaw dimensions (without tool stand) are from 27 to 31 inches deep, 12 to 13 inches wide, and 15 to 20 inches high.

The frame houses most of the parts of the jigsaw. The frame

**FIGURE 4-2** / The jigsaw is the simplest and safest of the bench power tools, making it ideal for use by all of the family.

size determines the maximum width or diameter of a circular workpiece that can be cut on the jigsaw. The maximum size is determined by the *throat* which is the distance from the back of the blade to the frame. Jigsaw sizes are specified in *throat* dimensions; thus, a jigsaw with a 16 inch throat can cut a workpiece of width or radius 16 inches (diameter 32 inches). Throat sizes range from about 10 to 20 inches. The frame is bolted to a power tool stand or workbench.

The tilting table supports the workpiece for cutting. The table surface is machined; it ranges from approximately 8 by 9 inches to 12 by 12 inches, and has a hole in the center that holds a *table insert* through which the cutting tool passes. The table can be tilted in its support trunnions to the left or right—usually 45° to the right and at least 15° or more (up to 45°) to the left depending upon the location of the drive pulley. The table insert is easily removed for easy access to the lower plunger assembly for the changing of cutting tools; it must be removed when files or sanding cutting tools are used.

Jigsaw blades cut on the down stroke. Therefore, a hold down assembly is needed to firmly hold the workpiece against the table during the blade up stroke; the hold down prevents workpiece vibration that can cause inaccurate cuts and blade breakage. The height of the hold down assembly is adjustable from the table to a maximum of about 2 inches. (The height is restricted by the

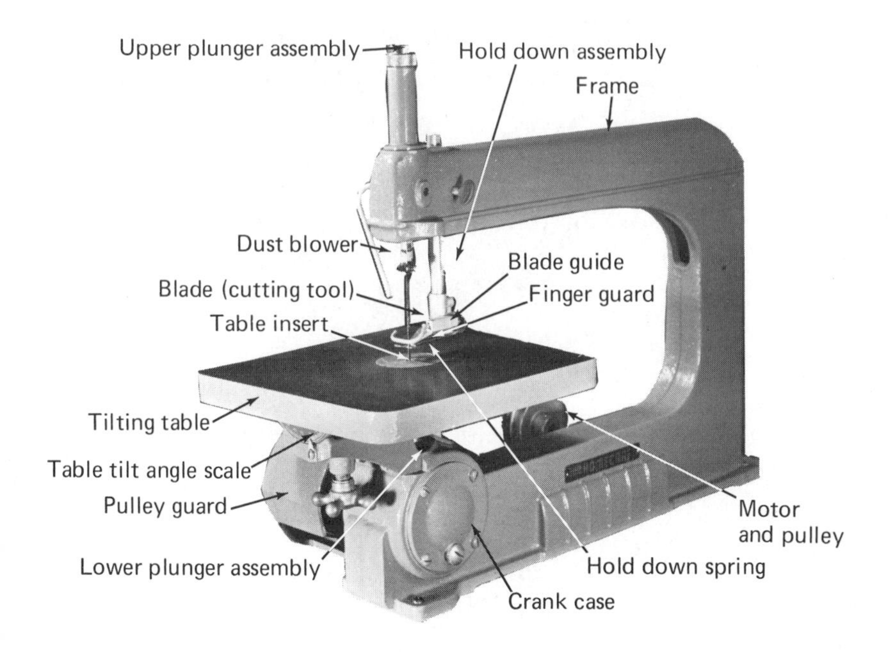


**FIGURE 4-3** / The jigsaw has only a few major parts and adjustments.

down stroke of the upper plunger assembly and blade chuck.) The hold down assembly usually consists of a steel hold down spring, blade guide, finger guard, and an adjustable column with a thumb locking screw. The steel hold down spring on some models can be rotated by loosening a cap screw so that the spring tightly clamps the workpiece when the table is tilted (Fig. 4-4); with other models, only one side of the hold down spring can be used when the table is tilted. The blade guide fits very close to the blade and aids in keeping the blade from twisting or bending when a workpiece is cut; the guard position is adjustable for different width blades. Some blade guards have notches on the left and right sides (in addition to the center notch) to guide the blade when it is turned 90° left or right. The finger guide aids in preventing the operator's fingers from coming into contact with the blade.

On some jigsaws, the rotary motion of a motor, drive belt, and pulley is changed by means of a crank shaft into an up and down motion that drives the lower plunger assembly. The crank shaft and part of the lower plunger assembly are housed in the base of the

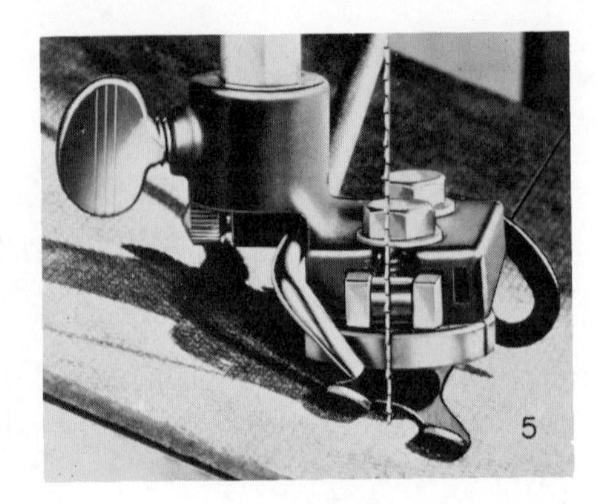


**FIGURE 4-4** / The hold down spring is adjusted to the angle of tilt of the table.

frame where an oil reservoir lubricates them by splashing. The crank shaft can be run in either direction, and, hence, it is possible to locate the motor on either side of the frame. The lower plunger assembly contains a universal chuck that accommodates standard jeweler's and saber saw blades or shafts of files or sanding attachments up to 1/4-inch in diameter in flat and V-groove jaws.

A magnetic jigsaw has no motor or drive system. The blade is driven at about 7200 cutting strokes per minute by means of a diaphragm. This type of jigsaw can cut moderately thick wood and soft metals such as copper, aluminum, and brass.

The jigsaw (excluding the magnetic type) upper plunger mechanism has a spring assembly that keeps the blade tension constant. The upper plunger tube operates as an air pump that blows air through a tube to remove sawdust and chips from the workpiece cutting line. The upper plunger mechanism also houses the upper blade chuck. Both the upper and lower blade chucks can be rotated 90° in some models for use of the jigsaw in ripping unlimited length workpieces from the left or right (the width of the workpiece is limited by the throat dimension).

The drive mechanism causes the lower plunger mechanism and cutting tool to move in an up and down stroking motion of about 1 inch. The upper plunger assembly moves with the lower plunger assembly because of the direct mechanical drive of the lower plunger through the blade to the upper plunger.

Heavier duty jigsaws are usually powered by 1/4-hp motors at

1725 rev/min, but 1/3-hp may also be used. The jigsaws should be operated at about 1275 strokes per minute (check your owner's manual) which means that the motor speed should be reduced at the jigsaw by the use of the proper selection of pulley sizes. With a 4 inch jigsaw drive pulley, a 3 inch motor pulley on a 1725 rev/min motor is about correct (refer to Sec. 1-7).

In selecting your jigsaw, select a vibrationless model that can cut the capacity of the workpiece you require—up to 2 inches in thickness and up to a maximum center cut of a 40 inch circle (20 inch throat). A jigsaw with the greatest workpiece capacities and jigsaw features is needed by the most demanding shop.

## 4-2 / BLADES

There are two main types of blades for the jigsaw: the *jeweler's* blade which is held between the upper and lower blade chucks and is thin for making fine cuts; and the *saber* blade which is heavier and wider than the jeweler's blade and is held only in the lower blade chuck. The saber blade is used for the majority of the heavier sawing operations, for cutting straight lines with no intricate turns, and for making cutouts in odd shaped workpieces where shifting from one opening to another is required.

The jeweler's blades are 5 inches or longer and from 0.035 to 0.250 inch wide; they are used for intricate scroll work. Some jigsaws accommodate blades longer than 5 inches, but if they don't, simply snip the end of the blade off. If the blades have pins, drive the pins out.

Saber blade lengths are from 3 to 4-1/4-inches long. The longer blade lengths are usually for cutting wood. Two forms of blade teeth are available for most general work—the stagger tooth blade and the wavy tooth blade. The stagger tooth blade has teeth that are set in an alternating pattern of right, left, right, left, etc. This blade is most often used on soft materials such as wood, plastics, and aluminum. The wavy tooth blade is used for cutting ferrous metals up to 1/4-inch thick and nonferrous metals up to 1/8-inch thick. Blades vary in number of teeth from 3 teeth per inch used in cutting soft materials to 32 teeth per inch used in ferrous metal cuttings.

With either the jeweler's or the saber blades, always use the widest blade possible, a sharp blade, and the correct blade (number of teeth) for the cuts to be made. Remember, the wider the blade, the smaller the turning radius in the workpiece. Wider blades make straight cuts more easily and the blade is not as likely to break. Narrower blades are used for intricate cuts and sharp curves of small radii. Dull blades should not be used because they do not cut freely; they require excessive pressure for cutting causing drag on the mechanisms and motor which eventually results in excessive wear. Discard worn blades.

Coarse blades with large cutting teeth are used for relatively thick pieces of wood and soft materials. Closely spaced fine tooth blades are used for cutting thin metal sheets or tubes. If the correct blade with the proper number of teeth has been chosen, at least two teeth will rest simultaneously on the workpiece (and the wall of a tube). Figures 4-5 and 4-6 are included as aids for selecting the correct blade for the material to be cut.

| Material Cut | Width In. | Teeth Per In. | Blade Full Size |
|---|---|---|---|
| Steel, Iron, Lead, Copper, Aluminum, Pewter | .070 | 32 | |
| Asbestos, Paper, Felt | .070 | 20 | |
| Steel, Iron, Lead, Copper, Brass | .070 | 15 | |
| Aluminum, Pewter | .085 | 15 | |
| Asbestos, Wood | .110 | 20 | |
| Asbestos, Brake Lining, Mica, Steel, Iron, Lead, Copper, Brass, Aluminum, Pewter | .250 | 20 | |
| Wood Veneer, Plastics, Celluloid, Hard Rubber, Bakelite, Ivory, Extremely Thin Materials | .035 | 20 | |
| Plastics, Celluloid | .050 | 15 | |
| Hard Rubber, Bakelite | .070 | 7 | |
| Ivory, Wood | .110 | 7 | |
| Wall Board, Pressed Wood, Wood, Lead, Bone, Felt, Paper, Copper, Ivory, Aluminum | .110 | 15 | |
| Hard and Soft Wood | .110 | 10 | |
| | .187 | 10 | |
| | .250 | 7 | |
| Pearl, Pewter, Mica | .054 | 30 | |
| Pressed Woods, Sea Shells | .054 | 20 | |
| Jewelry, Metals, Hard Leather | .085 | 12 | |
| Saber Blades for Hard and Soft Wood | .187 | 9 | |
| | .250 | 7 | |

FIGURE 4-5 / It is important to use the proper jeweler's blade for the intricate cuts to be made.

| | Blade type | Description of blade and use | Type of cut | Speed of cut | Blade length | Teeth per inch |
|---|---|---|---|---|---|---|
| | Flush cutting | Hard or soft wood over $\frac{1}{4}''$ thick. | Rough | Fast | 3'' | 7 |
| | Plaster cutting | Special V-tooth design provides constant abrading action which is most effective in cutting plaster, masonry and high density plastics. | Rough | Fast | $3\frac{5}{8}''$ | 9 |
| | Double cutting | Most wood and fiber materials. Tooth design allows for cutting in both directions with equal speed. | Rough | Fast | 3'' | 7 |
| | Double cutting | Cuts most wood and fiber materials. Tooth design allows for cutting in both directions with equal speed and quality of cut. | Medium | Medium | 3'' | 10 |
| | Skip tooth | Cuts most plastics and plywood. Special tooth design with extra large gullets provide extra chip clearance necessary for cutting plywood and plastic. | Rough | Fast | 3'' | 5 |
| | Wood cutting coarse | Cuts soft woods $\frac{3}{4}''$ and thicker. Canted shank provides built-in blade relief, thus helping to clear the saw dust and cool the blade. | Rough | Fastest | 3'' | 7 |
| | Wood cutting fine | Cuts soft woods under $\frac{3}{4}''$ thick. Canted shank provides built-in blade relief, thus helping to clear the saw dust and cool blade. More teeth per inch allows for finer quality of cut. | Medium | Medium | 3'' | 10 |
| | Wood cutting hollow ground | Hard woods under $\frac{3}{4}''$ thick. Hollow grinding provides no tooth projection beyond body of blade, thus imparting an absolutely smooth finish. Canted shank for blade clearance. | Smooth | Medium | 3'' | 7 |
| | Metal cutting | For cutting ferrous (iron) metals $\frac{1}{16}''$ to $\frac{3}{8}''$ thick and nonferrous (aluminum, copper, etc.) $\frac{1}{8}''$ to $\frac{1}{4}''$ thick. | Medium | Medium | 3'' | 14 to 32 |
| | Hollow ground | For cutting plywood and finish materials $\frac{1}{2}''$ and thicker where fine finish is desirable. Hollow ground for very smooth finish on all wood products. Provides the longest life woodcutting blade possible. | Fine to medium | Medium | $4\frac{1}{4}''$ | 6 to 10 |
| | Knife blade | For cutting leather, rubber, composition tile, cardboard, etc. | Smooth | Fast | 3'' | Knife edge |
| | Fleam ground | For cutting green or wet woods $\frac{1}{4}''$ to $1\frac{1}{2}''$ thick. Fleam ground provides shredding type cutting action which is most effective in sawing hard, green or wet materials. Provides longest cutting life possible. | Smooth to coarse | Medium | 4'' | 10 |
| | Scroll cut | For cutting wood, plastic and plywood $\frac{1}{4}''$ to 1'' thick. Set teeth and thin construction allows this blade to make intricate cuts and circles with radii as small as $\frac{1}{8}''$. | Smooth | Medium | $2\frac{1}{2}''$ | 10 |
| | Wood cutting coarse | Cuts most plastics and wood up to 4'' thick. Special tooth design with extra large gullets provide extra chip clearance for fast cutting in thicker materials. | Rough | Fast | 6'' | 3 |

**FIGURE 4-6** / It is important to select the proper saber blade for making heavier straight line cuts and for making cutouts in workpieces where shifting from one opening to another is required.

## 4-3 / OPERATING CONTROLS AND ADJUSTMENTS

Proper use of controls and the making of proper adjustments take only a few minutes and will compensate you with successful operation. The controls and adjustments found on most jigsaws include (Fig. 4-7): table tilt, workpiece hold down spring, hold down spring angle, blade guide, finger guard, dust blower, and lamp.

1 / *table tilt*—Loosen the table tilt adjustment (usually a star wheel or wrench type handle). Rotate the table in the trunnion to the angle of cut desired as indicated on the table tilt angle scale. Tighten the table tilt adjustment. The table tilt angle is limited on one side of the jigsaw by the pulley/belt guard. Remove the guard temporarily if necessary to increase the angle of tilt slightly; you can also turn the workpiece over and cut with the table tilted to the opposite direction—but compensate in your marking because of the angle.

2 / *workpiece hold down spring*—Loosen the hold down adjustment thumb screw and raise the assembly. Place the workpiece against the side of the blade under the spring. Lower the assembly to the workpiece and tighten the thumb adjustment screw. Some jigsaw models use a T-shaped spring (Fig. 4-8) rather than an assembly. In this case, lift the spring, slide the workpiece under it and release the spring.

3 / *hold down spring angle* (not available on all models)—After the table tilt angle has been set and the workpiece hold down assembly has been raised, loosen the hold down spring angular adjustment screw. Place the workpiece against the blade, lower the hold down assembly, and place the hold down spring flat against the workpiece. Tighten the hold down spring angular adjustment and the hold down adjustment. Figure 4-4 illustrates the correct position.

4 / *blade guide*—Loosen the blade guide adjustment screw. Move the blade guide forward until it barely touches the blade. When the blade is running free with no workpiece,

the blade should not touch the guide. Tighten the blade guide adjustment screw. When cutting from the left or right side of the saw, loosen the blade guide adjustment screw and adjust the applicable side slot for the blade (that has been rotated 90°). Retighten the blade guide adjustment screw.

5 / *finger guard*—This may be a spring clip that can be pulled out of the assembly when changing blades. Pull out; push back into the force-fit slot. Some models use the hold down spring as a finger guard.

6 / *dust blower*—Swing the nozzle into the best position for cleaning dust and chips from the workpiece guideline.

7 / *rotation of blade*—To rotate a blade 90°, first remove the blade (Sec. 4-9). Loosen the setscrew in the upper plunger assembly and rotate the casing; retighten the setscrew. Perform the same procedure in the lower plunger assembly.

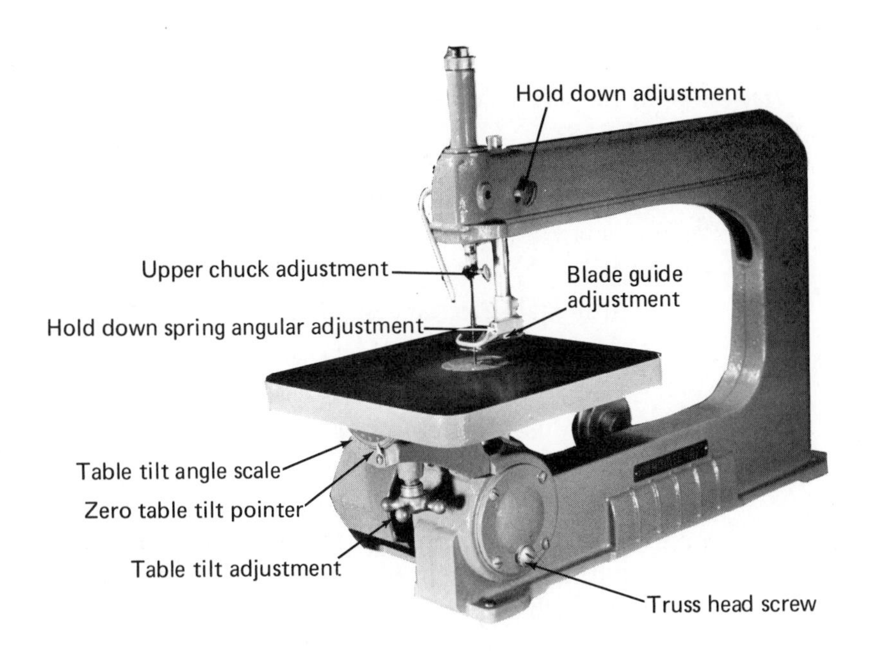


**FIGURE 4-7** / Proper adjustments take only a few moments and reward you with successful operation.

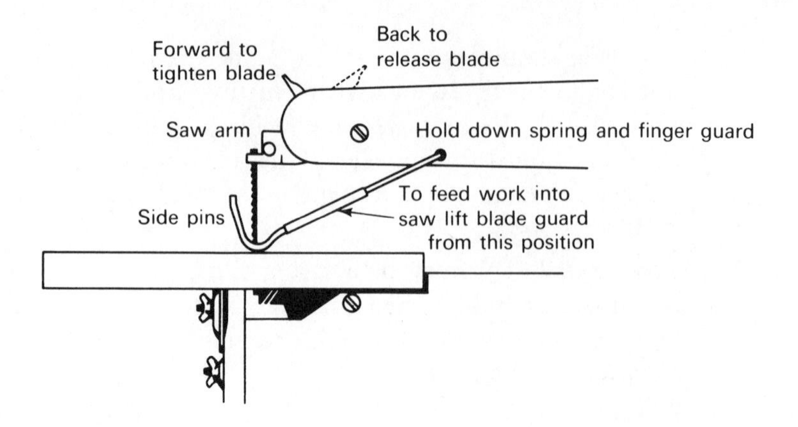


**FIGURE 4-8** / Small jigsaws have a spring loaded hold down spring that also acts as a finger guard.

## 4-4 / OPERATION

Perform the following procedures to operate the jigsaw:

### *CAUTION*

***Review all of the safety precautions in Sec. 1-16.***

*1* / Insert the correct cutting tool (blades, Sec. 4-2; files, Sec. 4-6; or sanding attachment, Sec. 4-7).

*2* / Set the jigsaw for the proper cutting speed (Secs. 4-5, 4-6, 4-7 and 1-7).

*3* / Set the tilting table to the desired angle.

*4* / Set the workpiece hold down spring and hold down assembly.

*5* / Adjust the dust blower toward the cutting line at the blade.

*6* / Grasp the drive belt and move the cutting tool through one complete stroke to ensure that all parts have clearance before the motor is started. This procedure can save you from breaking blades.

*7* / Apply electrical power to the motor and perform the sawing, filing, or sanding procedures (Secs. 4-5, 4-6, and 4-7, respectively).

## 4-5 / SAWING PROCEDURES

Guide and feed the workpiece (Fig. 4-9) into the blade lightly and steadily, and also maintain a slight downward pressure on the workpiece to the table. Don't push the work too fast; let the blade do the work at its own rate. When possible, cut just to the outside of your pattern; for internal cuts such as in a puzzle, follow the line directly.

The minimum radius of a curve that can be cut depends on the amount of tooth set in relation to the thickness and width of the blade. The back of the blade must run to one side of the saw kerf. Don't force the blade around a curve that is sharper than the blade is intended to cut. Instead, cut a series of short arcs or segments. You can finish the cuts smoothly by sanding or filing.

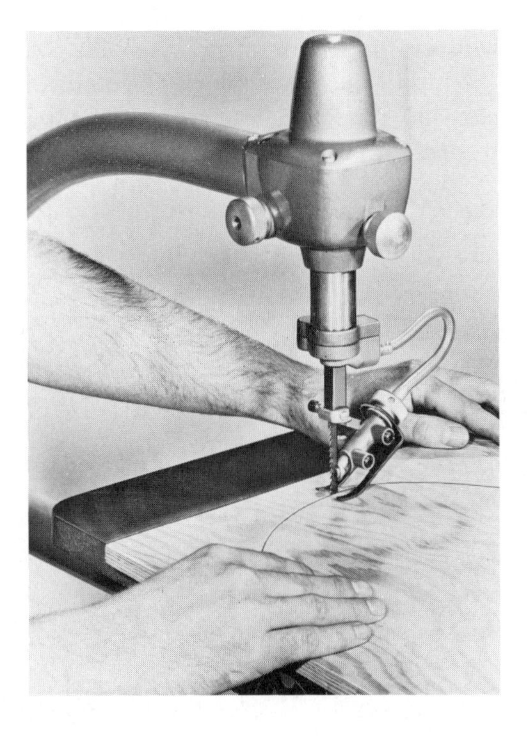

**FIGURE 4-9** / Guide the workpiece into the blade lightly and steadily and also maintain downward pressure. Where possible, cut just to the outside of the pattern in the scrap wood.

In cutting very thin materials, use a saw blade with many teeth—at least two teeth should be in the workpiece at a time. When only one tooth is cutting, it causes the workpiece to chatter and there is frequent blade breakage. Also feed the workpiece slowly and carefully. It is recommended that a thin workpiece be sandwiched between two pieces of thicker waste material such as 1/8- or 1/4-inch wood; the pattern must be on the top piece of scrap, and the materials should be tacked together—in the scrap area, if possible. This will result in a smoother cut of the workpiece with less burrs; the blade will also last longer.

Although the jigsaw is primarily a freehand saw, it can be used for straight line rip and crosscutting operations. Refer to Sec. 1-7.

One of the major advantages of the jigsaw compared to other bench saws is its ability to make internal cuts in workpieces (Fig. 4-10). To make an internal cut, bore a hole with a diameter larger than the blade width through the workpiece. With your hand, rotate the jigsaw drive belt until the lower plunger assembly is at the lowest point of its stroke and raise the hold down assembly. Release the jeweler's blade from the upper chuck; this, of course, is not required for saber blades. Place the blade through the hole (and reinstall the jeweler's blade into the upper chuck). Lower and tighten the hold down assembly and you're ready to make internal cuts.

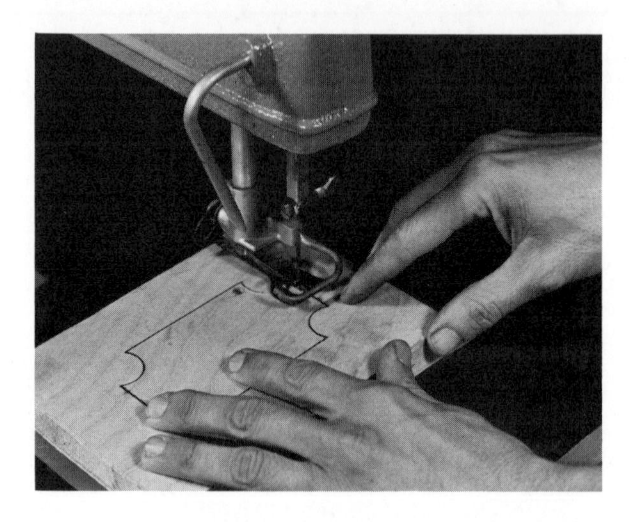

**FIGURE 4-10** / Intricate internal cuts can easily be made on the jigsaw.

Circles can be cut on the jigsaw fairly easily with the use of a jig. Cut a piece of 1/2- to 1 inch thick scrap plywood the size of the jigsaw table. Cut a hole through the center of the scrap wood for the blade to pass through. Clamp the scrap wood to the jigsaw table. Locate a pin (such as a piece of 1/8-inch dowel or rod) at a point equal to the distance of the radius of the circle to be cut directly opposite (at a right angle to) the teeth at the flat side of the blade (Fig. 4-11). Cut a hole the size of the dowel through the center of the workpiece, and rough cut the workpiece about 1/4-inch outside the proposed circle. At one point on the proposed circle, make a cut all the way to the circle line and out again leaving a 1/4-inch cut for the blade. With the power off, place the workpiece on the dowel with the blade at the 1/4-inch cut. Turn the power on and rotate the workpiece slowly as it is cut (Fig. 4-11).

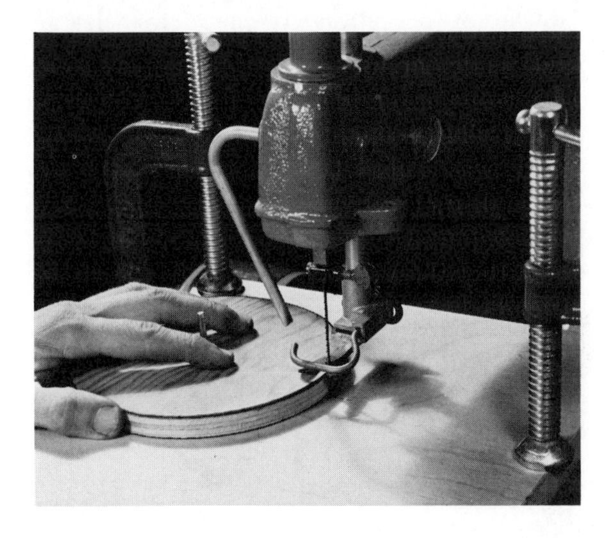

**FIGURE 4-11** / This jig is used to cut circular workpieces.

Wood, plastic, and similar materials are cut at a maximum speed of about 1275 strokes per minute (SPM). Metals are cut at about 800 SPM. An occasional drop of light oil will aid metal cutting. Jigsaw cutting speeds are considered as: slow, 650-900 SPM; medium, 900-1300 SPM; and fast, 1300-1750 SPM. (With the jigsaw, 1 rev/min at the jigsaw pulley—the driven pulley—equals 1 SPM).

## 4-6 / FILING

The jigsaw is capable of performing filing operations (Fig. 4-12) when a file (about 3-1/4-inches, Fig. 4-13) with a 1/8- or 1/4-inch round shank is placed into the V-groove of the lower chuck and the speed is reduced to about 800 strokes per minute (Sec. 1-7). Except for very thin files, the standard table insert must be removed; if the workpiece is thin and needs support under it, a special table insert with a 1/2-inch diameter hole can be made from aluminum or plastic using the standard insert as a pattern, or a piece of plywood with a 1/2-inch center hole can be clamped to the table instead of the special insert. The hold down accessory must be raised out of the way. If the machine file is not perfectly straight, rotate it in the chuck or work from the side of the table and tilt the table. Check straightness with a square block. Use your hand to rotate the jigsaw through one cycle of operation to check for clearances before applying electrical power to the motor.

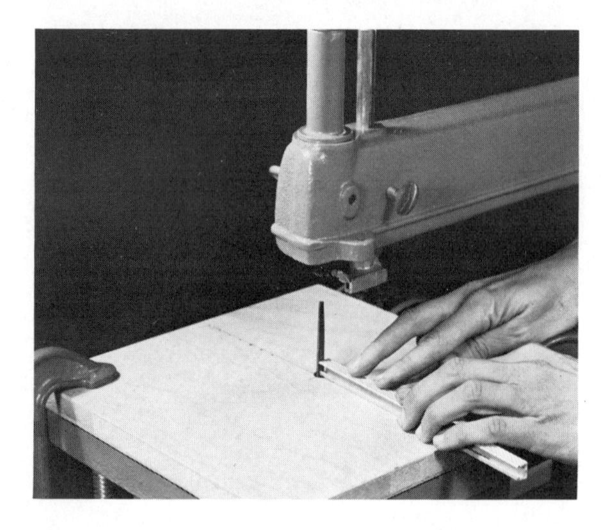

**FIGURE 4-12** / Run the jigsaw at about 800 strokes per minute for filing. You can make a special table insert or use a piece of plywood as shown here to support the workpiece.

Chalk may be rubbed into the rows of teeth of the file to help prevent particles of metal from clogging the teeth. When the teeth become clogged, the file slips, scratches, and is inefficient. Clean the file as required with a file card or brush by drawing it in a direction

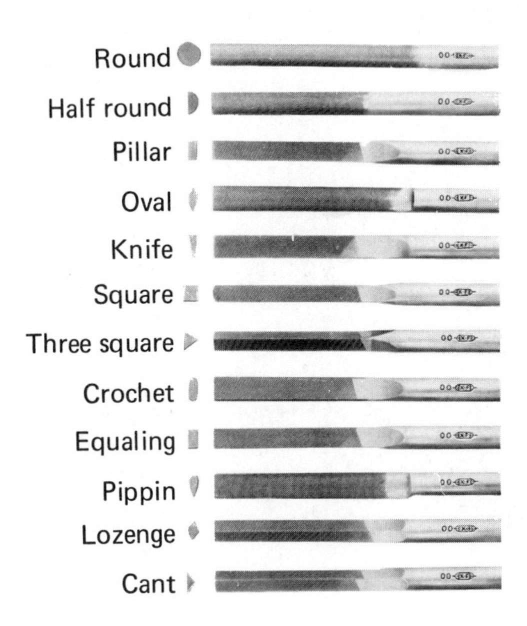


**FIGURE 4-13** / Files for the jigsaw are available in 12 patterns with 1/8 or 1/4 inch shanks.

parallel to the rows of teeth. Individual rows may be cleaned with a sharp point such as an ice pick or a nail.

## 4-7 / SANDING

The jigsaw can save you a lot of energy in smoothing a workpiece if you install a sanding attachment (Fig. 4-14). Commercial sanding attachments have 1/4-inch diameter shanks, are approximately 15/16-inch wide, 1/2-inch thick, and 2-1/2-inches long, and are shaped with a flat surface, a half-round surface, and fairly sharp corners. A knurled knob controls an expanding body that holds the quickly interchangeable sleeves securely. Various grades of coarseness are available.

The sanding attachment is held in the V-groove of the lower chuck. The standard table insert is removed, and a special home built insert of aluminum or plastic with a cutout the size of the sanding attachment is located in its place; as a substitute for the table insert, a plywood table top with a suitable center hole can be clamped to the table top. The hold down assembly is raised out of the way and the speed is set to approximately 800 strokes per minute. Clogged

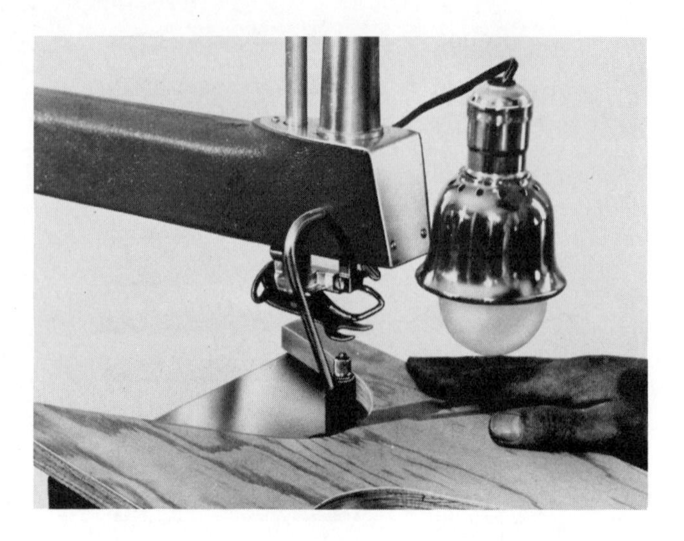

**FIGURE 4-14** / The sanding attachment smoothes workpieces quickly.

abrasive papers can be cleaned with a stiff brush, file card, or wire brush.

You can make sanding attachments of various sizes and shapes from a wood dowel of about 1 inch diameter and 2-1/2-inch length or from a wood block of approximately the same dimensions. Epoxy a metal shaft of 1/8- to 1/4-inch diameter into the center of the dowel. Glue abrasive paper to the outside.

## 4-8 / ACCESSORIES

The most useful jigsaw accessories available have been discussed because of their relative importance–jeweler's blades, saber blades, files, and sanding attachment. Several other accessories that add to the enjoyment of the use of the jigsaw are: lamp, self-centering lower chuck, and individual blade guides. The lamp is of great assistance to you when you are cutting intricate patterns. It holds a 15 to 25 watt bulb for illumination; it can be attached directly to the jigsaw and can be swung out of the way. The lamp shade is metal and becomes very hot during long periods of use. The self-centering chuck is handy for clamping very fine jeweler's blades. The chuck attaches easily to the lower plunger tube in place of the standard universal chuck. Individual blade guides are made for different thicknesses of blades. Personally, I have not found any need for the self-centering chuck nor for the individual blade guides.

Some smaller jigsaws have an auxiliary power connection (Fig. 4-15) for a disk sander or a buffing wheel. A special attachment

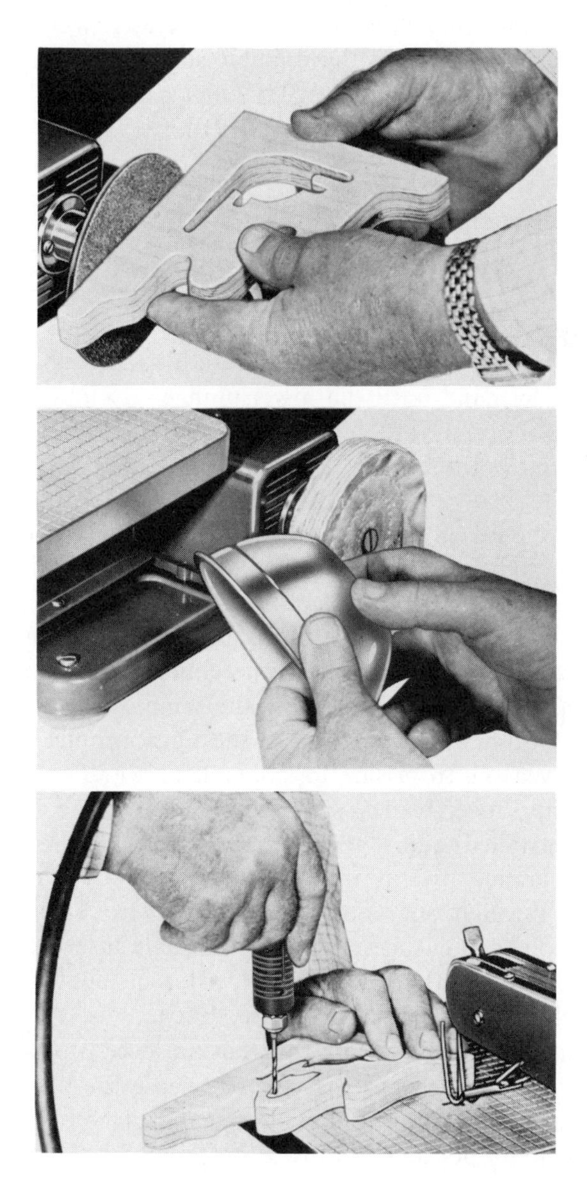

**FIGURE 4-15** / Some smaller jigsaws have an auxiliary power connection for a disk sander, buffing wheel, and a flexible shaft tool.

provides for the driving of a flexible shaft tool that can grind, drill, carve, rout, and deburr when the proper accessory is installed.

To connect accessories to the auxiliary power connection, first turn the motor off. Then line up the pin in the motor shaft with the slot in the adapter and press forward as far as it will go. Turn the wheel by hand slowly until the adapter setscrew comes into view. Tighten the screw lightly—the screw does not drive the shaft—it merely minimizes vibration and wheel drifting.

## 4-9 / BLADE REPLACEMENT

To replace a jeweler's blade, remove the table insert and then rotate the drive belt by hand until the lower plunger assembly is at the top of its stroke. Loosen the thumb screws in the upper and lower chucks and remove the blades.

Insert the new jeweler's blade with the teeth pointing down 1/2-inch into the lower chuck and tighten. Use a square, triangle, or a square block to assure that the blade is vertical. Pull the upper plunger down and insert the blade 1/2-inch into the upper chuck. Tighten the chuck. With a 5 inch blade, the tension will be correct. If the blade is longer than 5 inches (some chucks will accept the extra length), pull the upper blade plunger the same as for a 5 inch blade so that the tension will be correct. Blade tension must be correct or breakage or weaving from side to side will occur. If the chucks will not accept the longer blades, snip the blades off to 5 inches. When the blade is installed, adjust the blade guard, as required. Check the blade for clearance by rotating the drive belt by hand until the blade moves through one complete up-down stroke; this procedure will prevent blade breakage. Reinsert the table insert. Saber blades are installed only in the lower chuck; after installation, move the blade through one stroke manually (Fig. 4-16).

Some jigsaw models have a top tension lever to hold the blade (Fig. 4-8). Push the lever to the rear to release the blade. Hold the blade with the teeth pointing downward, and place it into the small slot of both the upper and the lower blade holder. Apply tension to the blade by pulling the lever forward.

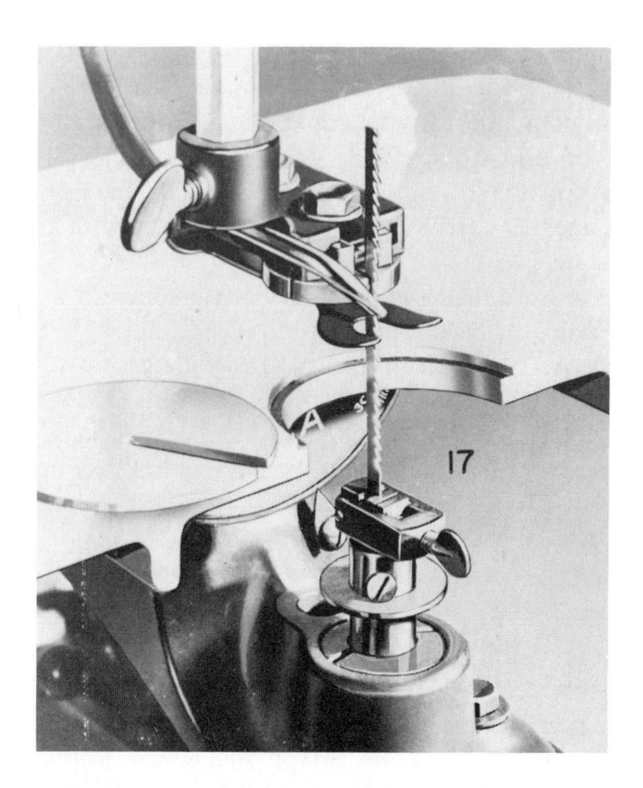


**FIGURE 4-16** / The saber saw blade is inserted in the straight or V chuck (shown) of the lower chuck assembly. Place the blade guide and hold down spring into position.

## *4-10* / CALIBRATION AND MAINTENANCE

The only portion of the jigsaw that requires calibration is the table tilt scale pointer. To calibrate, loosen the table tilt adjustment. Raise and secure the hold down assembly. Place a square or triangle against the flat side of the blade and move the table until it aligns squarely with the square or triangle. Tighten the table tilt adjustment. If the pointer does not point to 0°, loosen the zero table tilt pointer adjustment, set the pointer exactly to 0°, and retighten the adjustment. Lower the hold down assembly.

Maintenance tasks include lubrication and regrooving of blade guides. On jigsaws having an oil well, periodically check the well level by removing the truss head screw (Fig. 4-7). Add SAE-10 machine oil to bring the oil up to the level of the screw hole. Replace the screw.

Occasionally lubricate the upper plunger assembly by applying a few drops of oil into the hole at the top of the plunger. Also, occasionally oil the trunnions and other adjustable parts lightly to keep them operating freely. Wipe the table surface with an oily rag to prevent rusting.

To regroove a blade guide, reface the guide with a grinder or a file. Install the *blade* backwards into the blade chuck. With a piece of scrap wood, push the blade against the guide gently while the saw operates. Continue until the desired groove is cut.

With the smaller self-contained jigsaw, occasionally place a few drops of ordinary motor oil on the connecting link bearing.

## *4-11* / HINTS AND KINKS

A block of wood can be used to hold a blade perfectly vertical for you as you install it. Cut a thin slot into a square block of wood and hold the blade firmly in the slot of the block. Place the block on the table in the position for blade installation.

Cloth and paper can be cut on the jigsaw. Clamp the layers tightly between pieces of scrap wood and cut out the *sandwiched* pattern. Use a very fine blade for cloth and a medium fine blade for paper.

To cut a plastic workpiece, use a very thin blade with small teeth. Run the saw at a slow speed, and feed the workpiece into the blade slowly to prevent overheating and melting of the plastic.

To cut inlay pieces from different colors of wood, stack the various colors into one stack. Nail the outside edges carefully with small brads. The top piece of the veneer stack should have the pattern laid out on it. Cut all pieces of the stack simultaneously. The joining lines of the inlay can be made almost invisible by cutting the pieces at a bevel. Tilt the table from 1° to 5° to bevel cut the inlay pieces.

Coped saw joints between two workpieces such as molding can be made as follows. First, cut the end of one piece square and cut the other piece at a 45° angle. Lay the workpiece with the 45° angle cut flat on the jigsaw table. With the table at 0°, cut exactly *along* the "pattern line" made by the 45° cut. When the two pieces are joined, they will fit perfectly.

## 4-12 / INSTALLATION

When installing the jigsaw, place the rear of it toward the wall, and allow clearance to the left and right of the stand for long rip cuts from the side–about 4 feet of clearance on each side is ideal. Also allow clearance downward to the right for workpieces that project beyond the jigsaw table top when it is tilted 45°. Build the jigsaw table top at a convenient height of 40 to 42 inches.

Fasten the jigsaw securely to the stand top with carriage bolts of proper diameter. Mount the motor behind or below the driven pulley. (Refer to Sec. 1-7.) Check the supply of the oil in the crankcase and perform all of the calibration and maintenance procedures in Sec. 4-10.

# chapter five

# JOINTER

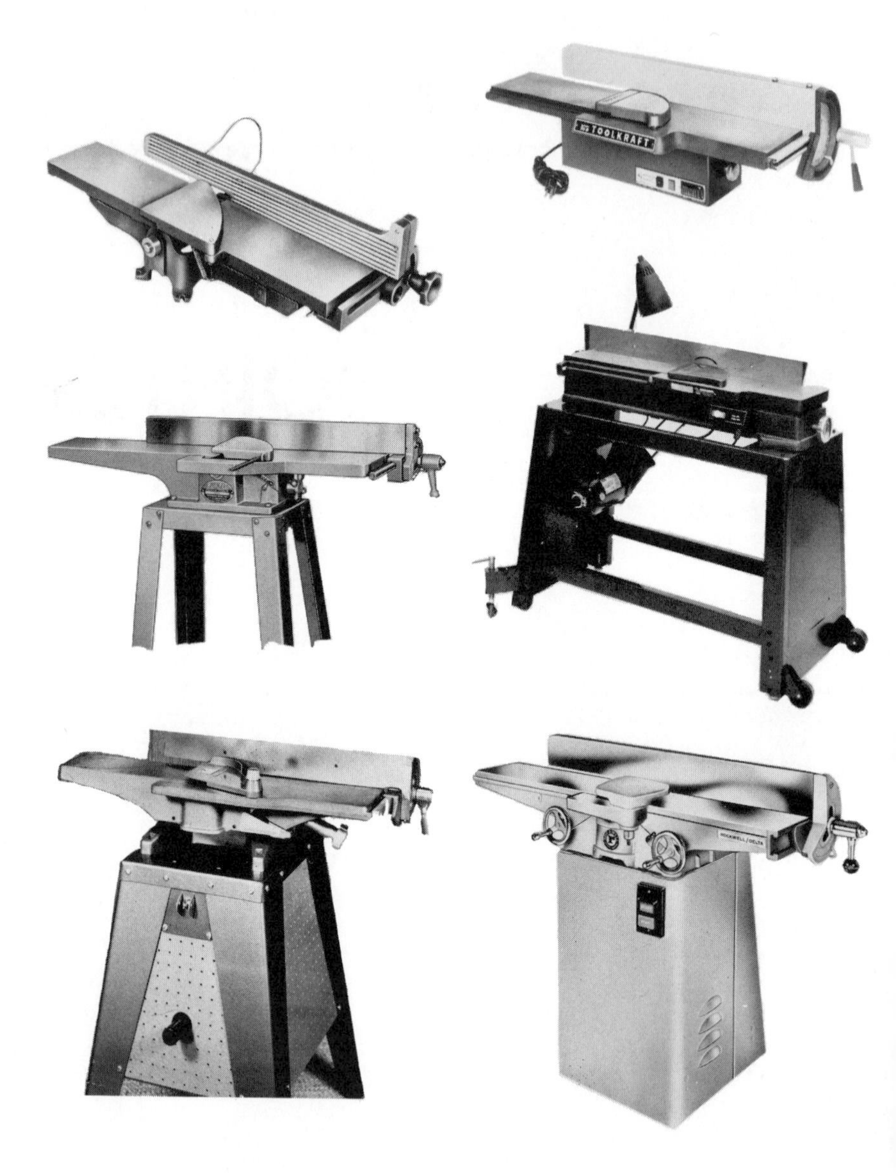


**FIGURE 5-1** / Jointers plane board edges to prepare the edges for joining together. Jointers also plane narrow boards.

The *jointer*, or *jointer-planer* as it is sometimes called, does the work of the hand plane; however, the jointer does it faster and better. The jointer gets its name from its primary function—that of planing board edges smooth for *joining* together with glue and dowels. The name of jointer-planer is also appropriate because the jointer can plane board surfaces as well as plane edges to be joined.

The primary function of the jointer, then, is to plane the edges of workpieces to be joined together, such as for the top of a table. Thus, the jointer is almost a necessity in order to build cabinets and furniture that require the joining of pieces of wood. The jointer is used with good results in planing boards smooth up to widths that are almost two times as wide as the knife length. The jointer is used to make rabbet cuts for doors, window frames, and table drawers. It also bevels edges, cuts chamfers and tenons, and can make taper cuts such as on table legs. The jointer can also take the warp out of a board.

The jointer operates by the action of three cutters, called knives, in a rotary cutting head revolving at high speed. The cutting head is located between two parallel table surfaces that are at slightly different levels, creating a step—the thickness of the cut. The workpiece is placed on the lower front table and is pushed into the revolving cutting head that removes excess stock. The *planed* area that has passed through the cutter passes onto the rear table that is slightly higher; thus, in a perfectly aligned jointer, the workpiece is always flat on the front table, the front and rear tables, or the rear table (after the workpiece has passed completely over the cutting head). In rabbeting, a special ledge called the *rabbeting ledge* supports the *uncut* section of a workpiece after the workpiece passes through the cutters. The finger guard has to be removed for rabbeting.

## 5-1 / DESCRIPTION AND MAJOR PARTS

The major parts of the jointer (Fig. 5-2) are the front table, rear table, cutting head with knives, fence, and finger guard. The front table raises and lowers on dovetail ways and adjustable gibs, or by rocker links, and thus it sets the difference in level—the depth of cut—between the front and rear tables. The front table also contains the rabbeting ledge used to support the *uncut* portion of the workpiece in making rabbet cuts and a slide rail that guides the fence into position across the tables. The fence is movable across the tables (right to left direction) on the slide rail to set the width of a rabbet cut and tilts usually from 45° right to 90° to 45° left for bevel cuts. On some models, the fence has positive stops at 45° and 90°. The fence is used as a workpiece guide to assure square cuts; during operation, the workpiece is held firmly against both of the tables and the fence. A bevel and width adjustment locks the fence for the desired bevel and rabbet width. On some models, this adjustment is a single locknut; on others, there is a dual control handle with two locknuts.

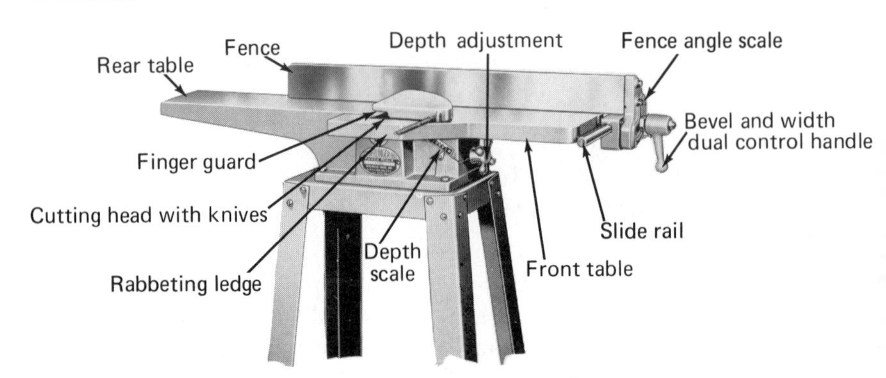


**FIGURE 5-2** / The major parts of the jointer.

The rear table is parallel to the front table and is fixed in position for operation on most jointers. The rear table may be adjusted (Sec. 5-6) to align it with (parallel to) the front table and at a height equal to the height of the knives in the cutting head. Figure 5-3 illustrates a jointer that has a rear table height adjustment within easy access; however, this adjustment is only made when cutter heads and knives are replaced. The front table height adjustment is changed quite often, depending upon the thickness of cut desired.

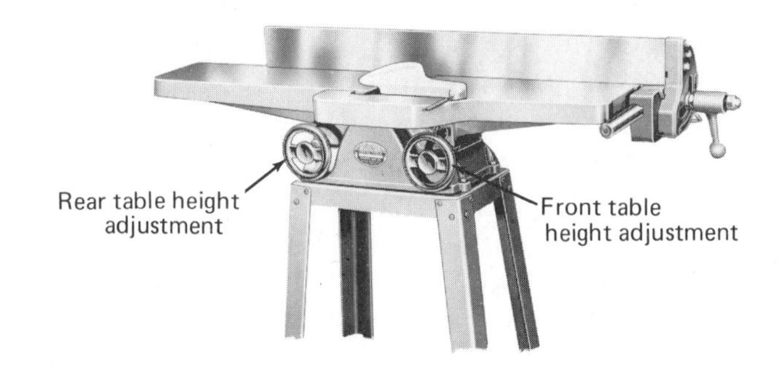


**FIGURE 5-3** / This 6 inch jointer has easily accessible front and rear table height adjustment wheels.

Located between the two tables and driven at a speed of 3000 to 4700 rev/min by the motor is the cutting head. The cutting head usually holds three high speed steel knives, although heads with two and four knives are available. The cutting head revolves in ball bearings, roller bearings, or sleeve bearings that are enclosed in a dustproof housing. Ball bearing supported cutting heads are lubricated for life.

Each knife is held in place by setscrews and is usually adjustable in height (if the height of the knife is not adjustable, then the rear table is adjustable) by means of two additional screws. The knives are *honed* in place but are removed for sharpening.

The finger guard covers the cutting head. It is moved out of the way on a pivot by the workpiece as the workpiece is pushed into the cutting head. The finger guard is always kept on the jointer except during rabbeting operations. Some jointers also have a finger guard on the right side to cover the cutting head when the fence is moved to the left for rabbeting. On some jointers, the guard can be moved from one side to the other.

A depth adjustment rotates a screw assembly to raise or lower the front table in order to set the desired depth of cut. A depth scale and pointer indicate the depth of cut (the difference in height of the two tables).

As previously indicated, the cutting head revolves at a speed of 3000 to 4700 rev/min. Some jointers have a built-in motor while others have the motor mounted below the jointer. A 1/3- or 1/2-hp motor is recommended for a 4 inch jointer, and a 1/2-, 3/4-, or 1 hp motor for a 6 inch jointer. Motor speed should be either 1725 or

3450 rev/min, depending upon the pulley sizes (refer to Sec. 1-7). Note that when the cutting head is traveling at 4000 rev/min, there are 12,000 cuts being made per minute.

Jointers with internal motors may have motor speeds as high as 15,000 rev/min. This speed is reduced by the pulley sizes, however, to a speed of about 4500-4700 rev/min.

The *size* of a jointer is specified as the width of a board that can be planed on one pass of a board through the cutting knives. Thus, a 4 inch jointer that is usually adequate for the home shop can plane a board 4 inches wide in one pass. Actually a board twice that width, or 8 inches, can be planed by making one pass and then turning the board around to make a second pass. Home workshop jointers are usually 4 or 6 inch sizes.

The total table size for a 4 inch jointer is from approximately 4-1/2- to 5-1/2-inches wide and 20 to 25 inches long; for 6 inch jointers, about 6 inches wide and 35 to 40 inches long. Fences are approximately 3 inches by 20 to 25 inches for the 4 inch jointer, and 4 inches by 28 inches for the 6 inch jointer. Overall sizes vary from approximately 9 inches high, 12 inches wide, and 32 inches long for the 4 inch jointer to approximately 10 inches high, 10 to 20 inches wide, and 40 inches long for the 6 inch jointer. Maximum depths of cuts for rabbeting on 4 inch jointers are from 1/4- to 3/8-inch and for the 6 inch jointers are from 3/8- to 1/2-inch.

All parts on the jointer come as standard equipment (except motor, belt, and motor pulley) unless the jointer is motorized. There are no accessories for the jointer except a power tool stand and a link rod used to start the motor.

## *5-2* / OPERATING CONTROLS AND ADJUSTMENTS

To make smooth final cuts or rabbet cuts on workpieces, it is important to make accurate adjustments of the depth of cut, fence position (width of rabbet), and the fence angle; the finger guard(s) should always be in place. Adjust the jointer operating controls and adjustments (Fig. 5-2) as follows:

*1* / *depth adjustment*—Rotate the depth adjustment clockwise to raise the table, thereby decreasing the depth of cut or counterclockwise to increase the depth of cut as indicated by the pointer on the depth scale. Cuts of 1/32-inch are normally used for final smoothing of an edge or a surface. If there is no depth scale on your jointer, place a straight edge across the rear table; as the front table is lowered, measure the distance between the straight edge and the front table. This is the depth of cut.

2 / *fence position* (width control)–The width control sets the distance from the left edge of the blade to the end of the rabbet cut. You have to use a ruler to measure and set the fence to the proper position. Loosen the locknut, which may be either loosened by a dual control handle or a concentric (one inside the other) shaft and knob. Position the fence and tighten the locknut. Make a final measurement check and readjust if necessary.

3 / *fence angle* (bevel)–The bevel control tightens the locknut that secures the fence at the desired angle for square (perpendicular) or bevel cuts. Loosen the locknut, which may be either loosened by a dual control handle or a concentric shaft and knob. Position the fence to the desired angle as indicated on the fence angle scale; for accurate angles, use a bevel or/and protractor to set the angle. Right angles (perpendicular to the table) can be set with a square. With the fence tilted at the desired angle, tighten the locknut. Some jointer fences have positive stops at 45°, 90°, and 135°. For these angles, engage the stop and tighten the locknut.

4 / *finger guards*–Guards should be kept in place at all times. The left guard (near the rabbeting ledge) is removed for rabbeting operations by pulling the guard and post up from the table. After rabbeting, reinsert the guard according to the manufacturer's instructions–usually, the guard is inserted through a hole in the front table. Be sure that the slot in the guard spindle aligns properly and is attached to the spring that holds the guard over against the fence.

## 5-3 / OPERATION

### CAUTIONS

*1 / Ensure that there are no nails in the workpiece. Nails can cause the knives to kick the workpiece back and will also nick the knives preventing further smooth cuts until the blades are reground.*

*2 / Never place your hands directly over the knives; keep your hands over the table and hold the workpiece firmly to the tables and fence.*

*3 / Always use a push block (Fig. 5-5) for thin stock and short pieces.*

*4 / Keep the finger guard(s) in place at all times.*

*5 / Observe the general safety precautions in Sec. 1-16.*

Perform the following procedures to operate the jointer:

*1* / Set the desired depth of cut.

*2* / Set the fence to the desired bevel.

*3* / Set the fence to the desired width of cut for rabbeting.

*4* / Apply electrical power to the motor and perform the applicable jointing and planing procedures in Sec. 5-4.

## 5-4 / JOINTING AND PLANING PROCEDURES

At first thought, it doesn't seem that there could be too much effort to jointing or planing a workpiece. But there are actually quite a number of considerations, procedures, and types of cuts. This section includes checking the direction of the wood grain for jointing and planing; holding the workpiece correctly; jointing and planing long, short, and thin workpieces; planing wide workpieces; end grain planing; rabbeting; tapering; beveling; chamfering; and smoothing warped workpieces.

The first consideration in planing is the direction of the workpiece grain. Determine the grain and plane with the grain, if possible, as shown in Fig. 5-4. There are times, as in planing wide boards when two passes are required, when you must plane against the grain. Make the against-the-grain pass first, followed by the with-the-grain pass. Feed the workpiece at half the normal feed speed when cutting against the grain; also approach the ends slowly to avoid splitting. If you can't determine the grain direction, make a thin test cut with the workpiece in one direction followed by a pass in the opposite direction. The pass producing the smoothest finish is the pass with-the-grain.

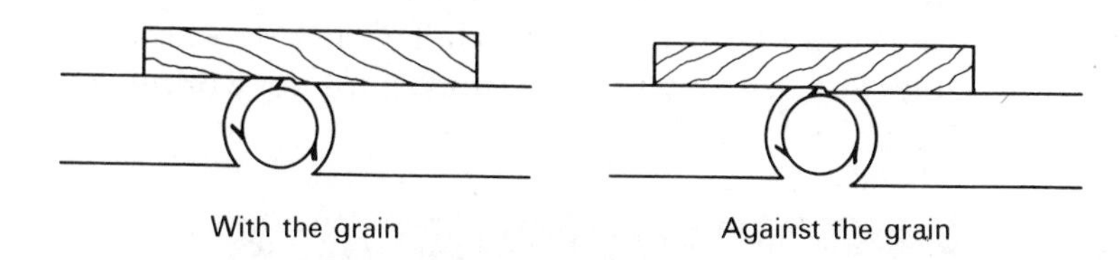


**FIGURE 5-4** / Cut with the grain whenever possible for the smoothest jointing and planing.

Thin cuts of not greater than 1/32-inch are made for *finish* cuts. Cuts of 1/64- to 1/32-inch are made in hardwoods, and as many passes as required are made.

### *CAUTION*

***The procedure in the following paragraph describes general planing techniques for edge planing and for planing very thick workpieces. If thin workpieces are being planed, use a push block—refer to Fig. 5-5.***

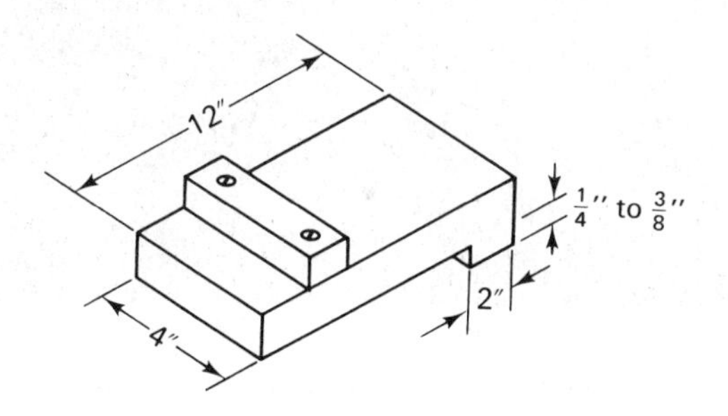


**FIGURE 5-5** / Construct a push block.

To cut any workpiece on the jointer, hold the workpiece firmly against the tables and fence with both hands until the workpiece has top of the workpiece and your left hand to the front and top of the workpiece (Fig. 5-6). Feed the workpiece with slow, even pressure on the front table into the cutting knives. When the workpiece has passed *over* the knives and onto the rear table, lift your left hand *over* the knives and hold the workpiece firmly down on the rear table and against the fence (Fig. 5-7). Let the workpiece slide under your left hand which remains just *beyond* the knives at the rear table as you feed the workpiece with your right hand. Continue with pressure against the tables and fence with both hands until the workpiece has passed over the knives.

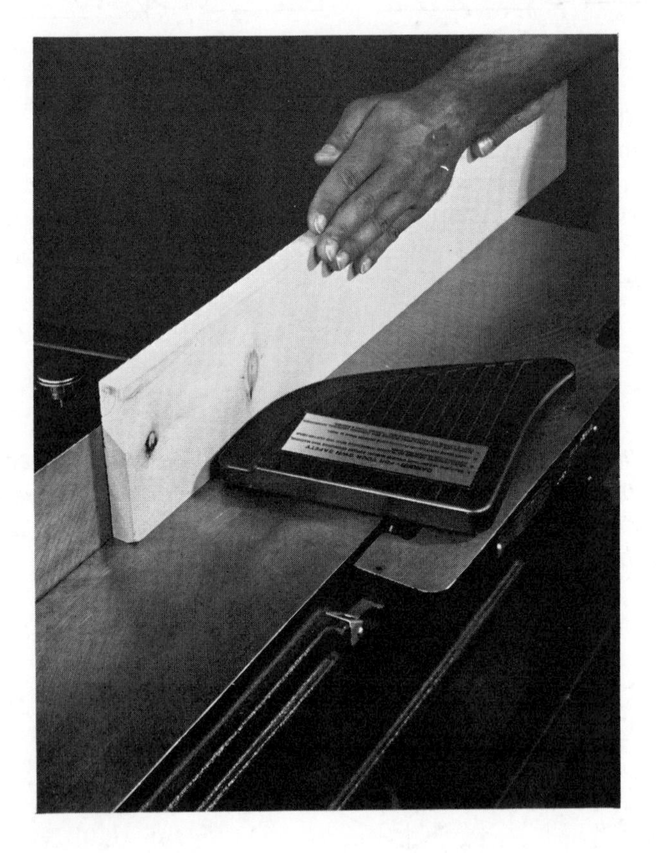

**FIGURE 5-6** / Hold the workpiece firmly against the tables and the fence.

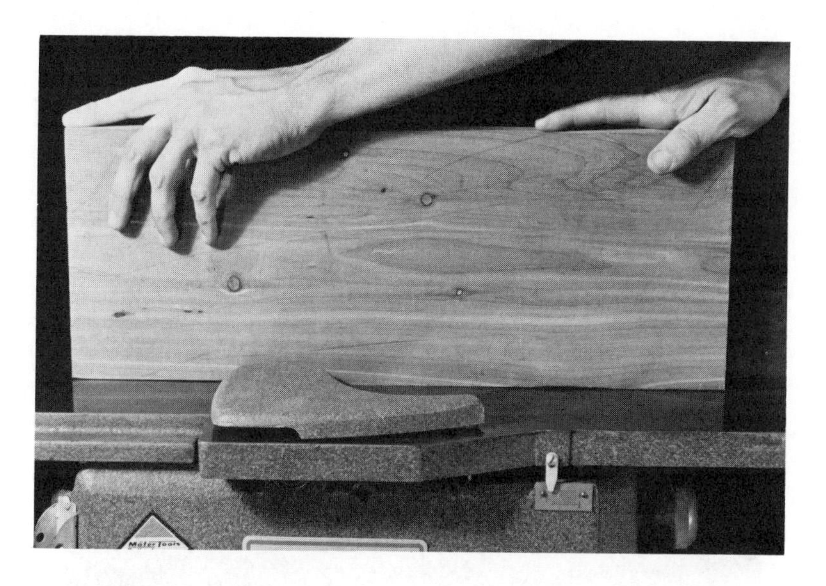

**FIGURE 5-7** / Do not place your hands over the cutting knives at any time—for safety's sake.

Long boards–over 3 feet–should have a support at the rear of the rear table to assure a uniform cut. You can use a workpiece support stand (Sec. 1-10) set to the height of the rear table. You can also clamp a hold down board to the end of the fence (Fig. 5-8).

When short or thin workpieces are planed, use a push block (Fig. 5-9). This assures an even cut, prevents workpiece kickback, and protects the hands of the operator.

If the edges of a workpiece to be jointed are very rough, pass the workpiece through a table, radial arm, or band saw prior to passing it through the jointer. On rough edges, push extra hard on the surface that is on the rear table. If the jointing is to be on the edges of *wide* boards, screw an auxiliary fence onto the existing fence to make the fence higher and hence more supporting (Fig. 5-10). Most jointer fences are drilled; insert wood screws through the drilled holes into the auxiliary fence.

The end grains of a workpiece can be planed quite smooth. However, you must use a special procedure to prevent the splitting of wood fibers at the very end of the workpiece. To prevent splitting, make a short cut on one end of the workpiece. Then turn the workpiece around and make the rest of the cut. Be sure to hold the

**FIGURE 5-8** / Either a workpiece support or a hold down board can be used when long workpieces are planed. Both are illustrated here.

**FIGURE 5-9** / Use a push block for short or thin workpieces.

workpiece firmly against the tables and fence, and use a slower than normal feed speed (Fig. 5-11).

Rabbet cuts are made using the left sides of the cutting knives (Fig. 5-12). Remove the left finger guard—if applicable, relocate the guard to the right side. Measuring from the left edge of the knives to

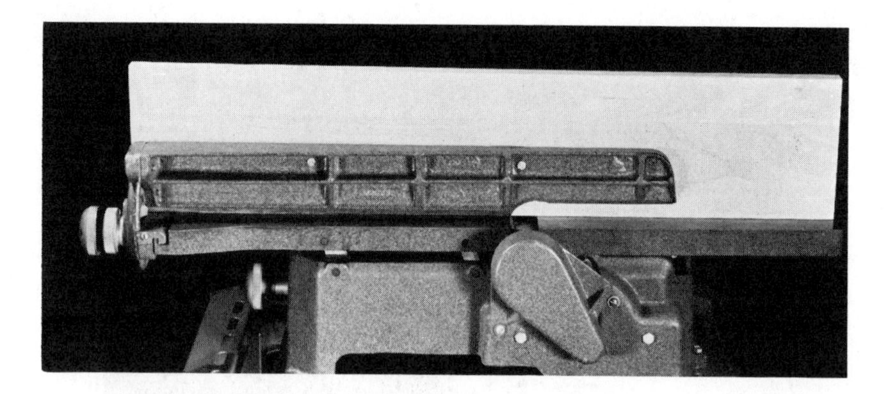

**FIGURE 5-10** / When extra wide workpieces are edge planed, add an auxiliary fence.

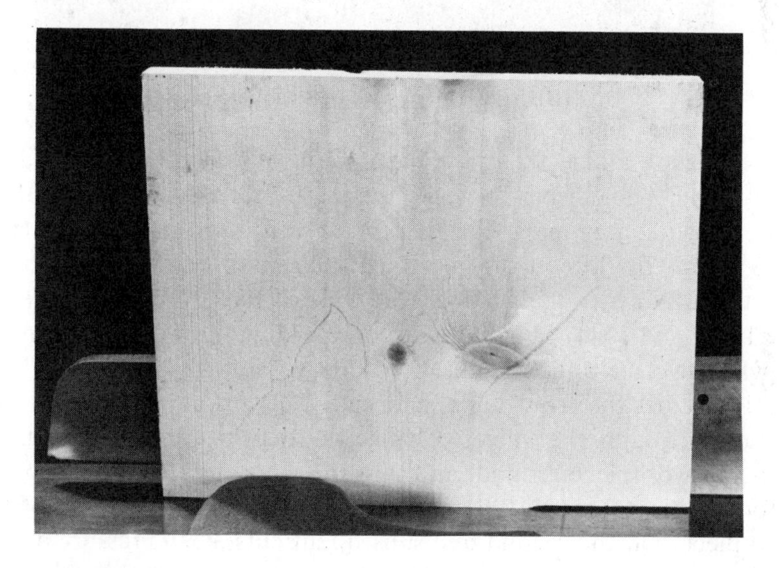

**FIGURE 5-11** / On end grains, make a short cut on one end followed by a cut from the other end.

the fence, set the fence for the width of the rabbet desired. Set the depth of cut from 1/8- to a maximum of 3/16-inch deep for each cut; make repeated cuts to attain the desired rabbet depth. Hold the workpiece firmly against the front table, rabbet ledge, and the fence, using a push block as necessary. The *uncut* portion of the workpiece will pass the outside left edge of the knives and will be supported by the rabbeting ledge. Use a slower feed so that the cutting head does not slow down appreciably; a slower cutting head makes a rougher cut.

**FIGURE 5-12** / Making a rabbet cut.

To cut a taper, determine the amount of taper desired per linear foot–say 3/16-inch per foot. Set the jointer for a 3/16-inch depth of cut. Measure and mark the workpiece 1 foot from one end (Fig. 5-13). With the jointer off, set the 1 inch mark on the workpiece at the top of one of the cutting head knives. Raise the workpiece off the knife and start the jointer motor. Holding the workpiece firmly, slowly lower it onto the rotating knives. Hold the workpiece *end* firmly against the front table, and pass the workpiece (the one foot section) through the knives. Change the depth of cut to 1/16-inch, turn the workpiece around, and pass the workpiece with the tapered 1 foot section through the cutters first, continuing to the end of the workpiece. On the second and subsequent cuts, keep pressure on the workpiece so that the tapered portion is always against first the front and then the rear table. Don't "rock" the workpiece. Plane the rest of the workpiece to the desired taper.

To make a bevel cut (Fig. 5-14), tilt the fence inward and lock the fence at the desired angle. When the fence is tilted inward, the workpiece is wedged between the table and the fence; this wedging holds the workpiece securely, resulting in cuts that are more accurate than when the fence is tilted outward. Hold the workpiece firmly against the fence, and make sufficient cuts to complete the bevel all the way across the edge of the workpiece.

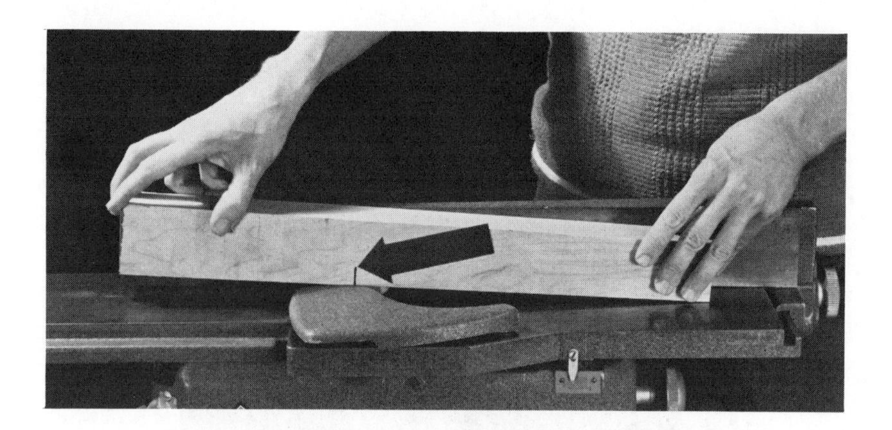

FIGURE 5-13 / Cutting a tapered workpiece.

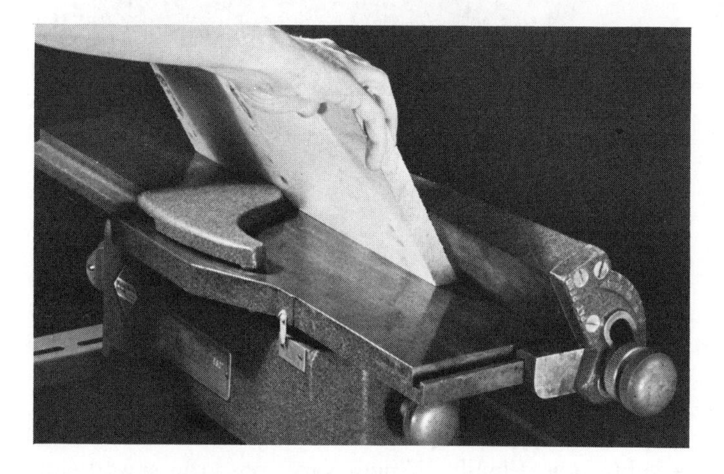

FIGURE 5-14 / Cutting a bevel.

Chamfers are cut on workpieces to remove sharp edges. Set the jointer up for a bevel cut; use a shallow depth of cut and make a single pass only (Fig. 5-15).

Warped boards, within the width capacity of the jointer, can be planed smooth. Surface plane the boards on the concave side; then plane on the convex side. On the concave cut, the board will set flat on the two edges; on the convex side, hold the board firmly on the tables and against the fence. Make sufficient cuts on each side to shape the board flat.

Another method of leveling warped boards is to smooth the concave side first on the jointer. Then hold the smoothed side against

**FIGURE 5-15** / Chamfers are cut on workpieces to remove sharp edges.

the table saw fence, and cut off the convex side of the warped board with the table saw. Finally, if necessary, pass the sawed side of the board through the jointer to further smooth it.

## 5-5 / KNIFE SHARPENING AND REPLACEMENT

The cutter knives should be honed occasionally with a fine abrasive stone (Fig. 5-16). The knives are *not* removed from the cutting head for this procedure. Rotate a cutting knife to a top position so that the beveled edge is parallel to the table surface; using a wedge of wood between the cutting head and table, fix the cutting head so it cannot rotate. Raise or lower the front table so that the honing stone is parallel to and lies flat against the full width of the knife bevel and on the table; place a piece of paper under the hone on the front table so that the hone does not scratch the table. Using kerosene or a light oil on the hone, stroke the hone lightly back and forth across the complete length of the knife. Use the approximate same number of strokes on each knife. Remove the burr on the flat side of the knife by rubbing it very gently with a fine slip stone or a piece of emery cloth.

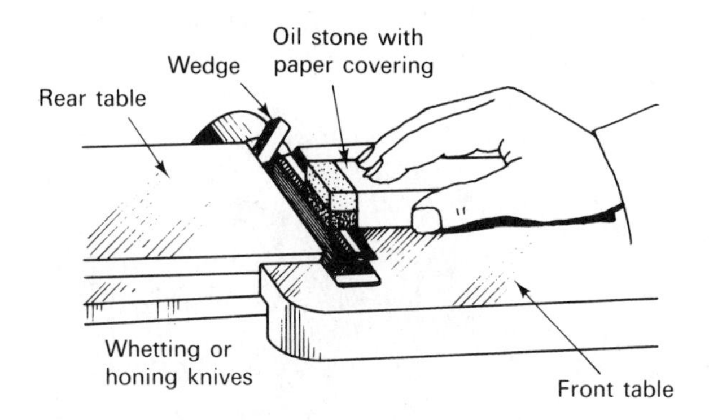


**FIGURE 5-16** / Honing a jointer knife edge.

## CAUTION

***In the following procedures, ensure that all setscrews that lock the knives to the cutting head are secure before applying electrical power to the jointer motor.***

To remove the knives from the cutting head for sharpening or replacement, loosen the setscrews on each knife and lift the knives out of the head. Regrind the knife edges, removing approximately the same amount of material from each knife. Grind at the same angle as the original beveled edge. Prevent the knives from being overheated during grinding.

To place the knives back into the cutting head, set the knives into place and locate them horizontally against a small block of wood that is situated between the rabbet ledge and the knives; this will gauge the position of each knife so that all knives are equally spaced horizontally. Tighten the setscrews for each knife, but do not tighten them securely. Set a straight edge from the rear table extending across the cutting head and knives (Fig. 5-17); a block of hardwood or a square is good for this purpose. Rotate each knife to its highest point. Using the knife height adjustment screws for each knife, set each knife height to *just touch* the hardwood block or square as the knife is rotated by hand under the block (a counterclockwise rotation of the adjustment screw raises the knife). Be sure that the knives are all flat against the adjustment screws. Now tighten the setscrews to secure the knives tightly. Rotate the cutting head by hand to check for knife clearance before applying electrical power to the motor.

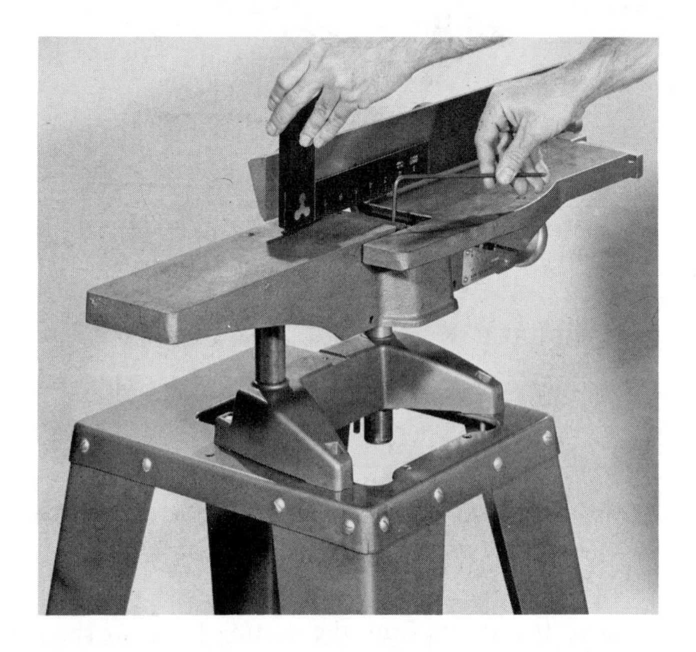

**FIGURE 5-17** / Setting the jointer cutting knives to proper height.

If your cutting head does not have knife adjustment screws, set the knives a little high in the slots. Rotate each knife to the highest position, and then use a hardwood block and a light hammer to tap the knives down into the cutting head slots to the correct depth. Secure the knives with the setscrews. Rotate the cutting head by hand to check clearance before applying electrical power to the motor.

On some jointers, the position of the knives may be fixed, but the rear table can be lowered to compensate for the grinding of the knives. If this is the case, use a straight edge and lower the table until it is the same height as the knives at their uppermost point. After the height is set, lock the table in position.

## 5-6 / CALIBRATION AND MAINTENANCE

As with all power tools, exact calibration adjustments are necessary for accurate work. This section describes how to make adjustments for cutting head alignment, depth of cut calibration, rear table alignment, and fence alignment. Maintenance steps are also included.

Visual indications of rear table height misadjustments are: a step or gouge at the end of a cut usually means that the rear table is too low; a cut that tapers from one end to the other indicates that the rear table is too high.

Jointer calibration alignments should be made in the following sequential order: cutting head alignment, depth of cut pointer, rear table adjustment, resetting cutting knives (refer to Sec. 5-5), and fence angle pointer and stops (45, 90, and 135°).

To check cutting head alignment, raise the front table to maximum height. Place a straight edge across the table and rotate the cutting head until a knife is at maximum height; it should *just* touch the straight edge. If it does not, and if the cutting head arbor is adjustable, raise or lower the arbor until the knife just touches the straight edge.

With the front table remaining at the maximum height, check that the depth of cut pointer indicates zero depth. If it does not, loosen the pointer setscrew, reposition the pointer, and retighten the setscrew.

Check the position of the rear table for height and for parallelism (level) with the front table as follows. Remove the fence from the slide rail. Place a straight edge across the front and rear tables trying all angles and positions on the tables to determine whether the tables are parallel with each other. If the tables are not parallel, proceed with the manufacturer's instructions for leveling; the instructions are usually to loosen lock screws, adjust three or four leveling screws until the rear table is level with the front table, and then tighten the lock screws. The lock screws and leveling screws are concentric. This procedure may take you a while, but it will be well worth the time.

If the knives have been resharpened, require honing, or need to be checked for proper alignment (height), refer to Sec. 5-5.

To align the fence, place it back on the slide rail. Loosen the fence bevel locknut, and set the fence perpendicular to the tables by using a square or right angle triangle as a gauge. Tighten the locknut. Check the pointer on the fence angle scale; if it does not indicate 0°, loosen the pointer setscrew, set the pointer to 0°, and tighten the setscrew.

Jointers having fence *stops* at 45, 90 and 135° (45° left) may have adjustments for the stops. Use a 45-45-90° triangle placed across the table and against the fence. Use a screwdriver to adjust the stops; once the stops are properly set, the fence will return to these stops accurately every time.

Jointers with cutting head arbors having bronze bearings on each side of the cutting head should be lubricated with several drops of oil on the shaft on both sides of both bearings. Lubricate before each use and during prolonged (15 minutes) running. Ball bearings are usually sealed and never need lubrication. All moving parts such as links, arms, and screws should be oiled occasionally with a light machine oil.

## 5-7 / HINTS AND KINKS

Fit a chute made of 1/4-inch plywood or Masonite to the bottom of the jointer stand, and have the chute empty into a box or can. Varnish and wax the inside of the chute so that shavings won't stick to it.

If a board is to be planed so thin that it slides under the rear edge of the fence, it is necessary to screw a flat board onto the fence. Set the board on the rear table top and use 3/4- or 1 inch stock and 3/4-inch wood screws.

## 5-8 / INSTALLATION

Fasten the jointer securely to a power tool stand or bench. The jointer tables should be from 32 to 35 inches above the floor.

Install the motor pulley directly under the jointer arbor driven pulley. Install the motor so that the jointer cutting head rotation is clockwise when viewed from the left (rabbeting ledge) side of the jointer.

Perform all of the calibration and preventive maintenance procedures in Sec. 5-6.

# chapter six

# LATHE

**FIGURE 6-1** / You can derive a great amount of satisfaction and pleasure by creating your own designs and then spinning lamps, legs, bowls, etc. on the lathe.

You can probably get more pleasure from a wood lathe than from any other power tool in your workshop. As a beginner, you can place a dirty, rough piece of wood into the lathe and turn out a perfectly smooth, symmetrical finished workpiece in a relatively short time. By following a pattern you've designed, you can turn lamps, table and chair legs, bowls, salt and pepper shakers, lamp bases, spindles, spirals, balls, balusters, and replacement parts for broken pieces of furniture. Wood, plastic, and nonferrous light metals can be precision turned in the wood lathe.

The lathe is a versatile tool when accessories are added to the basic machine—sanding (disk and drum), buffing, polishing, and horizontal drilling are thus easily performed.

There are two classifications of *turnings* made on the lathe: *spindle* and *faceplate* (Figs. 6-2 and 3). Spindle turnings—lamps, legs, balusters, and similar workpieces—are turned between centers mounted in the *headstock* and the *tailstock* of the lathe. Faceplate turnings—lamp bases, bowls, cups, etc.—are mounted to the headstock only on a faceplate. With the workpiece mounted as either a spindle or a faceplate turning, sharp *chisels* and *gouges* are used to cut away waste material as the workpiece material spins between the centers or on the faceplate.

Before any further discussion on the lathe, it is necessary to define several terms used in lathe work. You should understand these terms before proceeding to more detailed discussions. The terminology concerns the three types of *surfaces* from which material is removed and the two types of tools and operations used to remove the material.

With lathe work, material can be removed from one of three *surfaces* on a workpiece: the surface around the *circumference*, along

**FIGURE 6-2** / Spindle turnings are mounted between centers in the headstock and tailstock.

**FIGURE 6-3** / Faceplate turnings are mounted on the headstock spindle. Note that the craftsman is performing a scraping operation with the chisel resting on the right angle tool rest.

the *diameter*, or along a surface that is a combination of circumference and diameter (Fig. 6-4). In removal of material along a circumference, the surface being cut travels *under the edge* of a chisel like an endless belt. Examples of removal of surface material around a circumference include the outside of a cylinder and the outside wall and inside wall of a faceplate turning. Material can be removed from a *circumference surface* of a workpiece by either of two types of operations—*cutting* or *scraping*—to be discussed shortly.

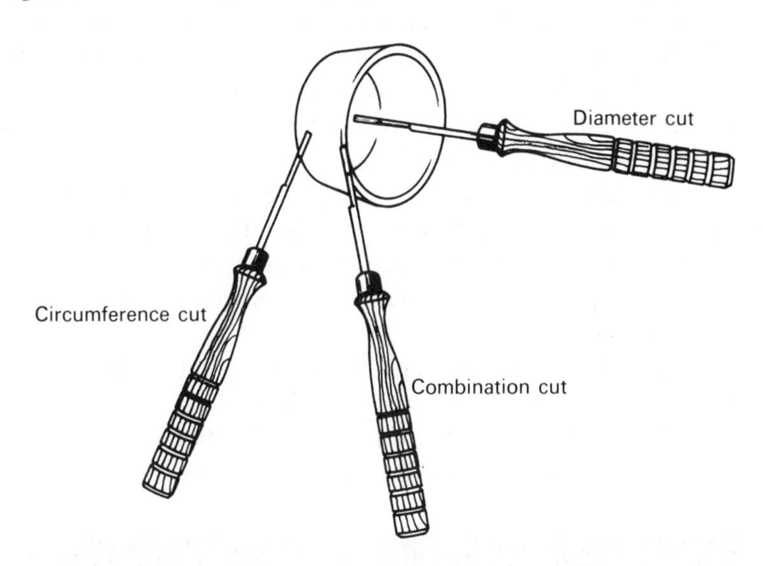


**FIGURE 6-4** / Material can be removed from a workpiece along a circumference, diameter, or combination circumference/diameter surface.

Material along a *diameter surface* is removed by a scraping operation of the lathe tool toward or *along* the diameter of the workpiece. Material on the *face* of a faceplate or on the side of a shoulder on a spindle is removed by a scraping operation. The surface being turned rotates like a disk *against the edge* of the chisel. Only a *scraping* operation is used for removing material along a diameter surface of a workpiece.

There are instances, such as cutting the corner of a bowl or a shoulder, when the operation of removing material approaches a combination of both *scraping* and *cutting* operations. *Cutting tools* may be used for both cutting and scraping operations, but *scraping tools* are practically never used for cutting operations. In general, don't try to use any tool to perform *cutting operations* when the workpiece "chatters" or "jumps"; instead, use a scraping operation.

There are two major categories of tools used with the lathe: tools to perform *scraping* operations and tools to perform *cutting* operations. The *scraping* tools are the *flat nose* (also called square nose) chisel, *round nose* chisel, and the *spear point* chisel. The scraping tools are *not* honed on the *flat* sides–when the tools are ground, the wire edge is left on as an aid in scraping. The *cutting* tools are the *gouge, skew* chisel, and *parting tool* chisel. The cutting tools are honed on *both* sides to razor sharp edges.

The cutting operation removes material faster than the scraping operation and gives a smoother finish; the materials removed are tiny shavings. Materials removed by scraping operations are tiny particles rather than shavings. Scraping dulls chisels fast, but the operation is easy to learn and control. Scraping operations are used for turning diameter surfaces, whereas cutting operations are performed only for turning circumference surfaces.

To perform a scraping operation, hold the lathe tool flat (horizontal) on the tool rest and the cutting edge parallel to the workpiece (Fig. 6-5). Hold the tool firmly. Always scrape in the *top* quadrant of the surface area where the workpiece is rotating *down*

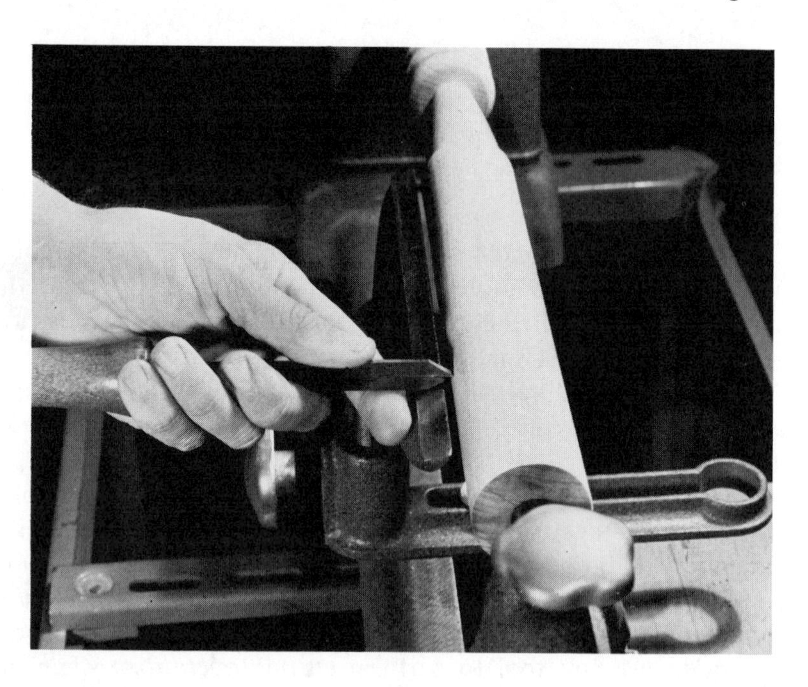

**FIGURE 6-5** / A scraping chisel is held with the cutting edge parallel to the center line of the workpiece. An unhoned edge aids the scraping action.

(Fig. 6-6). The tool is held horizontally and firmly against the tool rest which is located 1/8-inch below the diameter of the workpiece. If you try to scrape in the other top quadrant, the tool will be kicked into the air.

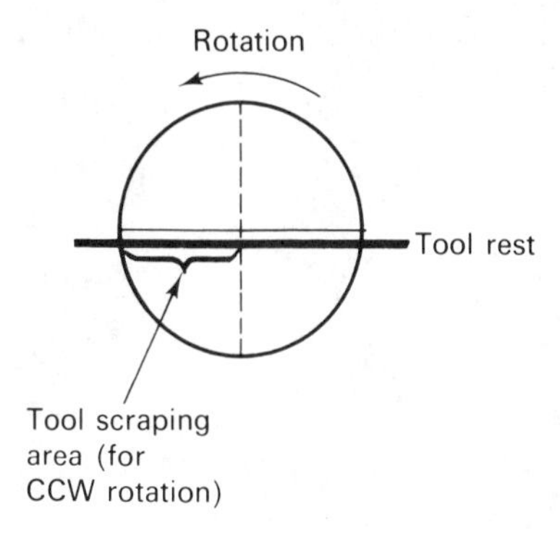


**FIGURE 6-6** / Location of the scraping tool for scraping operations along a diameter.

A cutting operation is harder to learn and takes more practice than a scraping operation. To use a cutting tool, hold the tool firmly against the tool rest so that the beveled cutting edge is *parallel* to the workpiece circumference and actually digs into the revolving work in such a manner as to peel the wood, as you would peel a potato (Fig. 6-7). Hold the tool steady using the tool rest as a fulcrum.

## *6-1* / DESCRIPTION AND MAJOR PARTS

Figure 6-8 illustrates the major parts of the lathe: headstock, headstock spindle, spur center, bed, way, tailstock, tailstock ram, and tool rest. The major parts of the *headstock* that hold the workpiece for faceplate turnings and one end of the workpiece for spindle turnings are the *spindle*, driven cone pulley (not illustrated), and an *indexing pin* and *lock*. The spindle is mounted with ball bearings or bronze bushings. A driven cone pulley drives the spindle (usually in a counterclockwise direction as viewed from the tailstock) at different speeds (refer to Sec. 6-6). The spindle is threaded to mount a faceplate (Sec. 6-16) internally for faceplate turnings or externally for larger faceplate turnings. Accessories such as a drill chuck may also attach to the spindle threads. A *Morse tapered spur*

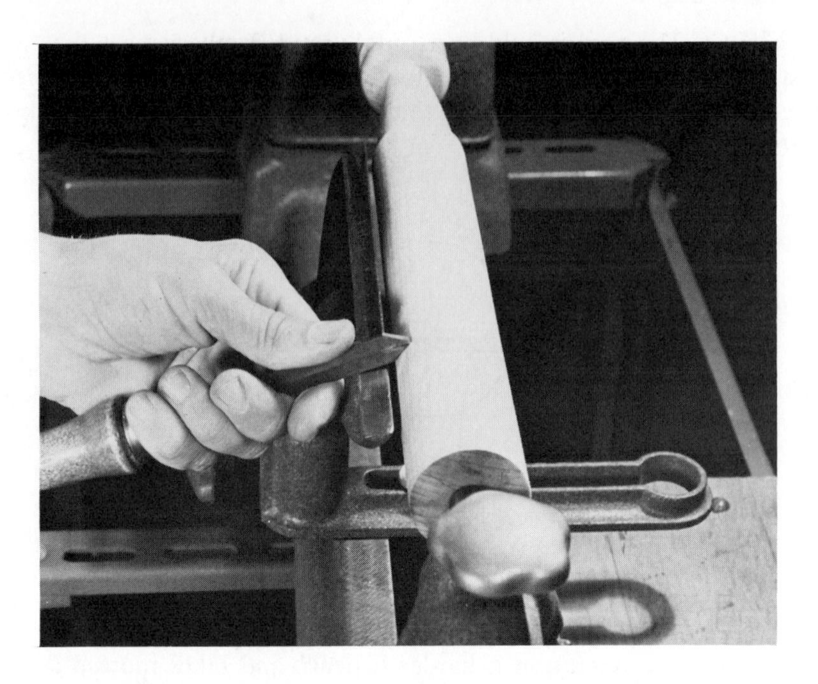

**FIGURE 6-7** / A cutting chisel is held so that the edge cuts into the workpiece in the same manner that the skin is shaved off a potato.

*center* is inserted into the spindle for use in driving a spindle mounted turning. Other accessories may also attach with a Morse taper fitting into the hollow headstock spindle. The indexing pin and

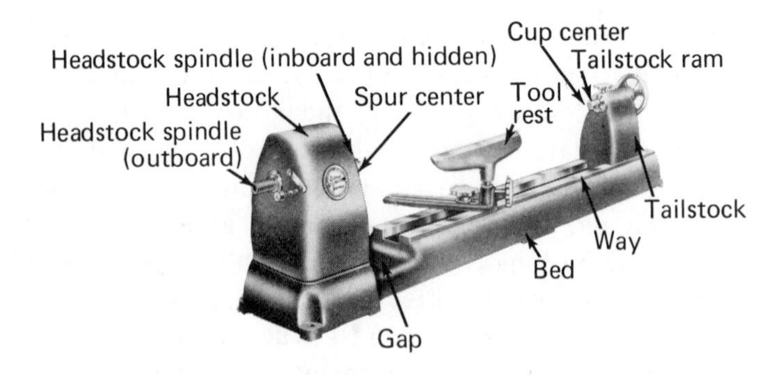


**FIGURE 6-8** / Major parts of the lathe.

lock are used to lock the lathe pulley and spindle in a fixed position so that operations such as fluting and reeding can be performed on the workpiece. The indexing mechanism allows for quick division of spindle and faceplate work.

The *bed* of the lathe provides alignment between the headstock and the tailstock and provides a path along the bed *ways* for the tailstock to pass over to adjust for different length workpieces. The bed may be a single piece of cast iron with precision ground ways or a tubular bed with one or two tubes with keyways for alignment of the tailstock. Cast iron lathes have a bed *gap* next to the headstock that allows workpieces with diameters greater than normal (spur to bed distance radius) to be turned.

The lathe *tailstock* supports one end of a spindle turning. It consists of a *ram*, a *center*, and some adjusting mechanisms. In use, the tailstock (with the ram retracted) is slid down the ways to approximately 1/2-inch from the spindle (already mounted to the headstock center). The tailstock is locked and the ram and center are extended to the workpiece. The center actually penetrates the workpiece slightly. The ram and center are then finally adjusted and locked into place. The ram travels up to approximately 2-1/4-inches. Various types of centers are available (Sec. 6-16). Some tailstocks are adjustable to compensate for misalignment between the headstock and tailstock centers because of unevenness of the bench surface.

Thus, it can be seen that a spindle shaped workpiece is placed between a driven spur center in the headstock and a center on the tailstock. Faceplates are attached to the threaded headstock spindle.

Lathe *sizes* are determined by the largest distance between the headstock and the tailstock centers and by the largest diameter that can be spun (inboard). Maximum capacities of lathes for home use range from 20 to 38 inches between centers, 6 to 12 inch diameters over the bed, and 6 to 14 inch diameters by 3 inches wide over a bed gap. Larger diameter workpieces can be accommodated by mounting the workpiece to the threaded outboard headstock spindle, and lathe bed extensions can be added to increase headstock-to-tailstock capacity. Overall lathe size is approximately 12 inches high, 56 inches long, and 11 inches wide.

The *tool rest* supports the turning tools, preventing them from being thrown from the operator's hands by the spinning workpiece. The tool rest is adjustable in height, angular direction, and in and out movement.

Motors of 1/4-, 1/3-, or 1/2-hp at 1725 rev/min are used with lathes. For 6 to 10 inch lathes, 1/3-hp is usually used; the 1/2-hp motors are for lathes larger than 10 inches. A three or four step cone pulley that matches the lathe pulley should be used on the motor.

When you buy a lathe, you should receive headstock, lathe cone pulley, tailstock, bed, tool rest and mount, a spur center, and a cup center for the tailstock. All other items including the lathe cutting tools, motor, motor pulley, and belt are considered accessories. (Refer to Secs. 6-2 and 6-16.)

## *6-2* / TURNING TOOLS

This section describes the purpose and the use of each of the lathe turning tools. There are six tools (Fig. 6-9) designed specifically for lathe turning: *gouge, round nose chisel, parting tool chisel, flat nose* (also called *square nose*) *chisel, skew,* and *spear point* (also called *diamond point*). There are also five other tools that, although not specifically designed for lathe turning, can be used: *wood rasps, files, molding knives, hand planes,* and *forming tools*.

Rough cuts to shape a square workpiece into a cylinder and to reduce the workpiece to working size (about 1/8-inch from finish size) are made with a *gouge*; the gouge is also used to make concave cuts and round grooves. The gouge rapidly cuts away large areas. Place the gouge on the tool rest with the convex side down and the cutting edge angled in advance of the handle; now roll the gouge approximately 30 to 45° in the direction in which it will be advanced along the tool rest. Because the gouge is a *cutting* tool, it is held with the handle down. Don't cut too deeply or feed too fast.

The gouge is a hollow, round nose tool with an outside bevel of 30°. Sizes range from 1/4- to 1-1/4-inches; 1/4-, 1/2-, and 3/4-inch gouges are generally used in home workshops.

The *round nose* chisel is a scraping tool used for diameter and circumference scraping operations such as rounding edges and bowl contours. Held in one position, the round nose chisel will scrape a round bottomed groove the opposite shape of the tool itself. If the tool is moved sideward, the groove is expanded into a cove. Hold this chisel in a horizontal position on the tool rest with the beveled side down; move the chisel into the work slowly.

Round nose chisels are like ordinary hand chisels, but with the end ground round. The cutting edge is beveled on one side to 40–45°. Widths are 1/4-, 1/2-, 3/4-, and 1 inch.

The most frequent use of the *parting tool* chisel is to cut narrow grooves as depth guides to facilitate the turning of the workpiece. It

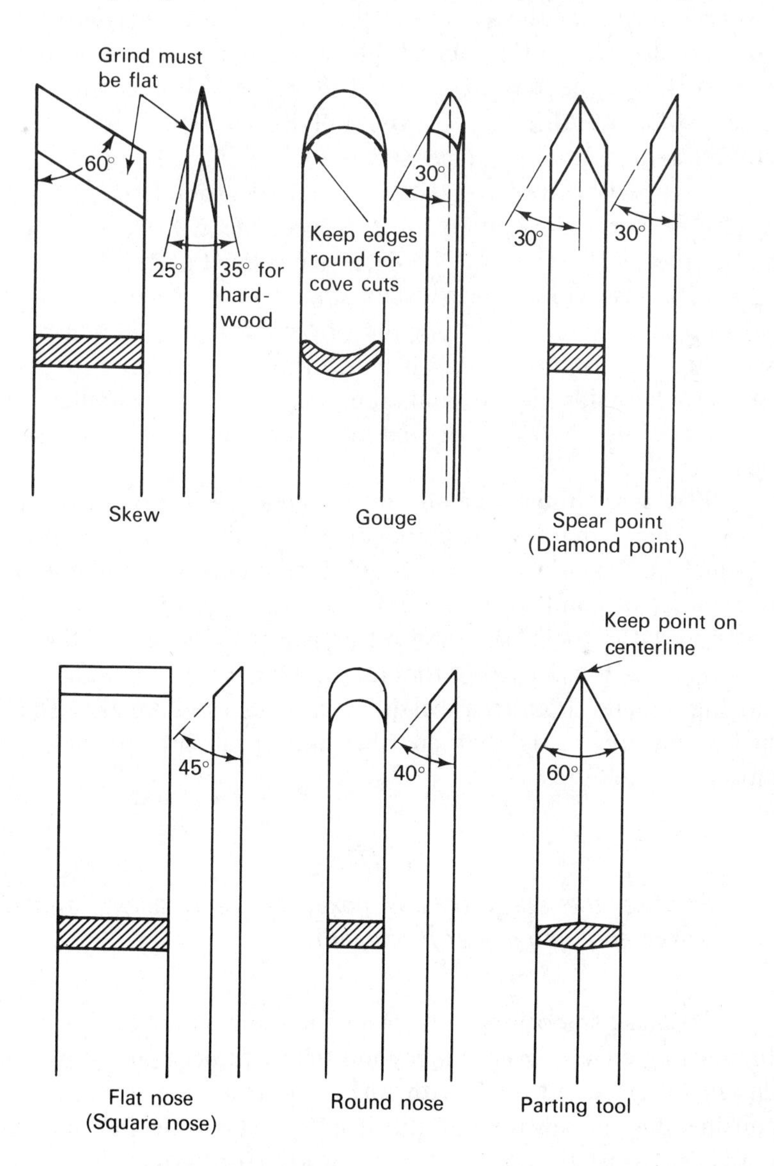


**FIGURE 6-9** / Lathe cutting tools and grinding angles.

is also used to *part* or cut off the workpiece and to square ends and shoulders; thus, it cuts straight into or through the workpiece. The parting tool is held with the narrow edge of the blade on the tool rest with the point of the tool above the centerline. It is fed into the workpiece so that the surface of the workpiece travels just under the cutting edge for cutting operations, or the cutting edge is pointed at the workpiece center for scraping operations. For cutting a workpiece off, cut through to about 1/8-inch, stop the lathe, and complete the cut with a hand saw.

The parting tool is a V-shaped chisel ground on two sides at angles of approximately 60°. It is available with 1/8-, 3/16-, and 1/2-inch cutting edges—the 1/8-inch size is most useful.

*Flat nose* chisels, also called *square nose* chisels, are used just prior to sanding for smoothing the workpiece and making it perfectly straight. The flat nose chisel is held firmly against the tool rest with the beveled side down and the scraping edge parallel to the workpiece; it is used for diameter and circumference scraping operations.

Flat nose chisels have one ground edge beveled on one side at an angle of 45°; the edge is perpendicular to the handle. Widths from 1/4-inch to 1-1/4-inches in 1/4-inch increments are available. If you have a set of hand wood chisels in your shop, you can use them as flat nose lathe tools—the only difference is the length of the handle.

The *skew* is a cutting tool used for smoothing cylinders and for cutting square shoulders, beads, V-grooves, and tapers. The skew makes finishing cuts that are the smoothest cuts possible with a chisel.

### NOTE

***Practice the steps of this next paragraph several times before applying power to the lathe.***

To make smoothing cuts, place the skew on the tool rest so that the cutting edge is over and beyond the workpiece, and the tool is at an angle of about 60° with the tool rest (the cutting edge is considerably in advance of the handle). The wide flat side of the chisel is against the tool rest and the *toe* (furthermost point on the chisel) is extended out. Now slowly draw the tool back toward you on the tool rest, and simultaneously raise the handle until there is one point of contact between the cutting edge and the workpiece, and the tool begins to cut. The contact point should be about 1/4-inch from the *heel* of the cutting edge. The correct vertical angle of the chisel is the angle where the base of the bevel is just about against the work. Advance the tool along the tool rest to continue the cut. Either the toe or heel of the skew can be used for taking light cuts, but about 1/4-inch from the heel is the best point. Take light cuts. Provide clearances for the cutting edge to prevent burning the tool.

The skew can be used also as a scraping tool. Hold the skew horizontally and firmly against the tool rest with the cutting edge parallel to the workpiece. Take lighter and lighter cuts. This is the easiest method to use until you become more proficient.

To round off corners, place the skew with the narrow heel side on the tool rest. Cut the workpiece with the heel, turning it gradually until the corner is rounded. To smooth shoulders, position the tool in the same manner, but with the handle down. Gradually raise the handle as the heel cuts into the workpiece, until the shoulder is squared and smooth.

The skew is a double ground chisel similar to the flat chisel except that the cutting edge is 60° with respect to the handle. Skews are available in increments of 1/4-inch from 1/4- to 2 inches. General use sizes are 1/2- and 1 inch.

The *spear point* lathe tool, also called a *diamond point*, is a scraping chisel used to delicately *scrape* shallow V-cuts, corners, beads, chamfers, and parallel grooves. It can also be used to mark the workpiece for other operations. Hold the spear point chisel horizontally on the tool rest with the beveled sides down. The spear point chisel has a diamond shaped tip with two beveled edges. Widths of 1/2-, 3/4-, and 1 inch are available; the 1/2-inch size is most often used.

In addition to the tools already described which are designed especially for lathe work, you can also use wood chisels (refer to flat nose), *wood rasps* and *files, molding knives, hand planes*, and *forming tools. Wood rasps* are used for rough work and leave a rough finish. *Files* may be used for beads, coves, and V-grooves. Files work best on hardwoods. Support rasps and files *firmly* against the tool rest (you may need to raise it a bit), and beware of kickbacks from the workpiece catching in the teeth. Keep rasps and files clean (they clog very quickly) by using a file card or wire brush.

*Molding knives* normally used with shaper heads can be used to make designs in the workpiece faster and easier than if a combination of lathe tools are used. Bolt the molding knife firmly to an old chisel, and be sure that the knife cannot move on the old chisel shaft. You can grind a flat area on the shaft to mate with the knife. Use the *scraping* operation rather than the cutting operation to remove material from the workpiece.

*Hand planes* are used as lathe cutting tools to produce a very smooth finish by extending the blade only slightly. Raise the tool rest to the top of the workpiece, and use the rest to support the rear of the plane (Fig. 6-10). Hold the plane on top of the tool rest with the blade on the workpiece; angle the plane at about 45° in the direction of travel of the plane along the workpiece. Keep the plane moving. Your little finger can run along the tool rest to guide the plane for the depth of cut.

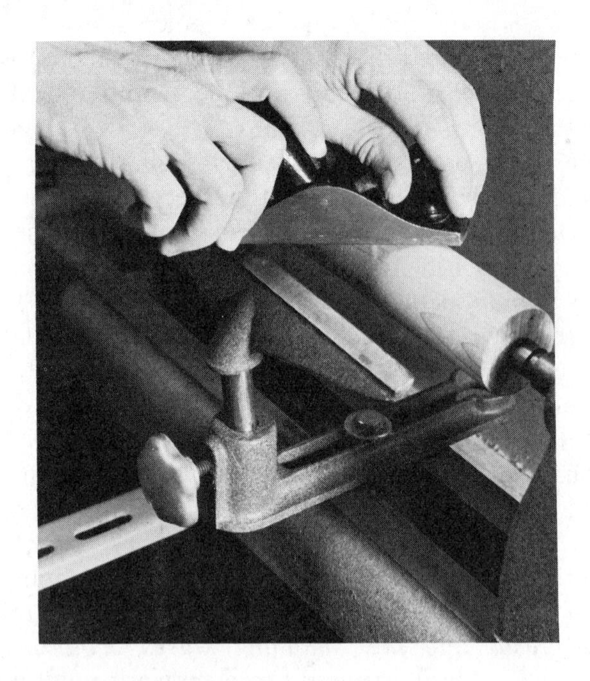

**FIGURE 6-10** / The hand plane produces a very smooth finish.

The *forming tool* is used on straight cylinders and tapers. It produces a rough finish. The open wood fiber clearing holes in the blade help to prevent clogging. Hold the forming tool firmly on top of the tool rest with the blade on the workpiece; angle the tool at about 45° in the direction of travel of the tool along the workpiece. Keep the tool moving.

Turning tools are made from special high alloy steel with precision ground cutting edges. Some turning tools are also tipped with carbide; these tools stay sharp many times longer than ordinary steel tools—and they cost quite a bit more too; but if you plan on a lot of turning, the carbide tipped tools may be for you. Carbide tipped tools are for turning wood, plastic, brass, and aluminum. Turning tool handles are approximately 10 inches long with diameters of 1-1/4-inches.

## 6-3 / OPERATING CONTROLS AND ADJUSTMENTS

Once the workpiece has been installed onto the lathe (Sec. 6-5), there is only one remaining adjustment made during operation of the lathe: positioning of the tool rest. The tool rest moves up and down, 360° around, and in and out. Adjust as follows:

1 / Turn the lathe off.

2 / To raise or lower the tool rest, loosen the tool rest post clamp (Fig. 6-11), raise or lower the tool rest, and retighten the post clamp.

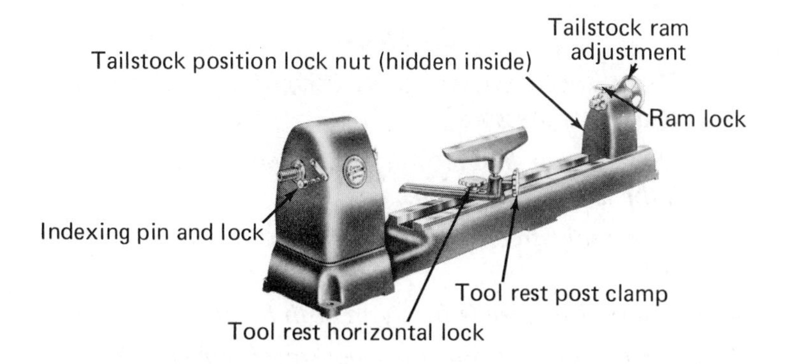


**FIGURE 6-11** / Lathe operating controls and adjustments.

3 / To move the tool rest in or out, along the bed, or in a circular path, loosen the tool rest horizontal lock. Reposition and retighten the lock. The tool rest should not be more than 1/8-inch away from the stock, and it should be parallel to the surface to be cut or scraped.

4 / Spin the workpiece by hand to ensure that there is adequate clearance between the tool rest and the workpiece. Check that all locking devices are secured.

5 / Stand aside and momentarily apply power to the lathe. Presuming all is clear, proceed with the operation procedures of Sec. 6-4.

Another control that is on the lathe is an indexing pin and lock. The pin is pushed through the headstock and into a drilled hole in the flange of the cone pulley, thus locking the position of the pulley and, therefore, the workpiece. The lathe is *not* operated when this pin is inserted in the pulley; instead, other operations such as fluting and reeding are performed on the workpiece.

To fix the headstock spindle, pulley, and workpiece in a stationary position, lift the index lock, insert the index pin into a pulley hole, and relock the pin (spring loaded to a disengaged position).

## 6-4 / OPERATION

Observe the following cautions prior to operating the lathe:

### *CAUTIONS*

*1 / Sharp tools are safe tools because they cut rapidly with little pressure.*

*2 / Don't stand in the line of the workpiece when the lathe is first turned on.*

*3 / Make adjustments and measurements with the lathe off.*

*4 / Hold turning tools firmly in both hands.*

*5 / Stand aside from the workpiece when electrical power is applied in the event that the workpiece is not correctly attached and is thrown from the lathe.*

*Likewise, position your body slightly to the side of the cutting tool in the event the tool catches in the workpiece and is thrown.*

6 / *The tool rest should be placed 1/8-inch from the workpiece and parallel to the surface to be cut and 1/8-inch above the centerline of the workpiece (unless otherwise directed). The tool rest should be used to maximum benefit for tool support in all operations. Reposition the tool rest as necessary as material is removed from the workpiece. Always spin the workpiece by hand to check workpiece clearance and adjustments before applying power to the motor.*

7 / *Observe the general safety precautions in Sec. 1-16.*

There are some general procedures that are practiced for every lathe turning operation; these are covered in this section. Completing a project consists of mounting the workpiece, rough cutting to cylindrical shape, cutting to rough dimensions, final cutting, sanding, finishing, and removal of the workpiece from the lathe. Read this entire *section* before any cutting is begun. Practice each step with electrical power off; then apply power and run the lathe at a low speed. For practice, turn pine wood first. Follow this with harder woods or wood from one of *your* trees (dried).

1 / Center the workpiece and place it in the lathe (refer to Sec. 6-5).

2 / Set the lathe belt/pulley combination for the proper speed (refer to Sec. 6-6).

3 / Position yourself in a natural position in front of the workpiece with one side of your body slightly nearer the lathe than the other side. The cutting tool, when placed on the workpiece, should be just to the side of your body.

4 / To rough cut the workpiece to a cylinder and to rough cut to the approximate dimension (1/8-inch greater than finished dimension), use a gouge and position your hands as shown in Fig. 6-12. The tool rest is 1/8-inch from the workpiece and 1/8-inch above the workpiece centerline.

Turn the lathe on so that the top of the workpiece is rotating toward you. Hold the gouge firmly with the palm down and fingers wrapped around the gouge. The heel of your hand runs along the tool rest and guides the tool. The hand on the handle guides the angle of the tool. Make rough cuts at low speeds (refer to Tab. 6-1) removing waste material slowly. Refer to Sec. 6-7.

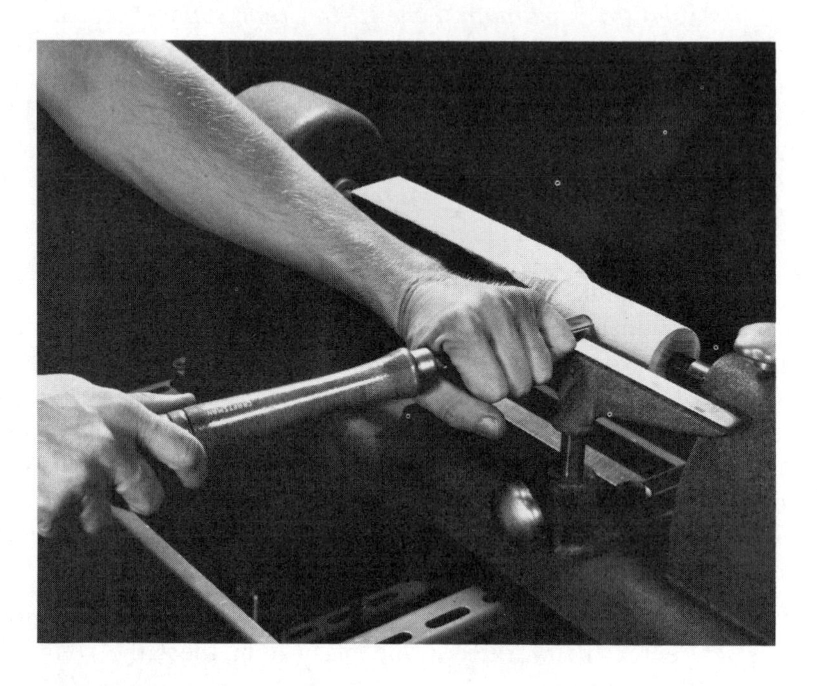

**FIGURE 6-12** / Position your hands as shown for rough cutting with a gouge.

*5* / Use the parting tool to approximate depths of cut at strategic points along the workpiece design. Refer to Sec. 6-8.

*6* / Cut from a larger diameter toward a smaller diameter on tapered cuts. Cut from the center of the workpiece toward one end and then toward the other end. Make sure you don't make any cuts to a depth likely to risk hitting the headstock or tailstock centers. Workpiece materials should allow sufficient extra length on each end for the centers. The material around the centers should only be cut to a rough cylinder to reduce the probability of vibrations. Cut from the center toward the ends and roll the tool off of the ends. Never start at an end because of the danger of the tool catching on the workpiece.

7 / Don't let the tool tip get so hot that the cutting edge is burned. If necessary, cool the tool frequently.

8 / Refer to the following sections to make the required type of cut:

| *Cut* | *Section* |
|---|---|
| rough | 6-7 |
| size | 6-8 |
| smoothing a cylinder | 6-9 |
| cutting a shoulder or end | 6-10 |
| cutting V-grooves | 6-11 |
| cutting beads | 6-12 |
| cutting rounded grooves | 6-13 |

9 / To finish cut, hold the chisel as shown in Fig. 6-13. Hold the palm of your hand up and let the side of your index finger act as a guide along the tool rest. Use light force and a lot of control. Take thin cuts to remove stock slowly. When you remove stock too quickly, the tool has a tendency to *dig* into the workpiece; this may require a lot of rework.

10 / When the finishing cuts are completed, the workpiece is sandpapered with abrasive strips to give it extreme smoothness (Fig. 6-14). Hold sandpaper strips with light pressure against the workpiece which should be revolving at a high speed. Don't hold the abrasive strips in one position; move them back and forth. Use progressively finer abrasive grits ending up with steel wool. Use small pieces of steel wool and be extremely careful as it has a tendency to catch in and wrap around the workpiece. If a motor reversing switch is available, try running the workpiece in the opposite direction for a smoother finish.

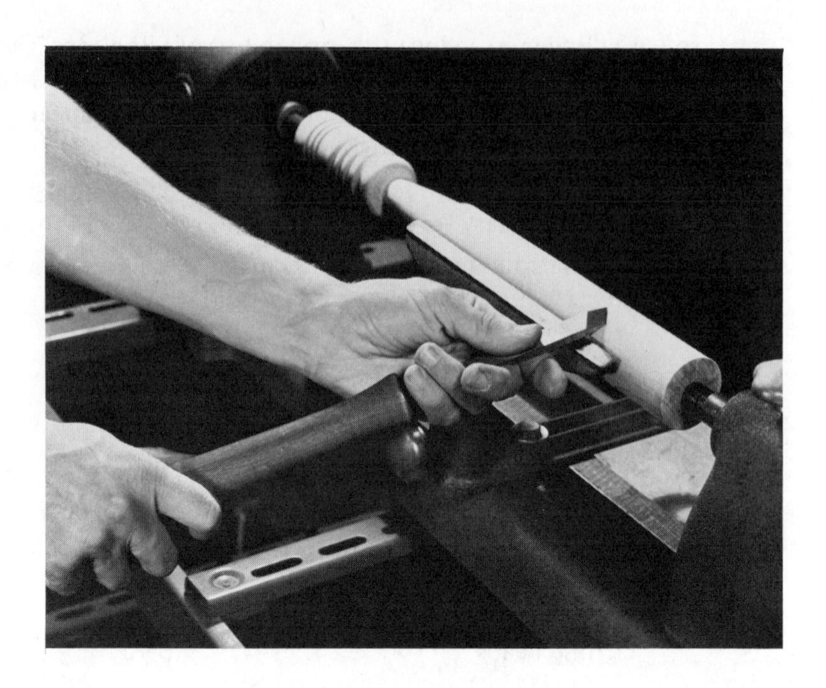

**FIGURE 6-13** / Chisels are held in your hands as shown for finish cuts.

11 / Stains and waxes can be applied (Fig. 6-15) while the workpiece is spinning at a slow speed. Apply a little stain or wax to a cloth and hold this against the workpiece. Too saturated a cloth will cause the stain or wax to be thrown from the workpiece in a spray. Stop the lathe for staining or polishing square portions of the workpiece.

## *6-5* / CENTERING SPINDLE AND FACEPLATE WORKPIECES

The workpiece must be properly centered to reduce vibration and chattering. Centers can be readily located on squared-off workpiece ends of square, circular, or irregular shaped stock. To locate the center of a square piece of stock for either spindle or faceplate turnings, simply draw diagonals (Fig. 6-16) from the corners; the intersection is the center.

The center of a circular workpiece is easily located with a jig as shown in Fig. 6-16. Cut an L-shaped right angle piece from 3/4-inch

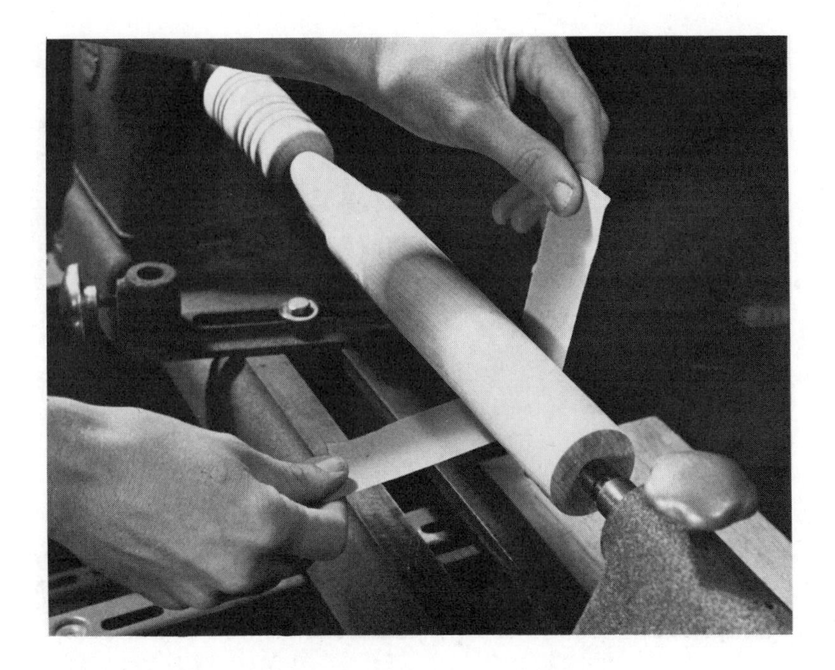

**FIGURE 6-14** / Sanding is done with abrasive strips; use finer and finer grits and finally steel wool for extremely smooth finishes.

scrap with legs about 6 inches long. Locate an 8 inch vertical member directly through the center of the L (at 45°); glue and screw this piece on. To locate the center of the stock, simply place it into the L and draw a line on the stock using the vertical member of the jig as a guide. Rotate the stock about 90° and draw another line; the intersection is the center.

The center of an irregular shaped piece of stock is located by drawing a set of lines parallel to the irregular edges across the squared end near the center. Estimate the center of the drawn figure (Fig. 6-16).

When the center of each end of the workpiece is located, use an awl (nail, punch, or ice pick) to make a starting center hole. Then drill a 1/8-inch diameter hole 1/8-inch deep at the center mark to receive the headstock and tailstock centers.

Stand the workpiece on end on your workbench, and with a rubber mallet, drive the point of a spur center into the predrilled hole until the spurs of the center pierce into the workpiece about 1/8-inch. In hardwood or plastic workpieces, it will be necessary to

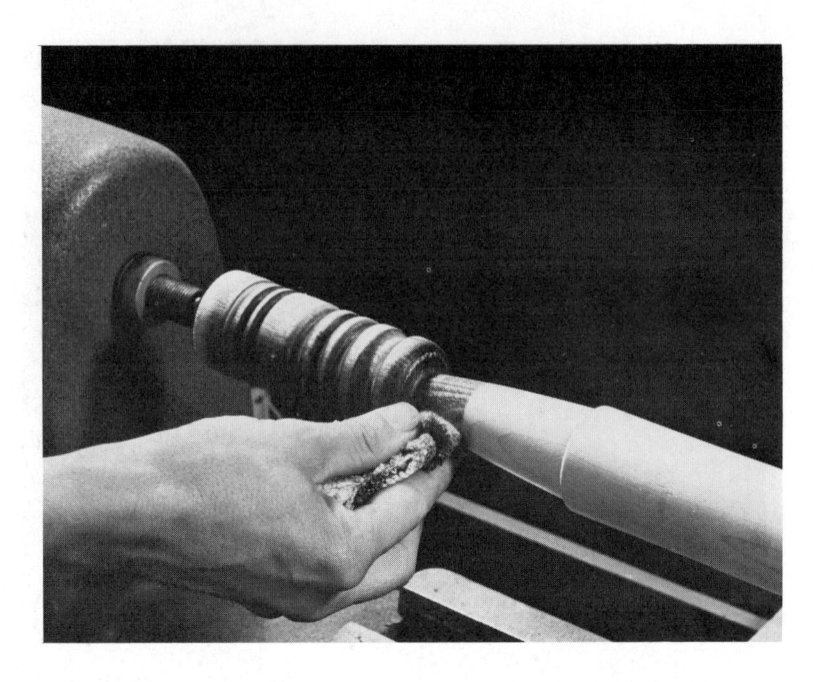

**FIGURE 6-15** / Stains and waxes can be applied while the workpiece is spinning.

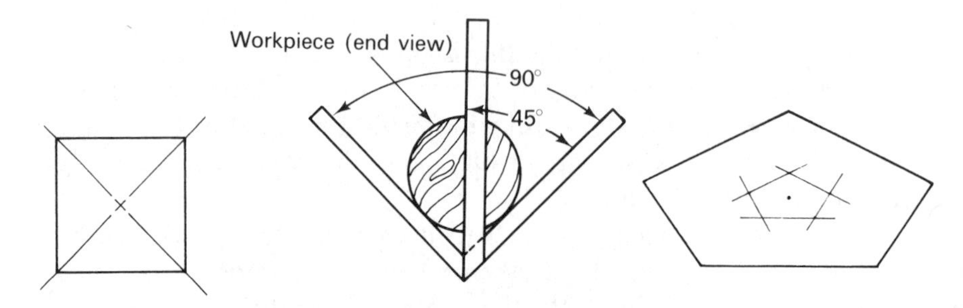


**FIGURE 6-16** / Locating the centers of stock.

make two saw slots perpendicular to each other through the center point and about 1/8-inch deep for the spurs to fit into. Tap the spur center. Be sure that the spur center is in the workpiece straight. Using a scriber, make a mark on one of the spur points (this mark permanently identifies that spur) and a corresponding mark on the workpiece. If the workpiece is removed from the spur center for any reason during turning operations, return the spur center into the same workpiece location by aligning the scribed marks.

Place the spur center (with workpiece attached) into the headstock spindle. *Never* drive the workpiece onto the spur center when the center is in the spindle; this prevents damage to the headstock spindle bearings. With the tailstock ram *retracted*, move the tailstock within 1/2-inch of the workpiece and lock it in place. Extend the ram and center into the predrilled hole in the workpiece. Rotate the workpiece by hand and continue to extend the ram and center until the workpiece is difficult to turn by hand. Now back off the tailstock ram adjustment one-half turn and tighten the ram lock. Place a little beeswax, grease, graphite, or machine oil on the cup center/workpiece interface to reduce friction and subsequent heat. (No lubricant is needed if a *live* ball bearing tailstock center is used.) Lubricate this interface frequently during lathe operation. Rotate the workpiece once again by hand to check for clearance. Stand back from the workpiece and apply electrical power to the motor.

To remove a spindle workpiece from the lathe, loosen the ram lock and rotate the tailstock ram adjustment. Pull the workpiece from the headstock spur center. To remove the headstock spur center from the spindle, insert a rod or dowel from the outboard side into the headstock spindle. Hold the spur center firmly in one hand and tap the center gently with the rod. To remove a tailstock center, simply retract the tailstock ram by rotating the tailstock ram adjustment until the center is free.

A faceplate is attached to a workpiece with flat head screws at least 3/4-inch long. Predrill holes in the workpiece using the faceplate as a template. The workpiece should also have as much waste material as possible removed from the workpiece by sawing with a band or jigsaw.

If the project does not permit screw holes in the workpiece, glue the workpiece to a piece of 1 inch scrap wood. Separation of the workpiece from the scrap wood will be easier if a piece of paper is glued between them. Screw the faceplate to the scrap wood. Screw the faceplate onto the headstock spindle and rotate the workpiece to check for clearance. Stand away from the workpiece and apply electrical power to the motor. Faceplate turnings are made by the scraping operation.

A *screw center* or *screw plate* is used for small workpieces such as knobs and rosettes. Locate the center of the stock, and predrill a hole about 1/2-inch deep and a little smaller than the screw center screw diameter. Place the stock on the screw and screw it on *straight*.

Place the screw center taper into the headstock spindle or onto the spindle as applicable to your lathe.

## 6-6 / TURNING SPEEDS

Table 6-1 suggests approximate lathe spindle speeds for various workpiece sizes and materials. Use the closest lower speed that your pulley arrangement allows. (Refer to Sec. 1-7 on how to determine tool speeds for various sized pulley arrangements. Once you've calculated the various speeds for your lathe, write them on a card affixed to your lathe.) In general, use low speed for all rough cuts, for heavy faceplate turnings, and until the workpiece is cylindrical; higher speeds are for light and finishing work. If the workpiece chatters or vibrates at a given speed, reduce the speed. Larger workpieces are turned at slower speeds for safety.

## 6-7 / ROUGH CUTS

Make rough cuts as follows:

1 / Reduce large spindle and faceplate workpieces on a band saw, if possible.

*CAUTION*

***Do not cut to a depth on either end of the workpiece that approaches the location of the headstock or tailstock centers. Always cut from the center of the workpiece toward the ends; never start at an end.***

2 / Round the complete workpiece first by making shallow cuts with the gouge. Start 2 inches from the tailstock and cut that. Then, starting 3 inches further toward the headstock, work again toward the tailstock. Continue in this manner until you are 2 inches from the headstock. Make this last 2 inch cut toward the headstock.

3 / Once the workpiece is cylindrically shaped, the lathe speed can be increased somewhat. Continue to rough cut until the workpiece is 1/8-inch larger than the final diameter.

Table 6-1
SPEED GUIDE (IN RPM)

| *Diameter of Workpiece (in inches)* | *Initial Cut Speed* | *Shaping Cut Speed* | *Finishing Cut Speed* |
|---|---|---|---|
| wood up to 2 | 900 | 2500 | 4200 |
| 2–4 | 800 | 2300 | 3300 |
| 4–6 | 700 | 1800 | 2300 |
| 6–8 | 700 | 1200 | 1800 |
| 8–10 | 700 | 900 | 1000 |
| wood over 10 | 700 | 700 | 700 |
| plastic to 3 | 2200 | 3100 | 3900 |
| plastic over 3 | 1000 | 1200 | 1700 |
| nonferrous metal to 3 (use carbide tipped tools) | 700 | 1300 | 3100 |

## *6-8* / SIZE CUTS

A *sizing* cut is a "square" groove cut at a workpiece dimension line to a depth of 1/8-inch less than the finished diameter (Fig. 6-17). A number of these grooves are made along the workpiece. A gouge is then used to cut the waste material by "eye gauging" between the grooves to 1/8-inch of the finished diameter. Make sizing cuts as follows:

*1* / Place the parting tool firmly on the tool rest.

*2* / Push the parting tool into the workpiece. Keep the tip pointing just above the centerline of the workpiece.

*3* / Some lathe operators hold the parting tool firmly in one hand and outside calipers in the other so that the groove depth can be gauged as the workpiece is cut. It is safer to use both hands on the parting tool, stopping the lathe before making caliper measurements.

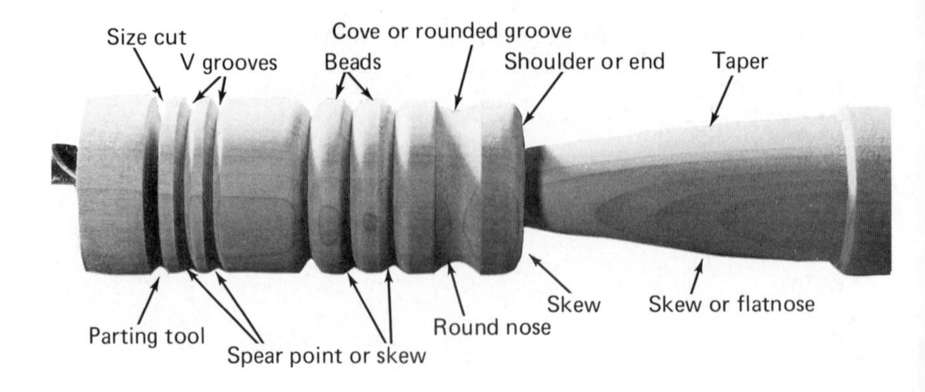


**FIGURE 6-17** / Cuts made on the lathe and the tools to make them with.

## *6-9* / SMOOTHING A CYLINDER

Smooth a cylinder as follows:

*1* / Use the skew to remove about another 3/32-inch of material. Leave 1/32-inch for final sanding. Either the *scraping* or the *cutting* operation can be used.

*2* / The skew provides the smoothest surface possible prior to sanding.

*3* / Smoothing may also be accomplished by use of a rasp, file, or block plane. The finish from rasps and files is slightly rough; a finish with a plane requires little sanding.

## *6-10* / CUTTING A SHOULDER OR END

A shoulder is a perpendicular *side* of a turned section, an end, or the side of a square portion left on the workpiece. Cut shoulders and ends as follows:

*1* / Using the parting tool, cut a groove 1/16-inch from the mark for the shoulder. The groove depth should be 1/8-inch less than the finished dimension.

2 / Remove any excess material with the gouge and smooth this area with the skew.

3 / Use the tip of the toe of the skew to finish the shoulder by removing thin shavings from the side of the shoulder. Cut to the required dimension.

## *6-11* / CUTTING V-GROOVES

Cut V-grooves (Fig. 6-17) as follows:

1 / Make one-half of the groove at a time taking shallow cuts.

2 / Place the skew on the tool rest to act as a pivot point. Using the toe of the skew, push into the workpiece slowly. Do not rotate the skew.

3 / The spear point chisel or a three-sided file may also be used to cut V-grooves. The spear point scrapes rather than cuts the V-groove.

4 / Deep V-grooves can be started with the parting tool and finished with the spear point.

## *6-12* / CUTTING BEADS

Cut beads (Fig. 6-17) as follows:

1 / To *cut* a bead, use the skew to make a vertical V at the point where the curved parts of the bead come together.

2 / Cut the V to the desired depth for the beads.

3 / Place the skew at a right angle to the workpiece to round off the bead. Rotate the skew toward the heel in a series of steps. Use the heel to do the cutting.

4 / To *scrape* a bead, use the spear point chisel. Hold the chisel firmly against the tool rest and slowly round off the bead.

## *6-13* / CUTTING ROUNDED GROOVES

Cut rounded grooves (Fig. 6-17) as follows:

*1* / Use the round nose chisel to scrape round grooves.

*2* / Widen the grooves into rounded valleys by pivoting the round nose chisel on the tool rest.

## *6-14* / WOODS FOR TURNING

Although many woods are suitable for turning, there are some woods more suitable in some applications than others. Well seasoned fruitwoods, pine, maple, and walnut turn beautifully. Ash and hickory are good handle material. Most oaks are very attractive, but mahogany is preferable for turnings of glued up pieces. Beech is brittle; fir and hemlock splinter and, if coarse grained, are difficult to sand smooth.

## *6-15* / MEASURING TOOLS

Three measuring tools are used in turning projects on the lathe: scale (ruler), inside caliper, and outside caliper. It's a safe practice to stop the lathe before using any of these measuring devices. Place the ruler next to the workpiece, and make a line about 1/2-inch long on the circumference at the measured locations. When the workpiece is spinning, the 1/2-inch mark will show lightly. Darken the mark by holding a pencil against the tool rest at the mark location, and press the pencil lightly against the spinning workpiece.

Calipers (Fig. 6-18) have curved legs that are bowed inward to obtain *outside* measurements and are bowed outward to obtain inside measurements. Calipers are used to obtain cylinder diameter measurements. They are particularly useful when using the parting tool to set workpiece diameters.

The legs of the calipers are held taut by a strong flexible bow spring. A screw with a special knurled nut allows for making rapid, accurate settings of the spacing between the hardened leg points. Tool lengths are from 3 to 12 inches; 7 inches is the correct size for general use.

To set calipers to a particular dimension, place one leg firmly on the one inch mark of a scale. Close the other leg to a measurement about 1/4-inch *less than* the desired dimension; then *back the nut off* allowing the leg to open until it is set at the proper dimension. Operate the dividers or calipers in this same method to set the legs to

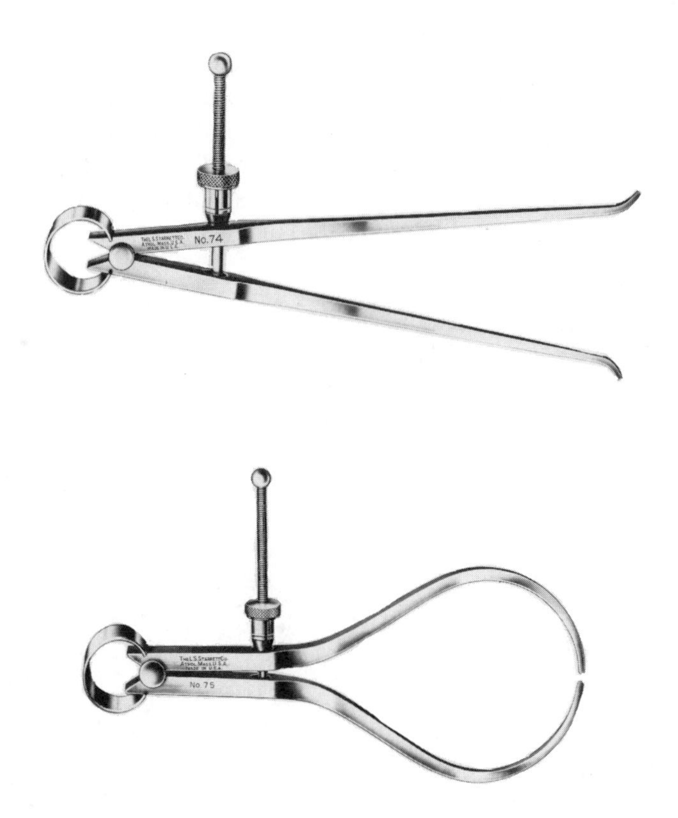


**FIGURE 6-18** / Inside calipers and outside calipers are used to measure workpieces turned on a lathe.

an unknown measurement on a workpiece or drawing. Then place one leg on the one inch mark on a scale, and make the dimension reading where the other leg meets the scale. Subtract one inch from the dimension to obtain the distance between the legs.

Remember that when you are using the gouge to rough the workpiece to a workable size, the workpiece dimension (and hence the caliper dimension) should be 1/8-inch larger than the finished size. With a scale, set the dimension on the calipers, and then slip the calipers over (or inside) the workpiece to compare the workpiece to the caliper dimension.

## *6-16* / ACCESSORIES

There are numerous accessories for the lathe which can be categorized into areas: accessories used for wood and plastic application; accessories for metal cutting; accessories to expand the applications of the lathe; and accessories applicable to all operations. Lathe turning tools themselves are considered accessories (Sec. 6-2).

Accessories used for wood, plastic, and light metal turning (Fig. 6-19) include bed extensions, centers, faceplates, tool rests, floor stands for tool rests, and a knockout bar. Bed extensions come in 12

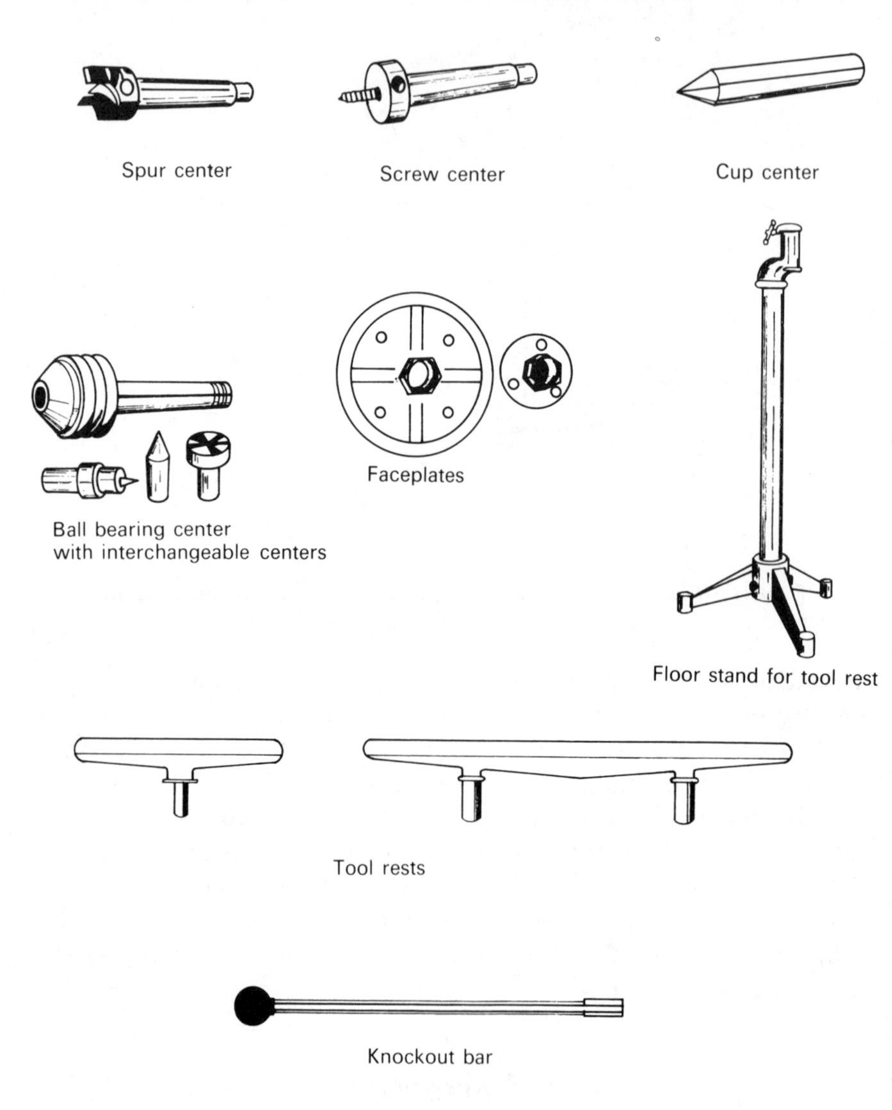


**FIGURE 6-19** / Accessories used for wood, plastic, and light metal turning.

and 24 inch lengths. One or more sections can be bolted onto the tool stand at the end of the lathe bed. Be sure the extension is aligned properly.

Two types of centers are available for the headstock (headstock centers are called "live" centers): spur (also called *drive*) and screw center. The spur center has a center point and four spurs for gripping into the workpiece. The spurs of the center are driven into the end of a soft workpiece or are placed into sawed slots in hardwood or plastic. Spur centers are a part of original equipment. The screw center holds small wooden workpieces such as knobs and cups. Both the spur and screw centers have Morse taper shanks. Instead of buying a screw center, you can screw a piece of 1 inch by 6 inch diameter wood to a 6 inch faceplate. Turn the wood to shape and balance it. Insert a number 8 two inch flat head wood screw through the exact center of the wood, leaving about 1 inch exposed for mounting small workpieces.

Two centers that fit the tailstock are the *cup* center and the *ball bearing* center. The cup center, usually supplied with the lathe, has no moving parts; the center pin can be replaced. Ball bearing centers prevent high heat buildup and subsequent burning of the workpiece because the center rotates with the workpiece. This center must be used for low melting temperature plastics; it is also recommended for high speed turning. Both centers have Morse taper shanks.

Faceplates are circular disks with threaded hubs for mounting workpiece stock for bowls, lamp bases, etc., to the headstock spindle. The disk hub has right hand threads for inboard mounting or left hand threads for outboard turning. Some faceplates attach with setscrews. Faceplates are available with 3 inch or 6 inch diameters. The 3 inch diameter faceplate sometimes has spurs and a removable center. Fasten the faceplate to the workpiece with at least 3 or 4 wood screws of 3/4-inch length.

In addition to the tool rest supplied with the lathe, you may want some other tool rests. Standard tool rests of 4, 6, and 12 inches are available commercially or you may want to weld a flat piece of iron to a solid rod—use your existing tool rest as a pattern for angle and rod diameter. A 24 inch tool rest is made for tool support along a long workpiece; two tool rest support bases are required. A 90° offset tool rest is used for faceplate turnings over a bed gap (Fig. 6-3). A tool rest floor stand is used to hold the tool rest for outboard turning.

Knockout bars are used to remove centers from the headstock spindle. Hold the center firmly in your right hand; insert the bar through the outboard side of the headstock spindle, and gently tap the center until it comes out. (Use a wooden 5/16-inch diameter dowel instead of buying a knockout bar.) Incidentally, tailstock centers are removed "automatically" by full retraction of the tailstock ram.

Accessories (Fig. 6-20) used to convert a wood lathe to a light metal lathe are: *compound slide rest, tool holder, boring bars, tool bits, 60° plain center,* and *jaw chucks*. The compound slide rest fits onto the lathe ways. Feed screws move the tool holder with its associated boring bar or tool bit into the workpiece for shaving away material. Boring bars are used to internally turn large diameter holes. Tool bits are made of high speed steel and include rough, finishing, left corner, and right corner bits.

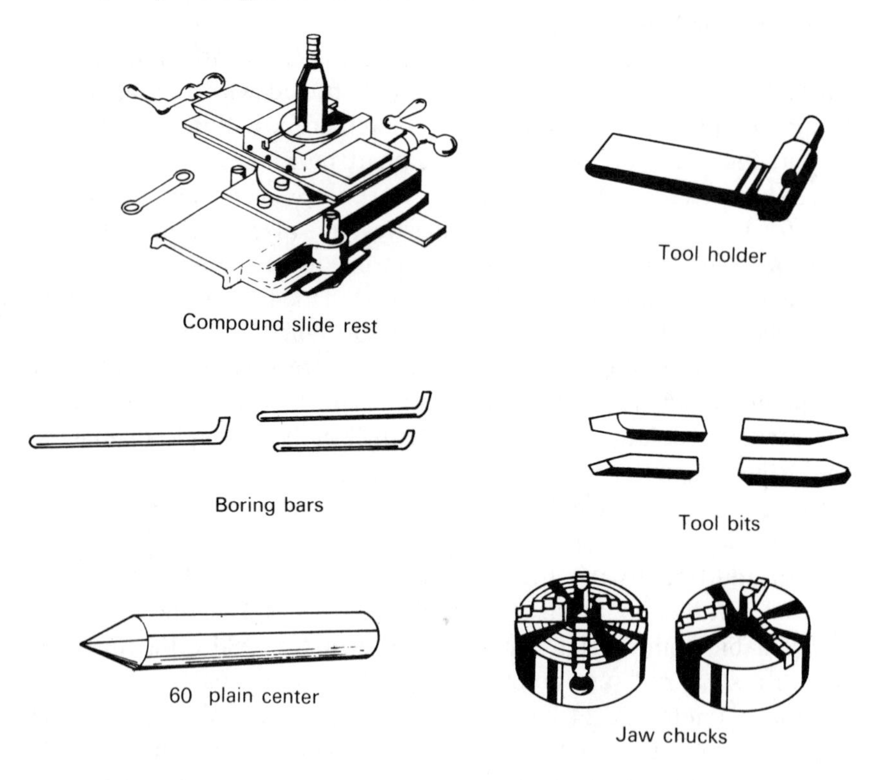


**FIGURE 6-20** / Accessories used to convert a wood lathe to a light metal lathe.

Three and four jaw chucks are available for attachment to the headstock spindle. The three jaw chuck is universal and has three internal and three external jaws. The four jaw chuck is an independent type chuck. There is one set of jaws that are reversible for internal or external work.

Accessories that expand the applications of the lathe are *sanding disks, sanding drums, buffing wheels, wire wheels, emery wheels, geared chuck,* and a *wood turning duplicator* (Fig. 6-21). *Sanding disks* are about 8 inches in diameter and mount onto the threaded headstock spindle. Abrasive disks are mounted to the disk with disk adhesive. Run the disks at the second lowest lathe speed. A sanding table with a surface up to about 12 by 12 inches can easily be constructed of 3/4-inch plywood to fit on top of the lathe ways. The top of the table should be even with the center of the spindle. A block and bolt assembly should be placed underneath so the table can be held firmly to the ways. Miter slots add to the versatility of the table.

Instead of buying a sanding disk, you might also turn one from wood on the faceplate. Attach abrasive paper to the wood with disk adhesive.

Various sizes of sanding drums mount by the use of an adapter to the headstock spindle. Sanding drums are expandable in size to accept and hold replaceable sleeves. The drums are used to sand irregularly curved shapes.

You can turn various cylindrical or tapered wooden drums on the lathe. Adhere abrasive paper to the drum with disk adhesive.

*Buffing wheels, wire wheels,* and *emery wheels* are fitted onto an arbor that screws onto the lathe headstock spindle. Buffing wheels polish and clean metal parts, wire wheels remove rust and burrs, and emery wheels grind. Use a workpiece support (such as the tool rest or sanding table) as necessary with any of these wheels. Without a support, workpieces should be held tightly in the hands or a clamp and then held against the lower quarter of the wheel so that the wheel runs off the work. Do not operate the wheels at any speed greater than that specified on the wheel. Buffing is done at next to the highest speed. Wheels come in diameters up to 6 inches and have 1/2- or 5/8-inch arbor mounting holes. Arbors designed for inboard mounting on the headstock spindle have right hand threads; left hand threads are for outboard mounting.

The *geared chuck* is used for horizontal drilling operations. It

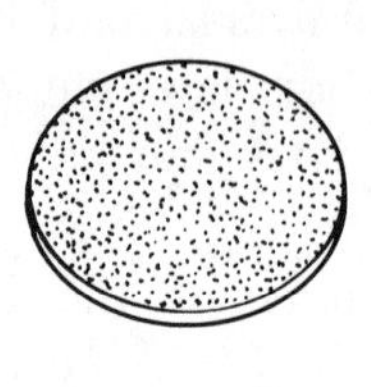

Sanding disk

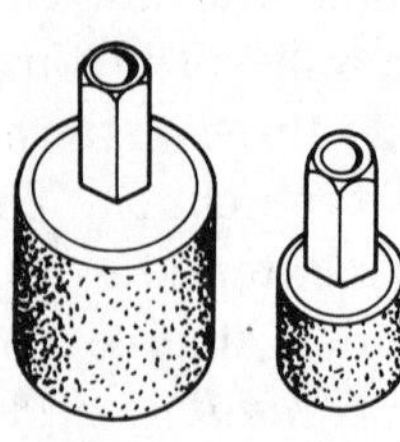

Sanding drums

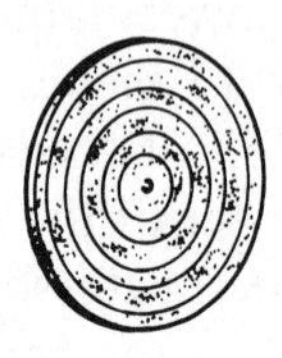

Buffing wheel

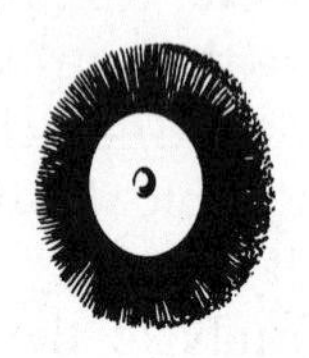

Wire wheel

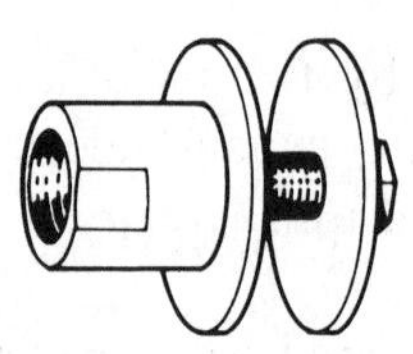

Screw-on arbor

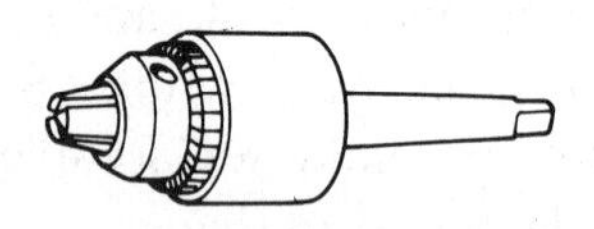

Geared chuck

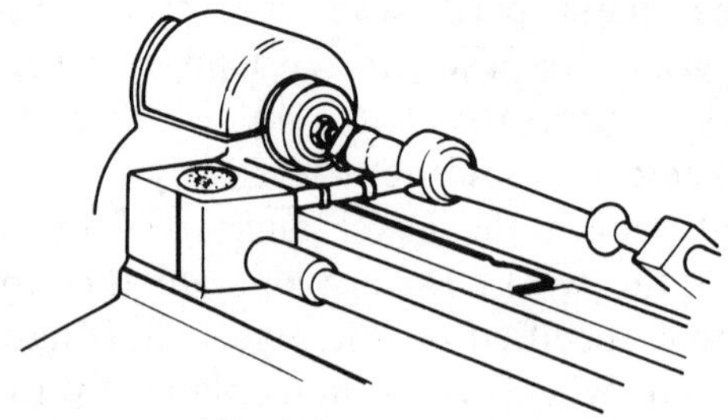

Wood turning duplicator

**FIGURE 6-21** / Accessories that expand the use of the lathe.

has a 0 to 1/2-inch drill size capacity and a Morse taper shank for mounting into the headstock spindle; some chucks mount onto the spindle threads. Small nonferrous metal workpieces such as brass and aluminum are easily mounted in a chuck. Use carbide tipped tools for metal turning operations.

*Wood turning duplicators* are for reproducing complex wood turnings. The wood turning duplicator saves valuable time and eliminates costly mistakes. You can purchase a duplicator commercially or you can build one yourself (Sec. 6-18).

Accessories that are suitable to all applications are the *switch rod* and the *counter shaft unit*. The switch rod provides a mechanical link to the motor on-off switch to enable the lathe operator to control the motor from an operating position. This is also a safety feature.

A *counter shaft unit*, also called a speed reducer, is for converting the 4 speeds of the lathe as determined by the drive and driven cone pulleys to a 16 speed lathe. The speed range is approximately 250 to 3450 rev/min. The counter shaft unit consists of hangers, line shaft, pulleys, V-belts, and collars, all in one kit.

## *6-17* / CALIBRATION AND MAINTENANCE

Maintenance of the lathe consists of lubrication and alignment of the tailstock center (if adjustable) with the headstock center. There are no calibrations. Lathe tools should be kept sharp at all times.

Ball bearing spindle mounts are usually sealed and require no lubrication. Bronze bearing chambers should be filled with light machine oil through holes in the headstock at intervals recommended by the manufacturer. Occasionally place a few drops of oil on the tailstock ram assembly and wipe the ways with an oily rag. Rather than wipe oil on the ways, you may wax them.

The tailstocks on some lathes have a threaded cross shaft underneath between the ways. The cross shaft is adjusted to align the ram center with the headstock center. Slide the tailstock down to the headstock. Using a screwdriver, adjust the threaded cross shaft.

## *6-18* / HINTS AND KINKS

To limit depth of cut of a lathe tool when rounding a cylinder, for example, clamp a small block of wood to the lathe tool so that it hits the top of the tool rest and prevents further penetration into the workpiece. The block should be tapered on one side to the angle of the tool rest taper.

Patterns or templates for single pieces or for duplicate turnings can be drawn to full scale on cardboard or thin wood. It is only necessary to draw one side (but the whole drawing gives you a better idea of what the final workpiece will look like). Cut the pattern out on one side; the *scrap* piece is your template. Hold up the template to the workpiece and mark significant points along the workpiece. As the cutting is continued, you can hold the template to the workpiece to determine where more cutting is required.

A *diameter board* is another method to use in setting up for duplicate turnings. The diameter board is used rather than resetting calipers to frequently used diameters. The diameter board has semicircular cutouts along its edge; each semicircle corresponds to the diameter of a certain location(s) along the workpiece. In use, the semicircular cutouts of the diameter board are placed around the workpiece at the given sizing cuts to check the diameters.

The use of a *template semaphore jig* is another method of making duplicate turnings. The jig is placed behind and parallel to the workpiece that is between the lathe centers. The semaphores are "arms" that are cut to length and spin on the jig. The arms are set on top of the spinning workpiece. When sufficient material is removed from the workpiece, the semaphores fall off the workpiece (and around the jig) indicating that the workpiece diameter at the location of the semaphore is correct.

You can make special lathe cutting tools from old files. Spear points and wide flat nose chisels are the easiest. Grind cutting edges onto the file; cool the file frequently in water to prevent overheating. Small files make ideal cutting tools for small lathe workpiece turning. Large wooden handles can be spun on the lathe.

Long slender spindles often vibrate during turning. To eliminate some of this vibration, make a *steady rest* as shown in Fig. 6-22; two models are shown. The first is cut from 3/4-inch plywood. The base of the V is cut at a distance exactly equal to the vertical distance from the way to the center point. Clamp the device to the lathe bed so that the turned cylindrical surface is just about touching the V with no tool pressure on the workpiece. When cutting pressure is applied, the workpiece will be supported by the steady rest.

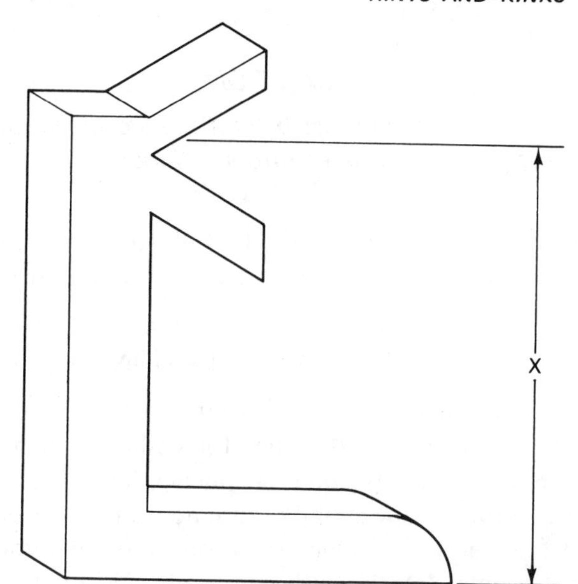
X
$\frac{3}{4}$ in. plywood
The X distance is equal to the exact vertical distance from the way to the cup center tip

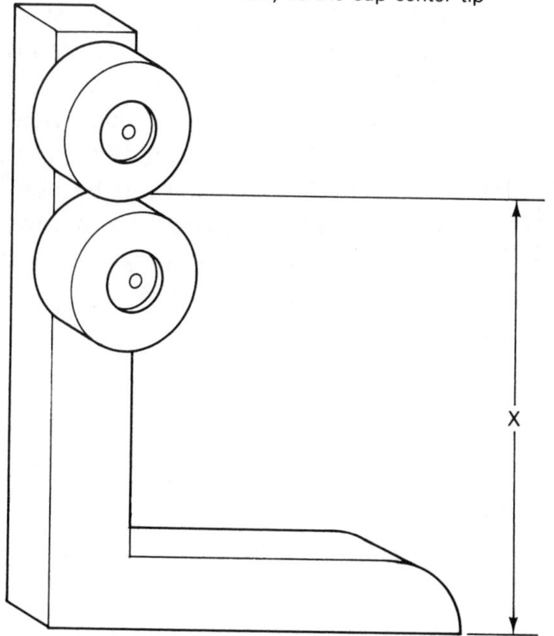
X

**FIGURE 6-22** / Two types of home workshop steady rests you can build.

### CAUTION

*Do not place a steady rest behind the workpiece until the workpiece has been shaped into a cylinder.*

Instead of the V shown in the first illustration of Fig. 6-22, you may use two roller skate wheels bolted to a piece of wood as shown.

## 6-19 / INSTALLATION

The lathe is mounted on a power tool stand or bench so that the height at the spindle is at the operator's elbows when his arms are down at his sides—this is about 42 inches high. The table can be located in a corner of the shop because no room is needed behind or on the sides of the lathe. (One exception to this is if you are turning a very large faceplate on the outboard headstock spindle.)

Make sure that the stand for the lathe bed is level and that the bed itself is level. This will prevent twisting of the lathe bed. Use shims where required and bolt the lathe to the stand. Mount the motor behind or below. Rigid mounting is okay, or a floating motor rail can be used to aid in speed changes. The headstock spindle rotates in a counterclockwise direction when viewed from the tailstock. Select two cone pulleys with four steps each (refer to Sec. 1-7). A speed reducer or jack shaft can also be used. A reversing electrical switch may be added if you have a reversible motor. Reverse direction is often desirable for sanding operations.

# chapter seven

# RADIAL ARM SAW

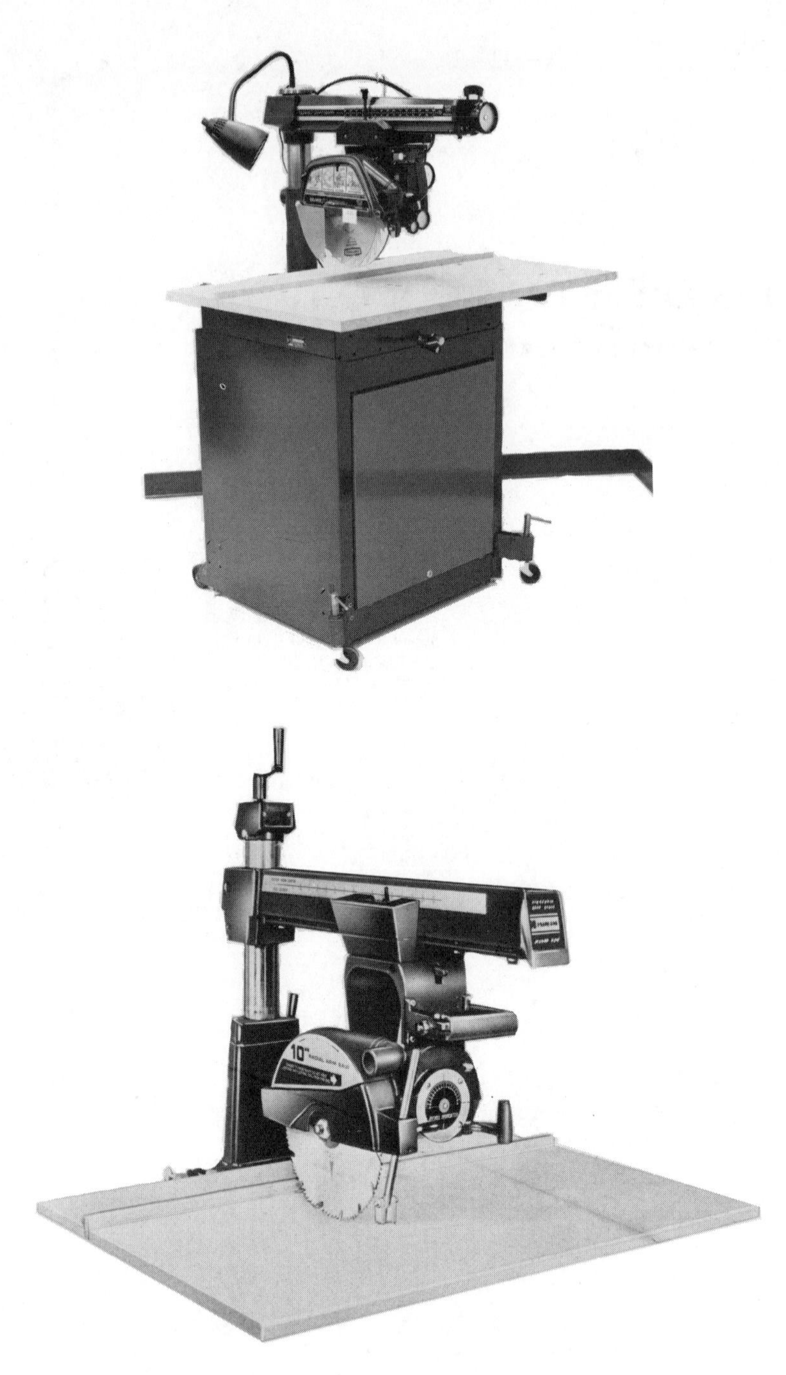

**FIGURE 7-1** / The radial arm saw is the most versatile power tool for the home workshop; it is the first bench power tool you should acquire.

The first operation performed on a workpiece is the cutting of the workpiece to size. To do this accurately, quickly, and conveniently, a bench saw is needed. You can choose either the radial arm saw or the table saw described in Chap. 11. The radial arm saw costs a little more, but it is worth the difference.

Both the radial arm saw and the table saw perform about the same functions. Both saws can make crosscut, miter, rip, bevel, and compound saw cuts. With accessories, both saws can shape, dado, and sand workpieces. With other accesories, the radial arm saw can perform additional functions that the table saw cannot perform: routing, surface planing, and drilling. Thus, the radial arm saw is more versatile than the table saw.

The blade of the radial arm saw is *above* the workpiece, whereas the blade of the table saw is *below* the workpiece (refer to Figs. 7-1 and 11-1). The fact that the blade on the radial arm saw is above the workpiece is the greatest advantage of the radial arm saw. With the cutting done from the top of the workpiece, you can *see* what is being cut–it is easier to follow the pattern line. This results in more accurately cut workpieces with less scrap from inaccurately cut lumber.

Because of its versatility, the radial arm saw is recommended as the first bench power tool for your workshop. The basic saw can cut *any* angle you'll ever need to cut and do the cutting exceptionally fast, accurately, and conveniently. Because workpieces are placed lengthwise on the work table for *both* the crosscut and the ripping operations, the radial arm saw can be located conveniently against a wall in your workshop.

## 7-1 / DEFINITIONS OF CUTS

Before the radial arm saw can be further discussed, it is necessary to define the following *cuts* that are sawed on this saw (and on the table saw as well): *crosscut, miter, rip, bevel,* and *compound.* A crosscut is a cut that is made *across* the grain of the wood. Most often, the crosscut is at 90° to the length of the workpiece. Cutting off the end of a piece of a 2 by 4 inch by 8 foot piece of lumber is a *crosscut* operation. Crosscuts are made by holding the workpiece against the fence and drawing the blade across the table and workpiece.

A *miter* cut is one that is at an angle to the length of the workpiece, but the blade remains perpendicular to the table. When the miter cut is at 0°, a crosscut is made. A miter cut is made by placing the workpiece against the fence, positioning the radial support arm at some angle between 90° left and 90° right, and pulling the blade across the table and workpiece.

A *rip* cut is made along the grain of the workpiece; the workpiece is "ripped" apart. In this operation, the blade is turned 90° (left or right) from the *crosscut position* to the *rip* position, and the carriage is locked into a fixed position on the radial support arm. Then the workpiece is fed through the blade using a fence as a guide. In the 90° left position (the blade nearer the rear), the radial arm saw is configured in the position known as the *in-rip* position; 90° right (the blade nearer the front) is the *out-rip* position. In the out-rip position, the blade can be located the farthest *out* (distance) from the column. In either rip position, the blade is always parallel to the fence.

A *bevel* cut is a cut at an angle to the surface of the workpiece when the angle is not 90° (perpendicular). Thus, the blade is at any angle other than 90° to the surface of the workpiece. A bevel cut can be made across the grain (crosscut) or with the grain (rip cut), but the blade is tilted. To make this cut, place the saw for either a crosscut or a rip cut and also tilt (bevel) the blade. The complete blade, arbor, and motor tilt together within the carriage assembly from 0° (perpendicular to the workpiece surface) to 90° in one direction (blade parallel to the table) to about 75° in the opposite direction (the blade is again nearly parallel to the workpiece, but it is near the radial arm instead of down near the table).

A *chamfer* cut is a bevel cut along the edge of a workpiece; the cut does not pass through the bottom surface of the workpiece. A *compound* cut is a cut that includes *both* a miter cut and bevel cut or a rip cut and a bevel cut.

By studying both your operator's manual and this book, you will become an expert in the complete use of this versatile power tool in a few evenings. Read–study–and saw plenty of scrap wood! You'll be able to accomplish operations you'd previously thought impossible.

## 7-2 / DESCRIPTION AND MAJOR PARTS

Figure 7-2 illustrates the major parts of the radial arm saw. The *motor,* sold as an integral part of the radial arm saw, is mounted in the *yoke.* The motor shaft is a directly driven, threaded, *arbor* that holds and turns the *blade* or other accessory. The arbor is usually 5/8-inch diameter with a threaded end (left hand thread) for the arbor nut. The *size* of the radial arm saw is determined by the diameter of the maximum size blade that can be placed on the arbor; sizes for the home workshop are 9, 10, and 12 inches with the 10 inch probably the most common size. Motors for the 9 and 10 inch sizes are 1 or 1-1/2-hp while a 2 hp motor is used for the 12 inch model. Input power is 120 volts on the smaller horsepower motors and 240 volts on the larger motors. Some motors can be used on either 120 or 240 volts by making simple wiring changes within the motor (directions supplied by the manufacturer). The motor arbor turns at 3450 rev/min clockwise as viewed in Fig. 7-2. Some motors also have auxiliary spindles that revolve at 3450 and 20,000 rev/min for accessories such as routing bits and drill chucks. Auxiliary spindles are located on the opposite side of the motor from the arbor and rotate in the opposite direction.

As a safety feature, many radial arm saw motors have braking devices within that brake the revolving cutter, eliminating coasting when electrical power is removed. Some brakes are automatic, and others are manual requiring the operator to push the manual brake to stop the blade almost instantly.

The blade is protected by a *blade guard* that attaches to the motor housing. The guard is removable and adjustable in position around part of the blade; however, keep the blade guard in position *whenever possible* because it protects your hands from entering the cutting area, and it also aids in preventing the workpiece and sawdust

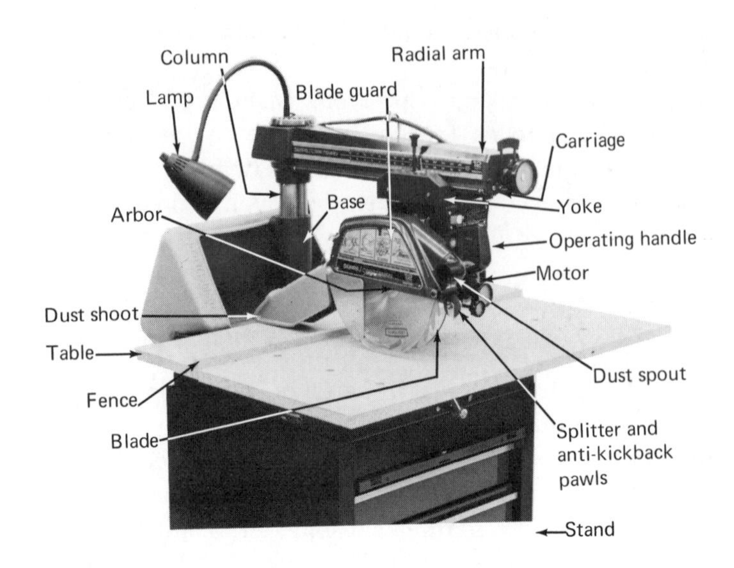


**FIGURE 7-2** / Major parts of the radial arm saw.

from being thrown or "kicked" at you. A dust spout in the blade guard directs the dust to exit from the side.

The *splitter and anti-kickback pawl* assembly is attached to the blade guard. Its position is adjustable. The splitter rides in the saw kerf during rip cut operations and prevents the kerf from closing on the blade which would cause the blade to bind in the workpiece and result in "kickback" of the workpiece at the operator. The anti-kickback pawls are pivoted metal tongues that allow the workpiece to pass through in one direction, but the tongues (pawls) dig into the workpiece if it attempts to move in the opposite direction. Thus, the pawls aid in preventing workpiece kickback. The splitter and anti-kickback pawl assembly is used for all ripping operations and should be placed in a lowered position to act as a partial blade guard during crosscut operations.

The *yoke* is a mounting frame that holds the motor to the *carriage.* The yoke permits the motor and blade to tilt for bevel cuts. The yoke rotates 90° (a full 360° is possible) in the carriage assembly from a crosscut position (Fig. 7-2) to a rip position (the yoke is *not* placed at any intermediate angles between crosscut and rip–it is in one or the other position). The *operating handle* is a part of the yoke and is used to *pull* the cutter (blade) through the workpiece.

The *carriage* supports the yoke on the radial arm. Sealed roller bearing guides in the carriage carry it over the length of the radial arm. The carriage can be locked in a fixed position. (The carriage is always locked for rip cuts, but never for crosscuts. It may be locked for operations with some accessories.)

A callout for a *head* is not identified on Fig. 7-2. However, the head is considered as incorporating the carriage, yoke, operating handle, motor, arbor, auxiliary spindles, cutting tool (blade), blade guard, and the splitter and anti-kickback pawls. Thus, it is correct to state that the head is moved from the rear of the radial arm to the front of the radial arm for crosscutting, etc.

The *radial arm* supports the head and allows the head to travel from one end to the other along the arm. The radial arm rotates 90° left and 90° right to set miter angles. In-rip and out-rip scales are along the radial arm to indicate by means of a pointer on the carriage the in-rip and out-rip distances from the fence when the fence is located at the rear of the table. (Some radial arm saws have two in-rip and two out-rip scales–one set is used when the fence is located *behind* the table, and one set is used when the fence is located *between* the rear sections of the table.)

Figure 7-2 illustrates a radial arm saw having one radial arm; Fig. 7-3 illustrates a saw with two radial arms termed the upper arm and the lower arm. Because of the configuration, the two arm saw has the advantage of additional, usable table workpiece support space when mitered cuts are made.

The *column* supports the radial arm. The column raises and lowers in the *base* that attaches the column to the saw structure (the base plate or the tool *stand*). The *lamp* is on a flexible gooseneck for positioning the light as required (the lamp is an accessory on most models). The *dust shoot* collects dust from the blade guard.

The *table* is a workpiece support made of two or four pieces of 3/4- or 1 inch plywood, masonite covered core, or chip board sitting on top of a frame that is adjustable for leveling the table. The *fence* is a piece of 3/4- or 1 inch stock; it fits between any of the table sections or behind the table. A four section table gives the operator more versatility in positioning the fence. The workpiece is held firmly against the table and fence for crosscut and miter cuts; the workpiece is slid along the table and fence for rip cuts. The fence and table are both sawed during normal operation of the saw and are easily replaced when necessary.

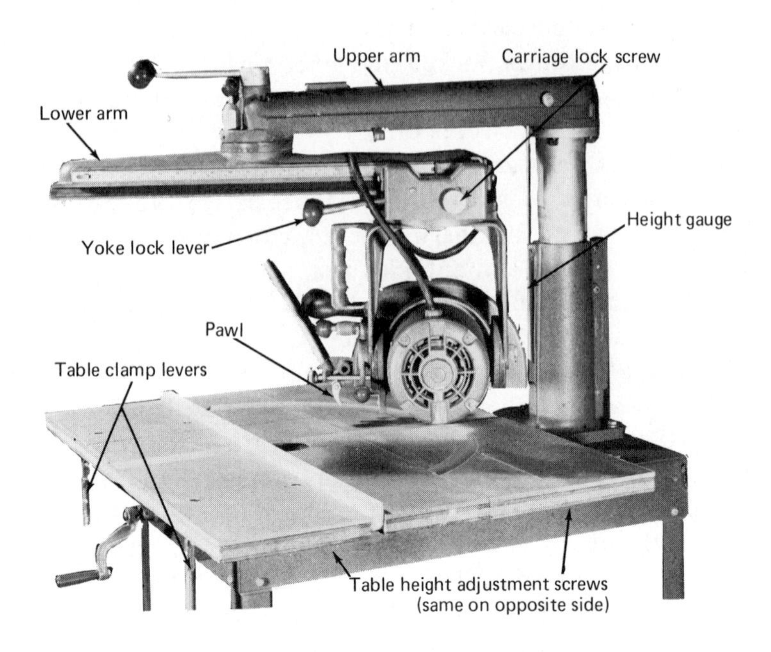


**FIGURE 7-3** / This is a two armed radial arm saw. It has more usable table surface when miter cuts are made because of the two arm configuration.

As previously mentioned, the size of a radial arm saw is specified by the diameter of the maximum blade that the saw is designed to use. The size of the blade determines the depth of cut in workpieces; the length of the radial *arm* and the table size determine the maximum crosscut capacities and the maximum rip capacities (the maximum size of the workpiece on the table as the overall workpiece is ripped). The average dimensions for these capacities are described in Table 7-1. Radial arm saws are about 24 to 27 inches high above the table.

## 7-3 / CUTTERS—BLADES, WHEELS, DADO HEADS, AND MOLDING HEADS

Saw *blades* and *wheels, dado heads* and *molding heads* are the cutters most often used on the radial arm saw and are therefore covered in

**Table 7-1**
**RADIAL ARM SAW CAPACITIES**

| | *Blade diameter (inches)* | | |
|---|---|---|---|
| | *9* | *10* | *12* |
| Depth of cut at 90° | 2-1/4 | 3 | 4 |
| Depth of cut at 45° bevel | 2 | 2-1/4 | 2-11/16 |
| Maximum crosscut capacity (3/4-in. stock) | 15 | 15 | 16 |
| Maximum rip capacity | 25 | 25 | 27 |
| Table size (average) | 26 x 32 | 26 x 36 | 29 x 40 |

detail in this section. A description of cutters used less frequently on the radial arm saw but more frequently on other power tools is covered in the applicable sections: shaping cutters, Sec. 10-2; router bits, Sec. 3-7; drills and bits, Sec. 3-2; sanding disks, Sec. 8-2; sanding drums, Sec. 3-6; and rotary planer, Sec. 3-11. However, the *procedures* for using *all* of these cutters on the radial arm saw are contained in this chapter.

*Blades*

The five types of blades most often used on the home workshop radial arm saw and the table saw (Chap. 11) are the rip, crosscut, combination, plywood combination, and carbide tipped blades (Fig. 7-4). The combination blade is the most desirable all-purpose blade.

The rip saw blade is designed for greatest efficiency when sawing a workpiece lengthwise in the direction of the grain. When a given job consists entirely of rip sawing, use of the rip saw blade will save time. Rip saw blade teeth act as a series of small chisels cutting into the workpiece.

The crosscut saw blade is designed to cut across the grain of a workpiece as in squaring and trimming to length. The teeth have an alternate face bevel or shear to enable them to sever the wood fibers. Use a crosscut blade for extensive cross-grain applications.

The combination blade is an all-purpose blade used for ripping, crosscutting, mitering and beveling. The blade is ground *flat* and the

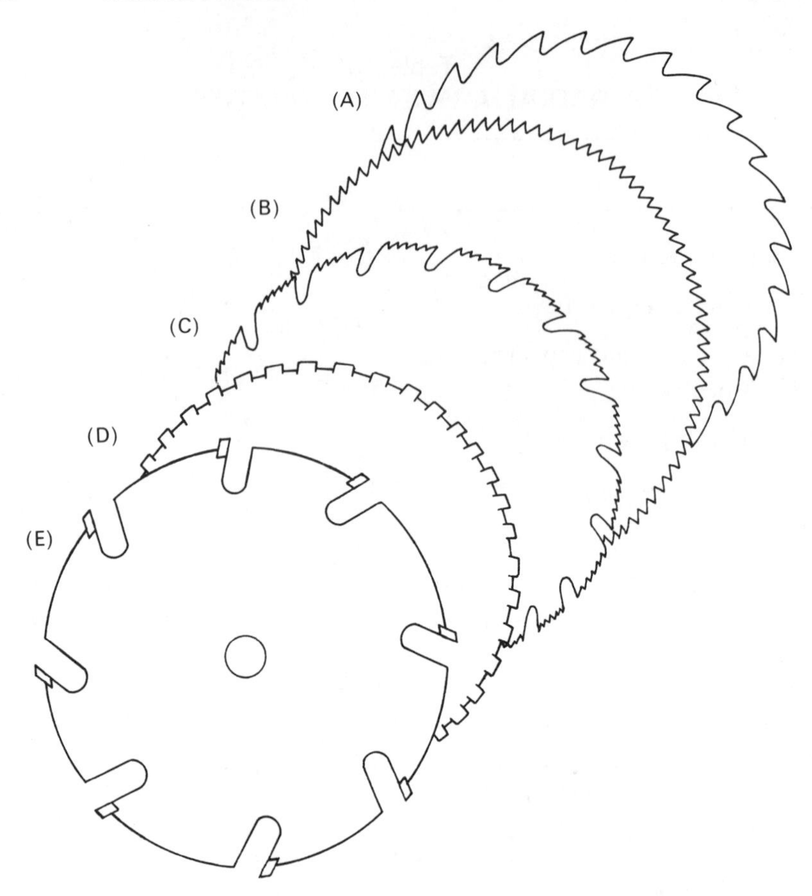


**FIGURE 7-4** / Radial arm and table saw blades: (A) rip; (B) crosscut; (C) combination; (D) plywood combination; (E) carbide tipped.

teeth are set for clearance. It has four (or sometimes two) *cutting teeth* and one *raker* or *cleaner* tooth per section. A *planer* combination saw blade is hollow ground and cuts smooth, thus eliminating sanding. The hollow ground blade is ground on both sides to prevent the blade from binding in the kerf.

The plywood combination blade cuts off plywood smoothly across the grain without splinters on the top or bottom and rips and miters plywood smooth enough so that no further sanding is necessary. The teeth are fine (small).

Carbide tipped blades outlast conventional chrome-nickel-molybdenum steel blades by more than ten to one. The blade teeth tips are made of tungsten carbide. These blades cut through very hard wood, laminates, plastics, formica, masonite, chip board, and other hard-to-cut materials with ease. These blades are not for cutting metals or masonry. Crosscuts, miters, bevels, and rip cuts are made with only slight chipping. Resharpening, though, is a job for the professional sharpener.

There are specialty blades too for cutting copper, brass, aluminum, sheet metal, and other materials. Consult your tool dealer.

Blades have 1/2- or 5/8-inch diameter arbor holes or have a 1/2-inch diameter hole with a 5/8-inch knockout that is removed for 5/8-inch arbors. Blade sizes range from 4 to 12 inches in diameter. The maximum useable size diameter blade for your saw should be used to give you maximum benefit in crosscutting and bevel cutting thick workpieces. You can, however, use smaller diameter blades which are less expensive. The carbide tipped blades are very expensive compared to conventional blades but they last much longer—and you may need a carbide tipped blade for your application.

### Wheels

Resinoid bond silicon carbide wheels are used on the radial arm saw and the table saw (Chap. 11) to cut tile, brick, ceramic, and slate. Resinoid bond wheels with aluminum oxide are used to cut steel. When used in these applications, be sure to clamp the workpiece to the table. Take small cuts.

### Dado Head

The dado head (Fig. 7-5) is used on the radial arm saw and the table saw (Chap. 11) to cut dadoes—grooves across the grain of a workpiece, ploughs—grooves along the grain of a workpiece, and rabbets—a groove along the edge of a workpiece to receive another piece to form a joint. The head can be used on either the radial arm or the table saw.

Dado heads are of two designs: a set of *blades* and *chippers,* and an *adjustable assembly.* The set consists of two outside combination saw blades, paper washers used to set a precise thickness of cut, four 1/8-inch chippers, and one 1/16-inch chipper. Depending on the configuration of the blades and chippers selected, the set can cut a minimum width of 1/8-inch (one blade) to 13/16-inches in 1/16-inch

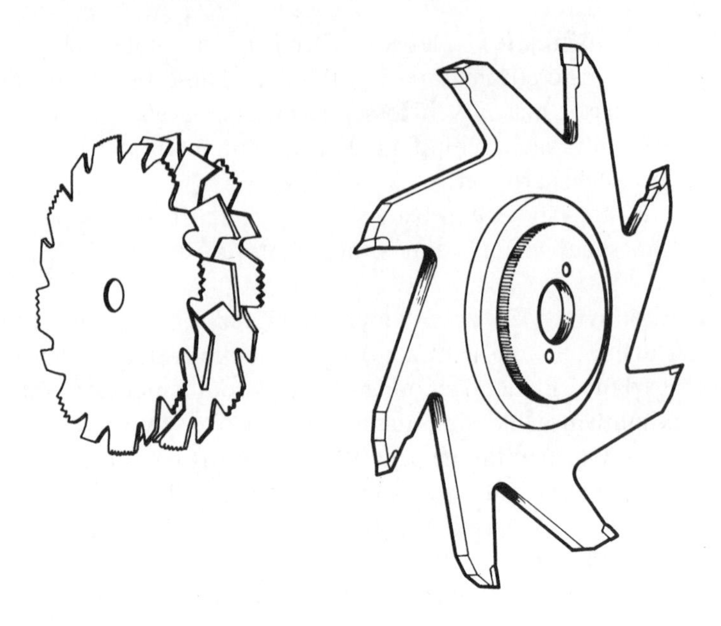

FIGURE 7-5 / Dado heads: (A) combination blades and chippers; (B) adjustable.

increments. Chippers are always "sandwiched" between the two blades; a blade and only a chipper are never used alone. The arbor hole is 1/2- or 5/8-inch, and heads with diameters of 6, 7, and 8 inches are available. A maximum depth of about 1-1/4-inches can be cut.

In placing the dado head set on the radial arm or table saw arbor, first place one blade on the arbor and then the required number of chippers. Space the chippers equally around the circumference to avoid vibration; the swaged or spread cutting edge of the chippers should coincide with the gullets (the space between tips of adjacent teeth) of the raker teeth of both saw blades. Finally, place the other saw blade on the arbor followed by the arbor washer and nut. (Eliminate the washer if there is insufficient thread capacity on the arbor.) Tighten the arbor nut securely and install the blade guard. Momentarily turn the power on and off to ensure that the blades have been installed in the correct direction of rotation.

The adjustable dado allows you to dial the desired width of the dado to be cut from 1/4- to 13/16-inch wide without removing the head from the arbor; just loosen the arbor nut, adjust, and retighten. The head is calibrated in 1/16-inch increments and has carbide tipped teeth. The depth of cut on different manufacturer's models varies from 3/4- to 2 inches. The head cuts hard and soft wood, plywood, and formica.

### Molding Head (Shaping Head)

The molding head, also called a shaping head (Fig. 7-6), is used on the radial arm saw and the table saw (Chap. 11) to shape decorative edges or surfaces on molding and furniture such as legs and table top edges. The heads accept cutters of many varying shapes (Fig. 7-7). Two types of heads are available: the triple and the single–the triple operates best because it makes three times as many cuts per revolution. The triple head is also more expensive as are the cutters since you need three of each pattern instead of one. A head comes complete with Allen wrench, spacer washer, and 1/2- and 5/8-inch arbor bushings.

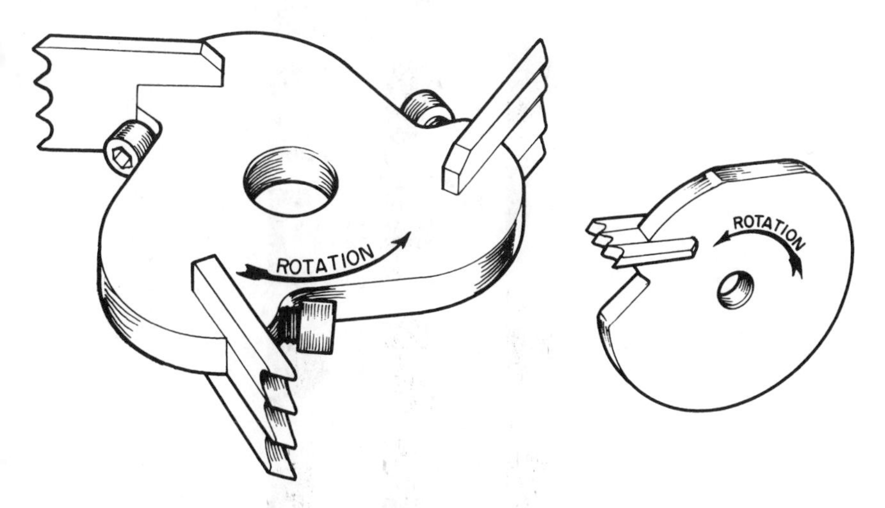


**FIGURE 7-6** / Molding head: (A) triple cutter molding head; (B) single cutter molding head.

To assemble the molding head, insert the cutters into the head with the cutting edge toward the lockscrew. (Many molding heads and cutters are "keyed" by means of a groove so that the cutters can not be installed backward.) Use the Allen wrench to secure the cutters with the lockscrews.

To install the molding head, select either the 1/2- or 5/8-inch

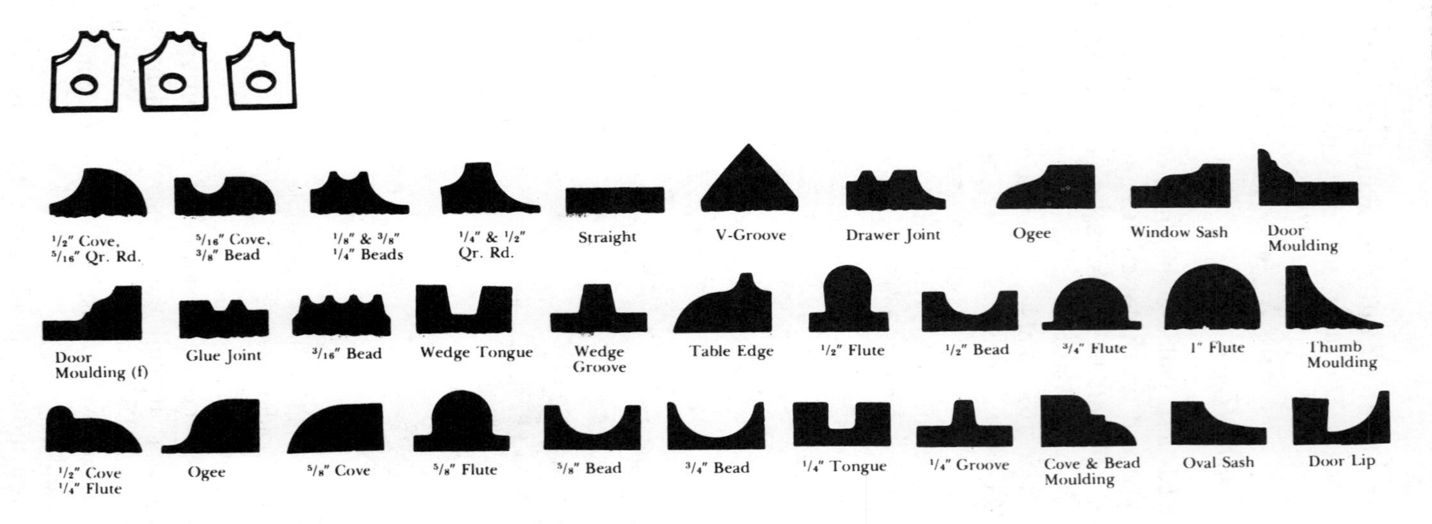


**FIGURE 7-7** / Typical molding head cutters.

bushing as applicable to your saw; place the bushing on the arbor. Place the spacer washer over the bushing and then place the molding head over the bushing. Install the radial arm saw arbor washer and nut and tighten securely. Install the blade guard. Rotate the shaper head by hand to check for clearance.

## 7-4 / OPERATING CONTROLS AND ADJUSTMENTS

Now that you are familiar with the nomenclature of the major parts of the radial arm saw, the operating controls and adjustments (Fig. 7-8) are discussed. Sit next to your radial arm saw while you read this section so that you can locate and operate the controls and operating adjustments on your saw. The major parts, controls, and adjustments are grouped by function in this section as follows: table leveling, table locks, cutter height, miter angle, bevel angle, yoke, carriage lock, rip positions, and guard lock.

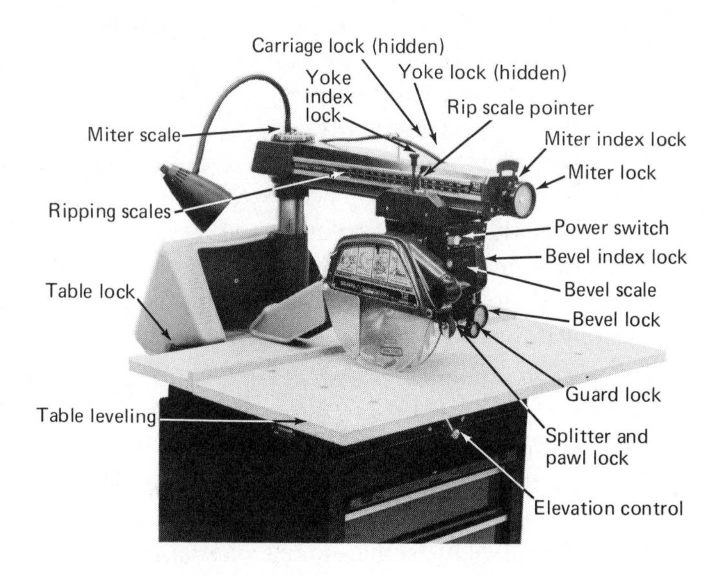


**FIGURE 7-8** / Become familiar with all of the controls and adjustments of the radial arm saw.

1 / *table leveling*—The *table leveling* screws are used to initially set all corners of the table to the same level, so that when the head is drawn across the radial arm at any

miter angle, the depth of cut into the workpiece at every point on the table is the same. The table is leveled (made parallel) with the radial arm, as opposed to leveling the table with the floor which can be done at the base of the stand. Once the table is set parallel to the radial arm at initial installation, it only needs a periodic check and readjustment as required.

2 / *table locks*–The *table locks* (one on each side of the table) are thumb screws (Fig. 7-8) or levers (Fig. 7-3) and can be located either in the rear or front of the table. The table locks secure the two or four sections of the table and the fence together. The locks are loosened any time the fence position is altered and are immediately retightened.

3 / *cutter height*–The *elevation* control raises and lowers the column and, hence, the radial arm and head of the saw to set the required depth of cut. One complete rotation of the handle may change the elevation by a fixed increment such as 1/8-inch; some models have a *height* gauge (Fig. 7-3) that is adjustable. For example, if you want to cut a 1/4-inch slot in a workpiece, you can place the workpiece under the blade (motor off) and lower the head until the blade teeth just touch the surface of the workpiece. Adjust the height gauge to 0 inches. Now remove the workpiece and lower the head by rotating the elevation control until the gauge indicates 1/4-inch. You are set for a 1/4-inch deep cut slot. The elevation control is also sometimes located at the top rear or front of the radial arm.

4 / *miter angle*–The *miter index lock, miter lock,* and *miter scale* function together to allow the operator to set, lock, and indicate the angle of miter cut from 90° left through 0° (crosscut) to 90° right. The miter index lock controls a pin that engages in a hole at common angles of 0, 45, and 90° left and right; some models may also index at 30 and 60° left and right. This indexing allows quick setups at the most frequently used angles. The miter lock secures the radial arm at the desired angle as indicated by the pointer on the miter scale.

5 / *bevel angle*–The *bevel index lock, bevel lock,* and *bevel* scale work in conjunction to permit tilting the motor–

arbor–blade to the desired bevel angles from 0 to 90° in a counterclockwise direction and to approximately 75° in a clockwise direction. The bevel index lock controls a pin that engages in a hole at common angles of 0, 45 and 90° counterclockwise and 45° clockwise; some models may also index at 30 and 60°. The indexing allows quick setups at the most frequently used bevel angles. The bevel lock secures the motor–arbor–blade at the desired angle as indicated by the pointer on the bevel scale.

6 / *yoke*–The *yoke index lock* (Fig. 7-8) and the *yoke lock* (Fig. 7-3) function together to allow the operator to position the motor–arbor–blade in either a crosscut *or* a rip position (there are no in-between positions) for miter and rip so that setups may be quickly made. The yoke lock secures the motor–arbor–blade at one of the two desired positions.

7 / *carriage lock*–The *carriage lock* (Fig. 7-3) secures the carriage at any desired position along the radial arm. The carriage is secured for rip sawing and when certain accessories are used with the radial arm saw. Lock the carriage by tightening the lock.

8 / *rip positions*–The yoke can be turned in a complete 360° path and locked at each 90° with the yoke index lock and yoke lock. Two of the four 90° positions are the rip positions. With the arbor pointing toward the column, the saw is in the *in-rip* configuration; with the arbor pointing toward the operator, the saw is in the *out-rip* position. The in-rip and out-rip *distances* are the distances of the blade from the fence when the fence is located at the back of the table (and also on some saws from between the rear fence sections). As the carriage is slid along the radial arm, a rip scale pointer on the carriage indicates the in-rip and out-rip distances on the *ripping scales.* In performing a rip operation, the yoke is turned to the in-rip or out-rip position, and the head is located for the desired rip dimension as indicated on the ripping scale. The carriage lock is then tightened to prevent the head from moving along the carriage.

9 / *guard lock*–The *guard lock* clamps the blade guard to the

motor housing. The guard is movable (and removable) around the blade and is positioned as required. The splitter and pawl assembly is attached to the blade guard and is secured in the required position by the *splitter and pawl lock.* The *power switch* applies electrical power to the motor. The switch may be a toggle or push button, or it may incorporate a locking device of some type to prevent unauthorized persons from operating the saw. The locking switch feature is of safety significance particularly when there are children in the home.

The controls and adjustments described in this section are typical of those found on all radial arm saws, regardless of size. The physical appearance of particular controls vary—some are knobs that turn a screw, some are levers that turn a nut or a bolt head, and some have ball knobs. Likewise, the relative position of the controls and adjustments may vary—some are up front, some on top, some on the sides, and some behind. Physical appearance is not critical to your operating satisfaction; however, location is important when considering ease of operation—the "up front" controls are easier to use.

## *7-5* / OPERATION

Observe the following cautions prior to *any* operations on the radial arm saw:

### *CAUTIONS*

1 / *Be sure all* required *adjustments and locks are secure before applying power.*

2 / *Do not force the radial arm saw at any time.*

3 / *Keep all guards in place. The splitter and anti-kickback pawl should be lowered in front of the blade to a height just above the table. This acts as an additional guard.*

4 / *Do not place your hands in front of the cutters at any time.*

5 / *Review all of the safety precautions in Sec. 1-16.*

Perform the following operating procedures:

1 / Plan ahead. Determine your cuts and plan to make all of the same types of cut on all similar workpieces.
2 / Select the correct blade, wheel, dado, or molding head (Sec. 7-3) and install it on the arbor. Tighten the arbor nut securely.
3 / Set the radial arm saw for the desired cut (crosscut, miter, bevel, rip, compound, etc.), lock all necessary locks, and position all guard devices (Sec. 7-6 through 7-15).
4 / Position the workpiece; clamp if necessary.
5 / Apply power and perform the applicable sawing (Sec. 7-6), dadoing (Sec. 7-7), surface planning (Sec. 7-8), molding and shaping (Sec. 7-9), routing (Sec. 7-10), disk sanding (Sec. 7-11), drum sanding (Sec. 7-12), buffing (Sec. 7-13), drilling (Sec. 7-14), or saber sawing (Sec. 7-15) procedures.

## 7-6 / SAWING PROCEDURES

The sawing procedures described in this section begin with the basic cuts: crosscut, miter, bevel and chamfer, compound angle, and rip cut. You should master the operating procedures for making the basic cuts first, then proceed to some more sophisticated cuts used for decorative projects. These cuts include: panel raising, dishing, taper cutting, and bending wood.

The procedures in this section assume that you have selected the correct blade (Sec. 7-3) and have installed it onto the arbor.

### *Crosscuts*

Crosscutting is cutting across the grain of the workpiece. In this procedure, crosscutting is considered to be at an angle of 0°. Other angles are considered as *miter* cuts and are subsequently covered. Crosscut as follows:

1 / Set and lock the yoke to the crosscut position (Fig. 7-9).
2 / Set and lock the head to a bevel of 0°.

3 / Set and lock the radial arm to a miter of 0°.

4 / Loosen the carriage lock and slide the carriage to the rear of the table. Lower the head to the bottom of the crosscut kerf.

5 / Place the fence in the table in front of the blade.

6 / Place the workpiece against the fence with the good side of the workpiece up and with the marked cutting line such that the blade cuts *along* the line, but in the scrap part of the board. Use one hand to hold the workpiece (not the scrap side).

7 / Turn the power on and draw the head forward slowly with your other hand–let the saw do the cutting. When the blade has cut completely through the workpiece, return the head to the rear of the table and turn power off.

**FIGURE 7-9** / Crosscutting.

You can crosscut a number of workpieces to the same size as shown in Fig. 7-10. Clamp a stop block—in this case a board—to the table at a distance from the blade equal to the length desired. Place all of the workpieces against the block and fence. Crosscut as previously described (also refer to stop blocks in Sec. 1-12).

**FIGURE 7-10** / Use a stop block to cut a number of equal length workpieces simultaneously.

If your workpiece is too wide so that the blade cannot complete the crosscut on the table, cut as much as you can. Then, return the head to the rear of the table, turn the workpiece around 180° and line up the marked cutting line with the blade. Pull the head forward on the radial arm to complete the cut.

*Miter Cuts*

Miter cuts are cuts across the grain at an angle of other than 0°. Cut miters as follows:

*1* / Set and lock the yoke to the crosscut position.

*2* / Set the bevel angle to 0°.

3 / Place the head to the rear of the radial arm, and lower the blade to the bottom of the miter trough.

4 / Set and lock the radial arm to the angle of the miter cut desired (Fig. 7-11).

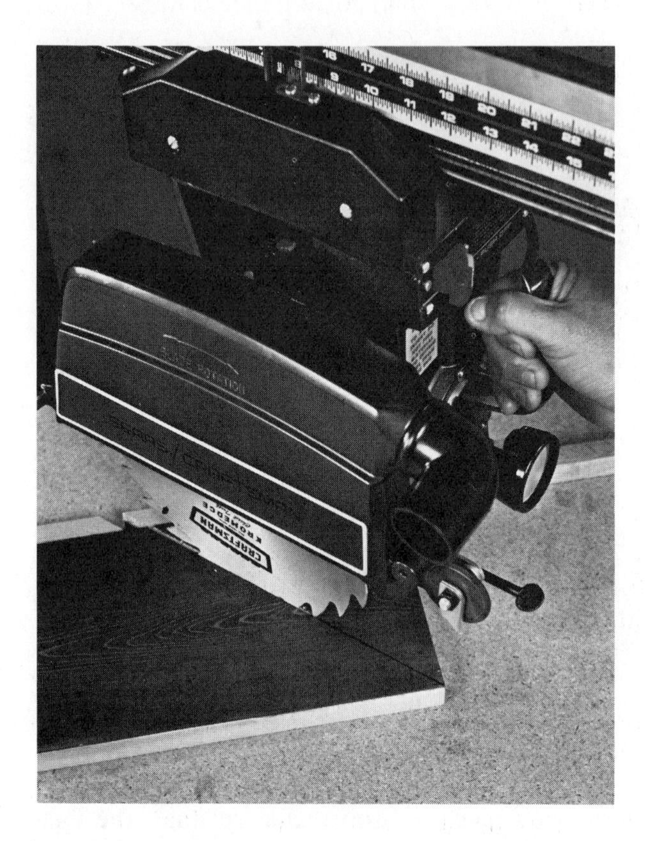

**FIGURE 7-11** / Cutting miters.

5 / Place the fence in the table in front of the blade. If your fence has a wide opening, place it in position where the blade will pass through.

6 / If there is no existing saw kerf in the table or fence for the miter angle set in step 4, turn the power on, and pull the head to the front of the radial arm cutting the kerf. Return the head to the rear and turn power off.

7 / Place the workpiece with the marked cutting line just to the side of the blade path so that the blade cuts *along* the

line, but in the scrap part of the board. Use one hand to hold the workpiece.

8 / Turn the power on and draw the head forward slowly with your other hand–let the saw do the cutting. When the blade has cut completely through the workpiece, return the head to the rear of the table and turn the power off.

### Bevel and Chamfer Cuts

A bevel cut is a cut at an angle to the surface of the workpiece when the angle is not 90°. A chamfer cut is a bevel cut that is on the edge of the workpiece but does not cut all the way through the workpiece. Cut a bevel or chamfer as follows:

1 / Set and lock the yoke to the crosscut position and the radial arm to 0°.

2 / Elevate the head.

3 / Set and lock the head to the desired bevel angle (Fig. 7-12).

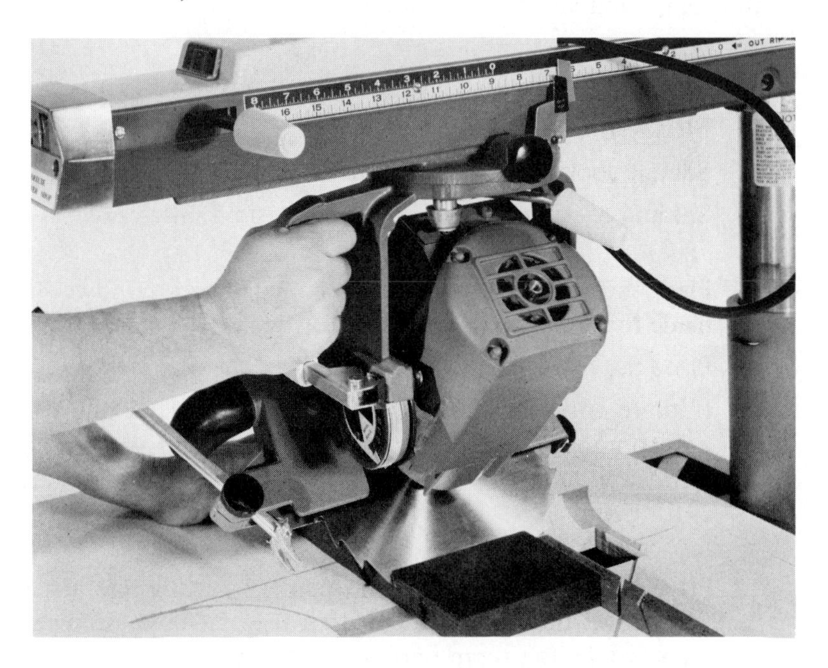

**FIGURE 7-12** / Cutting beveled angles.

4 / Place the head to the rear of the radial arm, and lower the blade to the bottom of the miter trough.

5 / Place the fence in the table in front of the blade.

6 / If there is no existing saw kerf in the table and fence for the bevel angle selected in step 3, turn the power on, and pull the head to the front of the radial arm cutting the kerf. Return the head to the rear and turn power off.

7 / Place the workpiece with the marked cutting line just to the side of the blade path so that the blade cuts along the line, but in the scrap part of the board. Use one hand to hold the workpiece.

8 / Turn the power on and draw the head forward slowly with your other hand—let the saw do the cutting. When the blade has cut completely through the workpiece, return the head to the rear of the table and turn the power off.

### *Compound Angle Cuts*

A compound angle cut includes both a bevel cut and a miter cut. Make the compound angle cut as follows:

1 / Set and lock the yoke in the crosscut position.

2 / Elevate the head.

3 / Set and lock the head to the desired bevel angle.

4 / Set and lock the radial arm to the desired miter angle (Fig. 7-13).

5 / Place the head to the rear of the radial arm, and lower the blade to the bottom of the miter trough.

6 / Place the fence in the table in front of the blade.

7 / If there is no existing saw kerf in the table and fence for the compound angle selected in steps 3 and 4, turn the power on, and pull the head to the front of the radial arm cutting the kerf. Return the head to the rear and turn power off.

8 / Place the workpiece with the marked cutting line just to the side of the blade path so that the blade cuts along the line, but in the scrap part of the board. Use one hand to hold the workpiece.

9 / Turn the power on and draw the head forward slowly with your other hand—let the saw do the cutting. When the blade has cut completely through the workpiece, return the head to the rear of the table and turn the power off.

**FIGURE 7-13** / Cutting a compound angle for a picture frame.

*Rip Cuts*

A rip cut is a cut along the grain of the wood. In rip cutting with the radial arm saw, remember it is the workpiece that moves—the blade remains stationary. Make rip cuts as follows:

1 / Set and lock the yoke in the in-rip or out-rip position (Fig. 7-14 shows the saw in the in-rip position) and the radial arm to 0°. (Use the transfer kerf to change from crosscut to rip.)

**FIGURE 7-14** / Rip sawing.

2 / If the rip cut is to be beveled, set and lock the head to the desired bevel angle. If necessary, lower the head to the bottom of the rip trough.

3 / After determining the desired width of the rip cut, move the carriage along the radial arm until the distance from the blade to the fence is the rip width. You may need to relocate the fence to the rear of the table. The rip width can be measured on the in-rip or out-rip scale or can be more accurately measured by measuring the distance with a rule.

4 / Lock the carriage.

5 / Momentarily place a piece of scrap wood the same thickness as the workpiece in front of the blade, and lower

the *infeed* end of the blade guard until it almost touches the workpiece. Secure the guard in place. (The *infeed* end of the blade guard is the end opposite the splitter and anti-kickback pawls.)

6 / Momentarily place the piece of scrap wood behind the blade. Lower the splitter and anti-kickback pawls until the pawls are about 1/16- to 1/8-inch lower than the workpiece. With the pawls in position on top of the scrap, try pushing the scrap wood *toward the blade.* The pawls should grab the wood and *prevent* it from moving; if they do not, readjust the height of the pawls until they grab the workpiece when it is pushed toward the blade.

7 / Place the workpiece against the fence in front of the blade with the good side *face down* to the table. Turn the power on.

### CAUTION

***Do not feed the workpiece from the splitter and anti-kickback pawl end of the blade guard.***

8 / Feed the workpiece against the fence and into the blade evenly with your hands positioned as in Fig. 7-14. Do not place your hands in front of the blade. Do not force the workpiece into the blade. Do not try to rip saw without the use of the fence as a guide. Give the blade a chance to cut the workpiece and use a push stick (Sec. 1-11) for narrow workpieces.

9 / Continue to feed the workpiece through the blade. Support long workpieces on the outfeed side with a workpiece support stand (Sec. 1-10). On long workpieces, you can walk around the radial arm saw and pull the final portion of the workpiece through the blade.

Wide workpieces are ripped with the head in the *out-rip* position and the fence at the rear of the table (Fig. 7-15). Be sure to properly set the pawls and to feed the workpiece to the infeed side of the blade guard.

**FIGURE 7-15** / Ripping large panels.

*Panel Raising*

Panel raising is a decorative effect made on doors. A thin beveled cut is taken along the top surface on all four sides of the panel (Fig. 7-16). Proceed as follows:

*1* / Set and lock the radial arm to 0° and the yoke to the rip position. Raise the head.

*2* / Set and lock the bevel to the desired angle (approximately 88° if set to out-rip or 92° if set to in-rip) on the bevel scale.

*3* / Locate the head on the carriage so that the distance between the blade and the fence is the desired width of the bevel. Lock the carriage.

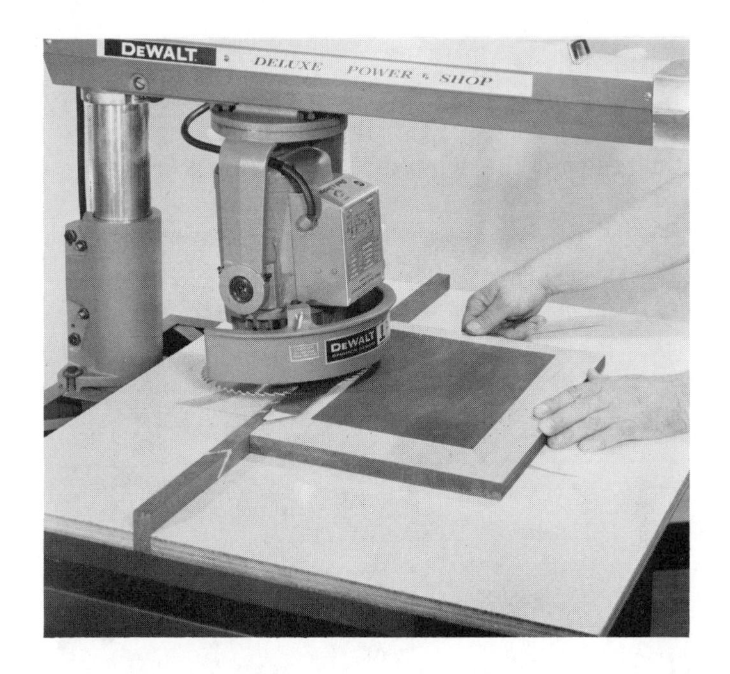


**FIGURE 7-16** / Panel raising.

4 / Lower the head until the tip of the blade (in front of the fence) is about 1/16-inch below the surface of the workpiece. If possible, use the guard or an accessory guard as shown in Fig. 7-16.

### *NOTE*

***It may be necessary to cut away part of the fence for blade clearance, or you can put a piece of scrap wood as an auxiliary table under the workpiece to raise it. Clamp the scrap piece to the table.***

5 / Turn power on and *slowly* feed the workpiece into the rotation of the blade. Hold the workpiece firmly against the fence. Cut the two across-the-grain edges first followed by the two with-the-grain edges. This sequence will cause the with-the-grain cuts to smooth off the splinters caused by the across-the-grain cuts.

### *Dishing*

Dishing is the process of making a concave cut into a workpiece surface (Fig. 7-17). The shape of the dish is determined by the bevel angle of the head and the depth of cut. Proceed as follows:

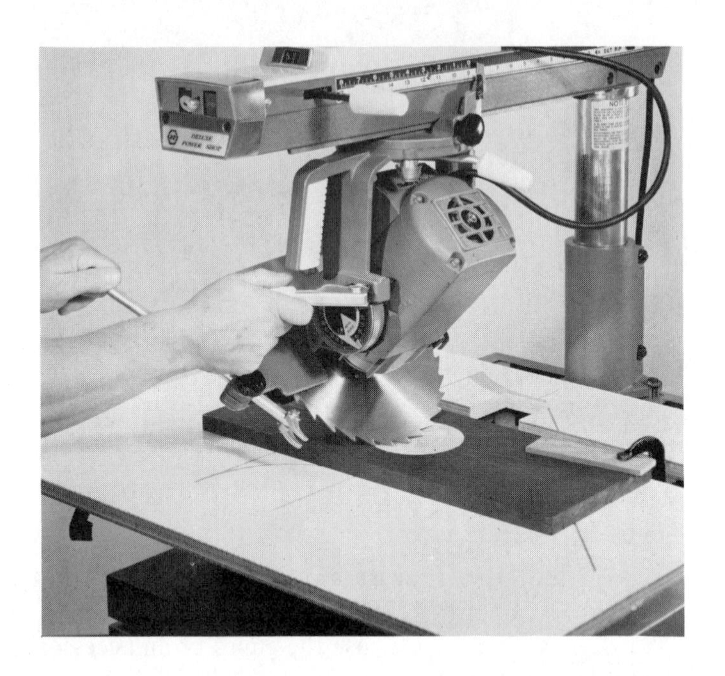

**FIGURE 7-17** / Dishing.

*1* / Place the radial arm saw in the crosscut configuration and set and lock the radial arm to 0°.

*2* / Set and lock the desired bevel angle on the head: the greater the bevel angle, the wider the dish.

*3* / Mark a cross at the center of the dish on the workpiece.

*4* / Lower the head until a tooth touches the center of the cross; move the carriage and workpiece as required.

*5* / Clamp or nail the workpiece to the table.

*6* / Lock the carriage lock.

*7* / Loosen the yoke lock slightly and the yoke index lock, and rotate the yoke 360° to check for clearance; make any clearance changes required.

8 / Apply power and rotate the yoke 360°.

9 / Increase the depth of cut in 1/32-inch increments and continue to make 360° swings of the yoke until the desired depth is reached.

### *Taper Cutting*

Taper cuts can be made by placing the workpiece against the fence. Proceed as follows:

1 / *Square* the workpiece. Mark the starting points of the taper on the squared end of the workpiece, and place the squared end against the fence.

2 / Place the radial arm saw in the crosscut configuration and set to the miter angle (taper) desired.

3 / Cut the taper.

4 / Now change the miter angle to the opposite side (example, 10° left and then 10° right), place the squared end of the workpiece against the fence with the mark in line with the blade and make the second cut.

The taper jig (Sec. 2-5) can also be used for making tapered workpieces; it is handy when you have a number of the same shaped workpieces required.

### *Bending Wood*

A strip of wood can be bent in an arc by sawing kerfs nearly through one side of the strip. Suppose you want to bend a piece of 3/4- by 2 inch wood around a 45° corner. Using scrap wood for a test, proceed as follows:

1 / Set up the saw for crosscutting.

2 / Saw kerfs across the width (2 inches) of the workpiece to a depth 1/16- to 1/8-inch less than the thickness of the workpiece. After the first kerf is cut, bend the workpiece until the kerf closes. Measure and mark off a distance from

the kerf toward the end of the workpiece equal to the radius of the intended bend (Fig. 7-18). Place the workpiece flat on the table with the kerf closed, and measure the distance from the table to the workpiece. This distance is about the correct spacing of the kerfs. Mark off spaces for the other kerfs.

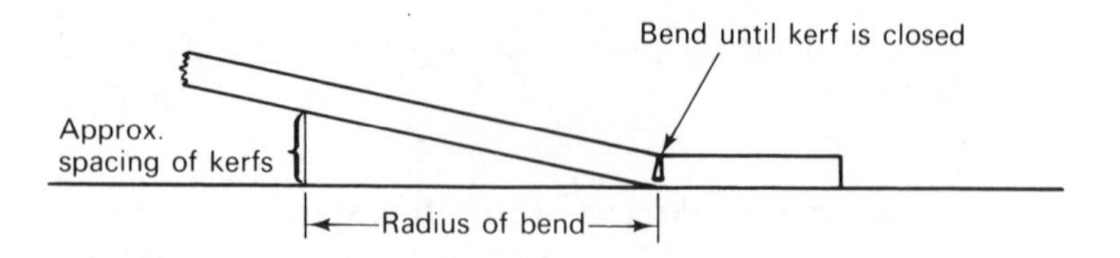


**FIGURE 7-18** / Determining the approximate number of kerfs needed for bending a workpiece. Refer to the text.

3 / Cut the remainder of the kerfs.

4 / Bend the workpiece and glue the kerfs closed. Clamp the workpiece until it is dry.

## 7-7 / DADOING PROCEDURES

Dadoing is the cutting of grooves across or along a workpiece; dado cuts along the workpiece are sometimes termed *ploughs.* The dado head also cuts rabbets–a groove along the edge of a workpiece. In dadoing, the basic cuts–crosscut, miter, bevel, compound, and rip–are performed nearly the same as described in Sec. 7-6. Dadoes are cut with a dado head (Sec. 7-3), although they may also be cut with a combination blade making repeated passes over the width of the desired groove.

The procedures in this section assume that the dado has been installed properly (Sec. 7-3), and that you are experienced in making the basic cuts (Sec. 7-6). The procedures in this section include: crosscut, mitered, rip, and beveled dado cuts; rabbeting; tongue and groove; box joint cutting; cutting decorative molding; and cutting a tapered groove.

*Crosscut, Mitered, Rip and Beveled Dado Cuts*

Crosscut, mitered, rip (Figs. 7-19, 7-20, and 7-21) and beveled dado cuts are made with the dado blades the same as making cuts with a single blade (Sec. 7-6) except for the following:

**FIGURE 7-19** / Crosscut dadoing.

1 / The width of cut is determined by the number of chippers and paper washers between the two blades. Repeat passes are made for wider cuts.

2 / The depth of cut is set as required.

3 / A kerf must be cut through the fence for the dado head.

4 / Cut scrap wood first to ensure that the width of cut is sufficient. Slightly wider cuts are made by adding paper washers between the blade and chippers.

*Rabbeting (Straight and Beveled)*

You can use the dado head to quickly make straight or beveled *edge* rabbets on long workpieces and *end* rabbets on narrow workpieces.

**FIGURE 7-20** / Beveled dadoing. In this design, equally spaced beveled dadoes are cut on one side of the workpiece and then on the other side. The depth of cut is slightly more than half way through the workpiece.

Edge rabbets are made from a ripping position as shown in Fig. 7-22; set the radial arm saw to the configuration described for panel raising in Sec. 7-6, except set the angle to 90° for straight rabbets or the angle desired for the bevel rabbet.

Edge rabbets are made with the saw in the *crosscut* configuration of Fig. 7-9. Place the workpiece lengthwise along the fence and draw the dado head over the workpiece to complete the edge rabbet.

### *Tongue and Groove Cuts*

Tongue and groove cuts are made to join two workpieces together. The tongue (the protrusion) can be made by making edge rabbet cuts

**FIGURE 7-21** / Rip dadoing (ploughing).

on each side of the workpiece; the groove is made with equal thickness and width (depth) as the tongue (Fig. 7-23). First cut all tongues followed by all grooves. Note in Fig. 7-23 that the fence has been cut partially away; you may also need to clamp a scrap board to the table under the workpiece. Feed the workpiece into the cutter.

### *Box Joints*

Box joints are made as shown in Fig. 7-24. A spacer (washer) of the required thickness is placed between the two dado blades. Chippers may be used, as necessary, between the combination blade and the spacer. Both workpieces to be joined are cut simultaneously.

A *tenon* can be cut by the above method. The same amount of workpiece material is removed by the dado head from each side of the tenon; a spacer determines the thickness of the tenon.

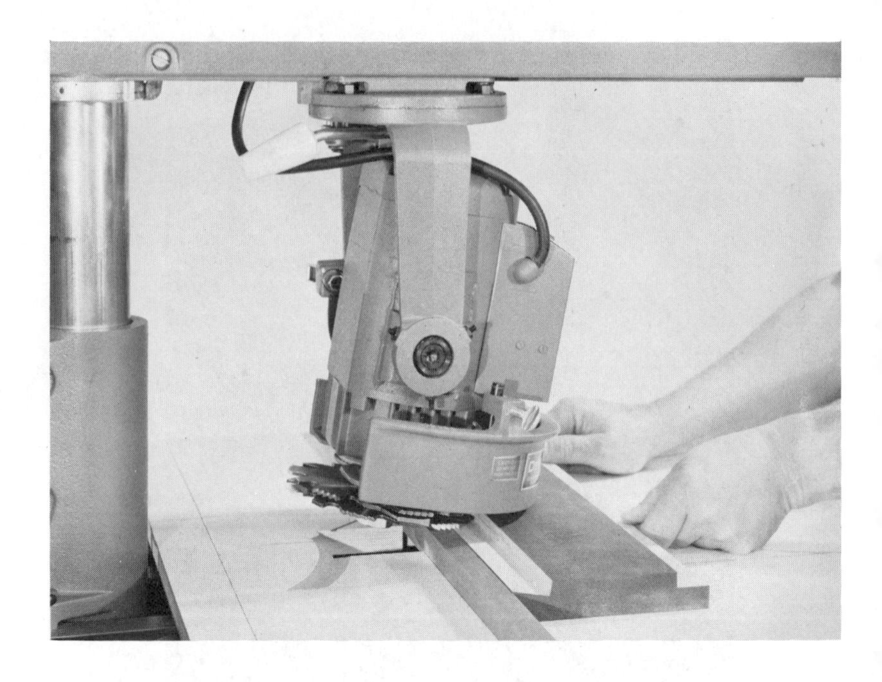

**FIGURE 7-22** / Straight and beveled edge rabbeting.

**FIGURE 7-23** / Tongue and groove cuts.

**FIGURE 7-24** / Cutting box joints.

*Decorative Molding*

You can make your own designed decorative moldings by cutting grooves in a workpiece that is already cut to the desired width (but not to the desired thickness). Cut the grooves with the dado (or molding head)—perhaps turning the workpiece over for every other groove. Then rip cut the workpiece into thin strips.

*Cutting a Tapered Groove*

A tapered groove is a groove in a workpiece that is shallow at one end and deep at the other end (Fig. 7-25). To cut the tapered groove, set up the radial arm saw for a crosscut operation. The dado head should be set to the desired width of the groove.

Place the workpiece against the fence; the shallow end of the groove will begin at the fence. Place a scrap piece of wood under the outer edge of the workpiece; and place the scrap so that the workpiece is slanted toward the fence at the desired taper. Set the radial arm head height to just touch the workpiece at the fence.

**FIGURE 7-25** / A piece of scrap wood is placed under the front of the workpiece to raise it for a sloped cut.

Apply power to the saw and draw the dado head across the workpiece cutting the taper.

## *7-8* / SURFACING PROCEDURES

Surface planing along workpieces, the cutting of rabbets, and panel raising can be accomplished with the addition of a rotary surface planing attachment to the saw. Follow the manufacturer's instructions on how to attach the planer in the proper direction of rotation and how to surface workpieces with it.

Place the radial arm saw in the configuration shown in Fig. 7-26. The fence is used as a guide; the carriage is locked in position, and the depth of cut is set very shallow–1/16 inch. Hold the workpiece firmly and advance the workpiece slowly. Cut with the grain of the wood.

**FIGURE 7-26** / Surfacing.

## 7-9 / MOLDING AND SHAPING PROCEDURES

The molding and shaping of workpieces are performed on the radial arm saw with the use of an accessory molding head (also called shaping head) and cutters (Sec. 7-2) and less frequently with shaping cutters (Sec. 10-2). These accessory cutters are attached to the radial arm saw arbor or auxiliary spindle as specified by the saw manufacturer; the molding or shaping head fits over the arbor and is secured by the arbor nut.

Place the cutters in the same direction of rotation as for a blade. The shaping cutters may fit a drill chuck or other adapter that is placed on the auxiliary spindle. Once installed, rotate the cutter by hand to check for clearance.

*CAUTION*

*Many shaper cutters can be installed for either clockwise or counterclockwise rotation by reversing their placement*

***on the arbor/spindle. Be absolutely positive that the cutter is installed in the proper direction. Many radial arm saws have an auxiliary spindle that travels in the opposite direction from the main arbor and should be used with shaper cutters. See your manufacturer's instructions.***

This section describes how to: shape designs into surfaces, shape edges, cut narrow strip edge molding, cut door lips, and shape freehand. Procedures using both the molding/shaping head and shaping cutters are included.

### *Surface Shaping*

Decorative surface shaping is done on the radial arm saw with the molding head and selected cutters. In Fig. 7-27, the radial arm saw is set as in rip sawing: yoke set and locked to rip position, carriage lock locked, bevel set and locked to desired angle, and the guard and pawls set for rip sawing. The fence is used as a guide, and the workpiece is fed against the direction of rotation of the cutter (feed from the end opposite the splitter and pawl assembly). Take shallow cuts and make repeat passes at increasing depths as required.

Figure 7-28 illustrates decorative surface cuts made with the radial arm saw in the rip configuration. Note that the workpiece is clamped to the table. The *arcs* are made by locking the yoke in the rip position, setting and locking the head at the desired bevel, and locking the carriage at the desired radius of the arc to be cut. The miter lock and miter index lock are loosened. The elevation is set to just nick the workpiece. With the motor on, the radial arm is moved slowly between the two desired points. Increase the depth 1/16-inch at a time, and make repeat passes until the desired depth of cut is reached.

The circles are cut by setting and locking the miter angle, bevel angle, and carriage. Lower the head to the surface and start the motor. Loosen the yoke lock and yoke index lock and rotate the yoke 360°. Gradually increase the depth of cut 1/16-inch at a time, and rotate the yoke until the desired depth of cut is attained.

FIGURE 7-27 / Surface shaping along a straight line.

*Edge Shaping*

The radial arm saw is placed in the same configuration for using all molding/shaping cutters with the exception that the height and the forward/backward position on the carriage may vary depending upon placement of the cut and the depth. Thus, the subsection describes the basic configuration for the radial arm saw for molding/shaping, *complete* and *partial* edge cutting, depth of cut, and fence positioning.

To perform molding/shaping cutting operations, set the radial arm saw in the following configuration:

*NOTE*

*The following sequence should not be completed and*

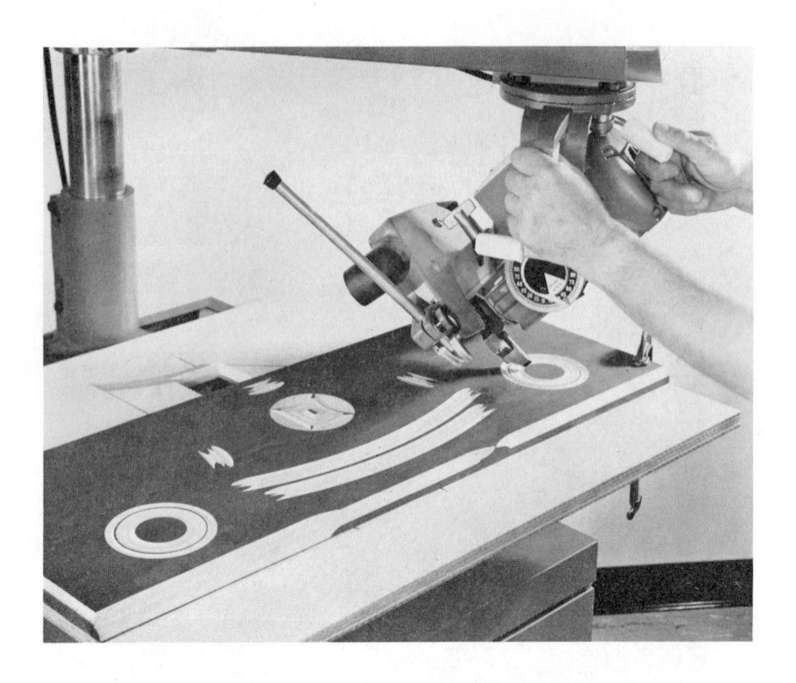

**FIGURE 7-28** / Decorative surface shaping.

***power should not be applied until this complete subsection (Edge Shaping) is read and understood.***

1 / Attach the cutting head with the desired cutters, and ensure that the correct direction of rotation is observed. Follow the manufacturer's specific instructions and Sec. 7-4.

2 / Set and lock the radial arm to 0°, bevel to 0°, and the yoke to the rip position.

3 / Install special guard for safety (some are sold as accessories).

4 / Install and adjust the molding/shaper fence (sold as an accessory) or shim a split fence (refer to subsequent text).

5 / Set the depth of cut by raising/lowering the head and by moving the head forward/backward on the carriage. (Small cuts will be taken with repeat passes as required.) Lock the carriage in position. (Depth of cut is subsequently discussed.)

6 / Hold the workpiece firmly against the table and fence, and feed the workpiece slowly through the cutter. Feed with the grain whenever possible. When shaping a rectangular workpiece, first shape the against-the-grain edges; then shape the with-the-grain edges.

The amount of material to be removed from the edge of a workpiece determines how you must position the fence; either a *partial* amount of the edge will be removed, or the *complete* edge will be removed. In removing only *part* of the edge of the workpiece, there is some material left remaining on the edge that is *constantly* against the radial arm fence so that true (straight) cuts are made. When *all* of the edge of a workpiece is removed by a cutter, the section of the fence (called the *outfeed* fence) beyond the cutter must be slightly forward of the *infeed* fence to compensate for the amount of material removed from the *complete* edge by the cutter. For example, the cutter in Fig. 7-29 is *not* removing *all* of the edge of the workpiece; a lip remains on the bottom that runs along a straight fence as a guide. But, the molding head *jointer* cutter shown in Fig. 7-30 will remove material from the *complete* edge of the workpiece. Therefore, the *outfeed* fence (in the foreground of the figure) must be forward of the *infeed* fence by the amount of the thickness removed in a single pass—in essence, the setup is like a jointer (Chap. 5) table turned on its side. Figure 7-30 illustrates an accessory fence that has an adjustable infeed table so that compensations for thickness can be made.

The depth of cut is determined by two factors: the height of the cutter in the workpiece and the position of the carriage on the radial arm. Your best method to set the depth of cut is to draw the pattern (using cardboard cutouts of the molding cutters that you have as templates) on the end of the workpiece; place the workpiece against the infeed fence with the pattern to the cutter. Adjust the elevation and position the carriage to make a small initial cut of about 1/16-inch. Later adjustments and subsequent passes will cut the edge to the pattern line.

The *infeed* fence must always be *in* (toward the rear of the table) from the outfeed fence when the complete edge of the workpiece is removed. This is easily accomplished with the adjustable fence accessory shown in Fig. 7-30 by moving the micrometer adjustment. First, set and lock the carriage on the radial arm so that

**FIGURE 7-29** / The molding/shaping head cutter is removing part of the edge of the workpiece; only a straight fence is required.

the cutter is even with the outfeed fence. Then adjust the infeed fence until it is behind the outfeed fence by the amount of the thickness to be removed from the complete edge of the workpiece by the cutter in a single pass. Use scrapwood to check—pass it through the cutter until it reaches the outfeed fence. Turn the power off and then make adjustments with the micrometer as necessary so that the outfeed fence will support the workpiece.

Without an adjustable fence, your task of offsetting the infeed fence is more difficult, but possible. You need to shim the fence. The easiest method of shimming is to clamp a thin strip of wood along the face (forward) of the outfeed fence section. The thickness of the shim where the workpiece meets it is equal to the depth of cut; again, set the cutters even with the outfeed fence and try a scrap workpiece first.

**FIGURE 7-30** / Jointing with the radial arm saw and molding/shaping head attachment. Note the accessory guard installed for safety and the adjustable fence, another accessory.

You may also find that, because of the table, the cutter cannot be lowered to the bottom of the workpiece. In this case, clamp or nail a scrap board to the table top in front of the table.

The jointer knives shown in the molding head on Fig. 7-30 are used to plane the edges of workpieces for joining. Rabbets can also be cut with the jointer knives by raising the cutter so that only a part of the wood is cut away. In this case, the fence sections are parallel because only a *part* of the edge is being cut away.

By raising the elevation of the head and by beveling the head, panel raising can be accomplished. Simulated louvers can also be cut by bringing the head almost to a vertical position; the yoke should be in the rip position. Make repeated passes of the workpiece under the jointer knives by feeding into the direction of rotation.

### *Narrow Strip Edge Molding*

Narrow strips of edge molding should be clamped with hold down fingers (Fig. 7-31) to hold the workpiece firmly against the table and fence. The hold down assembly is available as an accessory. In lieu of the accessory, you can clamp a guide onto the top of the table and parallel to the fence. The guide should be placed at a distance of the width of the workpiece, plus the thickness of a piece of paper for clearance. Stop blocks can be clamped to the fence above the workpiece. Use a push stick (Sec. 1-11) to push the narrow strips through the cutter.

**FIGURE 7-31** / Narrow strips of edge molding should be clamped with hold down fingers.

Whenever possible, avoid cutting narrow strips as shown in Fig. 7-31. Instead, shape the edge of a wider board and then cut the board to the proper width with the saw.

*Door Lips*

Cabinet door lips are cut as shown in Fig. 7-32. In cutting any four-sided workpiece, first cut the across-the-grain cuts and then the with-the-grain cuts. This produces a smoother workpiece because the latter cuts smooth any splinters on the edges caused by the across-the-grain cuts.

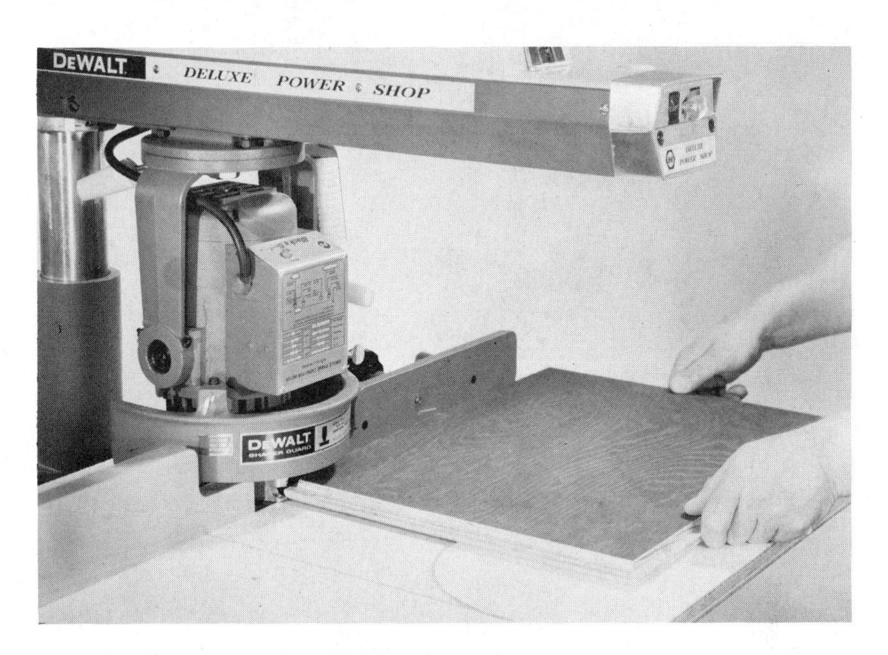


**FIGURE 7-32** / Shaping cabinet door lips. Do the across-the-grain cuts first.

*Freehand Shaping*

Freehand shaping can also be done on the radial arm saw (Fig. 7-33). A circular shaped guide is screwed securely to the table top. The depth of cut should begin shallow (1/16-inch) and the cuts repeated until the workpiece is shaped. Set the depth of cut by the positioning of the head on the carriage over the circle guide and by increasing or decreasing the elevation. Use the shaper guard. Hold the workpiece firmly and feed it in against the circle guard; the function of the guard is to prevent the workpiece from suddenly being jammed in the cutter causing a kickback. Also refer to the use of *pegs* in Chap. 10.

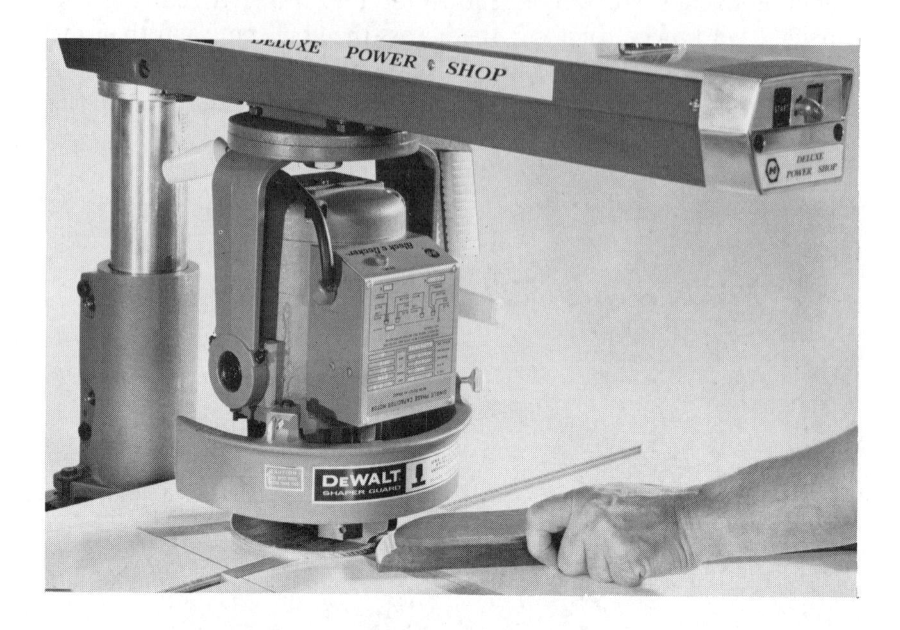


**FIGURE 7-33** / Freehand shaping. Note the guide circle attached to the table.

*Using Shaper Cutters*

The same shaping cutters used on the shaper (Sec. 10-2) and the drill press (Sec. 3-8) are used in a chuck attached to the radial arm saw. Workpieces are held firmly against the table and the fence (Fig. 7-34) and are fed slowly against the rotation of the cutter. Take small bites of wood on each pass. Refer to Chap. 10 for a complete discussion of shaper operations.

## *7-10* / ROUTING PROCEDURES

Routing bits are used to cut intricate contours, multicurved moldings and edges, relief panels, trim work on cabinets and bookshelves, sign engraving, and delicate grooves for intricate inlays in wood. Routing is performed on the radial arm saw by the use of router bits installed into a chuck that is screwed onto the radial arm saw *auxiliary spindle*

**FIGURE 7-34** / The same shaping cutters used with the shaper and the drill press are used with the radial arm saw.

that spins in the opposite direction from the arbor (Fig. 7-35). Router bits can be used up to speeds in excess of 20,000 rev/min, and they do cut smoother at the higher speeds; for this reason, some radial arm saws have auxiliary spindles at greatly increased speeds approximating 20,000 rev/min.

Edge routing, rabbeting, and surface routing should be performed where possible in the rip configuration with the applicable controls and adjustments locked. Use the fence as a guide. In the rip configuration, workpieces should be against the fence. Move the workpiece with the grain and into the cutter in the direction that forces the workpiece against the fence. When cutting across the grain, make shallow cuts and feed the workpiece slowly. In doing freehand work, lock all controls, take shallow bites into the wood, and feed

**FIGURE 7-35** / The radial arm saw becomes a router when bits are installed into arbor chuck.

slowly. Refer to Sec. 3-7 for more information on router bits and routing procedures.

## 7-11 / DISK SANDING PROCEDURES

The radial arm saw with a sanding disk attachment can be used to sand edges and surfaces of workpieces (Fig. 7-36 and 7-37) in all directions–mitered, beveled, crosscut, or rip. The disk spins at 3450 rev/min. Coarse, medium, and fine grit sanding disks are easily attached (Sec. 8-8).

As in all sanding operations, sand with the grain whenever possible to avoid scoring. Use coarser grits first followed by finer grits. Let the disk do the sanding–use light pressure and feed on the

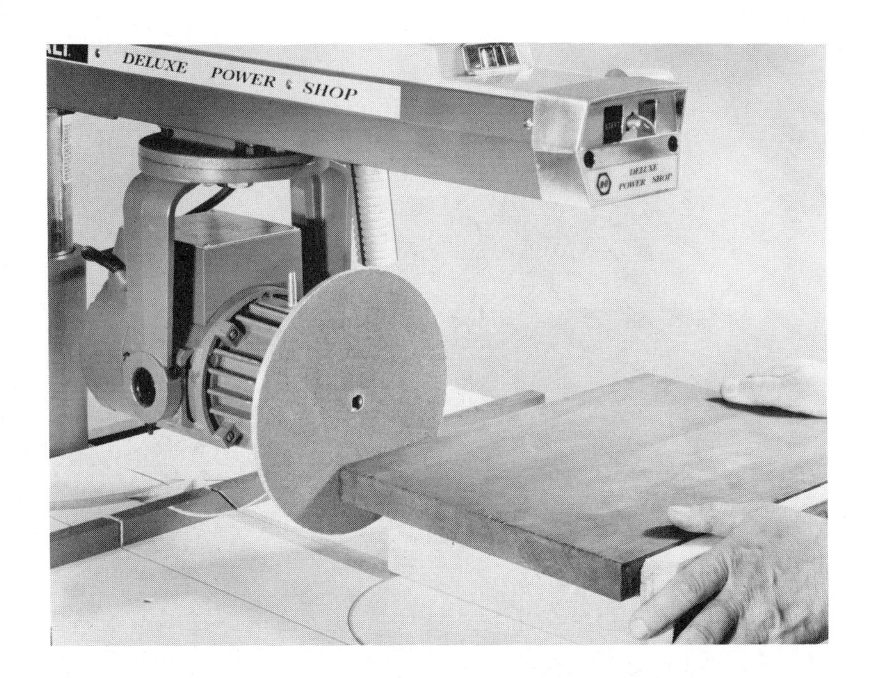


**FIGURE 7-36** / Edge sanding with a disk sanding attachment.

downside of the disk. Refer to Chap. 8 for detailed disk sanding instructions.

Figure 7-36 illustrates the setup for edge sanding. An auxiliary table is used so that the sanding disk can sand the entire edge of the workpiece. Note that the auxiliary table has a guide for running along the radial arm saw table. The radial arm saw is set with the radial arm (miter), bevel, and yoke all locked; the head is positioned and locked so that the disk will take a very light cut.

The surface of the workpiece in Fig. 7-37 is being sanded. The head is locked in position and the bevel is set for 90°. Use the fence as a guide and pass the workpiece from the infeed side under the disk slowly. For repeat passes, move the head and relock the carriage lock. Do not change the elevation of the head until all of the surface has been sanded.

## *7-12* / DRUM SANDING PROCEDURES

Drum sanding is particularly effective on irregularly curved edges (Fig. 7-38) and for sanding the internal edges of a workpiece (Fig.

**FIGURE 7-37** / The disk sanding attachment is also used for surface sanding.

7-39). The drum is attached to the arbor according to the manufacturer's instructions. The radial arm saw is set and locked so that the drum extends slightly through the hole in the table; this permits the complete edge of the workpiece to be sanded. By raising the head and placing the fence in front of the table hole, the fence can be used as a guide in sanding straight edges. This will necessitate the addition of a piece of scrap wood under the workpiece so that the complete edge will be sanded. Likewise, if your table has no hole in it, a scrap piece of wood is used. Feed the workpiece lightly against the drum. Start with a medium grit drum and then use a fine grit. The sanding sleeves are easily changed. Use firm supports for the workpiece whenever possible.

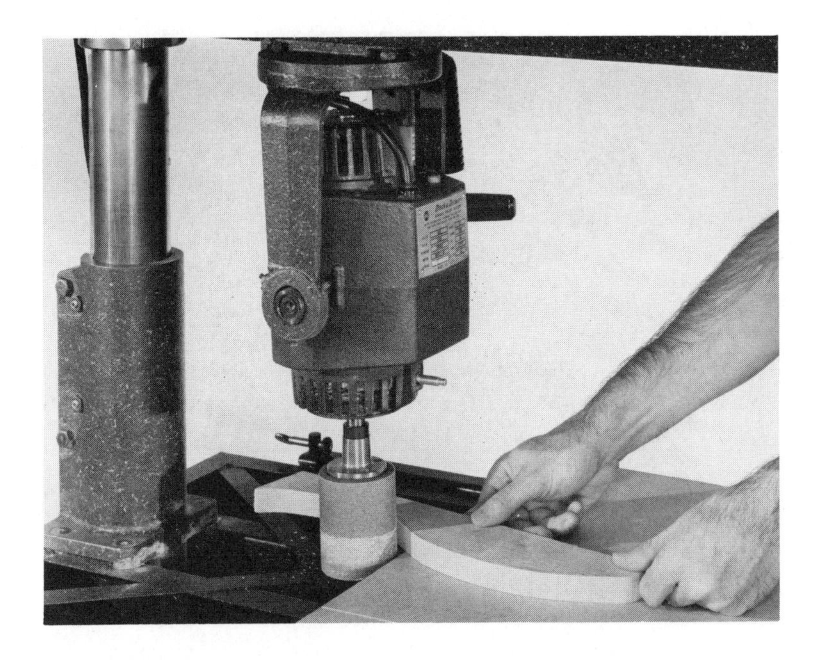

**FIGURE 7-38** / Irregularly curved workpieces are sanded as shown. A straight workpiece can be sanded by placing the drum just behind the fence and then using the fence as a guide.

## *7-13* / BUFFING PROCEDURES

The buffing wheel is attached to the arbor with adapters. Set and lock the radial arm controls into the desired position (Fig. 7-30). To polish, apply the applicable type of buffing compound (Sec. 9-10) to the wheel while the wheel is spinning; apply the compound to the downside edge of the wheel. Hold the workpiece firmly and apply with a gentle pressure to the *downside* of the wheel. Rotate the workpiece slowly.

## *7-14* / DRILLING PROCEDURES

Horizontal and angle drilling are easily accomplished on the radial arm saw providing you have an auxiliary spindle—the normal saw arbor spins in the wrong direction for drilling. You'll also need a drill chuck and perhaps an adapter. Install the chuck according to the manufacturer's instructions.

**FIGURE 7-39** / Drum sanding is effective in smoothing internal edges and irregular curved edges.

Figure 7-41 illustrates edge drilling. The saw yoke is placed so that the accessory chuck attached to the arbor is facing inward. Because the motor width prevents the lowering of the chuck to the table, it may be necessary to raise the workpiece on blocks so that the drill will meet the marked center line. Clamp the workpiece to a support (or the fence).

Advance the drill (wood boring) bit (Sec. 3-2) slowly by pushing the head across the radial arm. Occasionally pull the head and drill bit forward to remove dust in the hole.

Figure 7-42 illustrates the drilling of holes into the surface of a workpiece with a twist drill. Notice that a wide scrap piece of wood has been clamped to the fence to backup the workpiece, thus aiding in preventing the back of the workpiece from splitting when the drill comes through.

Holes may also be drilled accurately into the end of a workpiece. Rotate the radial arm saw yoke to the crosscut position. Locate the drill so that the fence may be used as a guide. *Feed the workpiece* along the fence and into the drill.

**FIGURE 7-40** / In buffing, hold the workpiece firmly and apply light pressure to the wheel.

## *7-15* / SABER SAWING

The radial arm saw is easily converted to a saber saw by attaching the accessory to the arbor; two knurled fasteners screw the attachment to the motor housing. Some provision must be made at the table for the saber blade that strokes up and down; either a hole can be drilled through the table or an auxiliary table with a hole can be clamped to the radial arm saw table.

As shown in Fig. 7-43, the saber saw attachment is versatile because it can cut internal and external cuts along straight, curved, beveled, and any other irregular line. Various saber saw blades (Sec. 4-2) permit the cutting of wood, fiber, plastics, thin ferrous metals, aluminum, copper, cardboard, leather, rubber, and other similar materials.

**FIGURE 7-41** / Horizontal drilling with the radial arm saw. The chuck is attached to the auxiliary spindle.

Install the proper blade for the material being cut. Place the radial arm saw in the crosscut configuration, and lock the radial arm, yoke, and the bevel (to the desired angle if applicable). Slide the head on the carriage until the blade is over the hole provided in the table for the reciprocating blade. Lock the carriage and lower the head to the desired height. Feed the workpiece into the blade and let the blade do the cutting.

## *7-16* / ACCESSORIES

Because accessories are so vital for the versatile applications of the radial arm saw, all of the important accessories have already been covered in this chapter: buffing wheel, dado head, disk sander, drill chuck and drills, drum sander, hold down fingers, molding/shaping

**FIGURE 7-42** / In this configuration for horizontal drilling, the head is moved along the carriage. Ends of the workpieces are drilled by rotating the yoke 90°; the workpiece is then fed along the fence into the drill.

head, router bits, saber saw, shaper cutters, shaper guard, and surface planer. Refer to the index for the location of information on these accessories.

Two other convenient accessories are a sawdust collector attachment and an automatic carriage return device. The dust collector eliminates sawdust and cuts down on clean up time. The plastic shroud collector catches chips and dust thrown by the blade and funnels them down a chute into a box or bag. A vacuum cleaner can also be attached.

The automatic carriage return pulls the head of the radial arm saw to the rear of the radial arm after each cutting stroke. The return consists of a spring with a steel guide wire.

## *7-17* / CALIBRATION AND MAINTENANCE

The radial arm saw must be in exact calibration if you expect it to do precision work. Four calibration checks should be made periodically;

**FIGURE 7-43** / Saber sawing on the radial arm saw.

if the checks are not satisfactorily completed, appropriate adjustments should be made in accordance with the manufacturer's directions. The four checks are: table parallel to the radial arm, blade perpendicular to the table, blade *travel* perpendicular to the fence, and *blade* perpendicular to the fence.

*Table Parallel to the Radial Arm*

In order that a consistent depth of cut can be made over the surface of the radial arm saw table, it is necessary for the plane of the table to be parallel to the plane of the radial arm. Place the radial arm saw in the configuration shown in Fig. 7-44. All controls must be set and locked before the final parallelism is checked at each location. By a combined movement of the head back and forth on the radial arm and right and left miter positioning of the radial arm, all corners of the table can be checked. If the table is not parallel to the radial arm as indicated by the arbor, adjust the table as required.

**FIGURE 7-44** / The table must be parallel to the radial arm.

*Blade Perpendicular to the Table*

To ensure 90° cutoffs of workpiece ends, the blade must be perpendicular to the table. Use a square to check perpendicularity (Fig. 7-45). Adjust as required and readjust the bevel zero degree scale pointer.

*Blade Travel Perpendicular to the Fence*

Accurate cutoffs of workpieces require that the blade travels perpendicular to the fence. Use a square to check for perpendicularity (Fig. 7-46). Adjust as required and readjust the miter zero degree scale pointer.

*Blade Perpendicular to the Fence (Heeling)*

The blade itself must be perpendicular to the fence to ensure narrow saw kerfs and to eliminate the splintering of workpieces. Check the blade with a square (Fig. 7-47) and adjust as required.

FIGURE 7-45 / Checking blade perpendicularity.

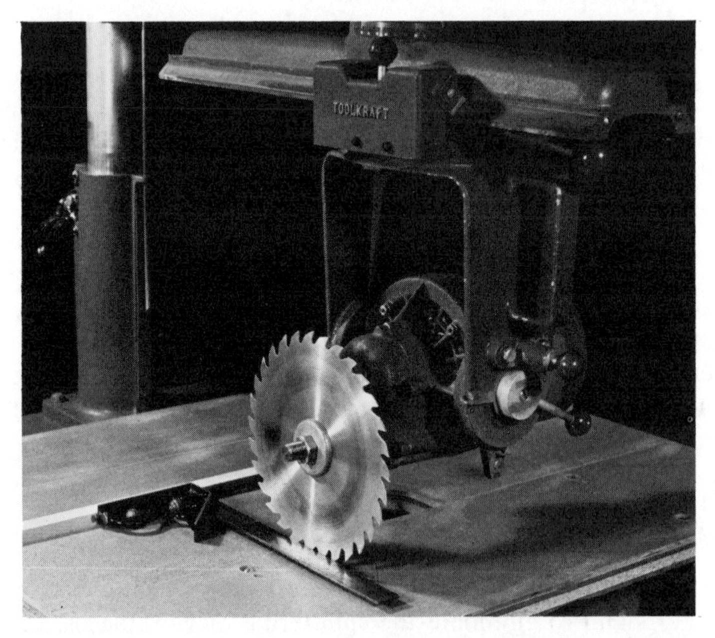


FIGURE 7-46 / The blade must travel perpendicular to the fence.

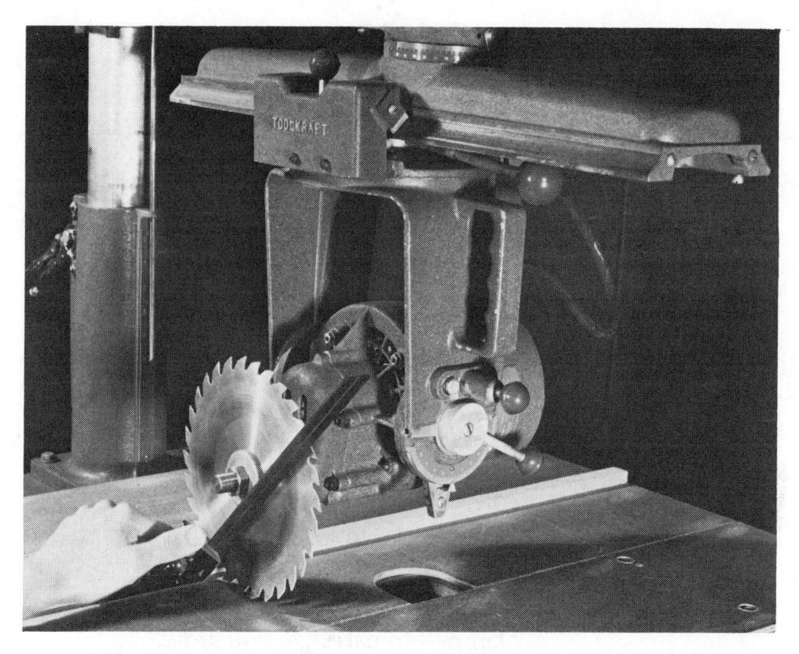

**FIGURE 7-47** / The blade itself must be perpendicular to the fence to provide narrow saw kerfs and to eliminate the splintering of workpieces.

Table 7-2 is an alignment guide for accurate cutting; it is included for your convenience. If you suspect the saw is cutting inaccurately, check its alignment. You are reminded, however, that changing one adjustment will affect another, so it is best to perform all of the alignment procedures in accordance with the manufacturer's instructions when correcting any one problem.

Keep all radial arm saw cutters clean and sharp. Remove pitch with a rag or toothbrush dampened with kerosene. Keep the motor air slots clean and free of chips; hold a vacuum nozzle to the slots to draw out the chips.

The radial arm tracks and bearing surfaces should be kept clean and dry. Periodically wipe the tracks with dry cleaner. Do not oil or grease the tracks.

**Table 7-2**
**ALIGNMENT GUIDE FOR ACCURATE RADIAL ARM SAW CUTTING**

| Problem | Possible Cause | Solution |
|---|---|---|
| 1. Saw will not make a square crosscut or a good 45° miter cut. | Radial arm is not perpendicular to fence. | Adjust crosscut travel with fence. |
| | Radial arm has excessive play at end. | Tighten adjusting screws. |
| | Column is loose in base. | Make proper adjustment. |
| | Too much play between radial arm and column. | Make proper adjustment. |
| | Carriage too loose in arm. | Adjust carriage correctly. |
| | Yoke too loose when clamped to carriage. | Adjust yoke lock handle. |
| | Saw dust between lumber and fence. | Keep table top clean. |
| | Table not parallel with radial arm. | Make proper adjustment. |
| | Fence not straight. | Replace fence. |
| | Rear edge of fixed board not straight. | Sand or replace. |
| 2. Lumber has a tendency to walk away from fence when ripping or ploughing. | Saw blade is not parallel with fence. | Make heel adjustment. |
| | Radial arm not perpendicular to fence. | Adjust crosscut travel with fence. |
| | Dull blade or cutters. | Sharpen or replace blade. |
| 3. Saw stalls when ripping or ploughing. | Fence not straight. | Replace fence. |
| | Feed rate too fast. | Slow feed rate. |
| | Wrong blade. | Use correct blade. |
| | Column too loose in base. | Make proper adjustment. |
| | Too much play between radial arm and column. | Make proper adjustment. |

**Table 7-2 (continued)**

| Problem | Possible Cause | Solution |
|---|---|---|
| | Carriage too loose in radial arm. | Make proper adjustment. |
| | Yoke loose when clamped to carriage. | Make proper adjustment. |
| | Saw dust between lumber and fence. | Keep table top clean. |
| 4. Saw blade scores lumber, not giving a good, finished cut. | Saw blade is heeling. | Make heel adjustment. |
| | Column too loose in base. | Make proper adjustments. |
| | Too much play between radial arm and column. | Make proper adjustments. |
| | Carriage loose in arm. | Make proper adjustments. |
| | Yoke too loose when locked to carriage. | Make proper adjustments. |
| | Bent blade or dull. | Replace blade. |
| | Not feeding saw properly. | Draw saw blade across lumber with a slow and steady pull. |
| | Using improper blade for finish cut desired. | Change blade. |
| 5. Saw blade or dado blades tend to push lumber to one side when cross-cutting. | Saw blade is heeling. | Make heel adjustment. |
| | Column too loose in base. | Make proper adjustments. |
| | Too much play between radial arm and column. | Make proper adjustments. |
| | Carriage too loose in radial arm. | Make proper adjustments. |
| | Yoke too loose | Make proper |

**Table 7-2 (continued)**

| Problem | Possible Cause | Solution |
| --- | --- | --- |
| | when locked to carriage. | adjustments. |
| | Fence not straight. | Replace. |
| | Dull blade or cutters. | Replace or sharpen. |
| 6. Cut depth varies from one end of stock to the other | Table top not parallel with radial arm. | Adjust table top parallel with radial arm. |
| | Column too loose in base. | Make proper adjustments. |
| | Too much play between radial arm and column. | Make proper adjustments. |
| 7. 45° bevel cut not accurate. | Saw blade not perpendicular to table top. | Make saw blade adjustment. |
| | Column too loose in base. | Make proper adjustments. |
| | Too much play between radial arm and column. | Make proper adjustments. |
| | Carriage too loose in arm. | Make proper adjustments. |
| | Yoke too loose when locked to carriage. | Make proper adjustments. |
| | Bevel lock handle loose. | Make proper adjustments. |
| | Table top not parallel with radial arm. | Make proper adjustments. |
| 8. Saw tends to advance over lumber too fast. | Carriage bearings not properly adjusted. | Adjust carriage bearing to radial arm. |
| | Dull blade. | Replace or sharpen. |

Table 7-2 (continued)

| Problem | Possible Cause | Solution |
|---|---|---|
| | Not feeding saw properly. | Draw saw blade across lumber with a slow and steady pull. |
| 9. Saw does not traverse smoothly in tracks. | Dirty tracks. | Clean. |
| | Bad bearing. | Replace bearing. |
| 10. Miter scale not accurate at various miter angles. | Scale pointer not properly adjusted. | Adjust scale pointer. |
| 11. Elevating handle slips when elevating or lowering saw. | Belt tension not sufficient. | Adjust belt tension. |
| | Setscrew in elevating arm loose. | Tighten setscrew. |
| | Base not adjusted properly. | Adjust base to column. |
| 12. Clamping force not sufficient at miter angles other than 45°. | Radial arm lock out of adjustment. | Adjust radial arm lock. |
| 13. Clamping force not sufficient at bevel angles other than 45°. | Bevel lock handle too loose. | Adjust bevel lock handle. |

## *7-18* / INSTALLATION

The installation of the radial arm saw requires more than just physical placement. It also requires that the saw be initially checked for calibration and corrected as required and that an initial set up involving the cutting of grooves into the table be performed. You can only expect accuracy from your radial arm saw if you keep it in calibration/adjustment.

The radial arm saw is usually purchased with a tool stand; however, if yours does not have a stand, build one according to the saw manufacturer's recommendations. The stand should be very sturdy and should place the radial arm table about 33 to 35 inches above the floor. Locate the saw against a wall; there should be room on either side for long workpieces to be placed on the table for crosscutting or pushed through the saw blade for rip cuts. (It is interesting to note that workpieces are placed laterally on the radial arm saw table for both crosscuts and rip cuts.)

Study and learn the use of all controls and adjustments in Sec. 7-4. Perform the calibration and maintenance instructions in Sec. 7-17, and then perform the initial steps of sawing kerfs and troughs into the table as described in this section. The procedures of sawing kerfs and troughs into the table are repeated anytime a new table top is placed on the radial arm saw table.

The most common kerf and trough cuts are sawed 1/16-inch deep into the table top initially so that the head (the head consists of the carriage, yoke, motor, arbor, blade, and blade guard) can be moved into different sawing positions without changing the elevation of the blade. A crosscut kerf, a transfer kerf (crosscut to rip), a rip trough, and a miter trough are cut as follows:

*NOTE*

***The following procedures are shown using a two arm radial arm saw with a four section table. The procedures for a one arm saw and a two section table are the same except that the fence should be placed between the two table sections for the*** miter trough ***cut. Practice this entire procedure once with the power off and the blade slightly elevated before actually making the cuts. Refer to Figs. 7-2, 7-3, and 7-8 for location of the controls and adjustments named in this section.***

*1* / Lock the radial arm to the 0° miter position, the head to the 0° bevel position, and the yoke to the crosscut position (Fig. 7-48). Loosen the carriage lock and place the head to the rear of the radial arm. Lower the blade with the elevation control to a point just barely above the table.

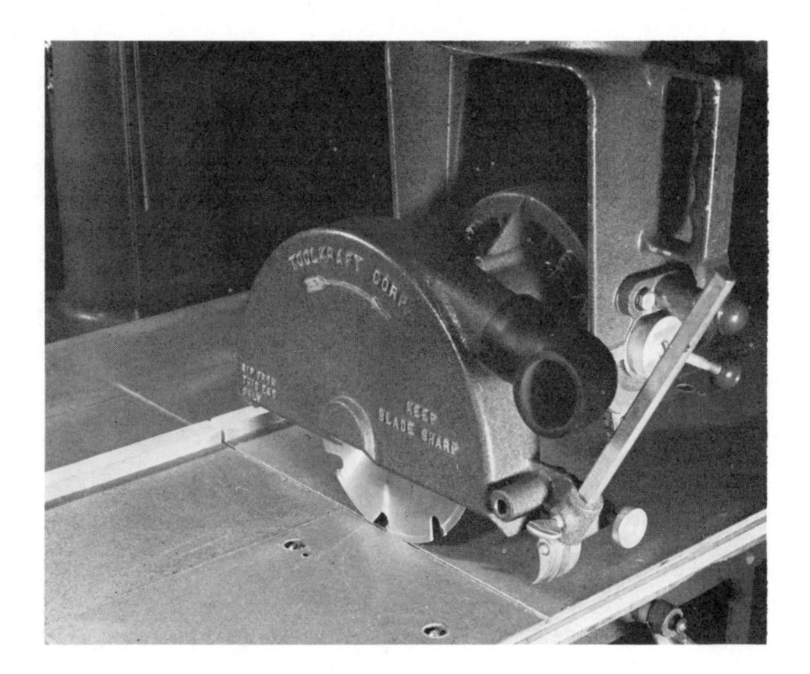


**FIGURE 7-48** / Cutting the crosscut kerf.

*2* / Turn the power on and hold the operating handle. Lower the head and blade with the elevation control until the blade is 1/32- to 1/16-inch deep in the table. Pull the head as far forward as possible and then lock the carriage with the carriage lock.

*3* / With the power still on, loosen the yoke lock, disengage the yoke index lock, and rotate the yoke to cut the transfer kerf (Fig. 7-49). In the rip position, the yoke index lock will again engage. Turn the power off and tighten the yoke lock. The head is now in the *in-rip* position.

*4* / Relocate the fence to the rear of the table (Fig. 7-50); ensure that the table sections are aligned. Turn the saw on. Loosen the carriage lock and *slowly* push the head to within 1/8-inch of the rear of the table. Then slowly pull the head back to the front of the saw and turn the power off. This is the *in-rip* trough.

*5* / Loosen the yoke lock and the yoke index lock. Rotate the

**FIGURE 7-49** / Cutting the transfer kerf.

**FIGURE 7-50** / Cutting the rip trough.

head from the *in-rip* to the *out-rip* position; the index lock will engage. Tighten the yoke lock. Apply power and *slowly* push the head toward the rear of the radial arm and then return it to the front of the arm. When completed, turn the power off; this is the *out-rip* trough. Using the transfer kerf, return the head to the crosscut position.

6 / Relocate the fence to the forward position (Fig. 7-51). Place the head to the rear of the radial arm and tighten the carriage lock.

**FIGURE 7-51** / Cutting the miter trough.

*NOTE*

*Figure 7-51 illustrates the miter trough that is cut by a* two arm *radial arm saw. The miter trough cut by a* one arm *radial arm saw will be the opposite curvature of the circle and should only be cut from 45° left to 45° right.*

7 / Apply power. Loosen the miter lock and disengage the miter index lock. *Slowly* rotate the radial arm to

the left to the fence (or to the rip position) and then to the right to the fence (or the rip position). Do not go more than 90° in either direction.

8 / Now place the saw in the miter positions you anticipate using, such as 30, 45, and 60°. Pull the head forward cutting the mitered kerfs in the table and the fence.

chapter eight

# SANDER (BELT AND DISK)

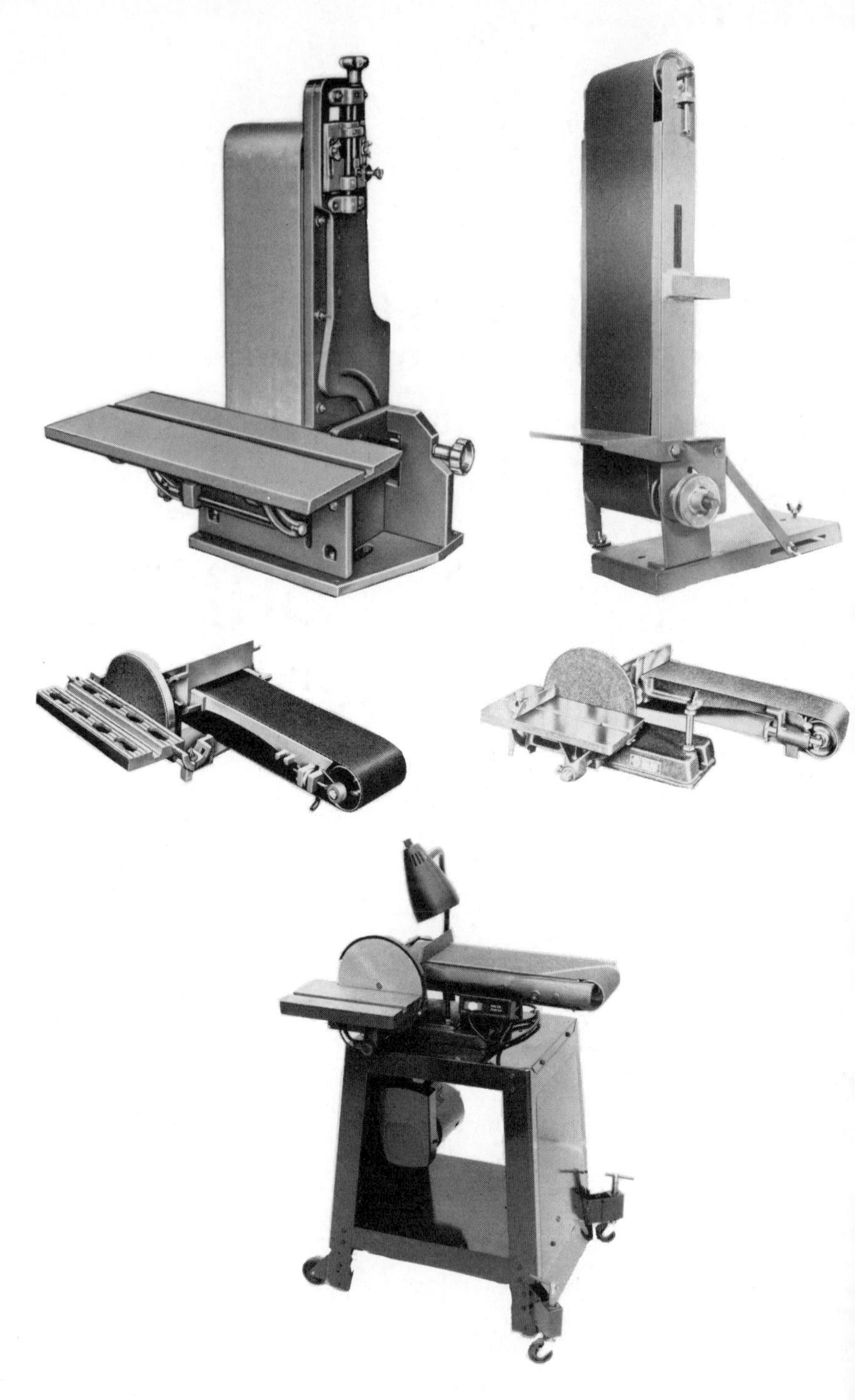

**FIGURE 8-1** / Belt and disk sanders eliminate the drudgery of hand sanding.

If there is one job in the workshop that most people despise, it is sanding—hand sanding that is. But, thanks to the belt and disk sanders, the hard work of hand sanding the edges and surfaces of small workpieces is nearly eliminated.

Belt and disk sanders are available individually or as a combination tool. It is best to choose the combination sander because of the variety of tasks the combination can perform. However, if you had to choose between the two, the belt sander would be the wiser choice; the disk sander can be added later as an accessory to a variety of other power tools you may already own, including the radial arm saw, table saw, and lathe.

The belt sander is a continuous revolving belt used to sand surfaces, edges, and ends of workpiece materials including wood, plastic, and metal. Flat, irregular, and curved surfaces can be sanded. The belt travels between two rollers; the top of the belt travels over a platen, but there is no support plate (platen) on the underside. The belt sander is usually positioned in a horizontal or a vertical position; many belt sanders can also be locked at any angle between horizontal and vertical. Belt sanders are specified by the width of the belt with 6 inches considered the standard width for home machines. You'll find that the wider the belt, the more useful the sander.

The disk sander is a revolving disk used to miter, square, and bevel sand the ends of workpieces. The work table tilts from 90° to 45° and may be locked at any angle. A miter gauge that slides in the work table slot holds the workpiece firmly and allows accurate sanding of workpieces. The disk sander is specified by diameter; a 9 inch diameter disk is usually used in the home workshop.

The combination belt and disk sander offers the most versatility because it combines the features and performs the functions of each separate tool. It needs only one motor and it is continually ready for use (as compared to a disk that is an accessory to another tool).

Sanders are used to smooth end grains, edges, and flat surfaces; to remove nicks, saw marks and deep scratches; and to miter or bevel ends of workpieces for precision fits.

## 8-1 / DESCRIPTION AND MAJOR PARTS

The combination belt and disk sander is shown in Fig. 8-2. The major parts of the *belt* sander are the rollers, abrasive belt, platen, belt alignment and locking screws, and the fence. There are two rollers—the *driven roller* (not illustrated) and the *idler roller.* The driven roller is powered by the tool driven pulley. This roller drives the abrasive belt around the idler roller, across the platen, and around the driven roller again in a counterclockwise direction as viewed in Fig. 8-2. The *idler* roller rotates because of the abrasive belt being driven by the *driven roller.* The idler roller is adjustable and moves either closer to or further from the driven roller to provide tension on the abrasive belt. Tension is adjusted by two *belt alignment screws* and held locked in place by two *belt locking screws*. The abrasive belt is always driven in the direction toward the *fence.* The abrasive belt removes excess stock from the workpiece as the workpiece is held against the belt. Abrasive belts are available in grits from coarse for heavy and rapid stock removal to fine grit for final sanding prior to finishing (such as painting). Abrasives are discussed in detail in Sec. 8-3. The abrasive belt passes over the *platen* that acts as a stiff backing or support for the belt; this assists in the rapid removal of stock and also provides a flat surface so the workpiece is sanded flat. Platens for the 6 inch belt sander are about 6-1/2- by 17 inches. The side of the abrasive belt opposite the platen has no support (platen); with the belt sander in a vertical position, this non-supported side of the belt is very effective in removing stock from curved workpieces. The *fence* acts as a backstop to help the craftsman keep workpieces from sliding off the end of the belt. The fence can be set at 90° to the abrasive belt, or at other angles, or can be removed.

Belt sanders for home use have belt sizes of 4 by 36 inches or 6 by 48 inches. Work tables are about 5 by 12 inches, fences 2 by 5 inches, and the rollers are from 2-1/2- to 3 inches in diameter.

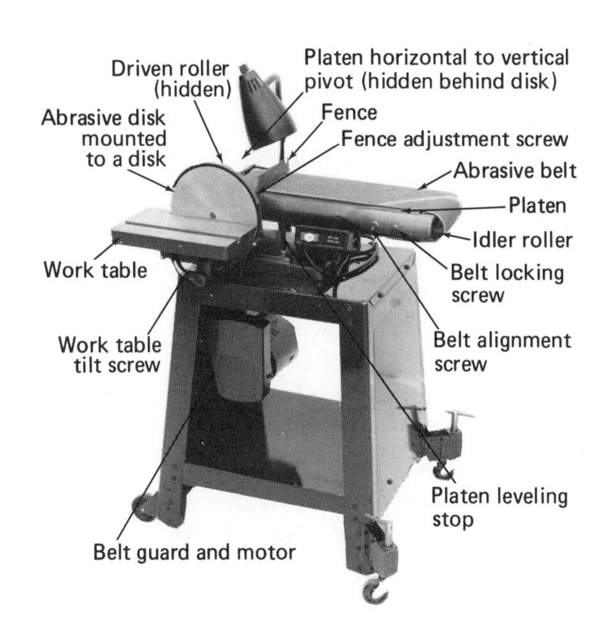


**FIGURE 8-2** / Major parts of the belt and disk sander.

Rollers in less expensive models have bronze sleeve bearings, whereas more expensive models (that expect more use and will last longer) have ball bearings.

Belt sander models (without combination disk sander) are available for horizontal sanding only; others are available for horizontal and vertical sanding. Sizes are 4 by 36 inches and 6 by 48 inches.

The disk sander consists of an *abrasive disk* mounted to a metal *disk,* a *work table,* and a *work table tilt screw.* The abrasive disks are available in grits from coarse to fine (Sec. 8-3) and are adhered to the metal disk either with a self sticking back, rubber cement, or other similar type of mastic made specifically for the purpose. The metal disk is mounted to a drive shaft that is driven by the motor, belt, and pulley assembly. The disk rotates counterclockwise as viewed in Fig. 8-2. Other accessories such as grinding wheels, wire wheels, and buffing wheels may be attached on some models to this drive shaft in place of the metal disk. If you intend to do a lot of coarse and then fine work with the disk sander it is suggested that you have two metal disks with the required abrasives adhered to them; then, changing grits amounts simply to changing metal disks on the drive shaft.

The work table supports the workpiece which is always placed against the *downside* of the spinning disk. The work table can be tilted from horizontal (90°) to 45° as indicated on a graduated angle of tilt scale. Better machines provide stops at the 90 and 45° positions. The work table tilt screw locks the table at any angle between 90 and 45°. A grooved slot in the work table is for a miter gauge that aids in holding the workpiece for beveled or compound angles. The work table is removable and relocatable for use with the belt sander when the belt is in a vertical position. Dust traps that attach to shop vacuums are provided on some models.

Thus, a good combination belt and disk sander for the home workshop has features that include: a belt sander that can be set to any angle from horizontal to vertical, a fence, a 6 inch belt and a 9 inch disk, and a tilting work table that can be located at either the disk or belt sander.

Recommended motors for a 6 inch belt sander are 1/3-hp for general use and 1/2-hp for production use. A 1/4- or 1/3-hp motor can be used for the 4 inch belt sanders. Either 1725 or 2450 rev/min motors in conjunction with the proper sized pulleys should be used as recommended by the manufacturer. The motor speed, pulley, and belt combination results in abrasive belt speeds of approximately 2700 feet per minute and disk speeds of approximately 3450 rev/min. Motors may be mounted below or in back of the tool.

## 8-2 / ABRASIVES

Abrasives are used to prepare wood for a final finish such as stain, varnish, paint, or lacquer. Abrasives are also used to a lesser extent in the home workshop to prepare metal and other materials for final finishing and to polish metals, stones, plastics, and ceramics to very smooth, bright finishes. They are also used to remove paint and rust and to clean workpieces.

Abrasives used on sanders are attached to backings and are often referred to as sandpaper, although the abrasive is not sand nor is the backing very often paper.

Abrasives are adhered to a backing, which may be paper, cloth, fiber, plastic, or paper and cloth combined. A paper backing is usually used as the abrasive backing for hand sanding; the other backing materials are used for machine sanding. Abrasives are manufactured in both open-coat and closed-coat forms. The area of open-coat backing is covered 50 to 70 percent with abrasive; this provides less cutting, more abrasive flexibility, and prevents the abrasive from becoming clogged with residue. With a closed-coat backing, the abrasive covers 100 percent of the backing. Self-cleaning papers are used with belt sanders to remove glue from surfaces. These self-cleaning papers have soap between the grains to prevent clogging. Backings are also classified as standard or wet; residue may be washed away from the wet type of backing.

Abrasive backings are also classified by letter designations: A, lightweight; C, heavier, for hand sanding; D, heavier, for machine sanding; J; and X, which is heavier and less flexible than J.

Abrasive papers are available in sheets, belts, tapes, disks, rolls, and cylinders. Sizes vary as shown in Table 8-1.

You may tear abrasive papers to fit a sanding block or a sanding machine as follows: fold the paper one way and crease it. Then unfold the crease and fold the paper in the opposite direction. Place the crease over a straight edge (as the edge of your workbench) and tear.

**Table 8-1**
**SIZES OF ABRASIVE PAPERS**

| *Format* | *Size* |
|---|---|
| Sheets | 9 x 11, 4-1/2- x 5-1/2-, and 3-2/3- x 9 inches |
| Belts | 2 to 12 inches wide |
| Cylinders | 1-1/2- to 3-1/2- inch diameters |
| Tapes | 1 to 1-1/2- inches wide |
| Disks | 3 to 14 inch diameters |

Clean clogged abrasive paper with a stiff brush, file card, or soft wire brush. Use a rotating motion. A light tapping will also remove some of the residue.

Table 8-2 lists the abrasives most commonly used by home craftsmen, hobbyists, and do-it-yourselfers. The abrasives listed are all adhered to backing. Table 8-3 lists the grades, grit number, number size, and uses of the various grades of abrasive papers for use on sanding machines. The grit number is the number of openings in a screen through which abrasives can pass. The openings vary from 40 (coarse grit) to 180 (very fine grit). The quality of the finished sanding depends upon the grit and the handling of the work. The

**Table 8-2**
**ABRASIVES**

| *Abrasive* | *Color* | *Description* | *Use* |
|---|---|---|---|
| Silicon carbide | Dark gray | Hard, brittle, sharp. | Cuts metals with low tensile strengths and plastics. Also for glass, porcelain, tile, stone, and composition. |
| Aluminum oxide | Brown | Long lasting, fast, tough. | Used on power sanders for sanding wood and metal with high tensile strength. Sharpens tools. Shapes and polishes metal. |
| Garnet | Reddish brown | Inexpensive, tough. | For hand sanding clean wood and general woodworking. Good for soft woods. |
| Flint | Yellow-white | Inexpensive, doesn't last long. Paper clogs easily. Soft. | For sanding painted wood or metal. For sanding gummy wood. |
| Emery | Black | Previously the best abrasive for metal, it has been superseded by silicon carbide and aluminum oxide. | For metal polishing (nonplated metals only). |

highest quality is obtained by first using a coarse grit abrasive for rough sanding followed by finer grits and lighter pressure for final sanding.

**Table 8-3**
**ABRASIVE GRADES**

| *Uses* | *Number* | *Grit No.* | *Grade* |
|---|---|---|---|
| Removal of rough stock; occasionally used on rough wood and for paint removal. | 1-1/2 | 40 | Coarse |
| | 1 | 50 | Coarse |
| | 1/2 | 60 | Coarse |
| Removal of light stock; polishing; deburring; sharpening; all-purpose for shop. | 1/0 | 80 | Medium |
| | 2/0 | 100 | Medium |
| Preparation for finish; fine polishing; sharpening; cabinet work | 3/0 | 120 | Fine |
| | 4/0 | 150 | Fine |
| | 5/0 | 180 | Fine |

## 8-3 / OPERATING CONTROLS AND ADJUSTMENTS

Operating controls and adjustments for the belt and disk sander (Fig. 8-2) include work table tilt, belt fence adjustment, and belt sander platen horizontal to vertical positioning. These adjustments are all made with the motor off.

1 / *work table tilt* and *position*—Loosen the work table tilt screw, position the table to the desired angle, and tighten the work table tilt screw. Stops are usually provided at 90 and 45°; angles in between are indicated on a tilt angle on some sanders. Accurate angles should be set with a bevel or protractor. Loosen the work table position screw, and position the work table to just clear the disk. Tighten the position screw. Note that if the work table can be used with either the disk or the belt sander, two position screws are available—one for belt and one for disk.

2 / *fence tilt*—Loosen the fence adjustment screw, position the

fence to the desired angle, and tighten the adjustment screw. A bevel or protractor should be used to set any accurate angles desired.

3 / belt sander *horizontal to vertical positioning*—Different models adjust differently; check your manufacturer's directions. Usually, two hex-headed bolts are passed through a pivot plate. Loosen the bolts, raise the belt sander to the vertical (or any other desired angle), and tighten the bolts.

## 8-4 / OPERATION

Observe the following cautions prior to any sanding operation:

### CAUTIONS

*1 / Hold the workpiece firmly to keep it from being driven from your hands. Use the fence at all times, if possible.*

*2 / On the disk sander, always sand on the* downside *of the disk and use the work table for support.*

*3 / Workpieces to be sanded should always be dry.*

*4 / Wear goggles or other suitable eye shield.*

*5 / Keep your fingers away from the rotating abrasives at all times. Don't stand in an awkward position.*

*6 / Don't finish any workpieces on the sanders that are too small to hold by hand.*

*7 / Do not attach a vacuum to the sander if iron, steel, or any other materials that create sparks are to be finished on the tool. Sparks can ignite the dust and start a fire.*

*8 / Observe the general safety precautions of Sec. 1-16.*

Perform the following operations before using either the belt or disk sander:

1 / Select and place the applicable grit or abrasive on the belt or disk (Sec. 8-8).

2 / Position the belt sander to the horizontal, vertical, or other required angle. Set the fence into position.

3 / Locate the work table to just clear the abrasive, and tilt it to the required angle.

4 / Apply electrical power to the motor, and let the motor run up to full speed. Check for proper belt tracking; if the belt is not tracking correctly, immediately turn power off and refer to Sec. 8-8.

5 / Perform either the belt sanding procedures (Sec. 8-5) or the disk sanding procedures (Sec. 8-6).

## 8-5 / BELT SANDING PROCEDURES

The belt sanding procedures that follow give you some general procedures for: producing quality finished workpieces, sanding very long workpieces, sanding wide workpieces, edge sanding, sanding warped boards, squaring and end finishing angled workpieces, contour sanding, and also for "drum" sanding.

Workpieces should always be sanded with the grain. If it becomes necessary to sand against the grain, try to hold the workpiece so that the grain is at a slight angle. Sanding with the grain will prevent the abrasive scratches from showing.

Surface sanding is performed on the platen side of the belt sander. Use a light, firm, even pressure to hold the workpiece against the abrasive and the fence (Fig. 8-3). For rapid removal of stock and rough sanding, hold the workpiece grain at a slight angle to the belt. At all times, move the workpiece slowly back and forth across the belt or in a slightly oval direction; this prevents the abrasive from "burning" the workpiece and from placing long lengthwise scratches in the workpiece. It also prevents the belt from becoming grooved. If the belt stalls or the rollers are slipping under the belt, increase the tension on the belt (Sec. 8-8).

The normal length that the belt sander accommodates is the length from the idler roller to the fence—about 16 inches on a 6 by 48 inch sander. If your workpiece is somewhat longer, remove the fence. Start the workpiece on the idler roller end, and gradually move the workpiece along the belt to the other end. For very long workpieces, use a workpiece extended beyond the sander.

Workpieces wider than the belt width are fed at a slant. Keep

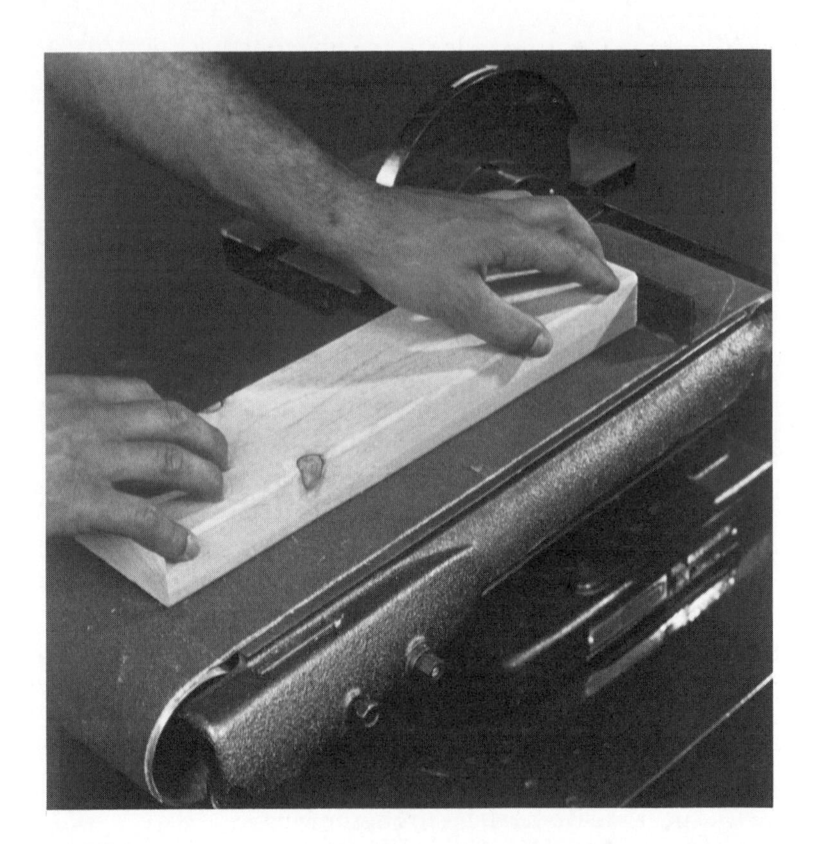

**FIGURE 8-3** / Hold the workpiece lightly but firmly against the belt and fence for surface sanding. Move the workpiece slowly across the belt, keeping your fingers away from the abrasive.

the angle of slant as small as possible; and move the workpiece continuously from end to end to sand the entire surface.

Use the fence when edge sanding (Fig. 8-4), and hold the workpiece steady at the desired angle. For square edges, you can clamp scrap pieces of wood to each side of the workpiece and sand the "sandwich"; this will aid you to sand the workpiece square. To get a true 90° edge sanding, add an accessory wooden fence along the length of the belt (Fig. 8-5). Some sanders are drilled for this accessory fence; if yours is not, drill holes and bolt on a hardwood fence or drill and tap and bolt on the fence. Hold the workpiece lightly against the belt and firmly against the fence.

Warped boards can be sanded flat on the belt sander. Use a coarse belt and hold the concave side of the workpiece flat against

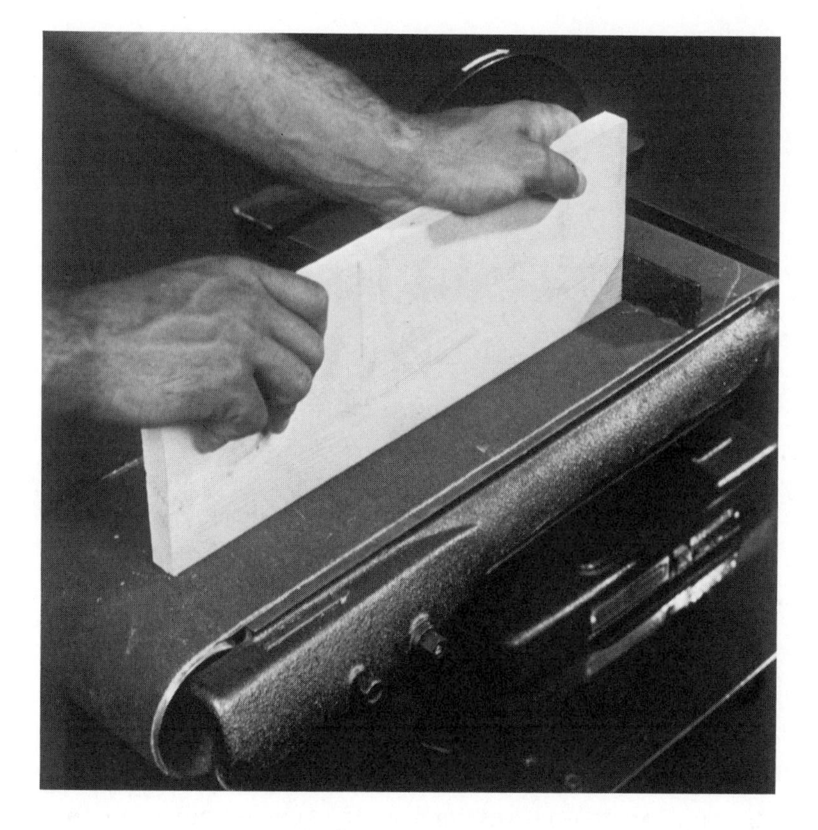

**FIGURE 8-4** / Edge finishing.

the belt. When the concave side is flat, turn the board over and, holding the convex side of the board parallel to the platen, sand the board flat. (For other treatments of warped boards, refer to Chaps. 5 and 12.)

To finish large workpiece ends square or at an angle, the belt sander can be placed in a vertical position. (Small workpiece ends are squared or angled on the disk sander, Sec. 8-6.) Attach the work table to support the workpiece (Fig. 8-6). Advance the workpiece gently into the moving belt, and move the workpiece back and forth across the belt. Remember that the work table can also be tilted to 45° and the miter can be used for increased accuracy.

Contour sanding of inside curves is done on the end rollers as shown in Fig. 8-7. This is similar to drum sanding done on other tools. Keep the workpiece moving.

The unsupported side (no platen) of the belt sander is used in

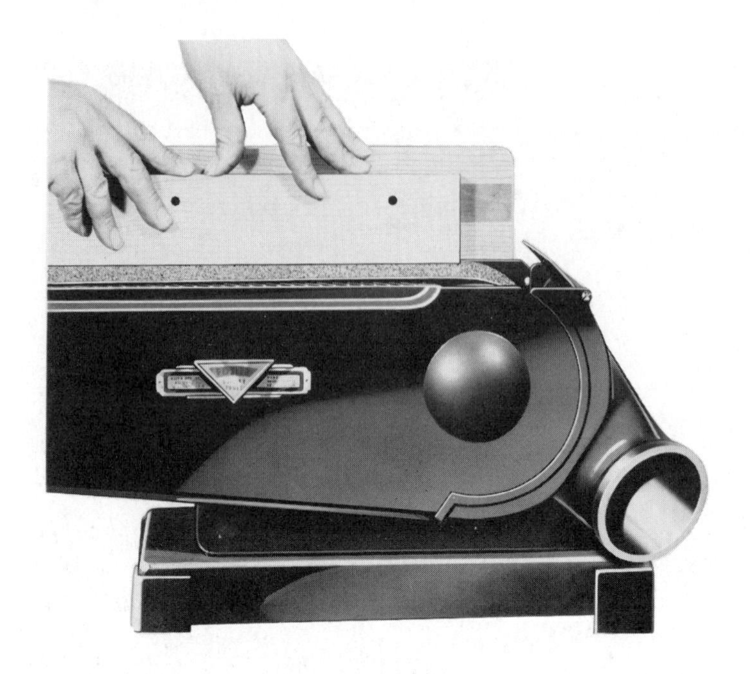

**FIGURE 8-5** / An auxiliary fence aids in producing true 90° sanded edges.

the vertical position for convex surfaces (Fig. 8-8). This is a good way to sand gradual curves such as the outside curve on rockers. Adjust the belt tension to suit the curve of the workpiece. Keep the workpiece moving to avoid burning it.

Very irregular workpieces can be effectively sanded by slashing the abrasive backing in strips about 1/8-inch wide. Short, uncut sections spaced randomly hold the strips together. The workpiece is sanded against the unbacked side of the sander in the vertical position.

## 8-6 / DISK SANDING PROCEDURES

Workpieces are always sanded on the *downside* of the disk (Fig. 8-9); this prevents the workpiece from being kicked up by the revolving disk. Hold the workpiece lightly against the disk, and move it back and forth slowly to prevent burning the workpiece and damaging the abrasive. The work table should always be used as a support for the

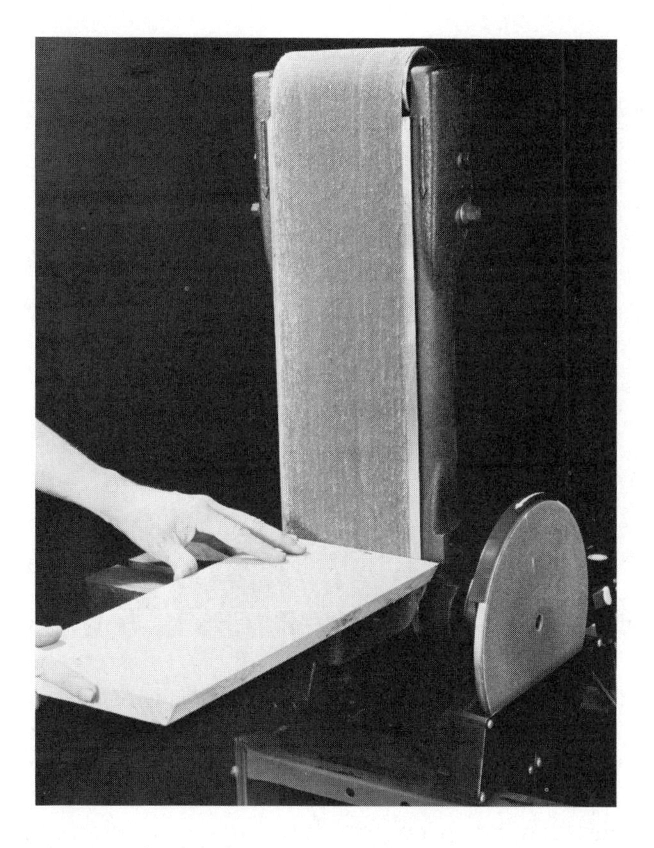

**FIGURE 8-6** / Large ends can be sanded with the belt sander in the vertical position.

workpiece. The table can be tilted from 90 to 45° for bevel cutting. The miter is a handy accessory that increases control of the workpiece against the revolving disk and allows for accurate mitered sanding including squared ends, chamfering, and angled ends. By use of the miter gauge and the tilting table, accurate compound angles can be finished smoothly on the disk.

Because of the revolving disk, the disk sander cuts across the grain. Therefore, if your workpiece demands final sanding for natural or stained finishes, the final sanding should be done with the grain on the belt sander.

In sanding convex curves on the disk sander, make a number of light passes of the workpiece against the disk. If you have a number of sanding operations to perform that require use of coarse and fine

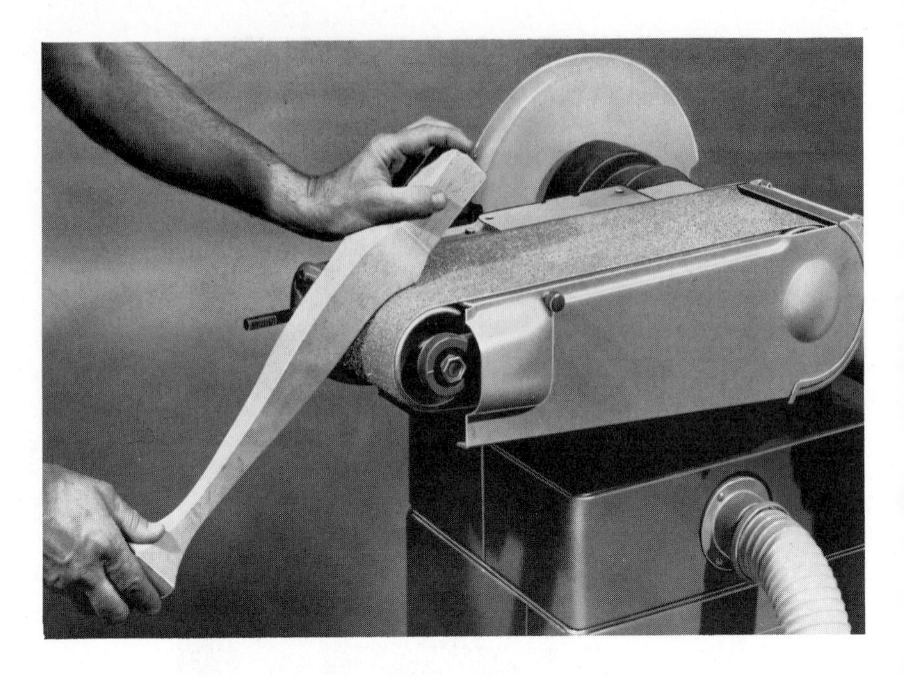

**FIGURE 8-7** / Contour sanding is done over the belt sander roller.

abrasives, obtain an extra disk. Attach a coarse abrasive disk to one and a fine abrasive disk to the other.

Pivot jigs can be made to allow for the accurate sanding of round workpieces. Clamp the jig shown in Fig. 4-11 to the work table in front of the disk sander. Placement should be such that the workpiece is sanded on the *downside* of the disk.

## 8-7 / ACCESSORIES

Accessories for the belt and disk sander that have been previously discussed include the miter gauge, the auxiliary fence, and an additional disk. In addition, the following accessories can be individually placed on the disk shaft: drum sander, grinding wheel, buffing wheel, wire brush, and rotary files and drills if a chuck can be installed onto the shaft. The work table can be used with each of these accessories; a lamp can also be attached to provide intense illumination of the work area. A shop vacuum hose can be attached to rid your shop of much dust.

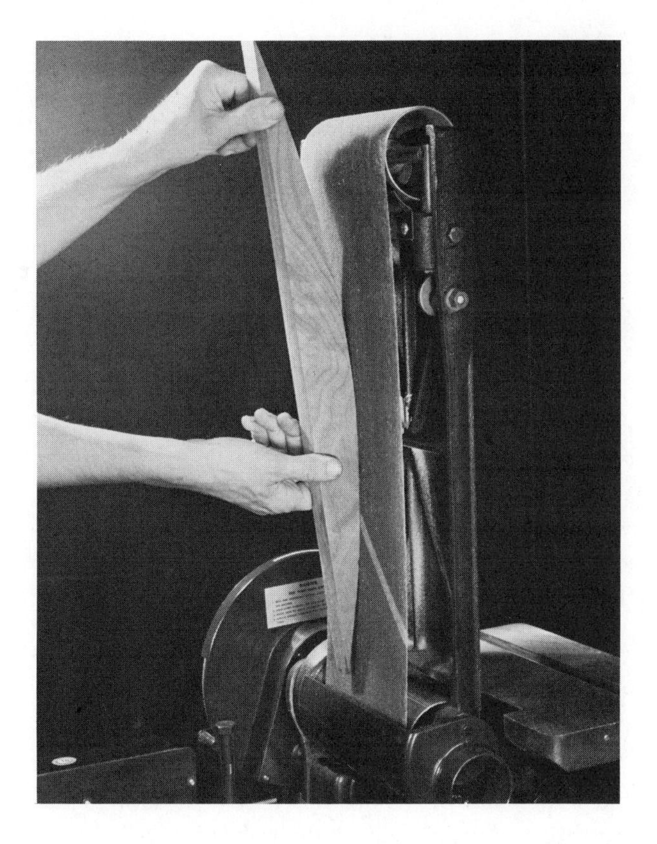

**FIGURE 8-8** / The unsupported side of the belt sander is used for gradually curved convex surfaces.

## 8-8 / BELT AND DISK REPLACEMENT

The abrasive belt is removed by sequentially loosening the two belt locking screws and the two belt alignment screws (Fig. 8-2); after loosening the locking screws, simultaneously loosen the alignment screws—the same number of turns on each side. This will permit rapid replacement with correct belt tracking on the rollers. When the belt is slack, remove it and replace it with another belt. The arrow on the inside of the belt is placed in the direction of rotation of the belt—toward the fence. Do not use any belt dressing.

With the belt placed in the center of the rollers, simultaneously tighten the belt alignment screws to draw the idler roller out and increase the belt tension the same on both sides. The belt tension can

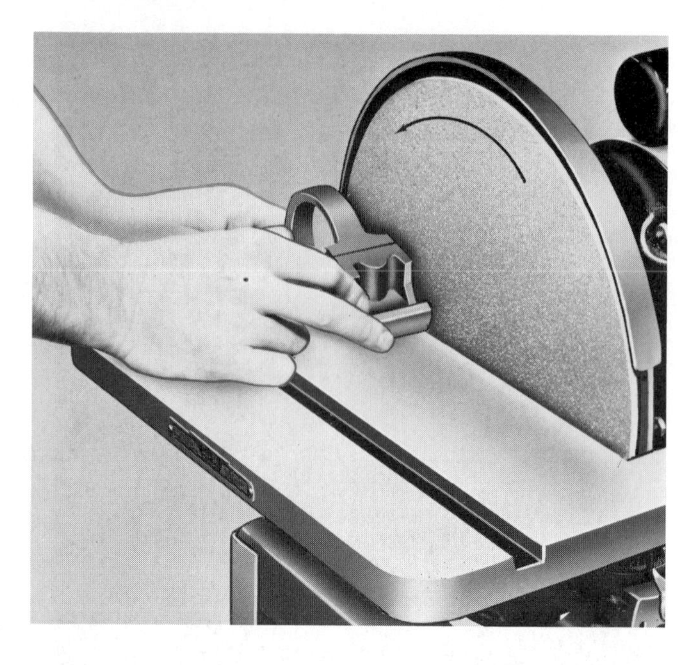

**FIGURE 8-9** / Sand workpieces on the *downside* of the rotating disk.

not be so tight that it stretches the belt and causes it to separate, nor so loose that irregular work is produced. The tension is about right if the side opposite the platen will deflect about 1/2-inch when pressed with moderate finger pressure. If in operation, the belt slips or the rollers turn faster than the belt, then the belt is too loose and additional tension is required. If you have a combination belt and disk sander, another method to check proper belt tension is to hold the disk with one hand while trying to push the belt across the platen with the other hand; if the belt does not slip very easily, the tension is proper. With the tension correctly set, tighten the belt locking screws.

Turn the motor on and observe the tracking of the belt over the rollers—if the belt remains centered, tracking is correct. If the belt moves to one side, turn the motor off immediately. If the belt moves to the right, loosen the right belt locking screw; turn the motor on, and adjust the right belt alignment screw until the belt runs in the center of the drive roller (the roller opposite the idler roller). Only a slight rotation of the belt alignment screw is necessary. If there is still a difficulty in adjusting the tracking, increase the tension on both sides. When the tracking is correct, tighten the right belt locking screw. If the belt moved to the left rather than the right, perform the preceding procedure using the left side belt locking screw and belt alignment screw instead of the right side screws.

Some belt sanders use a different arrangement for adjusting belt tension; the arrangement uses a lock knob and a tension lever. To adjust tension, the lock knob is loosened, the lever is moved, and the lock knob is retightened.

Sanding disks are available with pressure sensitive backs—simply peel off the back, align the disk with the metal disk, and set in place. Rub from the center out to get rid of any trapped air. Disks without pressure sensitive backs are applied by various disk cements or rubber cements available. One type of disk cement is in stick form and is applied to a rotating disk. When coated, the disk is stopped and the abrasive disk is applied. This type of cement is removed from the disk with a scraper or putty knife. Rubber cement is merely rubbed off with the finger.

## *8-9* / CALIBRATION AND MAINTENANCE

The calibration and maintenance procedures on the belt and disk sanders consist of making the abrasive belt horizontal to the floor, aligning the work table 45 and 90° stops, and lubrication. Paste wax can be applied to the work table for protection, but it should never be applied to the platen.

Check that the abrasive belt is level with the floor by placing a level on the abrasive belt along the length of the platen. If the abrasive belt and platen are not level, loosen the two adjustment locks on the platen horizontal to vertical pivot (Fig. 8-2) that permit the platen to move from horizontal to vertical. Loosen the locknut on the platen leveling stop. Screw the stop in or out until the table is level. Tighten the platen leveling stop locknut and the two adjustment lock bolts on the platen horizontal to vertical pivot.

The work table may incorporate 90 and 45° stops. Using a triangle or bevel, set the table to 90° and then 45° with respect to the disk. If the angles are not exact, loosen the respective stop locknut, and turn the stop in or out until the angle is correct. Tighten the locknut.

Lubricate the cams and shafts in the idler pulley mechanisms with light oil. If the rollers are on bronze bearings, place a few drops of oil on each side of the bearings on the shafts prior to each operation.

## *8-10* / HINTS AND KINKS

If you have a large number of similar curved workpieces to sand, you can build a form the shape of the long concave workpieces. Attach the form to the platen and use a longer sanding belt.

## *8-11* / INSTALLATION

Bolt the belt, disk, or combination belt and disk sander onto a firm work stand or table so that the work area is between 34 and 36 inches above the floor. The motor may be located either below or behind the sander and should be mounted so that the disk rotates counterclockwise when facing the disk; the abrasive belt should move toward the fence. Allow ample work space around the tool. Perform the calibration and maintenance procedures of Sec. 8-9.

# chapter nine

# SANDER-GRINDER

**FIGURE 9-1** / The sander-grinder sands, grinds, polishes, sharpens, and deburrs. It works well on wood, metals, plastics, and other materials.

The sander-grinder, a relatively new tool in the home workshop, lends itself to a variety of operations that include sanding, grinding, polishing, sharpening, and deburring. It is a valuable tool for finishing very small workpieces and contoured workpieces and for sharpening blades, chisels, lawn and garden tools, and lawn mower blades. The sander-grinder works well on nearly all materials including wood, metal, plastics, composition materials, leather, rubber, and ceramics.

All models of sander-grinders can be used for operations on *external* parts of workpieces. Some models can also be used for *internal* operations (Fig. 9-2) by rearranging idler pulleys and

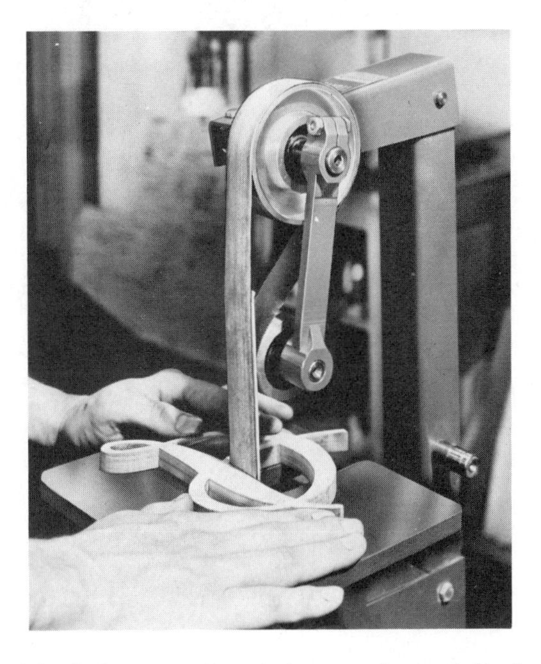

**FIGURE 9-2** / Some sander-grinders can be used for internal as well as external operations.

threading the abrasive belt through the workpiece. By removing a metal platen, the belt is free to assume the contour of the workpiece for sanding intricate designs. Some models operate in both a vertical and a horizontal position. Models may be portable or may be bolted to a bench or work stand.

## 9-1 / DESCRIPTION AND MAJOR PARTS

The sander-grinder (Figs. 9-3 and 9-4) has a replaceable driven abrasive belt that passes by a platen and a tilting table. The workpiece is placed on the table for support and is then pressed against the moving belt. The platen, located behind the belt, provides support to the belt to facilitate a high rate of stock removal from the workpiece and also provides for *square* grinding and sanding. The platen is removable on some models; with the platen removed, the

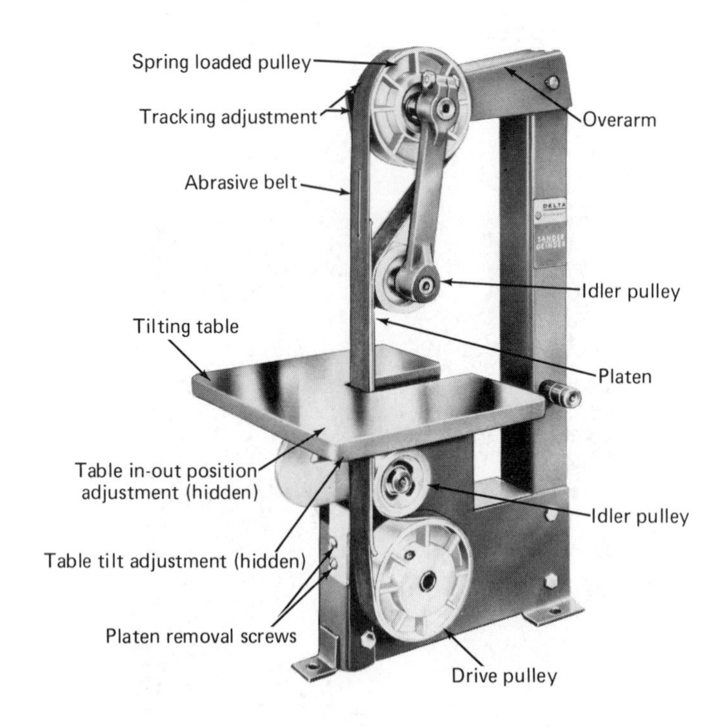


**FIGURE 9-3** / This sander-grinder operates on internal as well as external surfaces and has a removable platen.

belt is free to turn slightly and thus provide contoured cutting. On models without a platen, contoured cutting can sometimes be accomplished on the back side of the belt. (This is slightly hazardous, however, as the belt is moving upward with no table or other support for the workpiece.)

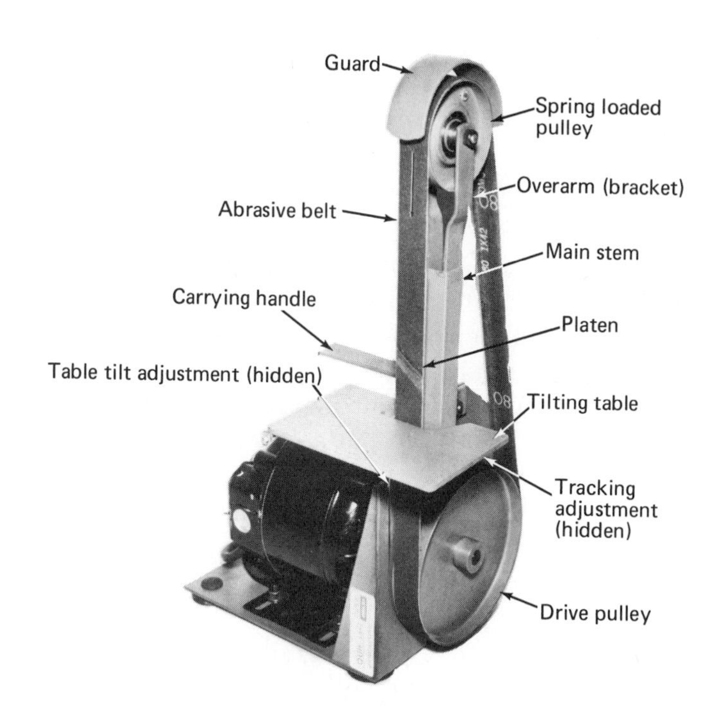


**FIGURE 9-4** / This sander-grinder has many features of the more expensive models but it does not make internal cuts and the platen is fixed.

The major parts of the sander-grinder are the abrasive belt, tilting table, platen, drive pulley, idler pulleys, and a spring loaded pulley. The abrasive belts are 1 by 42 inches on most models, but at least one model has belts of 2 by 48 inches. The abrasive belts are available with different types of grit materials and in grit sizes from coarse to fine (Sec. 9-2). The belts are driven at 2700–4000 SFPM by the stationary drive pulley. A tracking adjustment is set to align the belt on the pulleys. The tilting table is approximately 7 by 9 inches and tilts from 10° in to 90° out. The platen, as previously mentioned, backs up the abrasive belt for square cutting and aids in more rapid stock removal. The drive pulley, idler pulleys, and spring loaded pulley are ball bearing. The drive pulley, driven by the motor, provides the driving force to the abrasive belt. (On some models, the motor is mounted internally and directly drives the main pulley.) The idler pulleys control the direction of the abrasive belt for external or internal operations. The spring loaded pulley provides the correct tension to the abrasive belt during operation and is depressed to relieve tension when the belts are changed. The overall size of the sander-grinder is about 21 inches high, 10 inches wide, and 22 inches deep.

Check the manufacturer's recommendation for the proper motor speed—either 1725 or 3450 rev/min depending upon the size of the abrasive belt drive pulley. A 1/4-, 1/3-, or 1/2-hp motor is recommended for a 1 by 42 inch abrasive belt, whereas a 1/2-hp motor is recommended for a 2 by 48 inch abrasive belt.

In selecting your sander-grinder, try to anticipate your needs as compared to the other tools in your shop. For example, do you have a bench grinder now? Could you put an abrasive belt on your band saw (Sec. 2-6)? Do you have or do you anticipate buying a belt and disk sander (Chap. 8)? Will you use the sander-grinder for internal operations on workpieces? Purchase the sander-grinder that will meet your present as well as your future needs.

## 9-2 / ABRASIVE BELTS

Abrasive belts used on the sander-grinder are usually aluminum oxide or silicon carbide. The aluminum oxide is an all-purpose belt used with most materials. Silicon carbide is used in lapidary work, glass sanding, and on hard, brittle, low tensile strength materials. Grits run between sizes 50 and 320 or higher. The coarse grits—50 to 80—are used to quickly remove material. Medium grits of 100-150 are for polishing, deburring, and sharpening. Fine grits of 200 and up are for fine polishing and fine sharpening. Refer to Sec. 8-2 for more detailed information on abrasives.

All materials can be worked on a dry belt. For production work and for professional quality work, a low melting point grease is used on the belts for cooler cutting, a better finish, and long belt life. A lubricant should always be used when grinding aluminum and other soft metals such as brass and zinc to keep the abrasive belt from *loading.* The grease also prevents overheating when some kinds of plastics and steel are ground.

You may sometimes want an abrasive belt narrower than 1 inch. You can split a 1 inch belt by turning it inside out and cutting a slot in the belt at the desired width with a knife. Tear the belt a few inches at a time one way, and then reverse the tearing action. This reversal will help prevent the belt from unraveling.

## 9-3 / OPERATING CONTROLS AND ADJUSTMENTS

The less expensive sander-grinders (Fig. 9-4) have only one operating control: table tilt position. More sophisticated sander-grinder controls and adjustments (Fig. 9-3) include table tilt position, table in-out position, platen removal, and idler pulley positioning.

1 / *table tilt* position—This is a hex head bolt adjustment that is loosened, followed by table positioning to the desired angle and retightening of the bolt. A do-it-yourself homebuilt angle indicator can be added as suggested in Sec. 9-10, or a bevel, protector, or triangle can be used to set the desired angle.

2 / *table in-out* position—This is also a hex head bolt adjustment. Loosen the bolt; pull or push the table to the desired distance from the abrasive belt. Retighten the bolt.

3 / *platen removal*—To remove the platen for *strapping* operations on contoured workpieces, remove two round head screws and the platen. When desired, replace the platen and secure with the two screws.

4 / *idler pulley positioning*—The lower idler pulley is removed from front to rear or vice versa by removing a hex head screw from a shaft, removing the pulley and relocating it to the other shaft, and fastening securely with the screw. The upper idler pulley is moved forward or backward after the bolt in the idler arm is loosened. Once the idler arm pulley is in position, the bolt is retightened.

## *9-4* / OPERATION

Perform the following procedures to operate the sander-grinder, and observe the following cautions:

### *CAUTIONS*

*Always wear safety glasses or a face shield. Keep your hands away from the abrasive belts, and never wear gloves or hold the workpiece with a rag. Always perform operations on the downward side of the belt so that the work is held securely on the table. Review all safety precautions in Sec. 1-16.*

*1* / Select the desired abrasive belt (Sec. 9-2) and install it onto the sander-grinder for either external or internal operations (Sec. 9-8). Ensure that the arrow on the inside of the belt is pointing down when it passes the tilting table.

*2* / Set the tilting table to the desired in-out position and angle of tilt. Use a protractor, triangle, or bevel to set accurate angles.

*3* / Install or remove the platen, as required for the proposed operation.

*4* / Rotate the drive pulley and abrasive belt by hand to ensure that the abrasive belt is tracking properly, and that there is sufficient clearance between the abrasive belt and all sander-grinder parts.

*5* / Apply electrical power to the motor and perform sanding (Sec. 9-5) or grinding, polishing, and sharpening procedures (Sec. 9-6).

## *9-5* / SANDING PROCEDURES

Wood plastic, composition, or similar type workpieces are sanded by simply holding the workpiece on the tilting table and against the moving abrasive belt (Fig. 9-5). The table acts as a support for straight and angular sanding; it also prevents the workpiece from being "grabbed" from your hands and spun around the belt.

For fast removal of stock and for square removal of stock, leave the platen in place. For slower stock removal and for contoured surfaces, remove the platen (Sec. 9-3).

**FIGURE 9-5** / To sand, place the workpiece on the tilting table and press the workpiece against the moving abrasive belt.

*CAUTION*

***If any operations are performed on the back of the sander-grinder, or on the front with the tilting table removed, ensure a positive grip with both hands on the workpiece at all times. Also perform the operations in the center of the abrasive belt, not near the pulleys.***

To contour wood, remove the platen and install a coarse abrasive belt. Rotate and move the workpiece to and fro to get the desired effect. If the platen is not removable, you can contour on the outside of the rear of the abrasive belt by turning the sander-grinder around (Fig. 9-6).

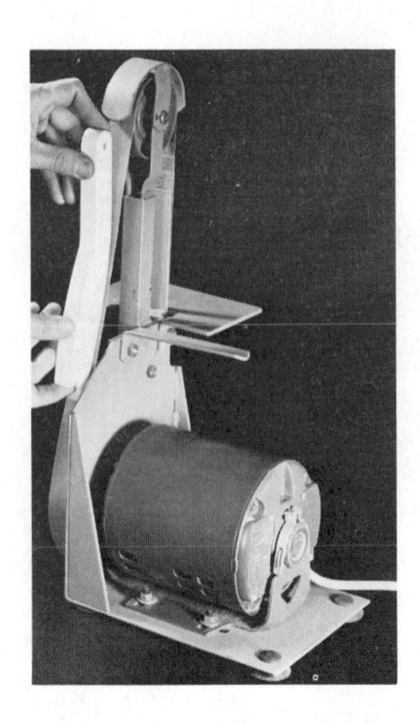

**FIGURE 9-6** / If the platen is not removable, contour sanding/polishing can be done on the rear of the belt but be sure to hold the workpiece firmly.

## 9-6 / GRINDING, POLISHING, AND SHARPENING PROCEDURES

These procedures are generally the same as for sanding, but you should always use the tilting table to prevent the workpiece from "grabbing" on the abrasive belt and being pulled from your hands (Fig. 9-7). When tools are sharpened, set the table to the original angle of the edge to be sharpened (Fig. 9-8). Sometimes you may find that a piece of wood clamped to the table helps to support the tool (for example, when grinding a short handled butt chisel).

You can sharpen circular saw blades using a 120 grit belt. Sharpen every other tooth on one side. Make a complete circle, and then turn the blade over and sharpen the other teeth.

When polishing aluminum or other soft metals, first cover the abrasive belt with ordinary blackboard chalk. This prevents the aluminum from clogging the belt, and it also gives a better polishing effect. The platen is often removed for polishing.

**FIGURE 9-7** / Hold metal workpieces firmly against the table.

**FIGURE 9-8** / When grinding or honing the edge of a tool, set the table to the original bevel of the tool.

## 9-7 / ACCESSORIES

Depending upon the different manufacturer's designs of sander-grinders, there are different accessories available including a disk sander attachment (refer to Chap. 8), motor switch rod, 1/2-inch flat platen for 1/2-inch wide abrasive belts, 1/2-inch radius convex platen for 1 inch belts, and a contact wheel. Other than the contact wheel, the accessories are self-explanatory.

The contact wheel is a grooved rubber wheel used in combination with an abrasive belt to remove flash, to deburr, to descale, and to remove excess stock. The contact wheel replaces the drive pulley (Fig. 9-2). The abrasive belt is mounted around the contact wheel and the spring loaded pulley; the idler pulleys are not used. To facilitate use of the contact wheel, the sander-grinder should be located to the extreme right hand side of the workbench or power tool stand. The workpiece is held against the abrasive belt at the contact wheel so that the contact wheel is backing up the belt at the point of contact of the workpiece with the belt. The platen and tilting table are removed during contact wheel operations.

## 9-8 / BELT REPLACEMENT

Belt replacement is easily accomplished. To remove the belt, depress the spring tensioned overarm to loosen the belt. Remove the belt. Arrange the idler pulleys for external (Fig. 9-9) or internal (Fig. 9-10) operations. With the overarm depressed, center the abrasive belt over the pulleys and over the front of the platen; the direction arrow on the inside of the belt should be pointing down at the table. For internal operations, the belt also has to pass through the workpiece. Release the overarm. Rotate the drive pulley (and hence the abrasive belt) by hand to ensure that the belt is tracking properly. If tracking is incorrect, refer to Sec. 9-9.

## 9-9 / CALIBRATION AND MAINTENANCE

The tracking adjustment is the only adjustment of a calibration nature required on the sander-grinder. To make a tracking adjustment, first disconnect power. Then rotate the abrasive belt by hand by rotating the drive pulley. Determine the direction (left or right) of

**FIGURE 9-9** / Arrangement of pulleys for external sander-grinder operations.

**FIGURE 9-10** / Arrangement of pulleys for internal sander-grinder operations.

the tracking error. Then adjust the tracking adjustment, according to the manufacturer's instructions, until the belt tracks in the center of the pulleys and platen. This usually involves loosening one screw and tightening another until the belt tracks correctly. The adjustment is usually very slight. Once the adjustment is satisfactory without power applied, apply power and make any final adjustment necessary.

On models that have a bracket fitting into the upper step, occasionally place a small amount of grease on the bracket so that it slides easily within the stem.

Abrasive belts can be cleaned by brushing the dirt from them with a whisk broom or soft metal brush. The motor is off during this operation.

## *9-10* / HINTS AND KINKS

Don't throw away your old abrasive belts. Instead, turn the belts inside out and apply jeweler's rouge liberally to the belt. Then use the belt to hone and polish workpieces. Red jeweler's rouge is used for gold and silver; white for aluminum, nickel, chrome, and stainless steel; and brown tripoli for brass, copper, and pewter.

I haven't seen a sander-grinder table with a tilt scale on it yet. But, you can make your own for the standard angles of 0, 30, 45, and 60°. Cut and bend a piece of wire for a pointer; epoxy the wire to the tilting table bracket so that the pointer points to a clear area on the frame. Using triangles, a protractor, or a bevel, set the table to the desired angles. Using a scribe, mark the location of the pointer onto the frame at the various table angles. Then letter the angles onto the frame with an artist's brush and paint, or a felt tip pen.

You'll probably find that you'll have to design a number of holding jigs for the various tools that you'll plan to sharpen. The jigs restrain the tool to a fixed angle and position for precision sharpening. Make the jigs from wood (Fig. 9-11).

## *9-11* / INSTALLATION

Portable sander-grinders having suction cup feet should be mounted to a smooth surface so that the cups hold. Sander-grinders may also be bolted to the workbench or to a power tool stand. Locate the tool near the front of the table or stand; the table height should be 40 to

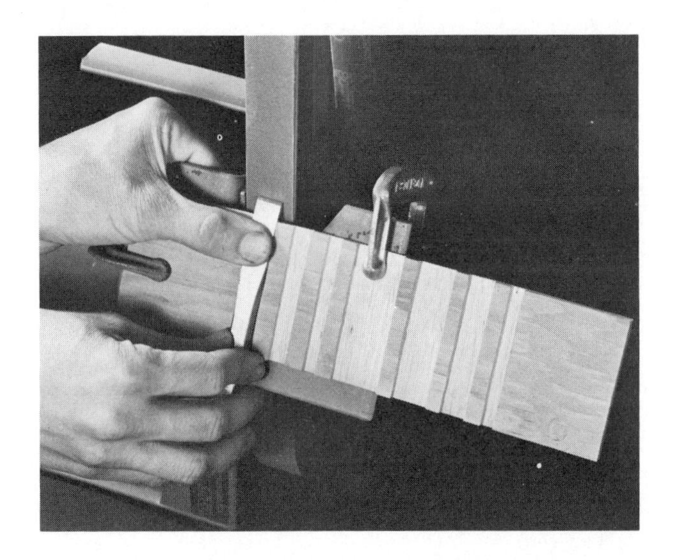

**FIGURE 9-11** / Jigs for supporting tools for grinding are made from wood.

42 inches. Some sander-grinder motors are mounted internally; others are mounted behind or below the tool.

Perform the calibration and maintenance procedures of Sec. 9-9.

# chapter ten

# SHAPER

**FIGURE 10-1** / Shapers are used to cut decorative designs along workpiece edges and moldings, and to shape edges for joining two workpieces together.

The shaper is probably the last power tool you need in your workshop. This is because there is seldom a need for its use and because you can now buy many decorative moldings, etc., in the lumber yards. Also, the functions of the shaper can be performed with accessories on other tools in your shop including the drill press, radial arm saw, table saw, and the router. The advantages of having a separate shaper tool are that it is immediately available for use without converting the other tools, and its larger table permits the shaping of large workpieces; it also operates at the most desirable speed.

One of the primary functions of the shaper is to decoratively shape wood—decorative molding, picture frames, straight, curved and irregular shaping, fluting, beading and scalloping (as along curved furniture edges), and the cutting of sash and door moldings. Another primary function of the shaper is to cut wood in preparation of joining two workpieces together—tongue and groove, drop-leaf joints, matched shaping, formation of glue joints, and rabbeting. The shaper also cuts cabinet door lips and can be used like a jointer to plane narrow workpiece edges. Basically, the shaper does the same work as the router, but the shaper head cannot be moved around freehand for "carving" as the router is sometimes operated.

The shaper cuts two kinds of shapes: *straight* and *irregular* (irregular in this case includes curved shapes). Straight shaping is the process of cutting a decorative edge or contour along the *straight edges* of tables, benches, or other furniture tops, and of cutting molding from straight pieces of lumber. *Irregular shaping* is the decorative cutting of irregular edges of workpieces, such as round or oval table tops, curved legs, etc.

The shaper has very few operating controls. It is simple to

operate and it does very good work quickly and accurately. The single, most important factor is that it operates at high speed—the higher the better. And sharp cutters are essential.

## 10-1 / DESCRIPTION AND MAJOR PARTS

Figures 10-2 and 10-3 illustrate the major parts of the shaper which include: cutter, spindle, fence, table, peg, hold down fingers, and motor. The shaper cutters do the actual cutting of the workpiece. They are placed on the spindle along with collars (cutters and collars are discussed in Sec. 10-2). The shaper cutters and collars are mounted on a permanently lubricated ball bearing mounted spindle and are secured with a nut. The spindle is almost always 1/2-inch in diameter to accept 1/2-inch bore cutters and collars; up to

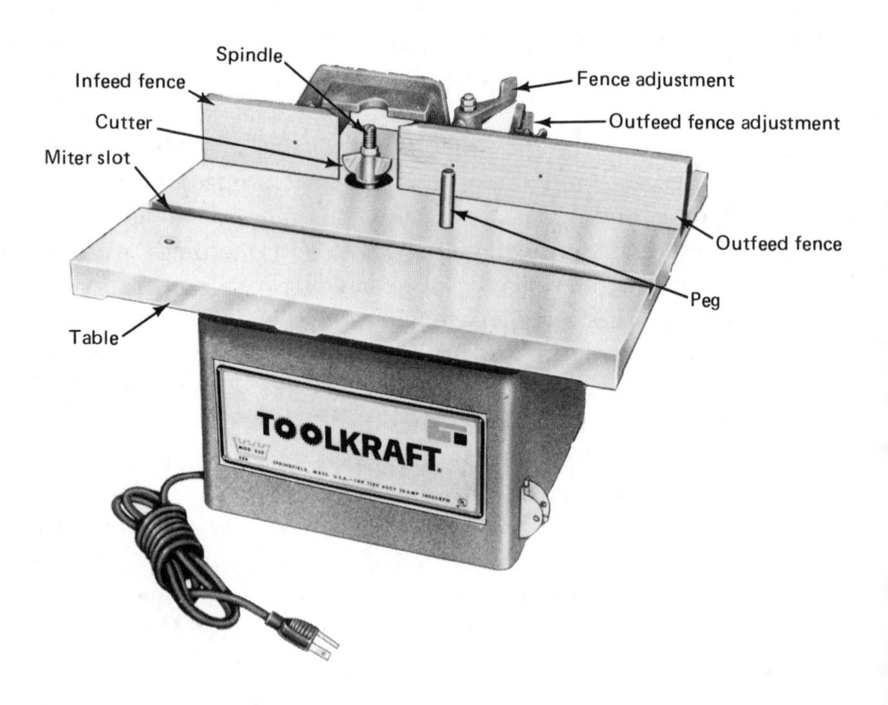


FIGURE 10-2 / Major parts of the shaper.

2-1/2-inches of cutters and collars can be placed on the spindle. The spindle, on some models, can be raised and lowered about 1 inch by means of a lever.

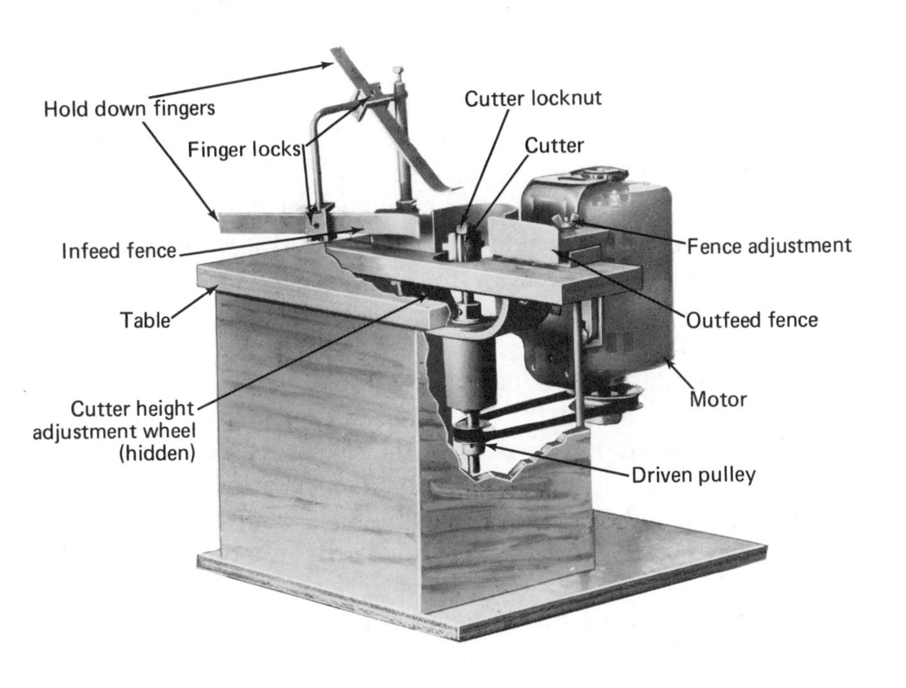


**FIGURE 10-3** / Major parts of another shaper model.

The shaper fence is actually two half fences that are adjustable front and rear and sometimes left and right. The *infeed* fence is the fence along which the workpiece is pushed *before* it passes through the cutter. The *outfeed* fence is the fence that supports the workpiece *after* the workpiece has passed through the cutter. Because some of the cutters can be inverted and the motor rotation reversed, the terminology "infeed" and "outfeed" may reverse on the sides of the cutter. The fence sections in Fig. 10-3 are labeled for a clockwise rotation of the cutter as viewed from the top; the workpiece feed is from left to right. Fences may be as large as 3 inches high by 11 inches on each side; shorter fences on smaller shapers can be enlarged by adding hardwood pieces to the existing fence sections.

The table supports the workpiece. It is approximately 18 by 20 inches—the bigger, the better. A table slot is provided for a miter that is used to support the workpiece when making cross grain and angle cuts. The table and base shown in Fig. 10-3 are not provided by the tool manufacturer. Thus, you can build the table and base (or stand) to your own dimensions, except that the cut out area for the cutter and the mounting hole locations of the motor mounts, spindle mount, and fence must be in the positions specified by the manufacturer. You can easily dado a miter slot into the wood table top. Pegs are used in the table to help support a workpiece during freehand operation (no fence). By pressing the workpiece against a peg and a spindle collar, the possibility of a kickback of the workpiece by the cutter is reduced.

Two adjustable hold down fingers are used to help hold the workpiece firmly against the fence and the table for straight shaping operations; they are not used when the shaper is used freehand. The fingers are especially useful when shaping narrow stock. The position, angle, and extension of the fingers are adjustable.

A ring guard, available on some shaper models, is situated (adjustable) directly over the cutter. The ring guard offers protection to your hands during the freehand cutting of curved and circular edge shaped workpieces. The ring guard can be used with or without the fence in place.

The approximate overall size of a shaper is 11 inches high, 20 inches deep, and 22 inches wide. A 3450 rev/min motor of at least 1/2-hp is recommended. The spindle speed should be 9000 rev/min or faster to produce smooth cuts that require little sanding. Slower speeds are acceptable if you feed the workpiece slowly.

## *10-2* / SHAPING CUTTERS AND COLLARS

Cutters for use on the shaper have three lips—three cutting edges. Many lip designs are sold by different manufacturers (Fig. 10-4) and are used in combination to form an almost infinite number of patterns for moldings and other decorative cuts. In addition to the patterns shown in Fig. 10-4, *straight* cutters that are used for edge planing and rabbeting are also available. The average cutter is 1 inch

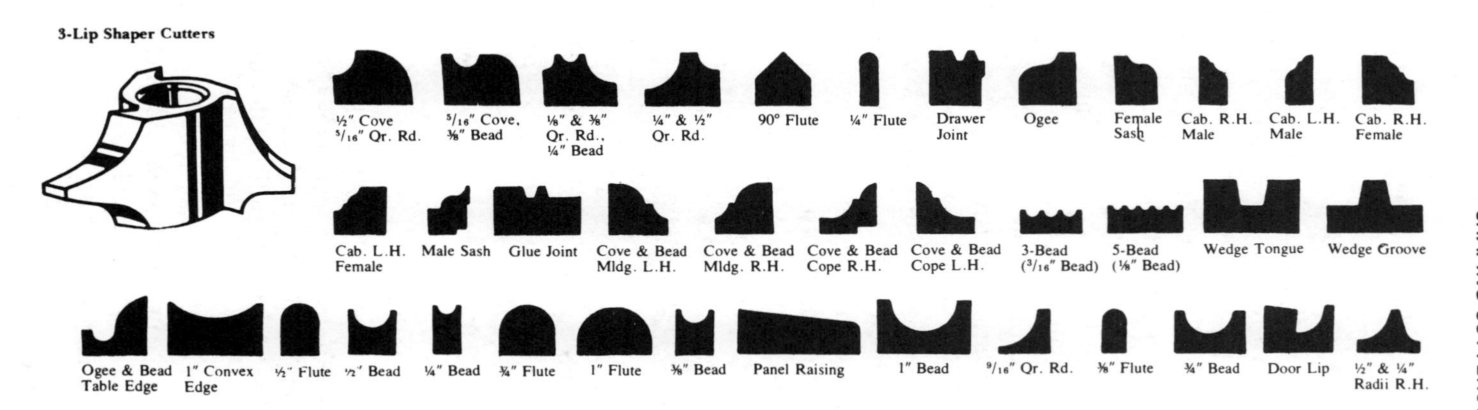


**FIGURE 10-4** / Shaper cutters. The cuts of different combinations of cutters produce an almost infinite number of patterns.

high and has a 1/2-inch bore for use with either the shaper or with an adapter for use on the drill press as a shaper.

An easy way to design your own patterns for shaping is to make cardboard cut outs of each shape in your possession. Then overlay the cutouts, turning them over and at angles as required until the desired pattern is attained. Place this pattern against the end of your workpiece stock, and draw a pattern line onto the end of the stock. Select one of the cutters for the first cut, and place it on the spindle using collars and jigs as required to set the cutter and workpiece to the position of the pattern. Cut a sample scrap piece to check the design. Then make *similar* cuts on *all* workpieces before changing the cutter, the cutter position, or the angle for subsequent cuts. Figure 10-5 suggests patterns for various designs.

Collars serve three functions: they take up spindle thread so that the spindle nut can secure the cutter; they control the depth of cut by virtue of the placement of the collars to raise and lower the cutter; and they provide for freehand shaping by acting as a bearing surface upon which the workpiece or a pattern presses. Collars have bores of 1/2-inch for installation on 1/2-inch shaper spindles. The thicknesses and outside diameters of collars vary, and you need an assortment of various sizes to set the depth of cut and space the workpiece from the cutter when shaping is done freehand. Outside diameters range from 3/4- to 1-7/8-inches with increments of 1/32- and 1/16-inches; thicknesses are 1/8-, 3/16-, 1/4-, and 3/8-inch. If the spindle and/or the cutter on the spindle are easily adjustable in height, you'll probably only need an assortment of outside diameters all of 1/4-inch thickness. Sets of five collars 1/4-inch thick with outside diameters of 3/4-, 7/8-, 1, 1-1/8-, and 1-1/4-inches are readily available.

A *cutterhead* (molding head) that holds three interchangeable shaped cutting knives and is used on a table saw or a radial arm saw for shaping operations can be used on the shaper if physical size limitations permit. Be sure that the knives are secured tightly in the cutterhead. (Refer to Sec. 7-3 for additional information on the molding head.)

Another type of cutterhead that holds two knives is also available. These knives are purchased as *blanks*, and you grind your own special molding pattern into them. The knives are 1/8-inch thick and are clamped into the head with setscrews at an angle of 30°.

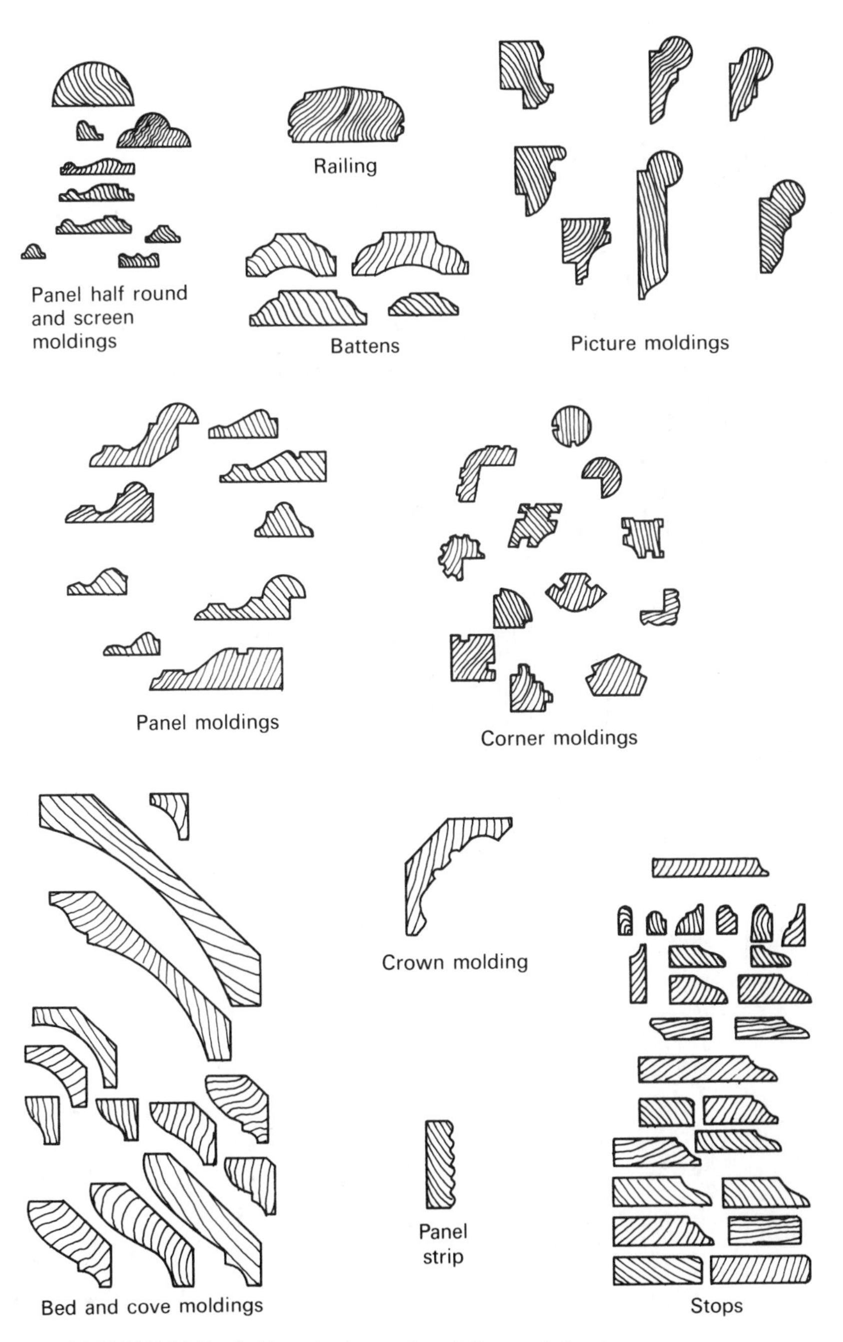


**FIGURE 10-5** / Standard wood molding and shaping patterns.

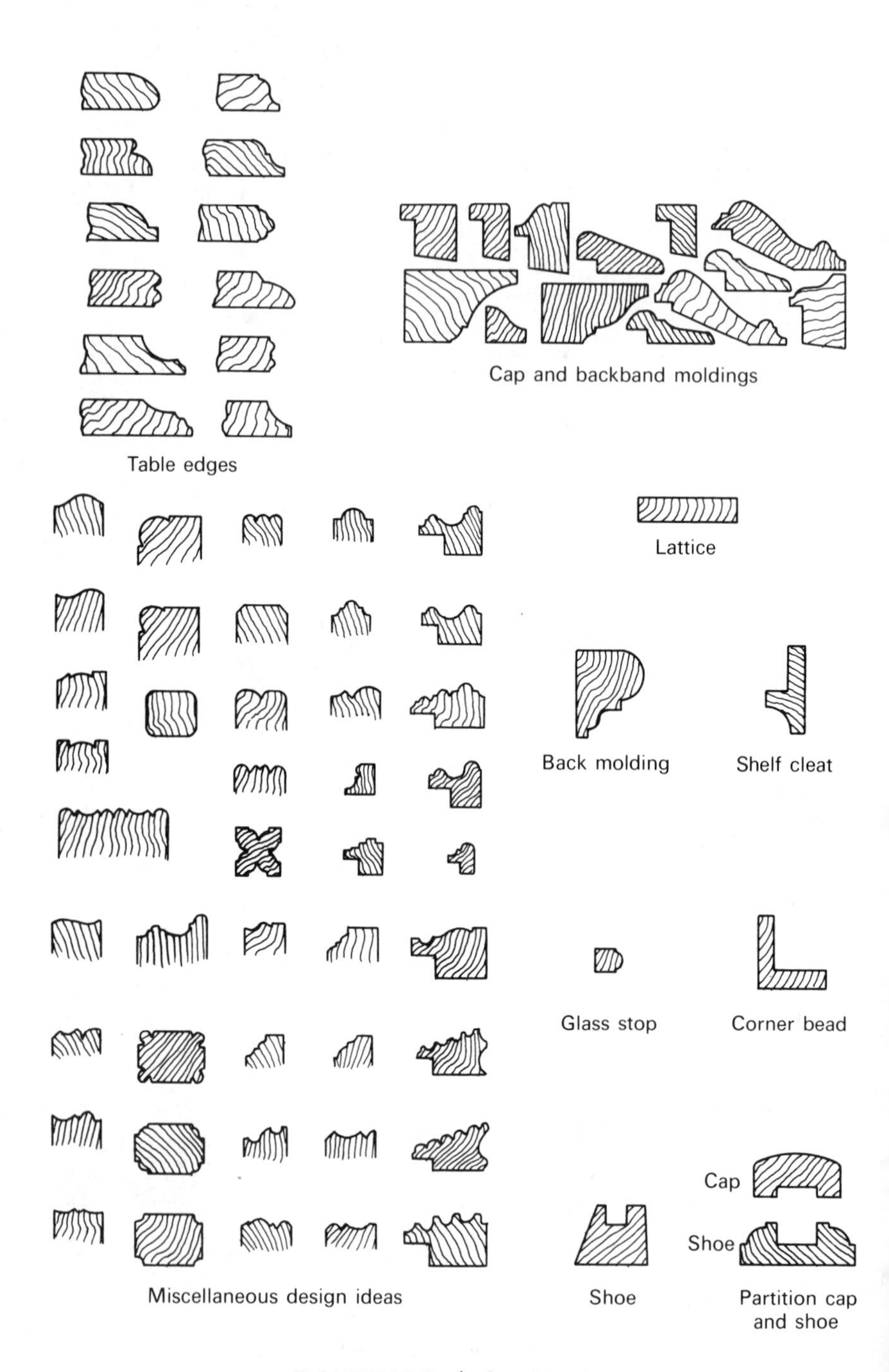


**FIGURE 10-5** / Continued.

## *10-3* / OPERATING CONTROLS AND ADJUSTMENTS

The setting of the cutter height, collar installation, infeed fence position, hold down fingers, ring guard, peg location, and outfeed fence position are the adjustments necessary to operate the shaper.

*NOTE*

*In setting up the shaper, use scrap pieces of wood of the same shape and material from which workpieces are to be made.*

*CAUTION*

*To adjust the outfeed fence, it is necessary to apply power to the motor. Observe the following cautions:*

*1 / Keep your hands away from the cutter.*

*2 / Adjust the hold down fingers correctly and use them. Locate the ring guard over the cutter.*

*3 / Grip the workpiece firmly with both hands and hold it against the fence and table.*

*4 / Take small cuts from the workpiece with repeated passes as required.*

*5 / Don't cut small workpieces. Instead, shape the edge of a larger workpiece, and then cut off the scrap with a table or radial arm saw.*

*6 / Review all safety precautions of Sec. 1-16.*

Perform the following procedures to set the shaper for operation (Figs. 10-2 and 10-3):

1 / *cutter height*—Place the scrap workpiece with the pattern marked on the end (Sec. 10-2) near the spindle, and place the desired shaper cutter on the spindle. Be sure it is correct for the direction of rotation of the spindle. Adjust the height adjustment wheel and/or place collars under the shaper cutter until the cutter lip is at the correct height of the pattern. If your shaper incorporates a control lever to

raise and lower the spindle, loosen the lock handle and make the final height adjustment; lock the handle. Place the locknut on the spindle with collars under it, if required, and tighten the nut securely.

2 / *infeed fence position*—Place the workpiece against the *infeed* fence. Loosen the infeed fence adjustment, and move the fence until the pattern on the workpiece aligns with the cutter. You may decide not to remove too much material on the first pass, so you may not align the cutter completely with the pattern line at this time. Lock the infeed fence in position. Use a ruler to check that the infeed fence is parallel to the miter slot on the table edge; if it is not parallel, readjust and tighten the infeed fence adjustment.

3 / *hold down fingers*—Loosen the hold down finger locks. With the workpiece against the table and fence, adjust the hold down fingers so that they force the workpiece in position against the table and fence. Tighten the finger locks. The hold down fingers position the workpiece against the *infeed* fence. Many shapers permit the fingers to be attached to either fence depending upon the direction of rotation of the cutter (which determines the infeed fence).

4 / *ring guard*—If your shaper is equipped with a ring guard, loosen its lock, swing it in position over the cutter, and lock it securely in position. The ring guard is specifically valuable as a safety feature when cutting curved and irregular workpieces where a fence is not used.

5 / *outfeed fence position*—If only a *part of the edge* of the workpiece is to be removed by the cutter, the outfeed fence is positioned in line with the infeed fence; loosen the outfeed fence adjustment, and place the outfeed fence against the board. Secure the fence. If the cutter will remove material from *all along the edge* of the workpiece, initially position the outfeed fence for the correct depth of cut. With the infeed fence, shaper, and hold down fingers in position, apply power to the shaper. Hold the scrap workpiece against the table and infeed fence, and slowly feed a part of the workpiece through and beyond the cutter about 2 inches (the workpiece is fed against the

rotation of the cutter). Remove power from the motor. Loosen the outfeed fence adjustment, and move the outfeed fence to the workpiece (Fig. 10-7). Secure the outfeed fence.

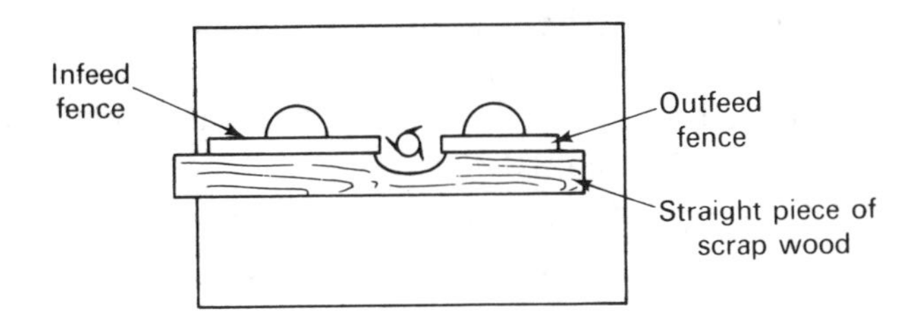


**FIGURE 10-6** / A piece of straight scrap wood with a semicircular cutout around the cutter is used to align the outfeed fence when only a part of the workpiece edge will be removed by the cutter.

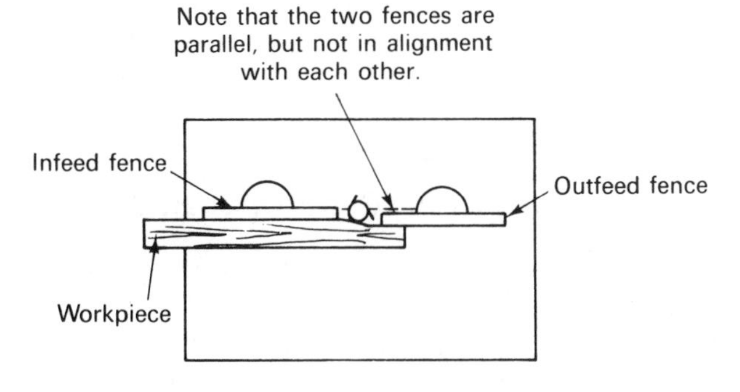


**FIGURE 10-7** / When the complete edge of the workpiece is removed by the cutter, pass about 2 inches of the workpiece through and beyond the cutter. Then, with the power off, move the outfeed fence forward to meet the workpiece.

6 / *peg location*—If the edge of a curved or irregular workpiece is to be shaped, the peg is located in one of its positions (the fence is not used). Screw the peg into the hole on the *infeed* side of the cutter.

## *10-4* / OPERATION

Once the adjustments of Sec. 10-3 are accomplished, you need only apply power and feed the workpiece through the cutter. Thus, this section is an abbreviated form of Sec. 10-3. Perform the following procedures to operate the shaper:

*1* / Observe all cautions listed in Sec. 10-3.

*2* / Place the desired cutter and collars on the spindle observing proper direction of rotation, and adjust for proper height. If a collar is to be used as a guide, position it correctly (Sec. 10-5).

*3* / Adjust infeed fence for desired depth of cut.

*4* / Position hold down fingers and ring guard.

*5* / Position outfeed fence.

*6* / If a fence is not used, position peg. If a fence is used, remove the peg.

*7* / Apply motor power in the proper direction, and perform the shaping procedures of Sec. 10-5. Repeat the above steps as many times as required to complete the shaping—remember, take small cuts and make repeat passes.

## *10-5* / SHAPING PROCEDURES

Since the fundamental procedures of shaping involve the design of the shape and the positioning of the cutter and workpiece by use of collars and location of the fence, it is important that you thoroughly understand these subjects before proceeding in this section. Reread the applicable parts of Secs. 10-2 and 10-3. This section discusses the four methods of shaping, and then gives general operation and safety procedures to be used at all times.

The four methods of shaping are: shaping with *guides* (the *fences* and miter), shaping with *collars,* shaping with an *outline pattern,* and shaping with *forms.* Shaping with the *fences* and the miter (Fig. 10-8) is the safest and most satisfactory way of working; this method should be used whenever possible. As previously discussed, the position of the fence (Fig. 10-9) limits the depth of cut by allowing as much or as little of the workpiece into the cutter as you desire. The straight fence is used for straight shaping, but you can design concave or convex fences that can be clamped or bolted to the shaper table to use as guides for curved workpieces. Special fences for odd shapes may also be designed.

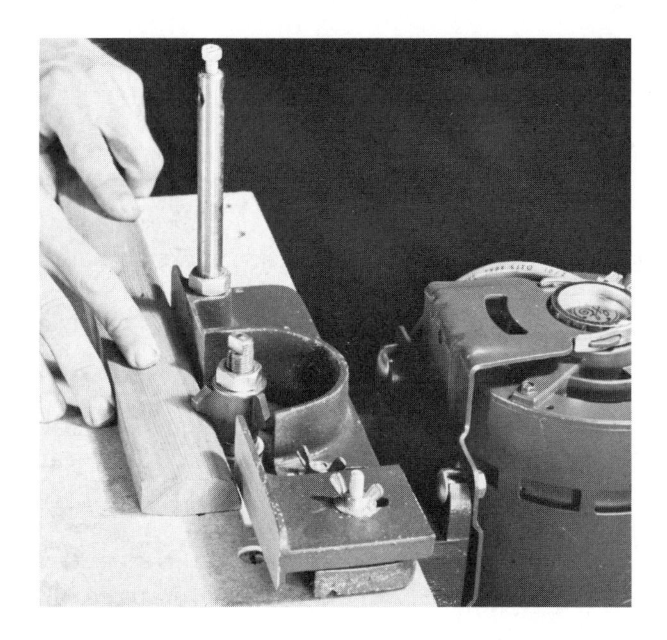

**FIGURE 10-8** / The fence is used as a guide for shaping straight workpieces.

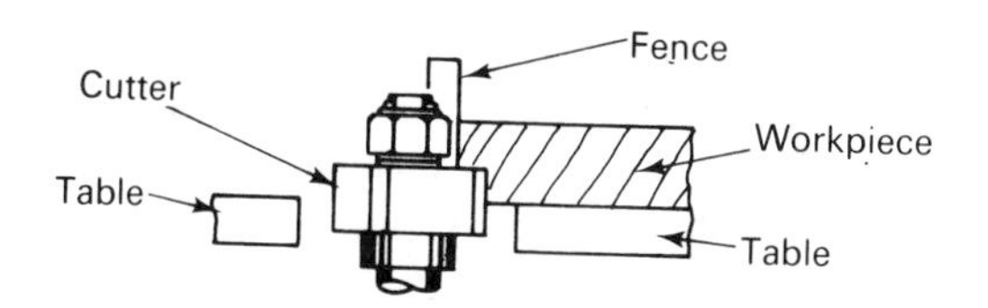


**FIGURE 10-9** / Hold the workpiece firmly against the fence. The position of the fence is one of the factors which determines the depth of the cut.

*Using a Fence as a Shaping Guide*

To shape with the fence as a guide, ensure that the fences, cutter, collars, and hold down fingers are secured. Hold the workpiece either flat or on an edge as applicable, against the table and infeed fence. Apply power and *slowly* and steadily feed the workpiece through the cutter and along the outfeed fence. One hand is initially positioned on top of the workpiece with the fingers positioned to feed the workpiece; the other hand is placed on the table with the fingers pushing the workpiece down and against the infeed fence. When the cutting is nearly complete, lift your hand on the table *beyond* the cutter, and hold the workpiece against the outfeed fence. Toward the end of the cut, use the hand on the outfeed fence side of the cutter to pull the workpiece the rest of the way through the cutter. A push stick can be used on narrow workpieces on the infeed side of the cutter. Do not place your hands in front of or over the cutters at any time. Make similar cuts on *all* workpieces before changing the setup for subsequent cuts.

### *Using a Miter as a Shaping Guide*

When cutting across the grain, hold the workpiece tightly against a miter. The depth of cut is determined by the cutter height and by how far the wood is pushed into the cutter. You must establish this depth and position and hold the workpiece on the miter at the correct position before advancing the miter and workpiece—take small cuts. Slowly and steadily pass the workpiece through the cutter.

### *Using Collars as Shaping Guides*

Shaping is done with collars (Fig. 10-10) when fences cannot be used, i.e., when curved and irregularly shaped workpieces are to be shaped. The rim of the collar rides against the workpiece, and the collar diameter limits the depth of cut. The desired collar must be placed on the spindle so that there is enough stock for the collar to ride on. The revolving collar slightly scores or burns the workpiece, but this is easily removed by light sanding. As the fence is absent in this shaping method, the ring guard should be put in position over the cutter as a safety device to help prevent your hands from coming into contact with the cutter. The peg is also installed on the infeed side of the cutter.

The peg is used as a guidepost when shaping with collars. Grip the workpiece tightly with both hands, place the workpiece against the peg, and very slowly feed the workpiece toward the cutter. When the cutter begins to shape the workpiece, advance the workpiece into the cutter until the workpiece is against the collar (Fig. 10-11). Continue to hold the workpiece against the peg and cutter collar as the workpiece is slowly and steadily fed through the cutter.

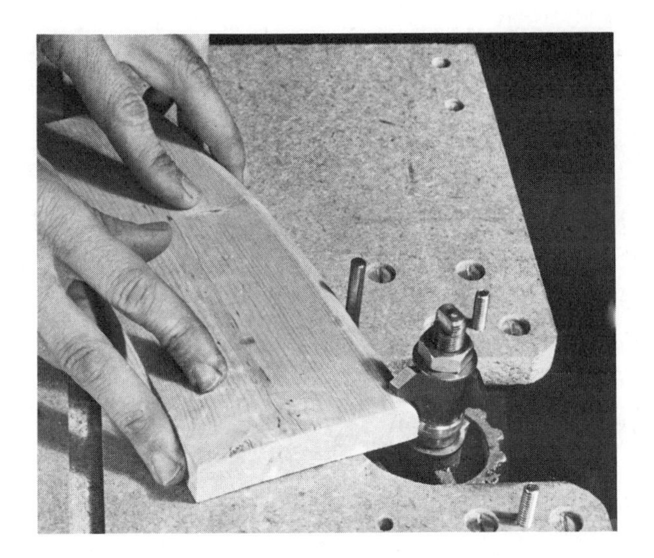

**FIGURE 10-10** / A collar is used as a guide for shaping curved and irregularly shaped workpieces. Hold the workpiece firmly with both hands and use the peg as a guide too.

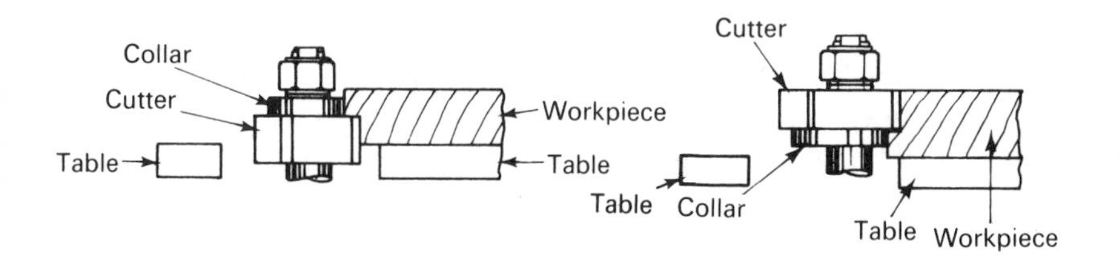


**FIGURE 10-11** / Hold the workpiece against the peg and collar.

*Using a Pattern as a Shaping Guide*

The third method of shaping is similar to the second method (collar) except that a *pattern* rides against the collar instead of the workpiece and thereby eliminates scoring and burning of the workpiece (Fig. 10-12). This method is good for repetitious workpiece shaping because the pattern can be used over and over again.

**FIGURE 10-12** / In pattern shaping, the pattern is pressed against a collar and peg. The pattern can be above or below the workpiece.

The pattern can be placed on top of or under the workpiece, but must be in a position to mate with a collar (Fig. 10-13). The pattern is attached to the workpiece by nailing brads or setting screws so that their points protrude slightly through the pattern and into the workpiece. Rough cut the workpiece on a band saw or jig saw to approximate the edge pattern before shaping is attempted.

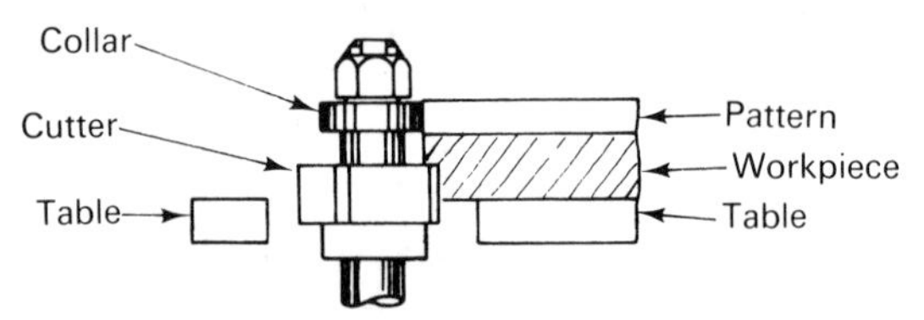


**FIGURE 10-13** / Rough cut the workpiece to the pattern shape before beginning to shape the edge.

When shaping with the pattern, also use the peg (on the infeed side of the cutter). Hold the workpiece firmly and use a slow and steady feed.

*Using a Form as a Shaping Guide*

The fourth and final method of shaping is accomplished with the use of a *form* (Fig. 10-14). A form is any device in which the workpiece is held so that the workpiece can be advanced to the cutter. A sliding miter and a sliding jig are the most common forms.

The depth of cut must be established before the workpiece is secured in the miter or jig—take small cuts. The workpiece is secured in the miter or jig and is advanced slowly and steadily through the cutter.

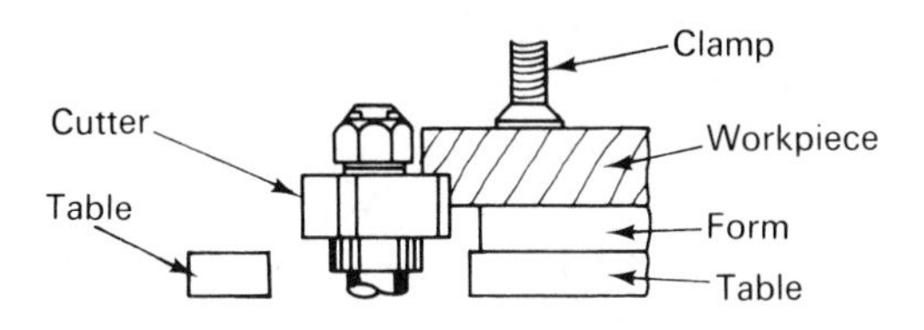


**FIGURE 10-14** / The fourth method of shaping uses a form—a device to hold the workpiece as it is advanced to the cutter.

*General Operating and Safety Procedures*

The following are general operating and safety hints that can help ensure quality workmanship in your shaping operations.

*1* / Make the cutting setups so that the cutter is *under* the workpiece (Fig. 10-12). In a sense, this makes the workpiece a guard in itself. If you slip and the workpiece raises, no damage is done to the workpiece.

*2* / Feed the workpiece so that your hands can never slip into the cutter. Remember that a clean table and sharp cutters are safe.

*3* / The workpiece is fed against the direction of rotation of the cutter. Thus, if the cutter is turning clockwise looking from the top, the workpiece is fed left to right (the left table is then termed the infeed table—the right, the outfeed table).

4 / The workpiece is held firmly against the table and the fence or collar and peg.

5 / Feed the workpiece into the cutter slowly and steadily. A slow feed produces a smooth finish.

6 / To get the full depth of cut desired, make repeat passes changing the position of the fence and spindle or diameter of the collars as required.

7 / Whenever possible, cut with the grain of the wood. To prevent splintering on cross cuts (across the grain), use an oversize stock workpiece, and then cut off the splintered ends on a bench saw. In shaping four sides of a workpiece, shape the two across-the-grain sides first; then shape the two with-the-grain sides which will smooth the rough edges made by the across-the-grain shaping.

8 / Never shape small or narrow workpieces. It is safer to shape the edge on a wide workpiece first, and then pass the workpiece through a bench saw to trim it to the proper size.

9 / Use *stops*—blocks of scrap wood—clamped to the fence to limit the length of cut when fluting, grooving, or molding edges.

10 / In matched shaping, as when constructing cabinets, interior trim, and similar work, a *pair* of cutters are used. One cutter is termed the male and the other female. Tongue and groove and drop-leaf cuts are examples of matched shaping.

11 / It is often advantageous to invert a cutter on the spindle which necessitates reversing the direction of travel of the spindle. This is accomplished by connecting an electrical reversing switch to the motor or by changing two wires within the motor. Refer to Sec. 1-7.

## 10-6 / ACCESSORIES

There are really no items that are considered accessories for the shaper. Some items such as hold down fingers and ring guards are not sold with every model of shaper and hence could be considered as accessories. Cutters and collars are seldom sold with the shaper unless a set of selected cutters is included. Be careful in buying a set though, because many times the set contains one or two cutters that you'll never have a need for.

You can sometimes buy a kit such as a sash and door cutting kit for making intricate cuts used on door and window frames. The kit includes spacer collars, sash cutter, recessed nuts and a hex key.

## 10-7 / CALIBRATION AND MAINTENANCE

There are no calibrations required, and maintenance of the shaper is minimal. Keep the cutters as sharp as possible—they cut easier and therefore are safer. When required, hone the cutter edges with a flat oil stone and a slip stone of the same material as the oil stone. Keep the cutting angle the same as the original. Remove as little material as possible. Always try to remove the same amount of material from each lip edge by counting the number of strokes. Keep the cutters oiled when stored to prevent rust—be sure to remove this oil before putting the cutter on the spindle.

The knives and the collars must be kept clean at all times to prevent burning the workpiece. Use a cloth soaked in kerosene to remove pitch; use a stiff brush with kerosene or steel wool to remove stubborn pitch.

## 10-8 / HINTS AND KINKS

A longer fence is helpful in guiding long straight workpieces through the cutter. You can increase the size of your fence by adding an auxiliary fence. Screw a piece of straight hardwood onto each section of existing fence. Make horizontal slots for the screws and a counterbore for the screwheads, and you have an adjustable fence.

You can clamp blocks of wood to the top of the fence and to the table if you do not have hold down fingers on your shaper. With power off, place the workpiece in position along the fence. Place a block of scrap wood on top of the workpiece with a piece of paper sandwiched between the block and the workpiece. Clamp the block to the fence with a C-clamp. The piece of paper will give the workpiece just enough clearance to slide freely under the block. A block can be similarly clamped to the edge of the shaper table to act as a hold down finger holding the workpiece against the fence.

If your shaper is one of the "kit" type shapers as shown in Fig. 10-3, make a larger table from 3/4-inch plywood to support your workpieces. Just be sure to keep the shaper cutter opening the same size, and drill the holes in the same location for mounting the spindle and fence.

If you're not quite convinced you need a shaper, perhaps you'd be better off buying shaping accessories for either your drill press, radial arm saw, or table saw (refer to Chaps. 3, 7, and 11, respectively). If you have a router, you can also use it as a shaper, and it can even be built into a table similar to that illustrated in Fig. 10-3. The router is bolted to the underside of the table. A fence can be made from wood with slots in it to allow each section to slide forward or backward.

## *10-9* / INSTALLATION

Place the shaper on a power tool stand so that the shaper table is 33 to 35 inches above the floor. The motor, if not built into the shaper, is located behind the shaper and is bolted to the table. Locate the shaper and power tool stand so that long workpieces such as molding can be passed from the infeed area through the cutter and out of the outfeed area.

chapter eleven

# TABLE (ARBOR, BENCH, CIRCULAR) SAW

**FIGURE 11-1** / Either the table saw or the radial arm saw is the first bench power tool required in the home workshop.

The first operation performed on a workpiece is the cutting of the workpiece to size. To do this accurately, quickly, and conveniently, a bench saw is needed. You can choose either the table saw or the radial arm saw described in Chap. 7.

The table saw can make crosscut, miter, bevel, compound, and rip saw cuts. (Refer to Sec. 7-1 for cut descriptions.) With accessories, it can also dado, shape, and sand workpieces. With the correct abrasive blade, it cuts wood, plywood, particle board, composition board, metals, plastics, bone, and stone. (The radial arm saw performs all of the functions of the table saw, and in addition, with accessories, it also shapes, routs, buffs, polishes, drills, and drum sands.)

As illustrated by the title of this chapter, the table saw is also called an arbor saw, bench saw, or circular saw. Whatever name is assigned to it by a manufacturer, it is still basically the same tool. Figure 11-1 illustrates several manufacturer's table saws.

The table saw is simply a circular blade driven by a motor. The blade projects through a slot in the top of the table. A fence or miter gauge is used to guide workpieces through the blade. (On the radial arm saw the workpiece remains stationary for crosscut, miter, and some bevel and compound cuts.) Elevating and blade tilting mechanisms position the combined movable motor-arbor-cutter assembly for crosscut, rip, miter, bevel, and compound angle cutting.

The table saw is superior in cutting straight lines. It is slightly less expensive than the radial arm saw. Its major disadvantage, compared to the radial arm saw, is that the cutter is beneath the pattern line where the operator cannot see the cut being made.

## 11-1 / DESCRIPTION AND MAJOR PARTS

The table saw (Fig. 11-2) has six major parts: *motor, cutter, table, base, fence,* and *miter gauge*. The *motor* is mounted on a trunnion either within the saw base or externally just behind the saw (Fig. 11-3). The trunnion allows the motor-arbor-cutter to move as one unit—appropriately named a *tilting arbor saw*—from 0° (the blade is perpendicular to the table) to a bevel of 45°. The cutter angle adjustment screw controls the position of the motor-arbor-cutter unit, and the cutter bevel angle is indicated by a pointer. Many table saws include adjustable mechanical stops at the 0° and 45° positions.

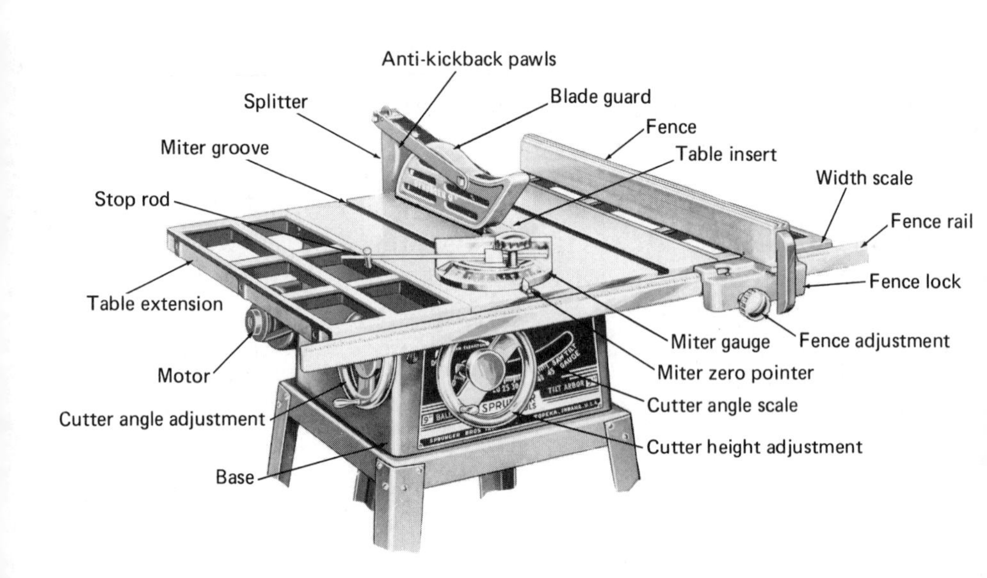


**FIGURE 11-2** / Major parts of the table saw.

Table saws are specified by the maximum diameter blade (cutter) that can be turned on the arbor. Table saws of 8, 9, 10, and 12 inches are available; the 8 and 9 inch saws are the most common saws used in home workshops. The approximate depths of cut at 0° and 45° are shown in Table 11-1. Arbor diameter is 1/2- or 5/8-inch.

**FIGURE 11-3** / The table saw motor is either mounted within or just behind the saw base. The motor, arbor, and cutter tilt together.

**Table 11-1**
**TABLE SAW DEPTHS OF CUT**

| | *Table Saw Capacities* | | | |
|---|---|---|---|---|
| Blade diameter (inches) | 8 | 9 | 10 | 12 |
| Depth of cut at 0° (inches) | 2-1/2 | 2-7/8 | 3-3/8 | 3-9/16 |
| Depth of cut at 45° (inches) | 1-3/4 | 2 | 2-1/4 | 2-3/8 |

The *table* provides support for the workpiece. The center section is solid cast metal with an opening for the cutter and a *miter groove* on each side of the blade for the miter gauge. Table inserts with various sized slots for blades, dado heads, and molding heads fit the table opening; the inserts provide workpiece support near the cutter. A slot or a fence rail is machined or attached to the front edge of the table for attachment of the movable fence; the fence rail sometimes incorporates a width scale that is used with the fence to indicate the distance in inches between the fence and the cutter. *Table extensions* bolt to either side of the table for additional support of wide workpieces.

Table sizes range from 11 by 13 inches to approximately 24 by 17 inches. With table extensions added, the total table size may increase to as much as 40 by 27 inches. Table heights range from approximately 10 to 17 inches. Floor models stand about 34 to 37 inches high.

The major table dimensions of concern are the distance from the blade (raised 1 inch) to the front of the table and from the blade to the rip fence on one side. The distance from the blade to the table front is the maximum width of a workpiece that can be crosscut. The distance from the blade to the rip fence is the maximum width of a workpiece that can be ripped.

The *base* supports the table and houses the motor, ball bearing arbor, cutter, and the elevating (cutter height) and tilting (cutter angle) screws and trunnions. Rotation of the screws causes the cutter to elevate or tilt to the desired height and cutter bevel angle. Some models may not have a cutter adjustment screw; in this case, the operator loosens a clamp and manually rotates the motor-arbor-cutter assembly to the desired cutter bevel angle as indicated on a scale, and then he retightens the clamp.

The *fence* is used as a guide for the workpiece during rip sawing operations. It moves back and forth across the table and is located at a distance from the blade equal to the width of the desired workpiece. On some models, the fence is positioned by a fence adjustment that moves on a geared mechanism along the fence rail; some rails include a width scale graduated in inches. A fence lock secures the fence to the table in a position that is parallel to the blade; the fence lock mechanism self-aligns the fence. Fences are approximately 2-1/2-inches high and extend from the front to the rear of the table.

The *miter gauge* is normally sold with a table saw. The miter gauge is used as a workpiece guide when crosscut, miter, or compound angle saw operations are performed. A locking knob is used to set and lock the head to the required angle between 0° and 45° left or right as indicated by a pointer on a scale. Some miter gauges have index stop pins every 15°. An adjustable stop rod is used as a stop block to set a fixed length for cutting a number of workpieces to the same length.

The *blade guard, splitter,* and *anti-kickback pawls* are part of one assembly that attaches to the trunnion frame, and thus the assembly tilts at the same angle as the motor-arbor-blade. The *blade guard*—sometimes see-through—protects the operator's hands from coming in contact with the cutter. The guard raises and lowers as the workpiece is fed through the cutter.

The *splitter* is aligned directly behind the saw blade. After the workpiece has passed through the blade, the blade kerf surrounds the splitter. The splitter prevents the kerf from closing on the blade causing the blade to bind in the workpiece resulting in a kickback.

The *anti-kickback pawls* are curved, tooth-shaped pieces of metal that ride on top of the workpiece as it passes the splitter. The pawls oppose any movement (kickback) of the workpiece toward the operator.

*Motor* sizes range from 1/2- or 3/4-hp for 8 inch saws up to 1-1/2- and 2 hp for 12 inch saws. Motor speeds are 1725 or 3450 rev/min to turn the blade at 3800–6000 rev/min. It is best to follow the table saw manufacturer's recommendations about horsepower, speed, and correct pulley size recommendations. Some motors incorporate safety clutches that allow the motor to continue to turn even if the blade binds in the saw kerf. If the saw binds, the power is turned off immediately by the operator, and the workpiece is pulled out.

## 11-2 / CUTTERS—BLADES, WHEELS, DADO HEADS, MOLDING HEADS, AND SANDING DISKS

Saw blades, wheels, dado heads, molding heads, and sanding disks are used on the table saw to cut, joint, shape, and smooth workpieces made of different materials. These cutters are the same as those used on the radial arm saw. Refer to the following sections for the description and installation procedures for the cutters: blades, wheels, dado heads, and molding heads—Sec. 7-3; sanding disks—Sec. 8-2. The procedures for using these cutters are contained within this chapter.

## 11-3 / OPERATING CONTROLS AND ADJUSTMENTS

The operating controls and adjustments are set prior to applying any power to the table saw. Proper setting of the controls and adjustments will enable you to operate the table saw accurately and safely. The table saw controls and adjustments include the following (Fig. 11-2): cutter angle, cutter height, fence positioning, miter gauge angle, and stop rod positioning.

1 / *cutter angle*—Rotate the cutter angle adjustment screw until the cutter-arbor-motor assembly is set to the desired bevel angle as indicated on the cutter angle scale. On table saws without adjustment screws, loosen the cutter angle tilt clamp, tilt the cutter-arbor-motor assembly to the desired angle as indicated on the scale, and retighten the clamp.

2 / *cutter height*—Rotate the cutter height adjustment to the required height as indicated on the height scale or as measured with a scale. The correct height of the dado head, molding head, and sanding disk is discussed in Secs. 11-6, 11-7, and 11-8, respectively. The correct blade height is normally 1/8- to 1/4-inch above the top surface of the workpiece.

3 / *fence positioning*—Loosen the fence lock and move the fence to the desired distance from the cutter as indicated on the width scale. If no width scale is available, use a scale to measure the distance between the cutter and the fence. When the fence is in position, tighten the fence lock. If the fence is not going to be used, remove it from the table.

4 / *miter angle*—To set the miter gauge to the desired angle, loosen the knob, rotate the head to the desired angle as indicated on the scale, and retighten the knob. If the miter gauge is not going to be used for the cutting operation, remove it from the table.

5 / *stop rod*—Loosen the wing nut or other adjustment screw, and slide the rod or stop to the desired workpiece length as measured between a blade tooth and the stop. Retighten.

## *11-4* / OPERATION

Observe the following cautions prior to any operations on the table saw:

### *CAUTIONS*

***1 / Be sure all adjustments and locks are secure before applying power.***

***2 / Do not force workpieces into the cutter at any time.***

*3 / Keep the blade guard in place.*

*4 / Do not place your hands in front of or on the cutters at any time. Likewise, if you are cutting a groove that does not come through the workpiece, do not place your hand on top of the workpiece over the cutter.*

*5 / Stop the saw before any adjustments are made, when stock is removed, or when cleaning dust from the table top.*

*6 / Ensure that the workpieces are free of nails.*

*7 / Hold the workpiece firmly against the miter gauge or fence.*

*8 / Review all of the safety precautions in Sec. 1-16.*

Perform the following operating procedures:

*1* / Plan ahead. Determine your cuts and plan to make all of the same types of cuts on all similar workpieces at one time.

*2* / Select the correct blade, wheel, dado, or molding head (Sec. 7-3), and install it on the arbor. Tighten the arbor nut securely.

*3* / Set the desired cutter bevel angle.

*4* / Set the correct cutter height.

*5* / Position and secure the fence as required.

*6* / Set the desired miter angle as required.

*7* / Position the workpiece and hold it against the fence or the miter gauge.

*8* / Apply power and let the motor reach full speed. Perform the applicable sawing (11-5), dadoing (11-6), molding and shaping (11-7), or sanding procedures (11-8). Note that all workpieces are fed from the front of the table saw toward the rear.

## *11-5* / SAWING PROCEDURES

The table saw easily executes the five basic types of cuts: crosscut, miter, bevel and chamfer, compound angle, and rip. These cuts are discussed in this section and should be mastered before you progress to the cutting of the joints and fancy cuts discussed later: resawing, lap joints, edge mortising and tenons, edge mortises, splined joints, taper cutting, panel raising, cove cutting, pattern sawing, and rabbeting. You may also want to scan through Chap. 7 on the radial arm saw because some of the same cuts can be made on the table saw, except that the table saw blade is beneath the workpiece rather than on top as with the radial arm saw.

Cutting on the table saw is difficult in two respects: first, the blade is under the workpiece, and second, the rear of the workpiece is cut first. These difficulties are compounded when cuts are made only part way through a workpiece. Two techniques that you can use to decrease the probability of making cutting errors are: using scrap wood for trial cuts prior to cutting the actual workpiece, and making sketch lines on the workpiece. The latter technique is explained by means of the following example. Suppose you want to cut a 30° bevel. Your simplest approach to avoid incorrect cuts is to mark the exact point where the saw blade is to begin its cut. Now, using a pencil, *sketch* a line across the edge and top of the board approximating the direction of the bevel. Place the workpiece on the table; observe the sketch line, and set the angle of the cutter. (The good side of the workpiece is always placed "face up" on the table to produce the smoothest cut on the face surface.) Now set the blade height so that it is 1/8- to 1/4-inch higher than the workpiece. Place the guard in position.

After power is applied, let the motor reach full speed before feeding the workpiece into the cutter. Do not feed the workpiece so fast that the motor slows down appreciably–let the cutter do the cutting. Stand to the side of the blade where you are holding the workpiece so that if kickback occurs you won't be directly in the path. Kickback is caused by binding the cutter–be sure the fence and blade are aligned, that the splitter is aligned and used, and that you hold the work extra firmly when knots are cut. Use a push stick (Sec. 1-11) to rip narrow pieces.

### *Crosscuts*

Crosscuts are made across the grain of the workpiece (Fig. 11-4). In this procedure, crosscutting is considered to be at an angle of 90°. Other angles are considered as *miter* cuts and are later covered.

**FIGURE 11-4** / Crosscuts are made across the grain of the wood. The miter gauge is used as a guide.

To crosscut, place the miter in a miter groove in the table top, and set the gauge to 90° (this is 0° on some miter gauges–at any rate, the miter head is perpendicular to the blade). Set the blade to the correct height and desired bevel angle (if any). Remove the fence from the table.

### *CAUTION*

***Always use the miter gauge for crosscut operations including 90° cutoffs, miters, bevels, and compound cuts.***

Place the workpiece with the good side face up with an edge against the miter gauge head. Position the workpiece so that the area to be cut off is beyond the blade, and the cutoff mark is in front of the blade. Position the workpiece cutoff line so that the blade kerf will be in the scrap part of the wood. Apply power. With a firm grip on the workpiece (Fig. 11-5) at the miter gauge, feed the workpiece into and through the blade. Do not hold onto the scrap part being cut off.

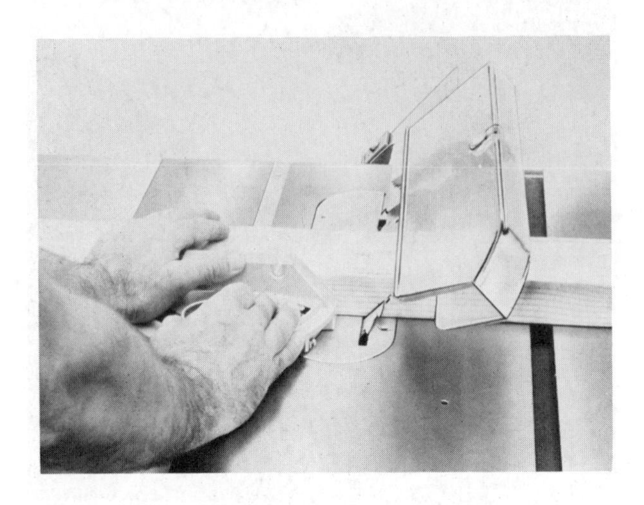

**FIGURE 11-5** / Hold the workpiece firmly against the miter gauge.

When long workpieces are crosscut, table extensions or some other means should be provided to support the workpiece (Fig. 11-4). A piece of hardwood screwed to the head of the miter will also enable more accurate cuts because the workpiece will be more evenly fed to the blade; space the hardwood 1/8-inch above the table for clearance. Some manufacturers also have an accessory clamp that can be added to the gauge to clamp the workpiece to the miter gauge (Fig. 11-4).

Workpieces that are wider than the distance from the blade to the front of the table are cut as follows: turn the miter gauge around so that it runs backward in the table miter groove. Feed the workpiece into the blade until there is sufficient room on the front of the table for the miter gauge. Turn the power off. Carefully, without altering the position of the workpiece on the table, reverse the miter gauge to its normal position. Apply power and continue the cut.

Another method of crosscutting very wide workpieces is to securely clamp a piece of straight scrap wood to the underside of the workpiece at a distance equal to the distance from the cutline to the edge of the table. Feed the workpiece to the blade while keeping the clamped scrap wood firmly against the table edge as a guide.

*CAUTION*

***Ensure that the stop rod is never set so that it can come near the cutter. Completely remove the stop rod from the miter gauge unless it is being used. In lieu of the stop rod on the miter gauge,* stop blocks *can be used.*** Refer to Sec. 1-12.

Duplicate sized workpieces can be cut using the miter gauge stop rod to determine the size of the duplicates. Adjust the stop for the workpiece length by measuring from the blade to the stop; set and lock the stop. Position the workpiece against the stop and the miter gauge head and secure the workpiece in position with your hand or miter gauge clamp (Fig. 11-6). Feed the workpiece into the blade cutting off the desired length. Place another piece in the miter gauge head and repeat.

**FIGURE 11-6** / Cutting duplicate length pieces.

### *Miter Cuts*

Use the same procedures for making miter cuts as for making *crosscuts*, except set the miter gauge to the required angle (Fig. 11-7). Hold the workpiece very firmly to the miter gauge head, and feed slowly to reduce the tendency of the workpiece to "creep" out of alignment along the head. To alleviate this creeping, use the stop rod and/or the miter gauge clamp, if available. In lieu of the stop rod and clamp, screw an auxiliary wooden face to the face of the miter gauge. Have several brad points sticking through the wooden face which will dig slightly into the workpiece and keep it from creeping. Another good trick to prevent creeping is to glue sandpaper to the face of the miter gauge.

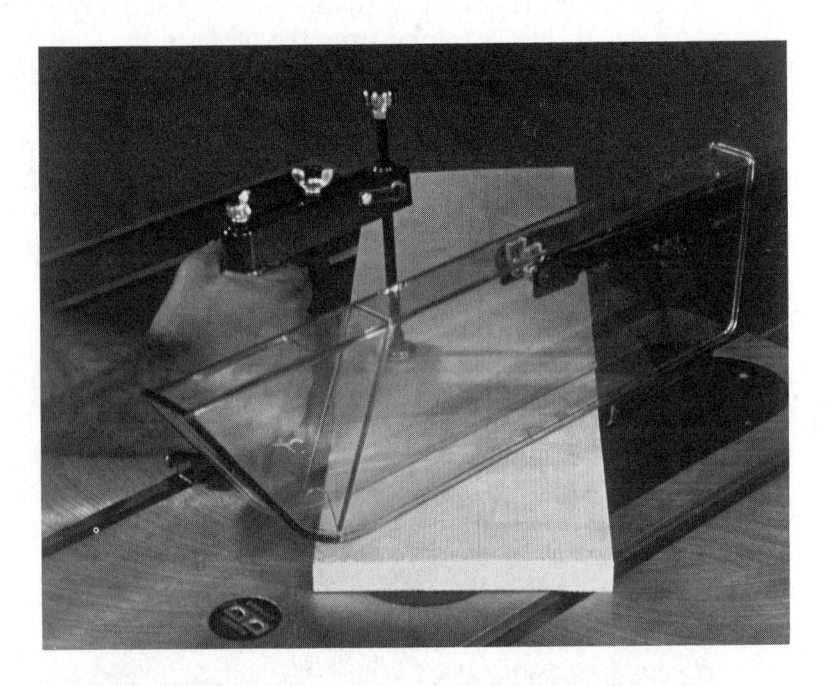

**FIGURE 11-7** / For miter cuts, position and lock the miter gauge to the required angle. As with all cutting operations, keep the blade guard in place.

### *Bevel and Chamfer Cuts*

A bevel or chamfer cut is made the same as the crosscut except that the blade is tilted (Fig. 11-8). The right hand miter groove should be used for the miter gauge.

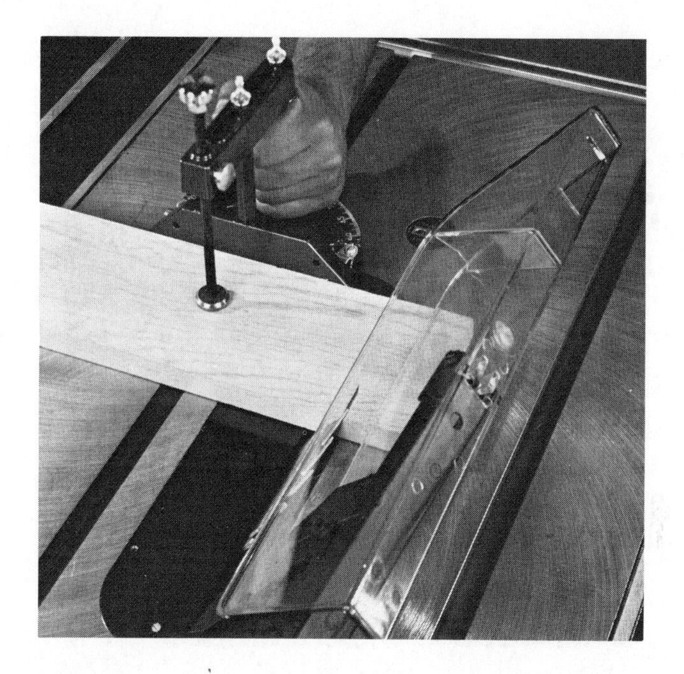

**FIGURE 11-8** / The blade–arbor–motor assembly is tilted for making bevel cuts.

*Compound Angle Cuts*

Compound cuts are combined miter and bevel cuts. Use the same procedures as in crosscutting, except set the blade-arbor-motor and the miter gauge to the required settings (Fig. 11-9). Use the right hand miter gauge slot. If the workpiece "creeps" out of alignment on the miter gauge, use one of the three methods previously described under *miter cuts* to solve the problem.

*Rip Cuts*

Rip cuts are made lengthwise along the grain of the wood (Fig. 11-10). Place and lock the fence to the desired ripping width. Use the width scale to set the width, or use a scale to measure the distance from the blade to the fence. Place a *straight edge* of the workpiece against the fence with the good face (side) of the workpiece turned up. One hand should hold the workpiece down and push it gently toward the fence; the other hand should be along the fence to push the workpiece through. It's a good idea to let the little finger of the hand along the fence curl over the fence to aid in preventing your

**FIGURE 11-9** / When compound angle cuts are made, both the blade and the miter are set to the required angles.

**FIGURE 11-10** / Rip cuts are made along the grain of the workpiece. Ensure that the blade guard, splitter, and pawls are installed and aligned properly.

hand from coming near the blade. Place your body on the side of the blade where the fence is located; in the event of workpiece kickback, your body will be out of the workpiece path.

*CAUTION*

***Ensure that the blade guard is in place and that neither your hands nor your body are in front of the blade.***

With the power on, firmly grip the workpiece and push it against the fence and into the blade. Let the saw do the cutting. Do not feed the workpiece so fast that the motor speed is appreciably decreased. As the workpiece passes the blade, it will surround the splitter that will keep the kerf from closing. After the workpiece has been sawed, continue to push it along the fence until it clears the blade. Remove the workpiece; turn power off *before* removing the cutoff scrap from the table.

If long workpieces are being ripped and the saw does not have a splitter, place wedges in the kerf as the workpiece exits from the blade. Failure to keep the kerf open can result in violent kickback of the workpiece when the kerf binds on the saw blade. If the saw begins to bind at any time, *stop the feed immediately and turn the power off*. Also turn the power off to remove a partially cut workpiece. If the cut is to be continued, turn the power on and let the motor reach full speed. Carefully feed the workpiece back into the blade. Keep the workpiece firmly against the fence.

Long workpieces must be supported when they exit from the rear of the saw. Use a workpiece support stand (Sec. 1-10). The table on the drill press can also be positioned as a support. After about one-half of the workpiece has been ripped, you may find it easier to walk around the table saw (hold the workpiece steady as you do so) and pull the workpiece through the blade.

When narrow workpieces are cut, use a push stick (Fig. 11-10). A design for a push stick is suggested in Sec. 1-11. Warped workpieces are cut with the concave side down against the table.

If rough stock is to be ripped and there is no straight edge along any edge of the stock, nail a straight piece of wood as a guide along one workpiece edge with finishing nails. Place the guide piece along the fence, and then rip off the opposite edge of the stock. Next, remove the guide and nails; using the cut edge as the guide edge against the fence, rip off the other rough edge. The other two edges can be cut square by crosscutting.

### *Resawing*

## *CAUTION*

***Ensure that your hands are not over the blade at any time, and that you stand to the side of the blade where the fence is located.***

Resawing is the cutting of a thick board into two thinner boards. Although more easily performed on the bandsaw (Sec. 2-5), resawing can be done on the table saw. Place the blade height to cut slightly less than one-half of the workpiece, and place the fence at the desired location. Remove the blade guard and splitter. Hold the board firmly against the fence; using a push stick, rip cut through the workpiece. (If the workpiece is of sufficient *width* that additional support is needed at the fence when the workpiece is turned on its edge, screw a hardwood auxiliary fence onto the existing fence.) Turn the workpiece end for end, but with the same side against the fence. Raise the blade so that its cut will overlap the first cut by 1/2-inch. Using a push stick, rip cut the second cut. This method described prevents collapse and binding of the wood.

### *Lap Joints*

Lap joints can either be cut with a universal jig (Fig. 11-11) or with the fence and a support as a guide. Lap joints can also be cut with a dado head (Sec. 11-6).

To cut the lap joint, first set the table saw for crosscuts. Set the blade to a height equal to 1/32-inch less than one-half the thickness of the workpiece. Place the workpiece flat on the table against the miter head, and make a cut across the grain at the top of the joint (do all similar workpieces while the table saw is set up). Turn the workpiece vertically, and use either the jig or the fence to make the second and final joint cut as follows. If a jig as shown in Fig. 11-11 is used, clamp the workpiece in a vertical position and at the proper location for the cut. Set the proper blade height. Pass the workpiece through the blade making the second cut.

**FIGURE 11-11** / Lap joints are cut with a jig or with the fence as a guide (refer to the text).

If a jig is not available, clamp a piece of straight scrap wood to the workpiece as shown in Fig. 11-12. Move the fence so that the blade will remove one-half the width of the workpiece. Lock the fence and set the proper blade height. Hold the clamped workpiece and the scrap wood tightly against the fence, and pass the workpiece through the blade making the second cut. The scrap wood support provides a safe method of preventing the workpiece from sliding, twisting, or upsetting on the table.

*End Mortises and Tenons*

End mortises are made in one of three ways: with a jig (Fig. 11-13), with the fence and a scrap board as a support, or with a dado head. Make the end mortises as described under *lap joints*, except that no cut across the width is required. Dado techniques are discussed in Sec. 11-6.

Tenons are made similarly to the end mortise, except for the position of the jig or the position of the fence and support in regard

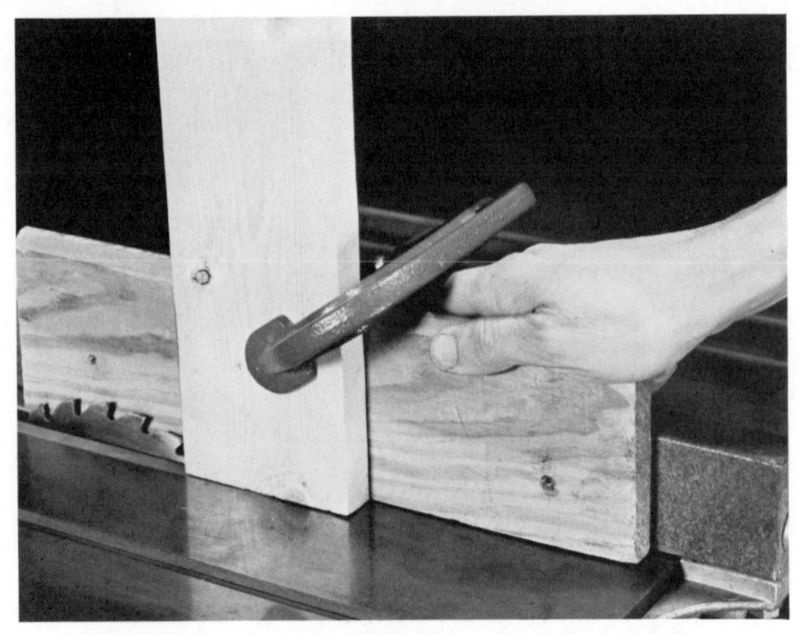

**FIGURE 11-12** / A scrap wood support should always be used to provide a safe means of making end cuts.

**FIGURE 11-13** / The illustration shows an end mortise being cut. Similar procedures are used to cut tenons and edge mortises.

to the workpiece. One side of the tenon is cut on one or more passes, as required; the workpiece is then turned around in the jig or the support and clamp, and the other side is cut.

### *Edge Mortises*

A mortise along the edge of a workpiece is made in the same manner as end mortises. In using the fence as a guide, however, a support is not required.

### *Splined Joints*

In a splined joint, a small piece of wood is added into the joint to give extra strength. Mitered joints at 45° are grooved (Fig. 11-14). Use one of the three cutting procedures described under *end mortises* to make the splined joint cuts.

**FIGURE 11-14** / Splined joints are made by cutting grooves into the mitered cuts.

### *Taper Cutting*

Tapers are often cut on table legs. The cutting is easily accomplished if a simple, adjustable, inexpensive taper jig is either purchased or built. The jig shown in Fig. 11-15 was purchased. To use it, the desired taper angle is set by opening the legs of the jig until the scale indicates the degree of taper desired. The jig is then locked.

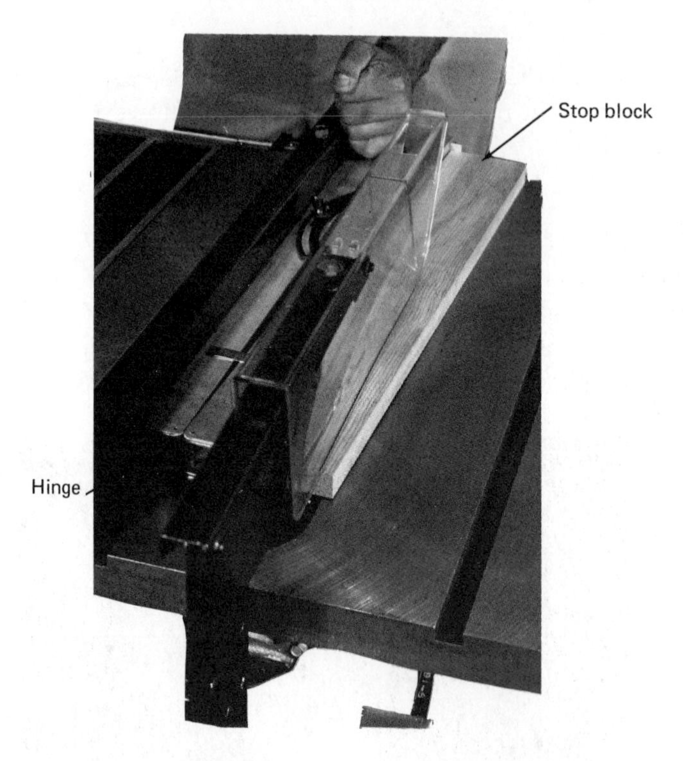


**FIGURE 11-15** / Cutting tapers on the table saw.

The jig is placed against the fence as shown, and the workpiece is placed against the jig stop block. The jig and workpiece are then pushed through the blade using the fence as a guide. To cut the taper on the other edge of the workpiece, the angle of the jig is doubled and the fence position is reset to correspond to the taper.

A taper jig similar to the commercial one illustrated in Fig. 11-15 can be constructed from two pieces of wood identically shaped. Hinge two ends of the legs together using a hinge that is slightly smaller than the cross section of the legs. From the hinged end of the taper jig, measure and mark the one foot location. By spreading the legs apart and measuring the opening at the one foot mark, the amount of desired taper, as 1/2-inch per foot, is easily set.

Using a piece of scrap wood across the top of the legs, nail the legs open to the desired taper angle. Glue and nail a stop block to the end of the outer leg as illustrated in Fig. 11-15.

A tapered pattern block can also be used if a number of duplicate tapered cuts are required. *Refer to Sec. 2-5.*

### Panel Raising

Panel raising—a decorative touch added to cabinet doors—is easily accomplished with the aid of an easily constructed jig. First, attach a high auxiliary fence made from a piece of hardwood onto the existing fence (Fig. 11-16). Then screw two other pieces of hardwood together to form a right angle.

**FIGURE 11-16** / Raised panels are cut using simple guides.

Raise the blade to the width of panel raising desired, and tilt the blade about 2°. Place the right angle next to the blade and parallel to the table edge. Clamp the angle in place and move the fence until it is a distance from the right angle equal to the thickness of the workpiece. Apply power to the saw, and make the across-the-grain cuts followed by the with-the-grain cuts.

If deep panel raising is desired, it is necessary to make depth cuts around the edge of the "raised panel" prior to making the angular cuts. The depth cuts are made with the panel flat on the table using the miter gauge and rip fence as guides.

### *Cove Cutting*

It is sometimes desirable to make a wide cove as shown in Fig. 11-17. The workpiece is passed over the blade at an angle, taking small successive cuts.

**FIGURE 11-17** / Cove cutting is accomplished by taking many successive cuts of 1/16 inch depth. Auxiliary fences are clamped to the table.

Clamp two auxiliary fences to the table as shown. For the first pass, set the blade depth to 1/16-inch; increase the depth by 1/16-inch on successive passes. Push the workpiece through the fences with a push stick; do not force the workpiece. When the inside of the cove is completed, the outside corners are cut off with the saw blade with chamfer cuts. If desired, the outside can be rounded to shape.

### *Pattern Sawing*

If a number of duplicate workpieces having straight line cuts are to be sawed, use a pattern. Clamp a right angle auxiliary fence onto the fence so that the auxiliary fence piece is about 1/16-inch higher than the thickness of the workpiece (Fig. 11-18). Put the pattern on top of the stock and tack the two together with brads. Place the auxiliary fence edge parallel to and flush with the far side of the blade. The blade height is set to cut about 1/16-inch above the workpiece thickness. Run the pattern along the auxiliary fence to cut out the duplicate workpiece.

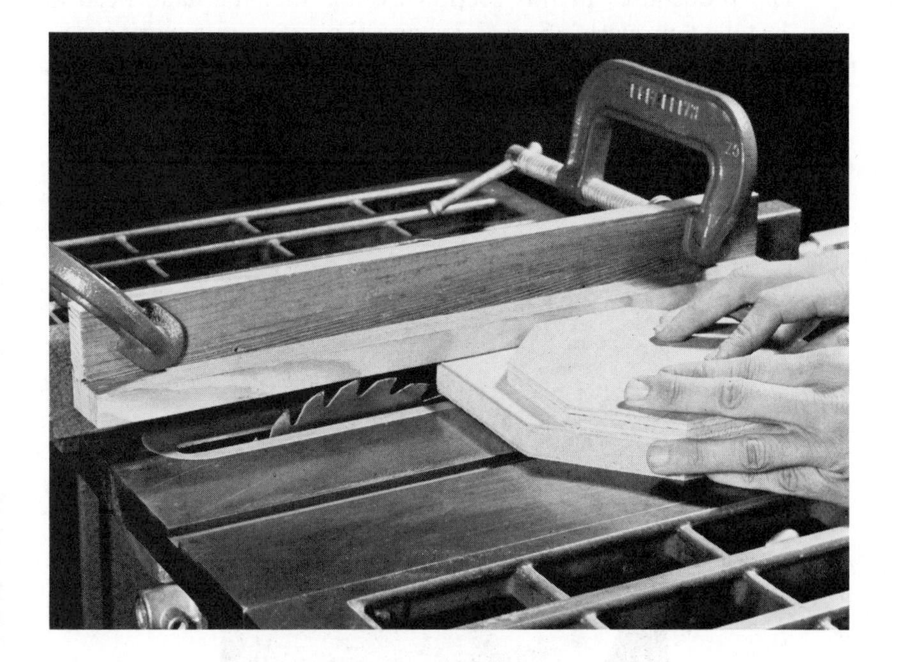

**FIGURE 11-18** / A pattern can be used to make duplicate straight cuts.

### *Rabbeting*

If a dado head is not available (Sec. 11-7), rabbet cuts can be made by making two passes on the table saw. The first pass should be made on the *edge* with the workpiece *face against the fence*. Use a push stick to feed the workpiece. The second cut is made with the workpiece flat on the table and against the fence as a guide.

## 11-6 / DADOING PROCEDURES

Dadoing is the cutting of rectangular grooves across or along a workpiece. Dado cuts along the edge or end of a workpiece are known as rabbet cuts.

In dadoing, the basic cuts–crosscut, miter, bevel, compound, and rip–are performed nearly the same as described in Sec. 11-5. Dadoes are cut with dado heads (Sec. 7-3), although they may also be cut with a combination blade by making repeated passes over the width of the desired groove.

The procedures in this section assume that the dado head has been installed properly (Sec. 7-3), and that you are experienced in making the basic cuts in Sec. 11-5. The dado head table insert also

**FIGURE 11-19** / Cutting a crosscut groove with a dado head.

must be placed in the table in place of the standard insert. The procedures in this section include: crosscut, mitered, rip and beveled dado cuts; rabbeting; tenons; tongue and groove; box joints; and cutting decorative molding.

### *Crosscut, Mitered, Rip and Beveled Dado Cuts*

Crosscut (Fig. 11-19), mitered, rip, and beveled dado cuts are made with the dado blades the same as making the cuts with a single blade (Sec. 11-5) except for the following:

1 / The width of cut is determined by the number of chippers and paper washers between the two blades. Repeat passes are made for wider cuts.

2 / The depth of cut is set as required.

3 / Cut scrap wood first to ensure that the width of cut is sufficient. Slightly wider cuts are made by adding paper washers between the blade and chippers.

### *Rabbeting*

Rabbeting cuts along the *edge* of a workpiece are made on the table saw as shown in Fig. 11-20 using a hold down finger assembly or in a different manner if the assembly is not available. The hold down finger assembly makes rabbeting a safer operation. As shown in Fig. 11-20, an auxiliary fence with a grooved cutout for the dado head is attached to the hold down finger assembly, and the complete unit is held to the existing table saw fence with thumb screws. The fingers are set to produce a spring force against the workpiece to hold it against the auxiliary fence and the table.

With the dado blade set to the desired width and the fence and hold down fingers adjusted, the workpiece is pushed through the dado head using the fence as a guide. If a rabbet wider than 13/16-inch is required, then the fence is readjusted to make a second pass.

Without a hold down finger assembly available, rabbets are made along the edge of a workpiece using the fence as a guide. Cuts are made on the *outside* edge of the workpiece *away from the fence*. Place the fence in position so that the outside dado blade extends

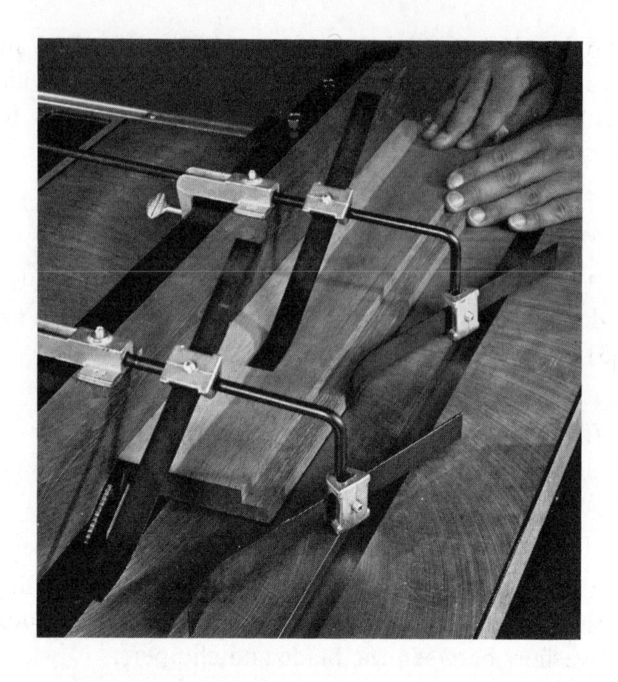

**FIGURE 11-20** / Rabbeting is accomplished easily with a dado head.

beyond the workpiece about 1/64-inch. Hold the workpiece as if a rip cut is to be made. Feed the workpiece slowly and maintain a slightly sideward force on the workpiece toward the fence. Let the dado cut. Do not place your hands over the area where the dado passes underneath. If a narrow workpiece is to be rabbeted, it is best to rabbet the edge of a wide piece of stock first; then rip the stock to the required workpiece width.

*End* rabbets are cut in the same method as a crosscut. Use the miter gauge as a guide.

### Tenons

Tenons are cut with a dado head and the table saw set for crosscuts (Fig. 11-21). Set the dado head width as desired for the tenon–if greater than 13/16-inch, then repeated passes are required. Set the blade height to remove the required material from one side of the workpiece. Place the workpiece against the miter gauge and a stop block that is located on the forward table edge as a position setting gauge when the workpiece is turned over for the backside cut on the tenon. Cut one side of the tenon; turn the workpiece over and cut the other side.

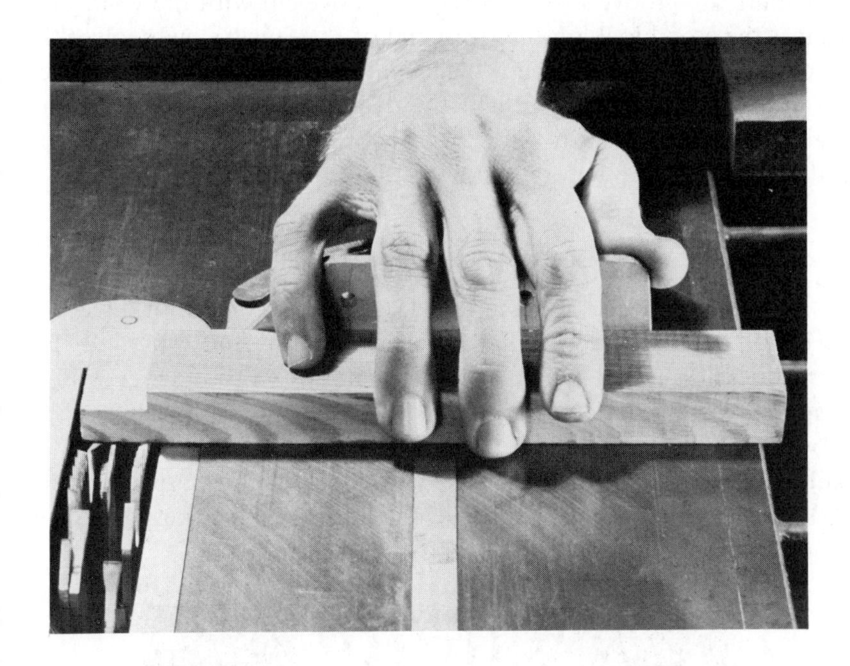

**FIGURE 11-21** / Cutting a tenon on the table saw.

*Tongue and Groove*

Tongue and groove cuts are made with the table saw in the rip configuration. A high auxiliary fence made from hardwood with a semicircular cutout is fastened to the table saw fence. (Observe the fence shown in Fig. 11-20.)

The grooves should be cut first (and cut all workpiece grooves at one time). Set the dado head width and height, and then place the fence so that the groove is cut in the center. Apply power and hold the workpiece against the fence as the groove is cut. Feed slowly.

Reposition the fence for cutting the tongues. Two methods are suggested: either cut one side of the groove and then turn the workpiece around and cut the other side, or place washers between the dado blades to provide space for cutting around the tongue. In the latter case, only one pass is required.

*Gains*—grooves with one closed end—and *stopped grooves*—grooves with both ends closed—are cut in a manner similar to cutting the grooves discussed. Clamp stop blocks to the fence at locations that limit the groove length. Start the groove cut with the workpiece against the stop block on the front end of the fence; slowly lower the workpiece onto the spinning blade until it touches the table. Then advance the workpiece through the dado until the workpiece stops against the stop block toward the rear of the fence. Remove power and let the saw stop before removing the workpiece.

### *Box Joints*

Box joints are cut as shown in Fig. 11-22. Clamp both workpieces to be joined together and set the dado head width. Space the cuts the *same* thickness as the blade kerf. Use scrap wood to practice with at first, and screw an auxiliary strip onto the miter head. Once the proper spacing has been ascertained by several cuts in scrap wood, a nail can be partially driven into the auxiliary strip for spacing cuts. Make the first cut; locate that cut on the nail and make the second cut; move the second cut to the nail and so on.

**FIGURE 11-22** / Cutting box joints.

### *Decorative Molding*

Decorative molding in designs of your imagination are made simply using the dado head and the table saw. Screw an auxiliary guide on the miter gauge as shown in Fig. 11-22, and drive a nail partially into the guide to use as a spacer. Using a wide workpiece, cut decorative dado cuts across the width of the workpiece, using the nail head as a spacer. Then rip cut the workpiece into thin strips.

## 11-7 / MOLDING AND SHAPING PROCEDURES

The molding and shaping of workpieces are performed on the table saw with the use of accessory molding head (also called shaping head) cutters (Sec. 7-3). These accessory cutters are attached to a head that is placed on the table saw arbor and secured by the arbor nut.

Place the cutters into the head as directed by the manufacturer (also refer to Sec. 7-3). Secure the head to the arbor ensuring that the head is placed in the correct direction of rotation. When the head is installed, rotate it by hand to ensure that there is clearance. Also replace the standard table insert with a molding head insert.

This section describes how to use the molding/shaping head to shape edges, ends, surfaces, and curved edges.

*CAUTION*

***Take small cuts on single passes with the molding/shaping cutters; increase the depth of cut in small increments. This method will prevent kickbacks and split workpieces.***

### *Edge Shaping*

The safest method of shaping edges on the table saw with the molding head cutters is to use an auxiliary fence with a semicircular cutout and a hold down finger assembly (Fig. 11-23). This method is used only if a *part of the edge of the workpiece is left remaining*. If the *complete edge* is removed by the cutter, then the area along the fence beyond the cutter has to be shimmed the thickness of the material cut off.

Attach the auxiliary fence and hold down fingers. Adjust the

**FIGURE 11-23** / Cutting edge molding on a workpiece. If the complete edge is removed, the fence beyond the cutters has to be shimmed.

fence into proper position. Raise the arbor so that the cutting head will take a small cut. Place the workpiece in position, and adjust the hold down fingers to hold the workpiece against the fence and the table. Apply power and feed the workpiece slowly through the cutters. Do not place your hands over the cutters or in line with the cutters. When part of the workpiece exits beyond the cutter, you can walk around the table and pull the workpiece the rest of the way through if necessary.

If hold down fingers are not available, the edge *away from the fence* should be shaped (rather than cutting along the fence). Position the fence (on either side of the cutter, depending upon the cutter) so that the edge of the workpiece is over the cutter; set the cutter to remove only a small amount of material on each cut. Reposition the fence and raise the fence as required until the edging is completed.

Depending upon the cutter, edges also may be shaped by placing the workpiece in a vertical position as shown in Fig. 11-24.

This position can only be used if a part of the edge *remains* on the workpiece.

**FIGURE 11-24** / Edges can also be shaped when the workpiece is held in the vertical position. However, if the *complete* edge is removed by the cutter, do not use this method. Refer to the text.

In cutting strip molding, shape the edge of a wide board. Then saw the edge off.

### *End Shaping*

The edges of workpieces are shaped by using the miter gauge as a guide. If possible, clamp the workpiece in the miter gauge. As previously mentioned, remove small amounts of material on each pass. Raise the height of the cutters as required. If both across-the-grain ends and with-the-grain edges are to be shaped, shape the ends first.

### *Surface Shaping*

Straight decorative shaping can be performed on the surface of workpieces. With the surface of the workpiece down, the cutter height low for shallow cuts, and the fence in position as a guide, pass the workpiece over the cutter. Increase the depth of cut until the required depth is reached.

### Shaping Curved Edges

Curved edges are shaped freehand by using a *U-shaped* guide (Figs. 11-25 and 11-27). The guide is undercut to clear the cutters. It is screwed into a straight board used as an auxiliary fence.

**FIGURE 11-25** / A U-shaped guide is used to guide the workpiece in freehand shaping.

Locate the fence in a position that will give the desired depth of cut from the cutter, and locate the U-shaped guide on the center of the arbor. Set the cutter height low for the initial cut, and raise it for successive passes of the workpiece. Stand at the front left of the table and very carefully approach the *downside* of the spinning cutter with the workpiece. Feed the workpiece into and against the *center* of the U-shaped guide block. Keep the workpiece firmly against the guide as the workpiece is shaped. Feed slowly.

## *11-8* / SANDING PROCEDURES

The table saw can be used as a disk sander by placing a disk on the arbor. You can either buy the disk or make a disk from plywood. Sometimes, you may want to place one abrasive grit size on one side of the disk and another grit size on the opposite side.

Raise the disk above the table only as far as required for the workpiece. Hold the workpiece firmly with both hands, and *touch* the workpiece against the disk on the *downside* spinning side (Fig. 11-26).

**FIGURE 11-26** / The table saw can be adapted for disk sanding.

When ends or mitered cuts of workpieces are to be sanded, use the miter gauge as a guide. When edges are sanded, the fence can be used as a guide.

## 11-9 / ACCESSORIES

Accessories for the table saw that have not already been discussed in detail include table extensions (some are adjustable) and molding and dado head inserts. Table extensions are useful, and, as a matter of fact, are almost a necessity for the table saw. The extensions provide additional supporting surface for wide boards. They are easily bolted on.

The molding and dado head table inserts have wider slots in them than does the standard insert. The inserts provide workpiece support near the cutter; the slot allows the cutter to pass through. The inserts are required when the heads are used.

## 11-10 / CALIBRATION AND MAINTENANCE

The table saw makes straight true cuts when it is properly aligned. Adjustments are easy. Check that the blade is perpendicular and parallel to the table, and that the fence is perpendicular and parallel to the table. Also periodically check that the fence width, miter gauge angle, and blade height scale pointers are correct, and that the leveling screws under the table insert are correct. Also lubricate and clean periodically as described.

Raise the blade to its maximum height, and use a square to check that the blade is perpendicular to the table when the cutter angle scale reads 0°. If it is not perpendicular, set it perpendicular and then reposition the pointer to the 0° mark. It may be necessary to reset the 0° *stop*—usually a bolt with a locknut on it. Also check the 45° stop using a 45° triangle or a combination square having a 45° angle; reset the stop as required.

Use a crayon to mark one blade tooth; rotate that tooth to the front of the table. Hold a pointed pencil against the miter gauge, and touch the pencil tip to the crayoned tooth. Rotate the blade tooth to the rear of the table, and holding the pencil exactly as it was previously, slide it to the rear of the table at the crayoned tooth. If the tip touches the crayoned tooth, the blade is parallel. If the blade is not parallel, loosen the table mount or arbor bolts and adjust. Recheck.

Check that the fence is parallel to the table and blade by aligning the fence on a miter groove; lock the fence. If the fence is not parallel, loosen the screws or bolts under the front casting, reset, and tighten.

Using a square, check that the fence is perpendicular to the table. If it is not, loosen the screws or bolts, realign the fence, and tighten.

If the saw has a fence scale, check its calibration by moving it over against the blade. If the pointer does not indicate 0 inches, reset the pointer.

Check that the splitter is in alignment with the blade by running a straight edge back from the blade to the splitter. Realign as necessary.

Remove the table insert and check whether or not it has alignment screws under it. If it does, adjust the screws as required to align the insert flush with the table top.

If the elevating screw handle turns from vibration causing the motor and blade height to change, tighten the tension by tightening the setscrews on the collar.

The arbor ball bearings are usually grease packed at the factory and do not require additional lubrication. A little graphite should be placed occasionally on the trunnion at the guides and on the elevating and arbor tilting screws at the thrust collars. The elevating screw nut, swivel pins, pivot pins, and other points where there is friction between two or more moving surfaces should be lubricated occasionally with no. 20 or 30 oil.

Keep the table and internal mechanisms free of sawdust and chips. Brush the dirt off. Keep the bevel *stops* and the arbor nut and washer clean so that no buildup occurs causing inaccuracies.

## *11-11* / HINTS AND KINKS

A piece of hardwood screwed onto the miter gauge (Fig. 11-27) will aid the gauge in supporting long workpieces that are to be cut off. In attaching the hardwood, leave about 1/8-clearance between it and the table.

Prior to installing the hardwood to the gauge, several brads can be driven through the wood. The exposed nail points dig into the workpiece being held against the miter gauge and prevent the workpiece from "creeping" when miter cuts are made. Instead of the

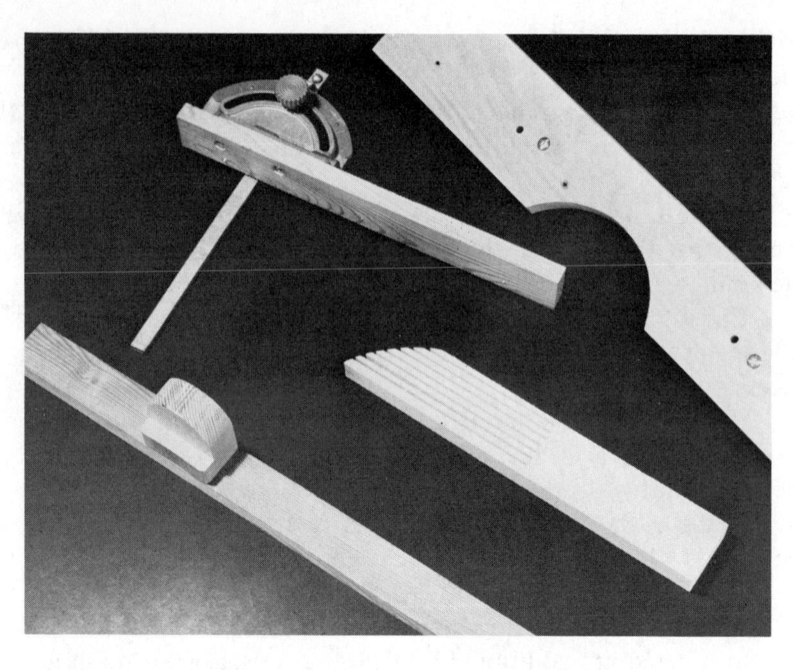

**FIGURE 11-27** / Helpful aids for the table saw: (A) miter gauge extension with brads; (B) auxiliary fence; (C) auxiliary fence with U-shaped guide; (D) spring stick.

brads, abrasive paper may be glued to the hardwood face; this also prevents the workpiece from creeping.

A piece of hardwood that is two or three times higher than the fence can be screwed to the fence to support large workpieces when edge cutting with the molding head or the dado head. Make a semicircular cutout in the hardwood for clearance of the dado and molding head cutters (Fig. 11-27).

When relatively narrow workpieces are to be shaped and no hold down fingers are available, a "spring stick" can be made (Fig. 11-27). Using a piece of 3/4- by 2 by 12 inch stock, cut lengthwise grooves each 1/4-inch for 4 inches along the length of the stick. Round off the top of the stick. Clamp the stick to the table in such a position that the workpiece is held against the fence.

## *11-12* / INSTALLATION

Because workpieces to be crosscut are placed crosswise on the table saw and workpieces to be ripped are placed lengthwise, workspace is needed on all four sides of the saw. The table is most ideally located in the center of the workshop—sometimes placed diagonally for a little space saving. The table saw should be placed on a sturdy stand with the table 34 to 37 inches above the floor. Casters facilitate relocating the saw if necessary to cut extra large workpieces; at least two of the four casters should have brakes.

Perform all of the calibration and maintenance procedures of Sec. 11-10.

chapter twelve

# THICKNESS PLANER

**FIGURE 12-1** / The thickness planer, a tool for the luxurious home workshop, is used to plane rough lumber and to smoothly plane wood to the desired thickness.

The thickness planer is a power tool for the luxurious home shop. You need a lot of money (over $400–without motor–for the most inexpensive model), and a need to do a lot of work to justify the cost.

The *thickness planer*, illustrated in Fig. 12-1, is used to clean rough lumber and to smoothly plane wood to the desired thickness. Other tools similar to the thickness planer, but more elaborate and expensive, are the *planer-molder* and the *planer-molder-saw*. Of the three, the thickness planer is the only tool that can be considered a home workshop tool. The other tools are for carpentry shops.

The thickness planer is self-feeding. Its maximum cut is 1/8-inch per pass; it accepts workpieces 12 inches wide by 4 inches thick and turns out smooth planed wood. Workpieces less than 1/16-inch thick or 6 inches in length cannot be planed.

The planer-molder performs both planing and molding operations in a single pass of the workpiece through the tool. A planer-molder-saw combines a sawing operation with the other two operations. These power fed tools trim rough lumber into moldings, trim, picture frames, and wood for furniture.

## *12-1* / DESCRIPTION AND MAJOR PARTS

A piece of wood with a flat surface is placed into the thickness planer on the infeed table (Fig. 12-2). With the thickness set, the motor running, and the feed rollers engaged, the workpiece is slid to the fluted infeed rollers. The infeed roller grips the wood and draws it at a rate of about 16 feet per minute into the overhead revolving cutter head that contains three high speed steel cutting knives. As the wood exits from the cutting head, it passes under the smooth outfeed roller that drives the wood along the outfeed table. A shaving hood provides the housing for the cutting head and drive rollers. The infeed/outfeed table has two passive rollers that reduce table friction as the wood passes over the table.

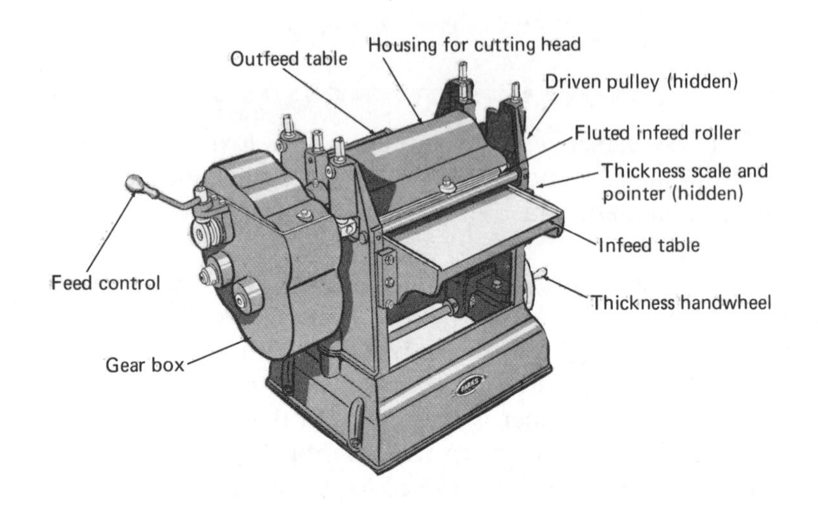


FIGURE 12-2 / Major parts of the thickness planer.

The thickness planer uses a motor of 1 to 3 hp. The 1 hp motor is for light duty service, whereas the 2 and up hp motors are for heavy duty. Either 1725 or 3450 rev/min motors are used with the proper sized pulleys to drive the cutting head from 4000 to 4200 rev/min. Double grooved pulleys and belts are also used.

## 12-2 / OPERATING ADJUSTMENTS AND CONTROLS

The only operating adjustments and controls on the thickness planer are the thickness adjustment and the feed control:

1 / *thickness adjustment*—the thickness adjustment—and hence the depth of cut—are made by rotating the thickness

handwheel (Fig. 12-2). The thickness—the distance between the cutter head knives and the table—is indicated by the pointer on the thickness scale. To set the depth of cut, the workpiece is first measured at its thickest part, or it can be placed under the knives with the power off and the knives lowered by rotating the thickness handwheel until the knives touch the workpiece. With the workpiece removed, the knives can then be lowered, as indicated on the thickness scale, an amount equal to the desired depth of cut (up to 1/8-inch).

2 / *feed control*—the feed control engages or disengages the infeed and the outfeed rollers.

## 12-3 / OPERATION

### *CAUTIONS*

1 / *Ensure that there are no nails in the workpiece nor any tools or other items on the planer tables.*

2 / *Provide a support, such as a workpiece support stand (Sec. 1-10), behind the outfeed table to support long workpieces. Without proper support, the weight of the overhanging end will make it difficult and perhaps dangerous to feed the work all the way through the machine.*

3 / *Stop the tool motor before attempting to dislodge a jammed workpiece or before removing loose chips from the tables.*

4 / *Do not try to exceed the maximum depth of cut for which your machine is designed. Do not force workpieces through the planer.*

5 / *Do not allow your fingers to get near the feed rollers or under the housing at any time when the motor is on. Keep your fingers at least 3 inches away from the infeed roller when feeding workpieces.*

6 / *Do not overload the motor by taking too deep a cut. If the motor slows down, disengage the rollers by use of the feed control until the motor returns to operating speed.*

***7 / Observe the safety precautions of Sec. 1-16.***

Perform the following procedures to operate the thickness planer:

*1* / Set the thickness for the desired cut. Remember, this is the thickness of the workpiece at the thickest part minus the thickness of the cut (usually not more than 1/8-inch. Refer to Sec. 12-2).

*2* / If required, position a workpiece support stand behind the outfeed table at a height level to the table.

*3* / Disengage the feed rollers.

*4* / Turn on the motor and let it reach maximum speed.

*5* / Engage the feed rollers and carefully feed the workpiece into the infeed roller so that the cutting knives are cutting with the grain. (Refer to Sec. 5-4, but remember that the thickness planer knives are overhead, whereas the jointer knives are underneath.)

*6* / Remove the workpiece from the outfeed table.

*7* / Repeat steps 5 and 6 for all workpieces that are the same thickness before changing the thickness for subsequent cuts.

*8* / To keep your workpieces from subsequently warping, plane equal amounts of stock from both sides.

Some thickness planers may not be power fed. In this case, push the workpiece through the cutting head at a feed speed that does not appreciably reduce the speed of the motor. When a sufficient section of the workpiece has gone through the cutting head onto the outfeed table, walk around to the rear of the thickness planer and pull the workpiece the rest of the way through. Do not allow your hands to get near the cutting head.

## *12-4* / PLANING PROCEDURES

Workpieces having at least one flat side are planed as detailed in Sec. 12-3. Workpieces requiring squaring, the planing of warped boards, and the planing of thin stock are discussed in the following paragraphs.

Workpieces that must be squared must first have two adjacent sides squared on a jointer (Chap. 5). The jointer fence is used in squaring the two sides. Mark the two sides squared on the jointer as *working sides*. Place one of the working sides flat down on the thickness planer, and plane the top surface until the desired thickness is attained. Then turn the other working side flat onto the thickness planer table, and plane the fourth side to the desired thickness.

Warped workpieces must have one side planed flat on a jointer (Chap. 5) before the workpiece can be planed on the thickness planer. This is because the pressure of the feed rollers would remove the warp as the workpiece passes through the planer, but as the workpiece emerges and the pressure is removed, the workpiece would again assume the warped configuration.

Thin workpieces of 1/4-inch or less must be backed with a backing board of 3/4- to 1 inch thickness and with a length and width slightly larger than the workpiece. Place the workpiece on top of the backing board, and pass the two simultaneously through the planer.

## 12-5 / KNIFE SHARPENING AND REPLACEMENT

Since the knives are 12 inches or longer in length, perhaps you should take the knives to a professional for grinding. After grinding, reset the knives into the cutting head by following the manufacturer's directions. Generally, one of two methods is followed. In the first method, a shim equal to the knife length is set into the bottom of each knife slot. The shims can be pieces of wire with a small diameter corresponding approximately to the amount of stock removed in the knife grinding. Insert the knives into the slots against the shims; tighten the setscrews securely against the knives.

The second method of resetting the knives consists of setting the knives to the table. Insert the knives into the slots in the cutting head, and tighten the setscrews just firmly enough to grip the knives. Place two pieces of hardwood of uniform thickness on the table at either end of the head. Raise the table so that the knife that is farthest out of the head is just scraping the wood. The other knives are then raised to the level of the highest knife by tapping lightly at the base of the knives on either side of the cutting head. The setscrews holding each knife are then securely tightened.

## 12-6 / CALIBRATION AND MAINTENANCE

Calibration consists of periodically checking the thickness scale and pointer for accurate indications; maintenance includes periodic lubrication. It may also be necessary to reset the feed rollers or pressure bar.

To calibrate the thickness scale and pointer, measure the thickness of a piece of hardwood, and then place the piece under the cutting head (with the motor off). Rotate the cutting head until one of the knives points straight down. Using the thickness handwheel, raise the table until the hardwood piece just touches the knife. Check the thickness scale and pointer for the proper measured thickness. If the indication is not correct, loosen the pointer setscrew, relocate the pointer to the correct indication, and tighten the setscrew.

The gear box is lubricated with 1/2- to 1 pound of soft pressure gun grease (available from gasoline service stations). The ball bearings are grease packed at the factory but should be lubricated twice a year if the planer has a lot of use. The table roller bearings and the feed rollers should be oiled with SAE 30 weight oil prior to each day's use if the planer is used continuously.

If it becomes necessary to reset the feed rollers or pressure bar, follow the manufacturer's instructions. Basically, the following procedures are performed (with the motor off). Two boards of equal thickness are placed on the table on each side of the cutting head. The table is then raised until the knives are touching the boards. The two feed rollers and the pressure bar are lowered until they also touch the two boards. The feed rollers, knives, and pressure bar are now even and parallel. The boards are removed and the fluted infeed roller is lowered one-half turn on the adjusting studs. The smooth outfeed roller is lowered one-quarter turn on the adjusting studs.

If the workpiece will not follow through, then the pressure bar must be raised slightly. Also, the table rollers should never be more than 1/64-inch above the table.

## 12-7 / INSTALLATION

The thickness planer is generally shipped factory adjusted. Only the motor, pulleys, and belts need be installed. Place the planer on a factory purchased table or another very sturdy flat surface so that the planer table is at a convenient height of about 32 to 35 inches. Clean all greased and coated surfaces before operating the planer.

# APPENDIXES

# A

# ENGLISH-TO-METRIC AND METRIC-TO-ENGLISH CONVERSION FACTORS

This appendix provides conversion factors from English to metric and from metric to English. To convert from one measurement unit in one system to another unit in the other system, multiply the first unit measurement by the conversion factor. Thus

$$\text{first system measurement and unit} \times \text{conversion factor} = \text{second system measurement and unit} \qquad \text{(A-1)}$$

*Example:* Convert 3¼ inches to centimeters.

Since the metric system is based on 10 (the decimal system), it is first necessary to change the fraction of ¼ to a decimal. Thus

$$\tfrac{1}{4} = 1 \div 4 = 0.250$$

Now, convert 3.250 inches to centimeters. Use the table on the following page to determine the conversion factor and equation (A-1) to find the answer:

$$3.250 \text{ inches} \times 2.540 = 8.255 \text{ centimeters}$$

*Example:* Convert 25 meters to feet. Use the table on the next page and equation (A-1):

$$25 \text{ meters} \times 3.281 = 82.025 \text{ feet}$$

| *To Convert* | *Into* | *Multiply by* |
|---|---|---|
| | English to Metric | |
| inches | millimeters | 25.40 |
| inches | centimeters | 2.540 |
| inches | meters | 0.0254 |
| feet | millimeters | 304.8 |
| feet | centimeters | 30.48 |
| feet | meters | 0.3048 |
| cubic feet | cubic meters | 0.02832 |
| cubic inches | cubic meters | $1.639 \times 10^{-5}$ |
| square inches | square millimeters | 645.2 |
| | Metric to English | |
| millimeters | inches | 0.03937 |
| millimeters | feet | $3.281 \times 10^{-3}$ |
| centimeters | inches | 0.3937 |
| centimeters | feet | $3.281 \times 10^{-2}$ |
| meters | inches | 39.37 |
| meters | feet | 3.281 |
| cubic meters | cubic feet | 35.31 |
| cubic meters | cubic inches | 61,023.0 |
| square meters | square feet | 10.76 |
| square millimeters | square inches | $1.550 \times 10^{-3}$ |

# B

# INCH-MILLIMETER EQUIVALENTS OF DECIMAL AND COMMON FRACTIONS

| Inch | ½'s | ¼'s | 8ths | 16ths | 32nds | 64ths | Millimeters | Decimals of an Inch[a] |
|---|---|---|---|---|---|---|---|---|
| | | | | | | 1 | 0.397 | 0.015 625 |
| | | | | | 1 | 2 | 0.794 | 0.031 25 |
| | | | | | | 3 | 1.191 | 0.046 875 |
| | | | | 1 | 2 | 4 | 1.588 | 0.062 5 |
| | | | | | | 5 | 1.984 | 0.078 125 |
| | | | | | 3 | 6 | 2.381 | 0.093 75 |
| | | | | | | 7 | 2.778 | 0.109 375 |
| | | | 1 | 2 | 4 | 8 | 3.175[a] | 0.125 0 |
| | | | | | | 9 | 3.572 | 0.140 625 |
| | | | | | 5 | 10 | 3.969 | 0.156 25 |
| | | | | | | 11 | 4.366 | 0.171 875 |
| | | | | 3 | 6 | 12 | 4.762 | 0.187 5 |
| | | | | | | 13 | 5.159 | 0.203 125 |
| | | | | | 7 | 14 | 5.556 | 0.218 75 |
| | | | | | | 15 | 5.953 | 0.234 375 |
| | | 1 | 2 | 4 | 8 | 16 | 6.350[a] | 0.250 0 |
| | | | | | | 17 | 6.747 | 0.265 625 |
| | | | | | 9 | 18 | 7.144 | 0.281 25 |
| | | | | | | 19 | 7.541 | 0.296 875 |
| | | | | 5 | 10 | 20 | 7.938 | 0.312 5 |
| | | | | | | 21 | 8.334 | 0.328 125 |
| | | | | | 11 | 22 | 8.731 | 0.343 75 |
| | | | | | | 23 | 9.128 | 0.359 375 |
| | | | 3 | 6 | 12 | 24 | 9.525[a] | 0.375 0 |
| | | | | | | 25 | 9.922 | 0.390 625 |
| | | | | | 13 | 26 | 10.319 | 0.406 25 |
| | | | | | | 27 | 10.716 | 0.421 875 |
| | | | | 7 | 14 | 28 | 11.112 | 0.437 5 |
| | | | | | | 29 | 11.509 | 0.453 125 |
| | | | | | 15 | 30 | 11.906 | 0.468 75 |
| | | | | | | 31 | 12.303 | 0.484 375 |
| | 1 | 2 | 4 | 8 | 16 | 32 | 12.700[a] | 0.500 0 |
| | | | | | | 33 | 13.097 | 0.515 625 |
| | | | | | 17 | 34 | 13.494 | 0.531 25 |
| | | | | | | 35 | 13.891 | 0.546 875 |
| | | | | 9 | 18 | 36 | 14.288 | 0.562 5 |

| *Inch* | *½'s* | *¼'s* | *8ths* | *16ths* | *32nds* | *64ths* | *Millimeters* | *Decimals of an Inch*[a] |
|---|---|---|---|---|---|---|---|---|
| | | | | | | 37 | 14.684 | 0.578 125 |
| | | | | | 19 | 38 | 15.081 | 0.593 75 |
| | | | | | | 39 | 15.478 | 0.609 375 |
| | | | 5 | 10 | 20 | 40 | 15.875[a] | 0.625 0 |
| | | | | | | 41 | 16.272 | 0.640 625 |
| | | | | | 21 | 42 | 16.669 | 0.656 25 |
| | | | | | | 43 | 17.066 | 0.671 875 |
| | | | | 11 | 22 | 44 | 17.462 | 0.687 5 |
| | | | | | | 45 | 17.859 | 0.703 125 |
| | | | | | 23 | 46 | 18.256 | 0.718 75 |
| | | | | | | 47 | 18.653 | 0.734 375 |
| | | 3 | 6 | 12 | 24 | 48 | 19.050[a] | 0.750 0 |
| | | | | | | 49 | 19.447 | 0.765 625 |
| | | | | | 25 | 50 | 19.844 | 0.781 25 |
| | | | | | | 51 | 20.241 | 0.796 875 |
| | | | | 13 | 26 | 52 | 20.638 | 0.812 5 |
| | | | | | | 53 | 21.034 | 0.828 125 |
| | | | | | 27 | 54 | 21.431 | 0.843 75 |
| | | | | | | 55 | 21.828 | 0.859 375 |
| | | | 7 | 14 | 28 | 56 | 22.225[a] | 0.875 0 |
| | | | | | | 57 | 22.622 | 0.890 625 |
| | | | | | 29 | 58 | 23.019 | 0.906 25 |
| | | | | | | 59 | 23.416 | 0.921 875 |
| | | | | 15 | 30 | 60 | 23.812 | 0.937 5 |
| | | | | | | 61 | 24.209 | 0.953 125 |
| | | | | | 31 | 62 | 24.606 | 0.968 75 |
| | | | | | | 63 | 25.003 | 0.984 375 |
| 1 | 2 | 4 | 8 | 16 | 32 | 64 | 25.400[a] | 1.000 0 |

[a] Exact.

# C
# DECIMAL EQUIVALENTS OF MILLIMETERS

| *mm.* | *Inches* | *mm.* | *Inches* | *mm.* | *Inches* | *mm.* | *Inches* | *mm.* | *Inches* |
|---|---|---|---|---|---|---|---|---|---|
| 0.01 | 0.00039 | 0.41 | 0.01614 | 0.81 | 0.03189 | 21 | 0.82677 | 61 | 2.40157 |
| 0.02 | 0.00079 | 0.42 | 0.01654 | 0.82 | 0.03228 | 22 | 0.86614 | 62 | 2.44094 |
| 0.03 | 0.00118 | 0.43 | 0.01693 | 0.83 | 0.03268 | 23 | 0.90551 | 63 | 2.48031 |
| 0.04 | 0.00157 | 0.44 | 0.01732 | 0.84 | 0.03307 | 24 | 0.94488 | 64 | 2.51968 |
| 0.05 | 0.00197 | 0.45 | 0.01772 | 0.85 | 0.03346 | 25 | 0.98425 | 65 | 2.55905 |
| 0.06 | 0.00236 | 0.46 | 0.01811 | 0.86 | 0.03386 | 26 | 1.02362 | 66 | 2.59842 |
| 0.07 | 0.00276 | 0.47 | 0.01850 | 0.87 | 0.03425 | 27 | 1.06299 | 67 | 2.63779 |
| 0.08 | 0.00315 | 0.48 | 0.01890 | 0.88 | 0.03465 | 28 | 1.10236 | 68 | 2.67716 |
| 0.09 | 0.00354 | 0.49 | 0.01929 | 0.89 | 0.03504 | 29 | 1.14173 | 69 | 2.71653 |
| 0.10 | 0.00394 | 0.50 | 0.01969 | 0.90 | 0.03543 | 30 | 1.18110 | 70 | 2.75590 |
| 0.11 | 0.00433 | 0.51 | 0.02008 | 0.91 | 0.03583 | 31 | 1.22047 | 71 | 2.79527 |
| 0.12 | 0.00472 | 0.52 | 0.02047 | 0.92 | 0.03622 | 32 | 1.25984 | 72 | 2.83464 |
| 0.13 | 0.00512 | 0.53 | 0.02087 | 0.93 | 0.03661 | 33 | 1.29921 | 73 | 2.87401 |
| 0.14 | 0.00551 | 0.54 | 0.02126 | 0.94 | 0.03701 | 34 | 1.33858 | 74 | 2.91338 |
| 0.15 | 0.00591 | 0.55 | 0.02165 | 0.95 | 0.03740 | 35 | 1.37795 | 75 | 2.95275 |
| 0.16 | 0.00630 | 0.56 | 0.02205 | 0.96 | 0.03780 | 36 | 1.41732 | 76 | 2.99212 |
| 0.17 | 0.00669 | 0.57 | 0.02244 | 0.97 | 0.03819 | 37 | 1.45669 | 77 | 3.03149 |
| 0.18 | 0.00709 | 0.58 | 0.02283 | 0.98 | 0.03858 | 38 | 1.49606 | 78 | 3.07086 |
| 0.19 | 0.00748 | 0.59 | 0.02323 | 0.99 | 0.03898 | 39 | 1.53543 | 79 | 3.11023 |
| 0.20 | 0.00787 | 0.60 | 0.02362 | 1.00 | 0.03937 | 40 | 1.57480 | 80 | 3.14960 |
| 0.21 | 0.00827 | 0.61 | 0.02402 | 1 | 0.03937 | 41 | 1.61417 | 81 | 3.18897 |
| 0.22 | 0.00866 | 0.62 | 0.02441 | 2 | 0.07874 | 42 | 1.65354 | 82 | 3.22834 |
| 0.23 | 0.00906 | 0.63 | 0.02480 | 3 | 0.11811 | 43 | 1.69291 | 83 | 3.26771 |
| 0.24 | 0.00945 | 0.64 | 0.02520 | 4 | 0.15748 | 44 | 1.73228 | 84 | 3.30708 |
| 0.25 | 0.00984 | 0.65 | 0.02559 | 5 | 0.19685 | 45 | 1.77165 | 85 | 3.34645 |
| 0.26 | 0.01024 | 0.66 | 0.02598 | 6 | 0.23622 | 46 | 1.81102 | 86 | 3.38582 |
| 0.27 | 0.01063 | 0.67 | 0.02638 | 7 | 0.27559 | 47 | 1.85039 | 87 | 3.42519 |
| 0.28 | 0.01102 | 0.68 | 0.02677 | 8 | 0.31496 | 48 | 1.88976 | 88 | 3.46456 |
| 0.29 | 0.01142 | 0.69 | 0.02717 | 9 | 0.35433 | 49 | 1.92913 | 89 | 3.50393 |
| 0.30 | 0.01181 | 0.70 | 0.02756 | 10 | 0.39370 | 50 | 1.96850 | 90 | 3.54330 |
| 0.31 | 0.01220 | 0.71 | 0.02795 | 11 | 0.43307 | 51 | 2.00787 | 91 | 3.58267 |
| 0.32 | 0.01260 | 0.72 | 0.02835 | 12 | 0.47244 | 52 | 2.04724 | 92 | 3.62204 |
| 0.33 | 0.01299 | 0.73 | 0.02874 | 13 | 0.51181 | 53 | 2.08661 | 93 | 3.66141 |
| 0.34 | 0.01339 | 0.74 | 0.02913 | 14 | 0.55118 | 54 | 2.12598 | 94 | 3.70078 |
| 0.35 | 0.01378 | 0.75 | 0.02953 | 15 | 0.59055 | 55 | 2.16535 | 95 | 3.74015 |
| 0.36 | 0.01417 | 0.76 | 0.02992 | 16 | 0.62992 | 56 | 2.20472 | 96 | 3.77952 |
| 0.37 | 0.01457 | 0.77 | 0.03032 | 17 | 0.66929 | 57 | 2.24409 | 97 | 3.81889 |
| 0.38 | 0.01496 | 0.78 | 0.03071 | 18 | 0.70866 | 58 | 2.28346 | 98 | 3.85826 |
| 0.39 | 0.01535 | 0.79 | 0.03110 | 19 | 0.74803 | 59 | 2.32283 | 99 | 3.89763 |
| 0.40 | 0.01575 | 0.80 | 0.03150 | 20 | 0.78740 | 60 | 2.36220 | 100 | 3.93700 |

# D

# ENGLISH SYSTEM OF WEIGHTS AND MEASURES

### Linear Measure (Length)

1000 mils = 1 inch (in.)
12 inches = 1 foot (ft.)
3 feet = 1 yard (yd.)
5280 feet = 1 mile

### Square Measure (Area)

144 square inches (sq.in.) = 1 square foot (sq.ft.)
9 square feet = 1 square yard (sq.yd.)

### Cubic Measure (Volume)

1728 cubic inches (cu.in.) = 1 cubic foot (cu.ft.)
27 cubic feet = 1 cubic yard (cu.yd.)
231 cubic inches = 1 U.S. gallon (gal.)
277.27 cubic inches = 1 British imperial gallon (i.gal.)

### Liquid Measure (Capacity)

4 fluid ounces (fl.oz.) = 1 gill (gi.)
2 pints = 1 quart (qt.)
4 quarts = 1 gallon

### Dry Measure (Capacity)

2 pints = 1 quart
8 quarts = 1 peck (pk.)

### Weight (Avoirdupois)

27.3438 grains = 1 dram (dr.)
16 drams = 1 ounce (oz.)
16 ounces = 1 pound (lb.)
100 pounds = 1 hundredweight (cwt.)
112 pounds = 1 long hundredweight (l.cwt.)
2000 pounds = 1 short ton (S.T.)
2240 pounds = 1 long ton (L.T.)

### Weight (Troy)

24 grains = 1 pennyweight (dwt.)
20 pennyweights = 1 ounce (oz.t.)
12 ounces = 1 pound (lb.t.)

### Angular or Circular Measure

60 seconds = 1 minute
60 minutes = 1 degree
57.2958 degrees = 1 radian
90 degrees = 1 quadrant or right angle
360 degrees = 1 circle or circumference

# E

# METRIC SYSTEM OF WEIGHTS AND MEASURES

### Linear Measure (Length)

1/10 meter = 1 decimeter (dm)
1/10 decimeter = 1 centimeter (cm)
1/10 centimeter = 1 millimeter (mm)
1/1000 millimeter = 1 micron ($\mu$)
1/1000 micron = 1 millimicron (m$\mu$)
10 meters = 1 dekameter (dkm)
10 dekameters = 1 hectometer (hm)
10 hectometers = 1 kilometer (km)
10 kilometers = 1 myriameter

### Square Measure (Area)

1 are = 1 square dekameter ($dkm^2$)
1 centare = 1 square meter ($m^2$)
1 hectare = 1 square hectometer ($hm^2$)

### Cubic Measure (Volume)

1 stere = 1 cubic meter ($m^3$)
1 decistere = 1 cubic decimeter ($dm^3$)
1 centistere = 1 cubic centimeter ($cm^3$)
1 dekastere = 1 cubic dekameter ($dkm^3$)

### Capacity

1/10 liter = 1 deciliter (dl)
1/10 deciliter = 1 centiliter (cl)
1/10 centiliter = 1 milliliter (ml)
10 liters = 1 dekaliter (dkl)
100 liters = 1 hectoliter (hl)
1000 liters = 1 kiloliter (kl)
1 kiloliter = 1 stere (s)

### Weight

1/10 gram = 1 decigram (dg)
1/10 decigram = 1 centigram (cg)
1/10 centigram = 1 milligram (mg)
10 grams = 1 dekagram (dkg)
100 grams = 1 hectogram (hg)
1000 grams = 1 kilogram (kg)
10,000 grams = 1 myriagram
100,000 grams = 1 quintal (q)
1,000,000 grams = 1 metric ton (t)

# F

# CONVERSION BETWEEN ENGLISH AND METRIC UNITS

| *English to Metric* | *Metric to English* |
|---|---|
| **Units of Length** | |
| 1 millimeter = 0.03937 inch or about 1/25 inch | |
| 1 inch = 2.540 centimeters | 1 centimeter = 0.3937 inch |
| 1 foot = 0.3048 meter | 1 decimeter = 3.937 inches |
| 1 yard = 0.9144 meter | 1 meter = 39.37 inches |
| 1 mile = 1.6093 kilometers | = 3.281 feet |
| | = 1.094 yards |
| | 1 kilometer = 0.62137 mile |
| **Units of Area** | |
| 1 sq. inch = 6.4516 sq. centimeters | 1 sq. centimeter = 0.1549997 sq. inch |
| 1 sq. foot = 0.0929 sq. meter | 1 sq. meter = 10.764 sq. feet |
| 1 sq. mile = 2.590 sq. kilometers | 1 sq. kilometer = 0.3861 sq. mile |
| 1 acre = 0.4047 hectare | 1 hectare = 2.471 acres |
| **Units of Volume** | |
| 1 cu. inch = 16.387 cu. centimeters | 1 cu. centimeter = 0.061023 cu. inch |
| 1 cu. foot = 0.028317 cu. meter | 1 cu. meter = 35.31445 cu. feet |
| **Capacity (Liquid)** | |
| 1 gill = 0.11829 liter | 1 liter = 8.4537 gills |
| 1 pint = 0.4732 liter | 1 liter = 2.1134 pints |
| 1 quart = 0.9463 liter | 1 liter = 1.0567 quarts |
| **Capacity (Dry)** | |
| 1 pint = 0.5506 liter | 1 liter = 1.816 pints |
| 1 quart = 1.1012 liters | 1 liter = 0.908 quart |
| 1 peck = 8.8096 liters | 1 liter = 0.1135 peck |
| 1 bushel = 3.52383 dekaliters | 1 dekaliter = 0.28378 bushel |
| **Units of Mass** | |
| 1 grain = 0.0648 gram | 1 gram = 15.432 grains |
| 1 ounce (avdp.) = 28.3495 grams | 1 kilogram = 35.274 oz. avdp. |
| 1 pound (avdp.) = 0.45359 kilogram | 1 kilogram = 2.2046 lbs. avdp. |
| 1 short ton (2000 lb.) = 0.9072 metric ton | 1 metric ton = 1.1023 short tons |
| 1 long ton (2240 lb.) = 1.016 metric tons | 1 metric ton = 0.9842 long ton |

# G

# METRIC CONVERSION TABLE

| | | | |
|---|---|---|---|
| Millimeters | × 0.03937 | = Inches |
| Millimeters | = 25.400 | × Inches |
| Meters | × 3.2809 | = Feet |
| Meters | = 0.3048 | × Feet |
| Kilometers | × 0.621377 | = Miles |
| Kilometers | = 1.6093 | × Miles |
| Square centimeters | × 0.15500 | = Square inches |
| Square centimeters | = 6.4515 | × Square inches |
| Square meters | × 10.76410 | = Square feet |
| Square meters | = 0.09290 | × Square feet |
| Cubic centimeters | × 0.061025 | = Cubic inches |
| Cubic centimeters | = 16.3866 | × Cubic inches |
| Cubic meters | × 35.3156 | = Cubic feet |
| Cubic meters | = 0.02832 | × Cubic feet |
| Cubic meters | × 1.308 | = Cubic yards |
| Cubic meters | = 0.765 | × Cubic yards |
| Liters | × 61.023 | = Cubic inches |
| Liters | = 0.01639 | × Cubic inches |
| Liters | × 0.26418 | = U.S. gallons |
| Liters | = 3.7854 | × U.S. gallons |
| Grams | × 15.4324 | = Grains |
| Grams | = 0.0648 | × Grains |
| Grams | × 0.03527 | = Ounces, avoirdupois |
| Grams | = 28.3495 | × Ounces, avoirdupois |
| Kilograms | × 2.2046 | = Pounds |
| Kilograms | = 0.4536 | × Pounds |
| Kilograms per square centimeter | × 14.2231 | = Pounds per square inch |
| Kilograms per square centimeter | = 0.0703 | × Pounds per square inch |
| Kilograms per cubic meter | × 0.06243 | = Pounds per cubic foot |
| Kilograms per cubic meter | = 16.01890 | × Pounds per cubic foot |
| Metric tons (1,000 kilograms) | × 1.1023 | = Tons (2,000 pounds) |
| Metric tons | = 0.9072 | × Tons (2,000 pounds) |
| Calories | × 3.9683 | = B.T. units |
| Calories | = 0.2520 | × B.T. units |

# H

# LUMBER CONVERSION CHART

*Lineal Feet to Board Feet*
*Example: 1 x 2 x 10 = 1–2/3 bd. ft.*

| | Length in (Feet) | | | | | | | |
|---|---|---|---|---|---|---|---|---|
| *Size* | *10* | *12* | *14* | *16* | *18* | *20* | *22* | *24* |
| 1 x 2 | 1-2/3 | 2 | 2-1/3 | 2-2/3 | 3 | 3-1/3 | 3-2/3 | 4 |
| 1 x 3 | 2½ | 3 | 3½ | 4 | 4½ | 5 | 5½ | 6 |
| 1 x 4 | 3-1/3 | 4 | 4-2/3 | 5-1/3 | 6 | 6-2/3 | 7-1/3 | 8 |
| 1 x 5 | 4-1/6 | 5 | 5-5/6 | 6-2/3 | 7½ | 8-1/3 | 9-1/6 | 10 |
| 1 x 6 | 5 | 6 | 7 | 8 | 9 | 10 | 11 | 12 |
| 1 x 7 | 5-5/6 | 7 | 8-1/6 | 9-1/3 | 10½ | 11-2/3 | 12-5/6 | 14 |
| 1 x 8 | 6-2/3 | 8 | 9-1/3 | 10-2/3 | 12 | 13-1/3 | 14-2/3 | 16 |
| 1 x 9 | 7½ | 9 | 10½ | 12 | 13½ | 15 | 16½ | 18 |
| 1 x 10 | 8-1/3 | 10 | 11-2/3 | 13-1/3 | 15 | 16-2/3 | 18-1/3 | 20 |
| 1 x 12 | 10 | 12 | 14 | 16 | 18 | 20 | 22 | 24 |
| 1 x 14 | 11-2/3 | 14 | 16-1/3 | 18-2/3 | 21 | 23-1/3 | 25-2/3 | 28 |
| 1 x 16 | 13-1/3 | 16 | 18-2/3 | 21-1/3 | 24 | 26-2/3 | 29-1/3 | 32 |
| 1¼ x 4 | 4-1/6 | 5 | 5-5/6 | 6-2/3 | 7½ | 8-1/3 | 9-1/6 | 10 |
| 1¼ x 5 | 5-5/24 | 6¼ | 7-7/24 | 8-1/3 | 9-3/8 | 10-5/12 | 11-11/24 | 12½ |
| 1¼ x 6 | 6¼ | 7½ | 8¾ | 10 | 11¼ | 12½ | 13-3/4 | 15 |
| 1¼ x 8 | 8-1/3 | 10 | 11-2/3 | 13-1/3 | 15 | 16-2/3 | 18-1/3 | 20 |
| 1¼ x 9 | 9-3/8 | 11¼ | 13-1/8 | 15 | 16-7/8 | 18¾ | 20-5/8 | 22½ |
| 1¼ x 10 | 10-5/12 | 12½ | 14-7/12 | 16-2/3 | 18¾ | 20-5/6 | 22-11/12 | 25 |
| 1¼ x 12 | 12½ | 15 | 17½ | 20 | 22½ | 25 | 27½ | 30 |
| 2 x 2 | 3-1/3 | 4 | 4-2/3 | 5-1/3 | 6 | 6-2/3 | 7-1/3 | 8 |
| 2 x 3 | 5 | 6 | 7 | 8 | 9 | 10 | 11 | 12 |
| 2 x 4 | 6-2/3 | 8 | 9-1/3 | 10-2/3 | 12 | 13-1/3 | 14-2/3 | 16 |
| 2 x 6 | 10 | 12 | 14 | 16 | 18 | 20 | 22 | 24 |
| 2 x 8 | 13-1/3 | 16 | 18-2/3 | 21-1/3 | 24 | 26-2/3 | 29-1/3 | 32 |
| 2 x 9 | 15 | 18 | 21 | 24 | 27 | 30 | 33 | 36 |
| 2 x 10 | 16-2/3 | 20 | 23-1/3 | 26-2/3 | 30 | 33-1/3 | 36-2/3 | 40 |

I

# DECIMAL EQUIVALENTS OF NUMBER AND LETTER SIZE DRILLS

*NUMBER SIZE DRILLS*

| No. | Size of Drill In Inches | No. | Size of Drill In Inches | No. | Size of Drill In Inches | No. | Size of Drill In Inches |
|---|---|---|---|---|---|---|---|
| 1 | .2280 | 21 | .1590 | 41 | .0960 | 61 | .0390 |
| 2 | .2210 | 22 | .1570 | 42 | .0935 | 62 | .0380 |
| 3 | .2130 | 23 | .1540 | 43 | .0890 | 63 | .0370 |
| 4 | .2090 | 24 | .1520 | 44 | .0860 | 64 | .0360 |
| 5 | .2055 | 25 | .1495 | 45 | .0820 | 65 | .0350 |
| 6 | .2040 | 26 | .1470 | 46 | .0810 | 66 | .0330 |
| 7 | .2010 | 27 | .1440 | 47 | .0785 | 67 | .0320 |
| 8 | .1990 | 28 | .1405 | 48 | .0760 | 68 | .0310 |
| 9 | .1960 | 29 | .1360 | 49 | .0730 | 69 | .0292 |
| 10 | .1935 | 30 | .1285 | 50 | .0700 | 70 | .0280 |
| 11 | .1910 | 31 | .1200 | 51 | .0670 | 71 | .0260 |
| 12 | .1890 | 32 | .1160 | 52 | .0635 | 72 | .0250 |
| 13 | .1850 | 33 | .1130 | 53 | .0595 | 73 | .0240 |
| 14 | .1820 | 34 | .1110 | 54 | .0550 | 74 | .0225 |
| 15 | .1800 | 35 | .1100 | 55 | .0520 | 75 | .0210 |
| 16 | .1770 | 36 | .1065 | 56 | .0465 | 76 | .0200 |
| 17 | .1730 | 37 | .1040 | 57 | .0430 | 77 | .0180 |
| 18 | .1695 | 38 | .1015 | 58 | .0420 | 78 | .0160 |
| 19 | .1660 | 39 | .0995 | 59 | .0410 | 79 | .0145 |
| 20 | .1610 | 40 | .0980 | 60 | .0400 | 80 | .0135 |

*LETTER SIZE DRILLS*

| | | | | | |
|---|---|---|---|---|---|
| A | 0.234 | J | 0.277 | S | 0.348 |
| B | 0.238 | K | 0.281 | T | 0.358 |
| C | 0.242 | L | 0.290 | U | 0.368 |
| D | 0.246 | M | 0.295 | V | 0.377 |
| E | 0.250 | N | 0.302 | W | 0.386 |
| F | 0.257 | O | 0.316 | X | 0.397 |
| G | 0.261 | P | 0.323 | Y | 0.404 |
| H | 0.266 | Q | 0.332 | Z | 0.413 |
| I | 0.272 | R | 0.339 | | |

## J

## COMMON JOINTS USED IN WOODWORKING

This appendix illustrates many of the common joints used in woodworking. The construction of many of these joints are discussed within this handbook (refer to the index).

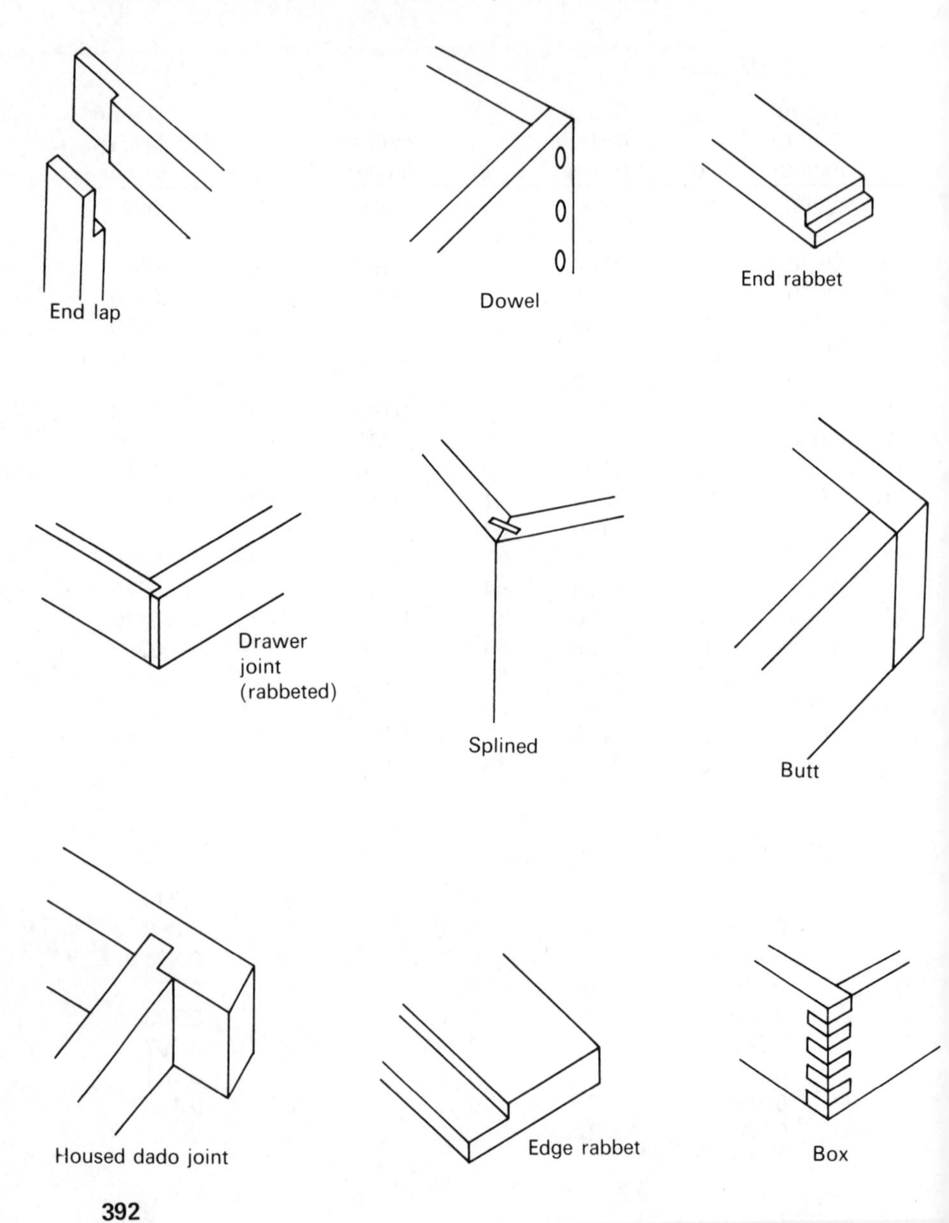

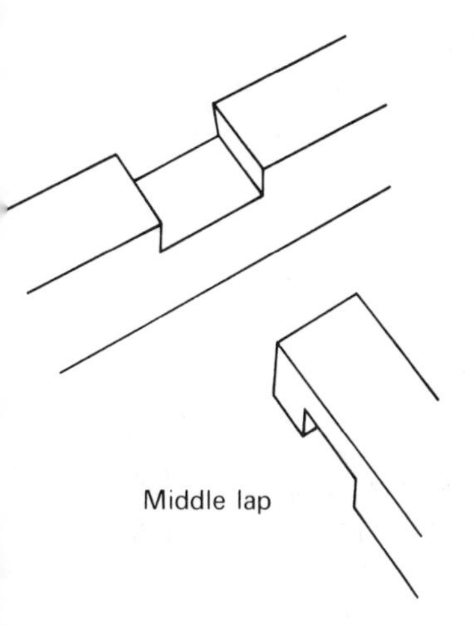

Middle lap

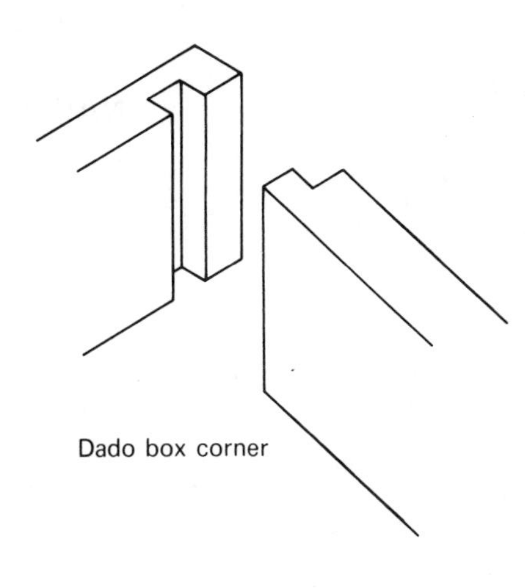

Dado box corner

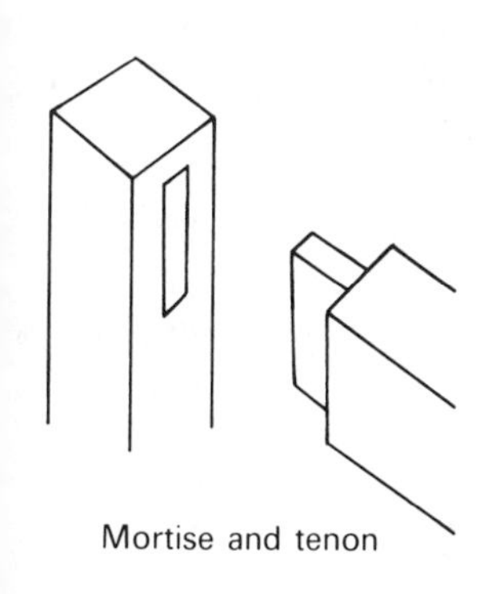

Mortise and tenon

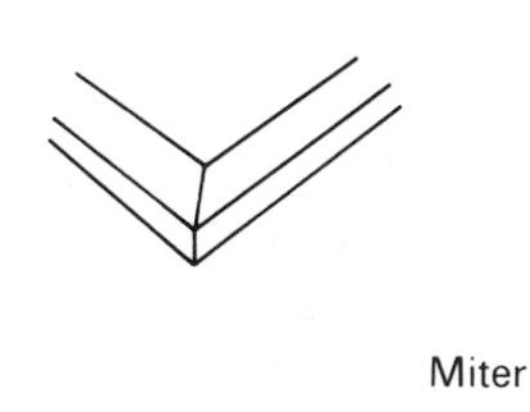

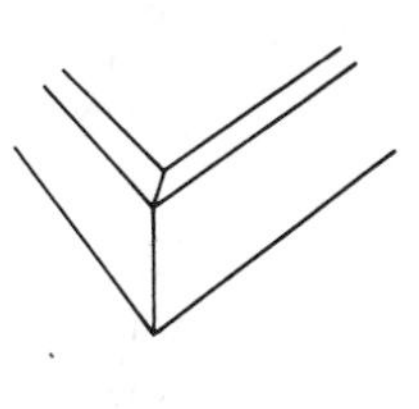

Miter

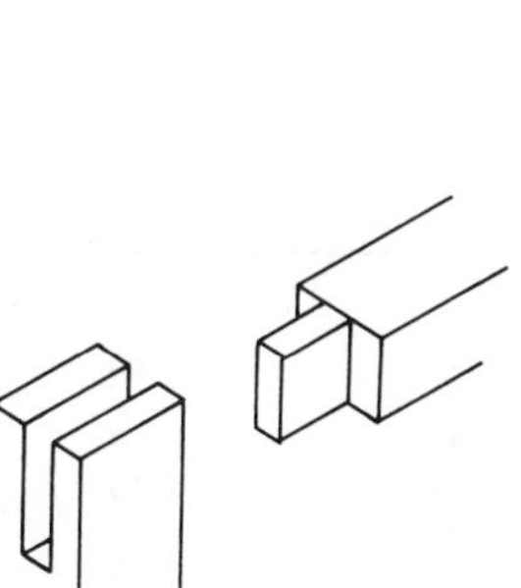

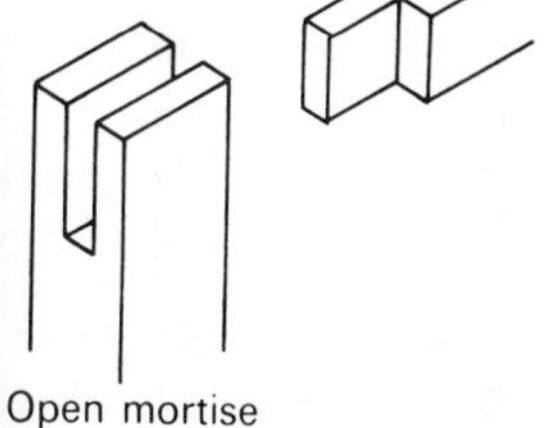

Open mortise
and tenon

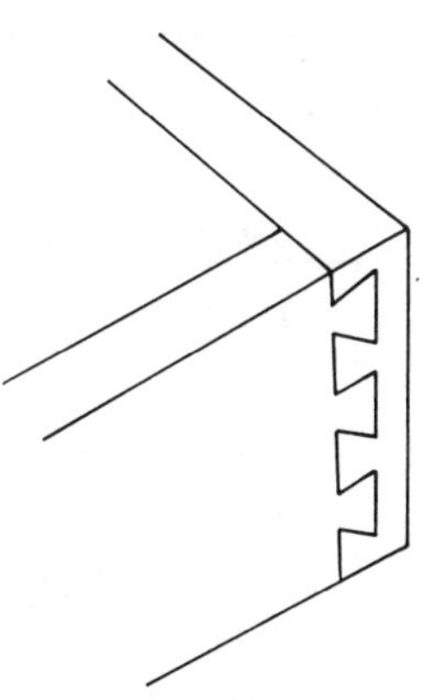

Dovetail

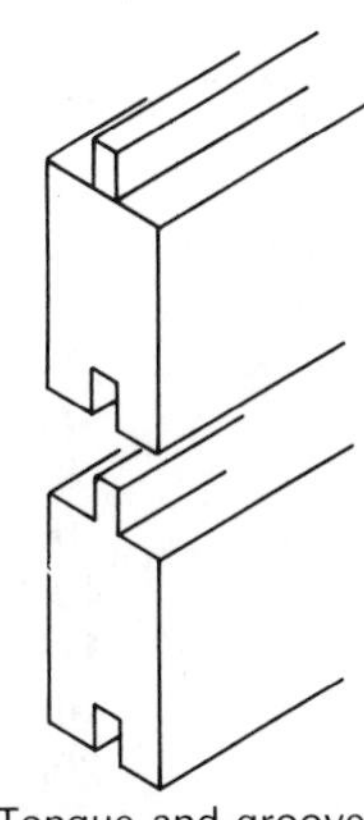

Tongue and groove

# K
# NAIL REFERENCE CHART

*COMMON WIRE NAILS*

| *Size* | *Length* | *Gauge* | *Approx. No. to lb.* |
|---|---|---|---|
| 2D | 1 In. | No. 15 | 876 |
| 3D | 1¼ | 14 | 568 |
| 4D | 1½ | 12½ | 316 |
| 5D | 1-3/4 | 12½ | 271 |
| 6D | 2 | 11½ | 181 |
| 7D | 2¼ | 11½ | 161 |
| 8D | 2½ | 10¼ | 106 |
| 9D | 2-3/4 | 10¼ | 96 |

| *Size* | *Length* | *Gauge* | *Approx. No. to lb.* |
|---|---|---|---|
| 10D | 3 In. | No. 9 | 69 |
| 12D | 3¼ | 9 | 63 |
| 16D | 3½ | 8 | 49 |
| 20D | 4 | 6 | 31 |
| 30D | 4½ | 5 | 24 |
| 40D | 5 | 4 | 18 |
| 50D | 5½ | 3 | 14 |
| 60D | 6 | 2 | 11 |

*FLOORING BRADS*

| *Size* | *Length* | *Gauge* | *Approx. No. to lb.* |
|---|---|---|---|
| 6D | 2 In. | No. 11 | 157 |
| 7D | 2¼ | 11 | 139 |
| 8D | 2½ | 10 | 99 |
| 9D | 2-3/4 | 10 | 90 |
| 10D | 3 | 9 | 69 |
| 12D | 3¼ | 8 | 54 |
| 16D | 3½ | 7 | 43 |
| 20D | 4 | 6 | 31 |

*FINISHING NAILS*

| Size | Length | Gauge | Approx. No. to lb. |
|---|---|---|---|
| 2D | 1 In. | No. 16½ | 1351 |
| 3D | 1¼ | 15½ | 807 |
| 4D | 1½ | 15 | 584 |
| 5D | 1-3/4 | 15 | 500 |
| 6D | 2 | 13 | 309 |
| 7D | 2¼ | 13 | 238 |
| 8D | 2½ | 12½ | 189 |
| 9D | 2-3/4 | 12½ | 172 |
| 10D | 3 | 11½ | 121 |
| 12D | 3¼ | 11½ | 113 |
| 16D | 3½ | 11 | 90 |
| 20D | 4 | 10 | 62 |

*CASING NAILS*

| Size | Length | Gauge | Approx. No. to lb. |
|---|---|---|---|
| 2D | 1 In. | No. 15½ | 1010 |
| 3D | 1¼ | 14½ | 635 |
| 4D | 1½ | 14 | 473 |
| 5D | 1-3/4 | 14 | 406 |
| 6D | 2 | 12½ | 236 |
| 7D | 2¼ | 12½ | 210 |
| 8D | 2½ | 11½ | 145 |
| 9D | 2-3/4 | 11½ | 132 |
| 10D | 3 | 10½ | 94 |
| 12D | 3¼ | 10½ | 87 |
| 16D | 3½ | 10 | 71 |
| 20D | 4 | 9 | 52 |
| 30D | 4½ | 9 | 46 |

*SMOOTH AND BARBED BOX NAILS*

| Size | Length | Gauge | Approx. No. to lb. |
|---|---|---|---|
| 2D | 1 In. | No. 15½ | 1010 |
| 3D | 1¼ | 14½ | 635 |
| 4D | 1½ | 14 | 473 |
| 5D | 1-3/4 | 14 | 406 |
| 6D | 2 | 12½ | 236 |
| 7D | 2¼ | 12½ | 210 |
| 8D | 2½ | 11½ | 145 |
| 9D | 2-3/4 | 11½ | 132 |
| 10D | 3 | 10½ | 94 |
| 12D | 3¼ | 10½ | 88 |
| 16D | 3½ | 10 | 71 |
| 20D | 4 | 9 | 52 |
| 30D | 4½ | 9 | 46 |
| 40D | 5 | 8 | 35 |

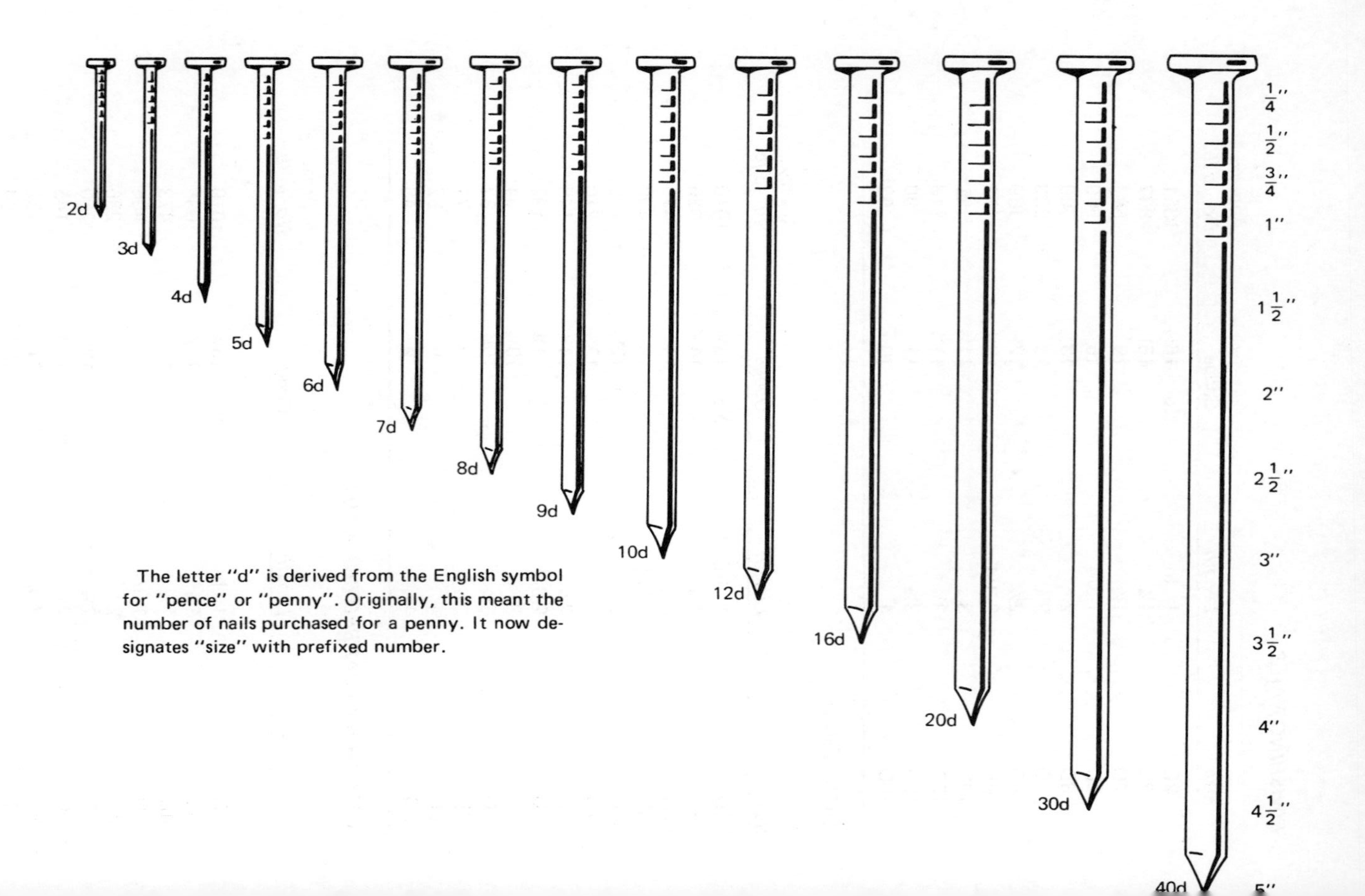


The letter "d" is derived from the English symbol for "pence" or "penny". Originally, this meant the number of nails purchased for a penny. It now designates "size" with prefixed number.

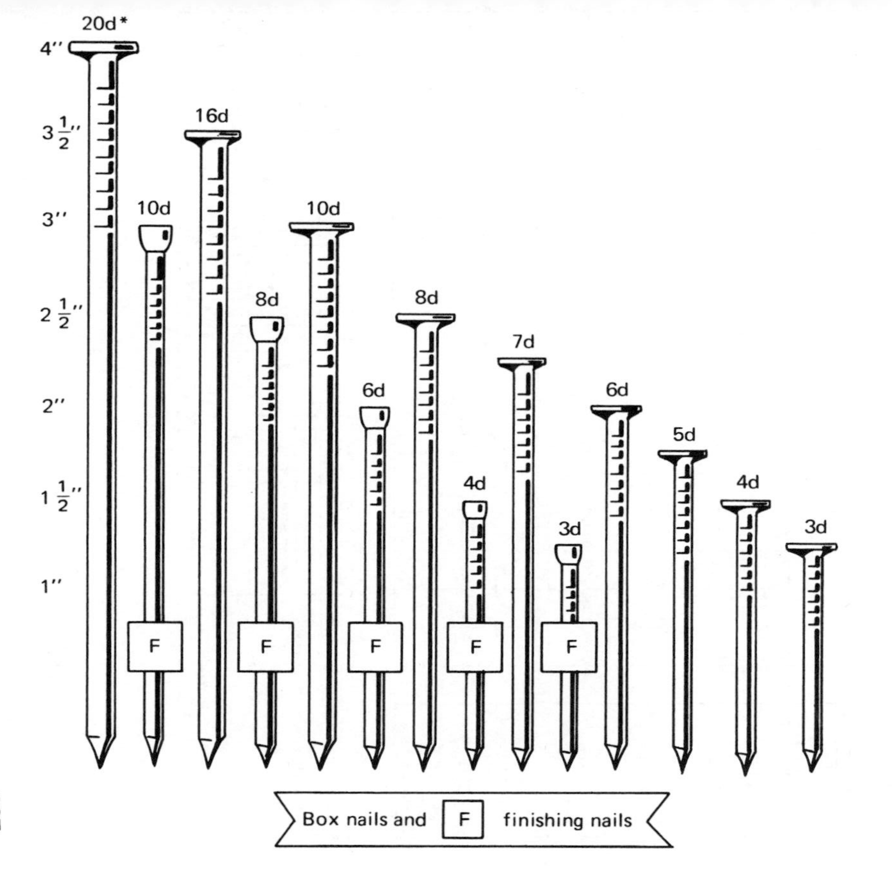


| Wire nails and brads | | | |
|---|---|---|---|
| Length | Gauges | Length | Gauges |
| $\frac{3}{16}$″ | 20 to 24 | 1″ | 7 to 20 |
| $\frac{1}{4}$″ | 19 to 26 | $1\frac{1}{8}$″ | 7 to 19 |
| $\frac{3}{8}$″ | 18 to 26 | $1\frac{1}{4}$″ | 6 to 17 |
| $\frac{1}{2}$″ | 14 to 24 | $1\frac{3}{8}$″ | 6 to 17 |
| $\frac{5}{8}$″ | 12 to 24 | $1\frac{1}{2}$″ | 4 to 17 |
| $\frac{3}{4}$″ | 10 to 21 | $1\frac{5}{8}$″ | 4 to 17 |
| $\frac{7}{8}$″ | 8 to 20 | $1\frac{3}{4}$″ | 4 to 17 |

*The letter "d" is derived from the English symbol for "pence" or "penny". Originally, this meant the number of nails purchased for a penny. It now designates "size" with prefixed number.

# L

# SCREW REFERENCE CHART

Listed below are screw lengths from $\frac{1}{4}$" to 4". Shank dimensions are shown from 0 to 24.
These sizes are most frequently used and are more generally available.

| Length | Shank numbers | | | | | | | | | | | | | | | | | |
|---|---|---|---|---|---|---|---|---|---|---|---|---|---|---|---|---|---|---|
| $\frac{1}{4}$ inch | 0 | 1 | 2 | 3 | | | | | | | | | | | | | | |
| $\frac{3}{8}$ inch | | | 2 | 3 | 4 | 5 | 6 | 7 | | | | | | | | | | |
| $\frac{1}{2}$ inch | | | 2 | 3 | 4 | 5 | 6 | 7 | 8 | | | | | | | | | |
| $\frac{5}{8}$ inch | | | | 3 | 4 | 5 | 6 | 7 | 8 | 9 | 10 | | | | | | | |
| $\frac{3}{4}$ inch | | | | | 4 | 5 | 6 | 7 | 8 | 9 | 10 | 11 | | | | | | |
| $\frac{7}{8}$ inch | | | | | | | 6 | 7 | 8 | 9 | 10 | 11 | 12 | | | | | |
| 1 inch | | | | | | | 6 | 7 | 8 | 9 | 10 | 11 | 12 | 14 | | | | |
| $1\frac{1}{4}$ inch | | | | | | | | 7 | 8 | 9 | 10 | 11 | 12 | 14 | 16 | | | |
| $1\frac{1}{2}$ inch | | | | | | | 6 | 7 | 8 | 9 | 10 | 11 | 12 | 14 | 16 | 18 | | |
| $1\frac{3}{4}$ inch | | | | | | | | | 8 | 9 | 10 | 11 | 12 | 14 | 16 | 18 | 20 | |
| 2 inch | | | | | | | | | 8 | 9 | 10 | 11 | 12 | 14 | 16 | 18 | 20 | |
| $2\frac{1}{4}$ inch | | | | | | | | | | 9 | 10 | 11 | 12 | 14 | 16 | 18 | 20 | |
| $2\frac{1}{2}$ inch | | | | | | | | | | | | | 12 | 14 | 16 | 18 | 20 | |
| $2\frac{3}{4}$ inch | | | | | | | | | | | | | | 14 | 16 | 18 | 20 | |
| 3 inch | | | | | | | | | | | | | | | 16 | 18 | 20 | |
| $3\frac{1}{2}$ inch | | | | | | | | | | | | | | | | 18 | 20 | 24 |
| 4 inch | | | | | | | | | | | | | | | | 18 | 20 | 24 |
| 0 to 24 diameter dimensions in inches at body | 0.060 | 0.073 | 0.086 | 0.099 | 0.112 | 0.125 | 0.138 | 0.151 | 0.164 | 0.177 | 0.190 | 0.203 | 0.216 | 0.242 | 0.268 | 0.294 | 0.320 | 0.372 |
| Twist bit sizes for round, flat and oval head screws in drilling shank and pilot holes. | | | | | | | | | | | | | | | | | | |
| Shank holes hard and softwood | $\frac{1}{16}$ | $\frac{5}{64}$ | $\frac{3}{32}$ | $\frac{7}{64}$ | $\frac{7}{64}$ | $\frac{1}{8}$ | $\frac{9}{64}$ | $\frac{5}{32}$ | $\frac{11}{64}$ | $\frac{3}{16}$ | $\frac{3}{16}$ | $\frac{13}{64}$ | $\frac{7}{32}$ | $\frac{1}{4}$ | $\frac{17}{64}$ | $\frac{19}{64}$ | $\frac{21}{64}$ | $\frac{3}{8}$ |
| Pilot hole softwood | $\frac{1}{64}$ | $\frac{1}{32}$ | $\frac{1}{32}$ | $\frac{3}{64}$ | $\frac{3}{64}$ | $\frac{1}{16}$ | $\frac{1}{16}$ | $\frac{1}{16}$ | $\frac{5}{64}$ | $\frac{5}{64}$ | $\frac{3}{32}$ | $\frac{3}{32}$ | $\frac{7}{64}$ | $\frac{7}{64}$ | $\frac{9}{64}$ | $\frac{9}{64}$ | $\frac{11}{64}$ | $\frac{3}{16}$ |
| Pilot hole hardwood | $\frac{1}{32}$ | $\frac{1}{32}$ | $\frac{3}{64}$ | $\frac{1}{16}$ | $\frac{1}{16}$ | $\frac{5}{64}$ | $\frac{5}{64}$ | $\frac{3}{32}$ | $\frac{3}{32}$ | $\frac{7}{64}$ | $\frac{7}{64}$ | $\frac{1}{8}$ | $\frac{1}{8}$ | $\frac{9}{64}$ | $\frac{5}{32}$ | $\frac{3}{16}$ | $\frac{3}{64}$ | $\frac{7}{32}$ |
| Auger bit sizes for countersunk heads | | | 3 | 4 | 4 | 4 | 5 | 5 | 6 | 6 | 6 | 7 | 7 | 8 | 9 | 10 | 11 | 12 |

| Twist drill sizes for round, oval and flat head screws in drilling shank and pilot holes. | | | | | | | | | | | | | | | | | | | |
|---|---|---|---|---|---|---|---|---|---|---|---|---|---|---|---|---|---|---|---|
| Screw sizes—common, slotted head | | 0 | 1 | 2 | 3 | 4 | 5 | 6 | 7 | 8 | 9 | 10 | 11 | 12 | 14 | 16 | 18 | 20 | 24 |
| Shank hole—hard and softwood | Fractional | $\frac{1}{16}$ | $\frac{5}{64}$ | $\frac{3}{32}$ | $\frac{7}{64}$ | $\frac{7}{64}$ | $\frac{1}{8}$ | $\frac{9}{64}$ | $\frac{5}{32}$ | $\frac{11}{64}$ | $\frac{3}{16}$ | $\frac{3}{16}$ | $\frac{13}{64}$ | $\frac{7}{32}$ | $\frac{1}{4}$ | $\frac{17}{64}$ | $\frac{19}{64}$ | $\frac{21}{64}$ | $\frac{3}{8}$ |
| | number- letter | 52 | 47 | 42 | 37 | 32 | 30 | 27 | 22 | 18 | 14 | 10 | 4 | 2 | D | I | N | P | V |
| Pilot hole—softwood | Fractional | $\frac{1}{64}$ | $\frac{1}{32}$ | $\frac{1}{32}$ | $\frac{3}{64}$ | $\frac{3}{64}$ | $\frac{1}{16}$ | $\frac{1}{16}$ | $\frac{1}{16}$ | $\frac{5}{64}$ | $\frac{5}{64}$ | $\frac{3}{32}$ | $\frac{3}{32}$ | $\frac{7}{64}$ | $\frac{7}{64}$ | $\frac{9}{64}$ | $\frac{9}{64}$ | $\frac{11}{64}$ | $\frac{3}{16}$ |
| | number | 75 | 71 | 65 | 58 | 55 | 53 | 52 | 51 | 48 | 45 | 43 | 40 | 38 | 32 | 29 | 26 | 19 | 15 |
| Pilot hole—hardwood | Fractional | $\frac{1}{32}$ | $\frac{1}{32}$ | $\frac{3}{64}$ | $\frac{1}{16}$ | $\frac{1}{16}$ | $\frac{5}{64}$ | $\frac{5}{64}$ | $\frac{3}{32}$ | $\frac{3}{32}$ | $\frac{7}{64}$ | $\frac{7}{64}$ | $\frac{1}{8}$ | $\frac{1}{8}$ | $\frac{9}{64}$ | $\frac{5}{32}$ | $\frac{3}{16}$ | $\frac{13}{64}$ | $\frac{7}{32}$ |
| | number | 70 | 66 | 56 | 54 | 52 | 49 | 47 | 44 | 40 | 37 | 33 | 31 | 30 | 25 | 18 | 13 | 4 | 1 |

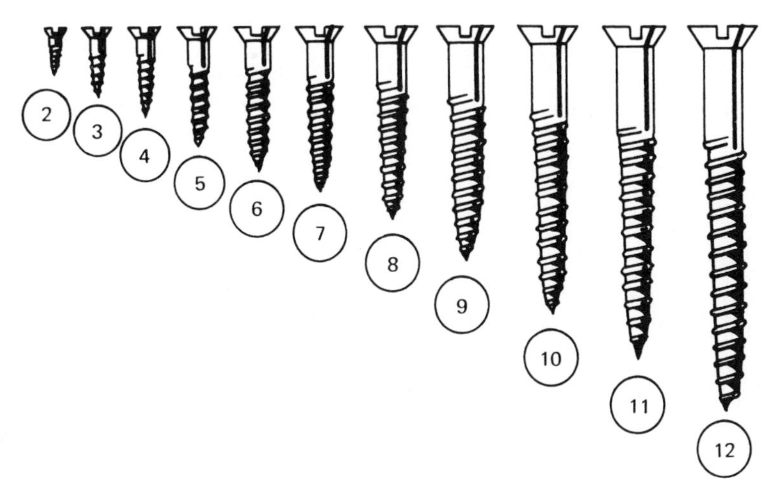
2
3
4
5
6
7
8
9
10
11
12

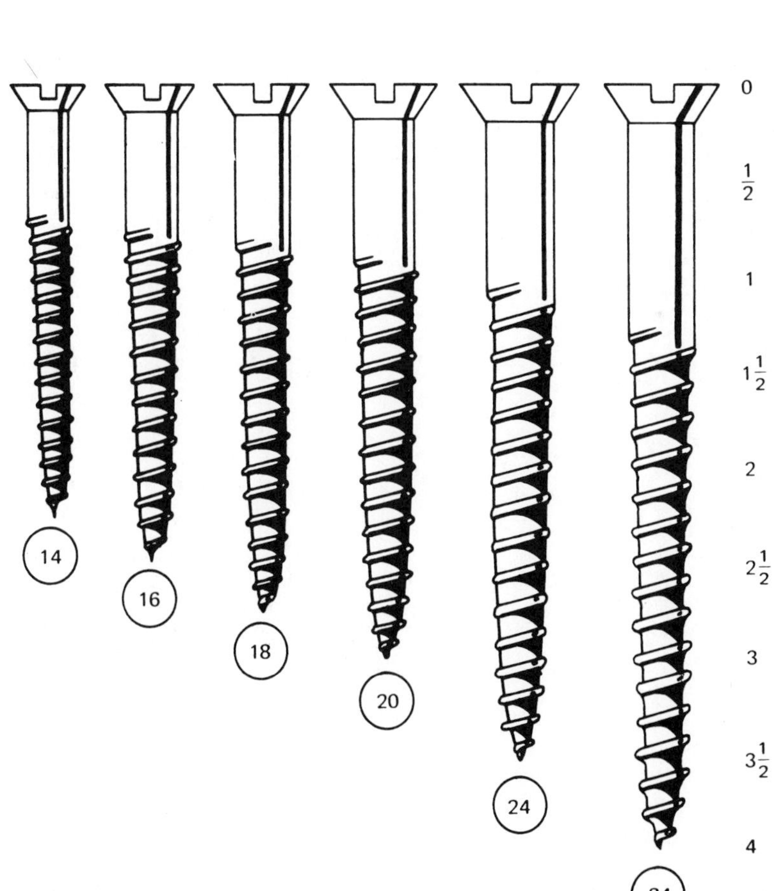
14
16
18
20
24
24
0
1/2
1
1 1/2
2
2 1/2
3
3 1/2
4

# GLOSSARY

This glossary lists shop and tool terms that are used in this handbook and with which you may be unfamiliar. Specific tool definitions are contained throughout the handbook—use the index to locate them.

**ARBOR** / a shaft on which a revolving cutting tool is mounted.

**BALUSTER** / an upright, often vase-shaped support for a rail; an object or vertical member (as the leg of a table or the stem of a glass) having a vaselike or turned outline.

**BEVEL CUT** / a cut made on one surface at an angle (except a right angle) to another surface; oblique.

**CHAMFER** / an oblique surface, usually 45°, cut on the corner or edge of a board or hole (or screw hole).

**CHISEL** / a metal tool with a cutting edge at the end, used in dressing, shaping, or working a workpiece. It is used for finish cuts; a smooth surface is produced.

**CIRCUMFERENCE** / the perimeter of a circle; the external boundary or surface of a figure or object.

**COLLET** / a metal band, collar, ferrule, or flange; used to hold small diameter bits.

**CONCAVE** / hollowed or rounded inward like the inside of a bowl.

**CONVEX** / curved like a circle or sphere when viewed from without; bulging and curved.

**COMPOUND CUT** / a cut that includes both a miter and a bevel cut.

**COUNTERBORE** / to enlarge the upper part of a hole to receive and allow the head of a screw or bolt to be recessed below the surface.

**COUNTERSINK** / to enlarge the upper part of a hole by chamfering to receive the cone-shaped head of a screw or bolt.

**CROSSCUT** / a cut across the grain of the wood.

**DADO** / to cut a rectangular groove into a workpiece; the blade used to cut the rectangular groove; a rectangular groove cut into a workpiece.

**DIAMETER** / the chord or length of a straight line through the center of an object.

**DIAPHRAGM** / a thin, flexible disk that vibrates.

**DOVETAIL** / resembling a dove's tail; a wood joint.

**DOWEL** / a pin fitting into a hole in an abutting piece to prevent motion or slipping; a round rod used especially for cutting into dowels.

**END GRAIN** / the grain at the end of a board, in the direction across the grain of the wood. See grain.

**FLUTE** / a rounded groove.

**GIB** / a plate of metal or other material machined to hold other parts in place, to afford a bearing surface, or to provide means for taking up wear.

**GOUGE** / a hollow blade chisel that is bevel ground inside or outside. The gouge is used for fast removal of material, but leaves a rough finish.

**GRAIN** / the stratification of the wood fibers in a piece of wood. Cutting *with-the-grain* is the process of cutting in the direction of the stratification.

**GULLET** / the space between the tips of adjacent saw teeth.

**HONE** / a fine grit stone for sharpening a cutting implement; to sharpen with a hone.

**HSS** / high speed steel.

**IDLER PULLEY** / a wheel, gear, or roller used to transfer motion or to guide or support something.

**JIG** / a device used as a guide or template to mechanically maintain the correct positional relationship between a workpiece and the tool or between parts of a workpiece during assembly.

**KERF** / the slot cut into a workpiece by a saw blade.

**LAPIDARY** / a cutter, polisher, or engraver of precious stones, usually other than diamonds; the art of cutting gems.

**MANDREL** / the shaft and bearings on which a tool is mounted; a tapered or cylindrical axle, spindle, or arbor inserted into a hole in a piece of work to support it during machining.

**METER** / the meter is the fundamental unit of length in the metric system and is equal to 39.37 inches or 3.281 feet. The meter is measured in cadmium–red light waves–and is equal to 1,553,164.13 of the waves.

**MITER** / the abutting surface or bevel on either of the pieces joined in a miter joint. A *mitered joint* is a joint formed when two pieces of identical cross section are joined at the ends, and where the joined ends are beveled at equal angles; a gauge for making mitered cuts.

**MITER CUT** / a cut made at an angle to the workpiece surface along the edge or through a workpiece.

**MORSE TAPER** / a tapered shank that is press fit into a cylinder; also known as American Standard Taper.

**MORTISE** / a rectangular cut of considerable depth in a piece of wood for receiving a corresponding projection (tenon) on another piece of wood to form a joint.

**PARALLEL** / lying in the same plane but never meeting, no matter how far extended.

**PAWL** / a pivoted tongue on one part of a machine that is adapted to fall into notches or interdental spaces on another part (as a ratchet wheel) so as to permit motion in only one direction.

**PERPENDICULAR** / vertical; upright; meeting a given line or surface at right angles.

**PILOT HOLE** / a small diameter hole drilled into a material to lead the point of a larger drill.

**PLATEN** / a flat metal plate that exerts or receives pressure.

**PLOUGH** / a dado cut along the grain of the workpiece.

**QUADRANT** / any of the four quarters into which something is divided by two real or imaginary lines that intersect each other at right angles.

**QUILL** / a hollow shaft surrounding another shaft and used in various mechanical devices.

**RABBET** / a cut, groove, or recess made on the edge or surface of a board to receive the end or edge of another board or the like which is similarly shaped.

**RADIAL** / arranged or having parts arranged like rays; relating to, placed like, or moving along a radius.

**RESAW** / the process of cutting a board through its thickness (depth) into two narrower boards. The work is usually accomplished on a band saw.

**RIP** / to saw or split with the grain of the workpiece.

**SET** / the slight bend of saw blade teeth alternately in opposite directions to aid in cutting and then the removal of chips.

**SFPM** / surface feet per minute. Denotes the speed of a motor belt, abrasive belt, or band saw blade.

**SHIM** / a thin, often tapered piece of metal or wood used to fill a space between things for support, leveling, or adjustment of fit; to level by use of a shim.

**SPLINE** / a key that is fixed to one of two connected mechanical parts and fits into a keyway in the other; a thin wood or metal strip used in construction of joints.

**SPLITTER** / a device used to keep the kerf of a saw blade from closing against the blade.

**TANGENT** / meeting a curve or surface in a single point if a sufficiently small interval is considered (as a straight line tangent to a curve).

**TAPER** / gradual reduction of thickness, diameter, or width in an elongated object; progressively narrowed toward one end.

**TEMPER** / to soften by reheating at a lower temperature; to harden (steel) by reheating and cooling in oil.

**TENON** / a projection fashioned on an end of a piece of wood for insertion into a corresponding cavity (mortise) in another piece of wood to form a joint.

**TENSILE STRENGTH** / the greatest longitudinal stress a substance can bear without tearing apart.

**THROAT** / the limiting space, or dimension, between a cutter and the frame of a tool. Tool sizes are determined by the throat size which is the maximum width of the workpiece that can be passed through the physical limits of the tool. Thus, a 16 inch jigsaw can cut a maximum width of 16 inches. This is also stated as the center of a 32 inch diameter circle.

**TRUNNION** / a pivot on which something (such as a jigsaw table) can be rotated or tilted.

**WAY** / the guiding surfaces on the bed of a machine along which a table or carriage (such as a tailstock) moves.

**WORKPIECE** / a piece of work that is to have sawing, sanding, cutting, planing, or some other operation performed on it.

# INDEX

## C



## D



## E



## I



## J

## L

## M



## N



## P



## R

## S

# T

## W